D1453842

Endgame

Endgame

*Britain, Russia and the Final
Struggle for Central Asia*

Jennifer Siegel

I.B.Tauris *Publishers*
LONDON ● NEW YORK

Published in 2002 by I.B.Tauris & Co Ltd
London and New York
www.ibtauris.com

In the United States and Canada distributed by St. Martin's Press, 175 Fifth
Avenue, New York NY 10010

ISBN 1-85043-371-2

A full CIP record for this book is available from the British Library
A full CIP record for this book is available from the Library of Congress

Library of Congress catalog card: available

Typeset in Perpetua by A. & D. Worthington, Newmarket, Suffolk
Printed and bound in Great Britain by MPG Books Ltd, Bodmin

Contents

To my father –
The Dean of Coaches

Foreword

During the second half of the twentieth century, international affairs were dominated by the rivalry between two superpowers, the USSR and the United States. No one doubted that the barometer of that relationship affected so many other aspects of politics – the domestic scene and public/congressional opinion in each country, the calculation of third parties, the unfolding of events in regions abroad, contested by Moscow and Washington.

A century earlier, admittedly in a multipolar rather than a bipolar world, international affairs were very much affected by the rivalry between the only two global powers, Great Britain and Russia. Both were empires of at least 400 years' standing, and both were still acquiring fresh territories. True, one of these imperial nations was a small island-state, while the other was a vast land-locked swathe of terrain. One was situated off the westernmost part of Europe, the other in the easternmost part. Their political relationships might have been similarly, and appropriately, distant but for a special shared interest – namely, in the fate of Central Asia. As the eighteenth and nineteenth centuries unfolded, British power pushed ever more into the Indian subcontinent and towards the Hindu Kush. Virtually in parallel, Russian military might surged through the Central Asian Khanates toward the Himalayan passes. As each player moved its chess pieces closer to the other, the 'Great Game' – a term popularized by Kipling but of older lineage – became more intense. The British regarded the Russian advance on their Indian domains as the greatest threat to the Empire's future. The Russians regarded Britain's neuralgic reactions as the greatest obstacles to the fulfilment of their imperial dreams in Asia. Most third parties, for example, Kaiser Wilhelm II and his advisers in Berlin, believed an Anglo-Russian war over Asia to be inevitable.

It was to the surprise of such observers, therefore, that in August 1907 Britain and Russia agreed to a delineation of their spheres of interest in Afghanistan, Tibet and, most importantly, in Persia. In many accounts of the Great Game, this was the termination point. In numerous studies of the origins of the First World War, this was the occasion when London and St

Petersburg buried the hatchet and turned in mutual accord, along with France, against the Central Powers of Germany and Austria-Hungary. The Anglo-Russian entente of 1907 was thus a stepping-stone to the First World War; and the treaty, once signed, marked a benign phase in the relations between the two Great Powers, the elephant and the whale.

But, as Dr Siegel's work reveals, this traditional view of Anglo-Russian relations in the years following their Asian entente is far too simplistic. To begin with, the 'Game' could not be played, and was definitely not played, by the British and Russian foreign ministries alone; local actors also played a part. In particular, contending forces among the Persian political elites manoeuvred both against each other *and* either for or against British and Russian influences. Since it was the Russians on the ground who were the more likely to attempt to advance their interests, this led to frequent Persian–Russian tensions and increasing British discomfort. Instead of buried hatchets, there were angry and anxious mutual protests between London and St Petersburg, threatening to affect the larger Anglo-Russian relationship.

Because of the availability of the archival sources, the British side of this tale has been told before, though never with the finesse and detail contained in *Endgame*. But Dr Siegel's greater accomplishment is to have mined the rich and hitherto unopened masses of Russian records in both Moscow and St Petersburg – an unintended but deeply satisfying consequence of the ending of the Cold War. (Whether this access by Western scholars to Russian archives will survive, fully, partially, or at all, remains an open question. Should Russian political reaction reduce such access, *Endgame* would become one of the few works to have benefited from this historical 'window of opportunity'.) This archival treasure trove provides wonderful examples of the makings of Imperial Russia's 'official mind', and of the complex relationships between centre and periphery. To this reader, at least, the on-the-ground reports from Russian diplomats and agents are an especially satisfying read.

Finally, *Endgame* is an important contribution to the intense scholarly debate over the determinants of British foreign policy in the years before 1914. Was that policy overwhelmingly driven by a rising fear of Wilhelmine Germany, its powerful navy, and its army's potential to crush France – a Eurocentric ordering of priorities that drove British statesmen to seek compromises with St Petersburg over Persia's convulsions in order to preserve the Anglo-French-Russian lineup against Berlin? Or, as some revisionist historians have suggested in recent years, was it the British obsession about preserving their hold upon India and the Persian Gulf in the face of Russia's seemingly unstoppable advances, that compelled them to view events in Asia as the most important of all – compelled them, finally, to enter the First

World War, *not* on account of the defence of Belgium and France but to mollify Russia's frustrations many thousands of miles away? Settling this age-old question was and is not Dr Siegel's chief purpose. But her detailed scrutiny of British sensitivities, plus her references to the wider context, should give each school food for thought.

And that, of course, is precisely what all good scholarly monographs should do.

Paul Kennedy

Acknowledgements

A book – especially a first book – is always a product of many people's inspiration, assistance, collegiality and support. This book is certainly no exception. For inspiration, I have been privileged to have worked with several outstanding scholars who fostered my interests in Anglo-Russian relations while teaching me what historians do – in the classroom, in the archives and at the computer. My initial debt lies with Professor Firuz Kazemzadeh, who not only set me on the path of Anglo-Russian relations when I was an undergraduate, but also wrote the classic study of Russian and British activities in Persia that is the starting point of my professional work. Similarly, Professors Robin Winks and Paul Bushkovitch have been venerable in their instruction and encouragement, helping me to be a better historian at every step. And, most obviously, my mentor and adviser, Professor Paul Kennedy, guided, fostered, supported and befriended me throughout the years that have been absorbed by this project.

With assistance, I have been equally fortunate. The personnel of the Archive of the Russian Imperial Foreign Ministry, the Russian State Historical Archive and the Russian State Military Historical Archive were overwhelmingly welcoming and tireless in their efforts to further my research in conditions that were, at times, uniquely designed to thwart any attempts at scholarship; the staffs at the Russian State Library, the State Public Historical Library and the Russian National Library were also very helpful. The staffs and collections of the Public Record Office, the India Office, the Admiralty Library and the British Library never ceased to remind me of all the reasons why I was attracted to the study of the British Empire in the first place.

I was also extremely fortunate to receive considerable financial assistance from various institutions that made the research and writing of this book possible. The MacArthur Foundation, the Smith Richardson Foundation, and the Bradley Foundation all supported the 18 months I spent in the archives. An Andrew Mellon Dissertation Fellowship allowed me to devote a year undistracted by teaching responsibilities to the writing of the dissertation on which this book is based. Post-doctoral fellowships from the Olin Foundation and Yale International Security Studies provided me with the opportunity to undertake the revisions necessary to transform a dissertation into a book. And I was most fortunate that the Sosnor family of Moscow and the Sheptitskii family of St Petersburg provided me with unending care and support during my time in Russia, while in Britain, Joanne Averiss and Ed Krawitt, Anneke Wyman de Boer, Kim and Stephen Davies, and Alison Russell opened their homes and made my time at the PRO sublime. Finally, Iradj Bagherzade, the chairman of I.B. Tauris, and Lester Crook, the history editor, have been magnificently helpful and encouraging. A chance meeting years ago has led to a professional relationship from which I have truly benefited.

I have also been blessed by outstanding and generous colleagues at Yale and beyond. David Stone, David Schimmelpenninck van der Oye, and Fernande Scheid provided a Russianist community that is unparalleled. My dear friends and compatriots, Michael Powell and Mark Lawrence, shared the triumphs and tribulations of the writing and revision process, vastly improving my own work by their influence. In addition, Harvard's Ana Siljak has proven both a friend and a scholar par excellence. David Laibson of the Harvard Economics Department was a tremendous assistance in the preparation of the trade statistics and an empathetic source of motivation. Wellesely's Will Hitchcock has contributed on so many crucial issues that it is impossible to thank him enough. Aaron Scholer's reading of the manuscript was above and beyond the call of duty. Liz Wilcox's extraordinary editorial dissection of the manuscript and invaluable suggestions were just another implementation of a 14-year treaty of mutual assistance. And the tireless spiritual and editorial support of C. Rodgers Palmer eased me through month after month and chapter after chapter, earning him six consecutive years in the Top Five.

For support, I have had my wonderful family. My parents, Naomi and Burt Siegel, sisters and brother-in-law, Debbi Siegel and Lilli and Jonathan Roth, and nephew and niece, Jeremy and Talia, were indefatigable in their love and motivation throughout the years of training and the preparation of this book. Furthermore, my mother's 11th-hour reading of the manuscript was a monumental effort for which I shall be eternally grateful. There is no one more fortunate in her family than I.

Finally, this book is dedicated to my father, whose love of history, devotion to his daughters, and understanding of life has inspired me each step of the way.

J.L.S.
Brookline, Massachusetts
July 2001

Note on Text

The calendar in Imperial Russia followed the Julian model, which was, by the twentieth century, 13 days behind the Gregorian calendar commonly employed in the West. Thus, for example, the British felt that they signed the Anglo-Russian Treaty of Rapprochement on 31 August 1907, but the Russian government considered the date to be 18 August 1907. Dates in this book are given, for the most part, according to the Gregorian calendar. When Russian dates are important and the Julian calendar is employed, the more commonly accepted Gregorian date is also offered, as in 18/31 August 1907.

Transliteration from Cyrillic in general follows the modified Library of Congress system, without diacritics. A number of exceptions exist, particularly with reference to people and places of great notoriety, whose westernized names are broadly known. For example, the tsars are Nicholas or Alexander, rather than Nikolai or Aleksandr. Furthermore, surnames of foreign origin, like Benckendorff or Hartwig, are in their original, not Russianized forms.

'Persia' is the mistaken nomenclature for the country that has always been known by its inhabitants as 'Iran'. The practice of using a name derived by the ancient Greeks from only one part of Iran, the modern province of Fars, was prevalent in the West. Since 'Persia' was the name employed by the Russian and British Empires in their interaction with the country before the First World War, it is, therefore, the name that most often appears in this study.

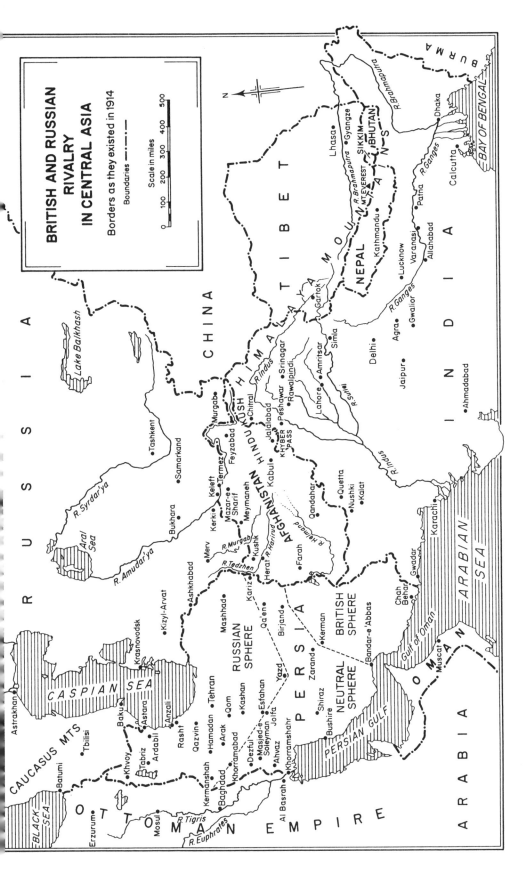

BRITISH AND RUSSIAN
RIVALRY
IN CENTRAL ASIA

Borders as they existed in 1914

Boundaries ━━━ ·━━

Scale in miles

0   100   200   300   400   500

N

RUSSIA

Lake Balkhash

CHINA

•Tashkent
•Samarkand
Bukhara•

R.Syrdar'ya

Aral
Sea

R.Amudar'ya

TIBET

HIMALAYA MOUNTAINS

Lhasa•
•Gyangze
SIKKIM
BHUTAN
MT.EVEREST
R.Brahmaputra

NEPAL
•Kathmandu
Gartok•

BURMA
R.Brahmaputra

•Dhaka

R.Ganges
•Calcutta
•Patna
Varanasi•
•Allahabad
•Lucknow

BAY OF BENGAL

Murgab•
Feyzabad•
HINDU KUSH
Chitral•
Jalalabad•
Peshawar•
KHYBER PASS
Kabul•

Simla•
Srinagar•
•Amritsar
Lahore•
Rawalpindi•
R.Indus
R.Sutlej

•Delhi
•Agra
•Jaipur

INDIA

•Gwalior
R.Ganges

•Ahmadabad

Termez•
Keleft•
Kerki•
Mazar-e
Sharif•
Meymaneh•

Kushk
R.Harirud
Herat•
AFGHANISTAN

Qandahar•
•Quetta
•Nushki
•Kalat

R.Indus

•Karachi

Merv•
R.Murgab
R.Tedzhen
Kariz•
Qa'en•
Farah•
R.Helmand

ARABIAN
SEA

•Ashkhabad
•Kizyl-Arvat
Mashhad•
RUSSIAN
SPHERE
Birjand•
Zarand•
•Kerman
BRITISH
SPHERE
Chah
Behar•
•Gwadar

Krasnovodsk•
•Muscat

CASPIAN SEA

•Tehran
Qazvin•
•Qom
Kashan•
Yazd•
PERSIA
NEUTRAL
SPHERE
Bandar-e 'Abbas•

OMAN

Gulf of Oman

Astrakhan•

Baku•
Astara•
•Anzali
Rasht•
•Hamadan
•Arak
Esfahan•
•Shiraz
•Bushire

ARABIA

Khvoy•
Tabriz•
Ardabil•
Dezful•
Masjed-e
Soleyman•
Jolfa•
Ahvaz•
Khorramshahr•

PERSIAN GULF

CAUCASUS MTS
•Tbilisi
Kermanshah•
Khorramabad•
•Al Basrah

Batumi•
Erzurum•

BLACK
SEA

OTTOMAN EMPIRE

Mosul•
R.Tigris
R.Euphrates

ARABIAN
SEA

Introduction

Without India the British Empire could not exist. The possession of India
is the inalienable badge of sovereignty in the eastern hemisphere.

GEORGE NATHANIEL CURZON, 1892[1]

England must not dictate our path to us; rather, we should direct her fate.
Above all remember that, not far from us, beyond the snowcapped
mountain range of the Eastern Hindu Kush, lies India, the foundation of
British power, and perhaps the political key to the whole world.

ANDREI EVGENEVICH SNESAREV, 1905[2]

Throughout the latter half of the nineteenth and early twentieth centuries, the empires of Russia and Great Britain seemed poised on the brink of war in Asia. Russia, whose traditional desire for territorial expansion and a warm water port in the west had been thwarted by the Crimean War, had turned its eyes eastward towards Central Asia and the Far East. Simultaneously, Britain was consolidating its position on the Indian subcontinent and constructing an empire in China. Britain was alarmed by Russian inroads in the Far East, but the steady advance of Russia towards India, 'The Jewel in the British Imperial Crown', was the most disturbing. The Russians, likewise, were convinced that everywhere they turned, east or west, the British were there to frustrate their imperial dreams.

Such conflicting Central Asian policies and ambitions increasingly pointed towards a Great Power clash with the ultimate prize of uncontested regional hegemony. This monumental competition between the two great Asian imperial powers came to be called 'the Great Game' – a term thought to have been coined by a young Bengal cavalry officer named Arthur Connolly in his 1835 *Narrative of an Overland Journey to the North of India*. Captain Connolly was an avid chess player and, in inventing the phrase, was paying a high compliment to the Russian proficiency at the game. But it was the use of the term 'Great Game' by that veteran great gamer, Rudyard Kipling, within the pages of his Victorian romances of Empire, that etched the images of a grand, glorious and irrefutably desperate competition for imperial survival upon the popular psyche. The idea of a great battle of wills and minds being played out across the mysterious mountains and fields of Central Asia took root in the British imagination, and was a driving force behind both government policy and cultural creativity throughout much of the nineteenth century. Although there is no such 'Great Game' phrase in Russian literature, the competition with Britain for supremacy in Asia was felt just as keenly in St Petersburg as in London.

As the new century began, it seemed clear that the struggle for Central Asian hegemony – which had so dominated the geostrategic landscape in the nineteenth century as one of the primary influences on both British and Russian foreign policy – would soon need to be resolved, either by diplomacy or armed conflict. Armed conflict, however, was becoming increasingly impracticable in the eyes of both Great Powers. The Second Boer War at the turn of the century had struck a sobering blow at Britain's sense of imperial security and fiscal well being. In 1902 Britain chose to end its traditional policy of 'splendid isolation' with its first twentieth-century alliance, an agreement with the unproven Asian power of Japan. This agreement alleviated several of Britain's Far Eastern security responsibilities, enabling the British to concentrate more of their resources on the defence of India. Similarly, in 1904, many of Britain's Middle Eastern and African concerns were mitigated by the conclusion of the Anglo-French Entente Cordiale, much reducing the risk of a colonial clash between London and Paris. But these steps were not enough. The British still considered themselves to be overextended and vulnerable in India, and a military clash with Russia might be more than the Empire could bear.

The year 1904 also marked the beginning of the Russo-Japanese War, the outcome of which left a much weakened and defeated Russia in turmoil after the Revolution of 1905. In the wake of the domestic unrest and international discomfort unleashed by Japan's victory, Russia sought to achieve a critical reorientation of its imperial strategy; a period of retrenchment and a simplification of the Russian international security environment seemed to be in order. Expansion in Central Asia, and the collision with Britain it would inevitably engender, was not a reasonable gamble for a war- and revolution-torn empire. Therefore, both parties considered the alleviation of the existing tensions in Central Asia through diplomatic means to be a principal aim of their foreign policies.

Thus, in March 1906, discussions began between the Russian and British governments towards the conclusion of a treaty of rapprochement. After months of heated negotiations, the two sides at last reached an agreement. The Convention of Mutual Cordiality, signed on 31 August 1907, formalized relations between these two competing nations in Central Asia, essentially establishing and guaranteeing the status quo in the buffer zones of Persia, Afghanistan and Tibet. The Great Power war between Russia and Britain that had been anticipated by so many for so long had been averted.

It is at this point, with the conclusion of the 1907 agreement, that the Great Game is commonly, but incorrectly, considered to have come to an end. The agreement has been traditionally represented as the diplomatic coup that allowed the former rivals to move from enmity to amicable accord in their opposition to the growing threat from Germany. This approach to the Anglo-Russian Convention interprets the rapprochement between Russia and Great Britain as demonstrating a deliberate shift of emphasis away from Asia and their respective imperial holdings to the European continent. Under this interpretation, the overriding importance of the 1907 agreement lay in its role as one of the principal diplomatic foundations of the European alliance structure, which so vividly contributed to the outbreak and evolution of the Great War; the maintenance of the Anglo-Russian relationship in Asia was, accordingly, significant for the two Great Powers almost exclusively as an essential component of their continental co-operation, not for its own merits.

But the final struggle for mastery in Central Asia was far from over in 1907. The last stages of the traditional Great Game – the game of Imperial Russia and Britain, not their later substitutes – were just beginning when the British ambassador and Russian foreign minister put pen to paper and signed the 1907 treaty. Central Asian concerns continued to play a crucial role in the formation of British and Russian policy well beyond the 1907 agreement. The priorities and aims that had driven British and Russian diplomatic, military and commercial strategy prior to 1907 continued to command attention and orient policy in Asia and Europe until the Great War and Bolshevik Revolution so altered the playing field that the Game could no longer be considered the same.

The importance of Central Asia to the policy makers and special-interest lobbyists in St Petersburg and London has been largely marginalized by scholars interested in British and Russian diplomacy before the First World War; only a strongly revisionist minority has challenged this Eurocentrism with regard to British policy, at times swinging the pendulum far the other direction and arguing for the precedence of the Russo-British Asian relationship over the Anglo-German or Russo-German antagonisms in the pre-War Great Power balance.[3] This book points somewhere in between. It does not seek to establish the nature of Britain's or Russia's relationship with Germany. It does, however, try to take fully into account the intense history of rivalry and continuing regional conflicts of interest that characterized Anglo-Russian relations, particularly in Central Asia. By offering a comprehensive examination of Anglo-Russian relations in Central Asia from the perspective of both principal parties, this book demonstrates that British and Russian foreign policy makers in 1914 were far more focused on all three of the countries that they had considered settled in the 1907 agreement than has previously been acknowledged.

From the conclusion of the agreement to the outbreak of the First World War, Anglo-Russian relations in Central Asia were marked by continued tensions and regional manoeuvrings on both sides, similar to those that had characterized the era before the rapprochement. By the outbreak of the European war in 1914, the Anglo-Russian Central Asian accord was on the verge of collapse on numerous fronts, threatening any further affinity in Europe. For the Russian foreign policy elite, the idea of a forward strategy in Central Asia had not only survived the 1907 agreement, it was, in many ways, a more vital concern than the buttressing of entente relations. For the British government, now committed to the maintenance of amicable Anglo-Russian relations, it had become clear by 1914 that British and Russian Central Asian policies could no longer be reconciled under the existing agreement. Despite the very real possibility that the breakdown of Anglo-Russian relations in Central Asia could lead towards a rupture of the European entente, Britain was unwilling and unable to tolerate further 'peaceful penetration' by the Russian regional presence.

The competitive progression from agreement in 1907 to crisis, re-evaluation and increasing conflict in 1914, was one that was fraught with friction and discord every step of the way. The contest was one in which one false move might lead Britain and Russia back into the state of Great Power cold war from which they had desperately sought to escape in 1907. It was a contest that could lead them once again to the brink of a war for regional hegemony in Central Asia. And it was a contest that bore a striking resemblance to that in which they had been engaged for so many years before the rapprochement. The rules may have changed – open animosity had been replaced by declared consensus – but the Game was just the same. And as each player grew increasingly to recognize that the conflict was far from over, their renewed pursuit of the Endgame proved the competition as heated as ever.

CHAPTER 1

The Great Game and
the 1907 Agreement

British influence in India began in the early days of the seventeenth century, with the establishment of the British East India Company. With the collapse of the Moghul Empire into separate warring states in the mid-1700s, a power vacuum was created into which the East India Company stepped, transforming itself from a commercial power into the leading political power in India within only a few years. By the early nineteenth century, Britain, in the form of the East India Company, was the dominant political and economic power throughout most of the subcontinent. The Company unified the majority of India under its rule until, in 1858, in the wake of the Sepoy Rebellion, the British government assumed direct control of the administration of the subcontinent.

By the 1880s India was absorbing approximately £270 million of British overseas investment and was purchasing 13 per cent of Britain's exports, making India the most important market for British manufactures in the Empire.[1] Throughout most of the nineteenth century, India was, from a military standpoint, a source of manpower rather than a drain. The Indian Army, although financed by Indian tax revenues, consistently sent troops to fight with those of the metropolitan power in conflicts that often had little direct relation to the defence of India itself. Dominion in India was seen as crucial to Britain's status as an imperial power; possession of the subcontinent was vital to Britain's sense of imperial glory and global might. Indian defence requirements were superseded in importance only by those of the British Isles themselves.[2]

In consideration of the pivotal role India played in the Empire, the British were naturally alarmed by the seemingly incessant southward extension of Russian territory in Central Asia. The origins of Russian involvement in Central Asia can be traced to the reign of Peter I. With the aim of making Russia the dominant intermediary in East–West trade, Peter had hoped to create a trading colony on the western and southern shores of the Caspian Sea. Wanting to emulate his European contemporaries, whose commercial empires in Asia he admired, Peter planned to create a Russian equivalent to those overseas colonies in the contiguous Caucasian and Caspian provinces. Towards this goal, his emissaries negotiated a commercial treaty with the Safavid government of Persia in 1717, but the weakness of the Safavid regime tempted Peter into attempting a military intervention in internal Persian political struggles. Although he abandoned the campaign long before reaching Teheran, the initial link between the Caucasus and the Russian metropolis was well established.

Beyond the Central Asian khanates, Russia had long cast its eyes towards the Indian subcontinent. The notion of direct Russian involvement in India had frequently been in vogue within certain Russian policy circles. Under their influence, Peter I had ordered an ill-fated force of 3500 men with Prince Bekovich-Cherkasskii in command to conquer Khiva and find the road to India; in addition, he sent a young officer, Artemii Volynskii, on to Persia to collect intelligence on, among other things, the routes from Persia and the Caspian Sea to India.[3] Similarly, at the end of the eighteenth century, Catherine II contemplated the dispatch of an expedition to India, a plan that was never carried out. But the idea of an advance on India persisted, and as late as January 1801, Catherine's son, Paul I, dispatched an army of 20,000 Cossacks to invade India.[4] Although the invasion force met with disaster crossing the Volga River, this failed offensive set a significant precedent.

The early nineteenth century for Russia was one of tremendous expansion in Asia. Alexander I – who wisely rescinded his father's invasion orders upon his succession in 1801 – is best remembered for his defeat of Napoleon and his championing of the idea of the Holy Alliance. But he was also responsible for the consolidation of Russian authority in the Caucasus. Nicholas I, who succeeded his brother Alexander, defeated Persia in 1828 and acquired much of Armenia and exclusive naval rights on the Caspian Sea. It was in the mid-to late 1800s, however, that the great thrust of Russian Central Asian expansion brought Imperial Russia's borders in that region close to the position they were at the time of the Revolution.

Russia's Central Asian expansion was largely a reaction to British antagonism in the rest of the world. As Count Vladimir Nikolaevich Lamsdorff, the Russian foreign minister, pointed out in February 1902: 'In Russia, Great Britain had for a century, at least, been regarded by the mass of the people as the one Power always to the fore in baulking at every conjuncture the national aspirations and barring the natural development and expansion of Russia.'[5] British concern over the potential growth of a competing naval power in the Mediterranean had motivated their push for a special provision in the Treaty of Paris in 1856, which ended the Crimean War and closed the Bosphorus and Dardanelles Straits to Russian ships. This Straits Convention effectively barred Russia from the Near East and stymied its territorial aspirations, resulting in an eastward shift of Russian imperial expansion from its traditional focus on the Ottoman Empire and Transcaucasia towards the khanates of Central Asia.

Russia's turn towards Asia was, therefore, both a defensive and offensive reaction to the disappointment of the Straits Convention, as the Russians strove both to expand in the only direction left open to them and to counter any British territorial ambitions in the region. Furthermore, Russia hoped to use its position in Asia as a bargaining point to regain access to the Straits; if the Russians were able to challenge British hegemony in Central Asia, they might impel Britain to support a revision of the hated Straits Convention. As General Mikhail Dmitrievich Skobelev wrote in 1881: 'To my mind the whole Central Asian Question is as clear as the daylight. If it does not enable us in a comparatively short time to take seriously in hand the Eastern Question, in other words, to dominate the Bosphorus, the hide is not worth tanning.'[6]

Russian strategic and economic interests in expanding their empire were bolstered by the romantic concepts of Russia's Asian heritage combined with its Orthodox mission. Evoking memories of Russia's conquest by the Mongols of the Golden Horde, Prince Esper Ukhtomsky, who accompanied Nicholas II on his tour of Asia in 1891, argued that 'All these [Asian] peoples of various races feel themselves drawn to us, and are ours, by blood, by tradition, and by ideas.'[7] Constantine Leontiev proclaimed the religious motivation for expansion in 1890: 'To the Russian mind, China is to be Russian, Persia is to be Russian, India is to be Russian. It is Russian power which is to restore the cross to Jerusalem.'[8] Furthermore, the Russians saw themselves as a civilizing force in the East, necessary to subdue their unstable, predatory neighbours. As Prince Gorchakov, Russian minister of foreign affairs under Nicholas I and Alexander II, accounted in 1864, Russia's position in Asia was that of all civilized states,

> which are brought into contact with half-savage nomad populations possessing no fixed social organization.
>
> In such cases it always happens that the more civilized state is forced, in the interest of the security of its frontier and its commercial relations, to exercise a certain ascendancy over those whom their turbulent and unsettled character make most undesirable neighbours.[9]

Russian nineteenth-century propaganda also emphasized Russia's ability to incorporate its subdued neighbours within its realm for the collective benefit of all involved parties. In this view, Russian Asianism, as opposed to its long-stressed European heritage, would allow Russia 'to easily fuse with the races brought under their subjection'.[10]

In addition to its territorial annexations in Central Asia and the Far East, Russia consolidated its position and its influence through the construction of an extensive railway system throughout its Asian holdings. In the Far East, the construction of the Trans-Siberian Railway between 1891 and 1903 was crucial to the development of Siberia and the extension of Russian suzerainty in the region. Central Asia was similarly transformed by the Russian railway revolution of the late 1800s. In 1880, construction began on the first line of the Trans-Caspian Railway, connecting the Caspian Sea with Samarkand and drawing near the Persian frontier at Ashkhabad. The Caspian–Samarkand line was completed in 1888, and in 1895 work commenced on lines connecting Samarkand with Andijan and Tashkent, the capital of Russian Central Asia; these lines were finished in early 1899. January 1899 also marked the completion of the highly strategic branch line from Merv up the Murghab River to Kushk, within 70 miles of Herat. In addition, work commenced that year on a rail line from Orenburg to Samarkand that, when completed in 1905, provided uninterrupted land transport from Russia to its Central Asian holdings, bypassing the Caspian Sea. This line doubled the potential supplies that could be transported into western Turkestan from Russia in the event of a military expedition from that territorial base.[11]

Furthermore, the wide dissemination in 1900 of a Russian pamphlet entitled 'Railways in Persia' strongly promoted the Russian intention to extend its railway lines through Persia and Afghanistan towards India. Written by a Russian staff officer, Captain P.A. Rittich, this unofficial but influential pamphlet emphasized the commercial, rather than the strategic value of an extended railway through Persia. Rittich projected that a rail connection with India would, 'place the whole trade of India and Eastern Asia with Russia and Europe in [Russian] hands'.[12] He readily acknowledged that such railway expansion would be neither welcomed by nor be particularly acceptable to an Indian government intent upon maintaining the British monopoly on Indian trade. But Britain could do little to prevent the Russian railway revolution; despite British opposition to further Russian railway expansion, the constructed and projected railways at the turn of the century in Russian Central Asia, Persia and Afghanistan resulted in a considerable increase in the Russian economic threat to British Central Asian holdings.

Railway expansion was an equally vital component in the development of the Central Asian strategic landscape. As Captain E. Peach of the Indian Army stated in 1901, 'the whole Central Asian question is practically one of railways.'[13] The Trans-Caspian and Central Asian Railways gave the Russians two primary lines of possible advance on India: the Qandahar and Kabul approaches. The Qandahar line utilized the Central Asian Railway, beginning at the Caspian ports and continuing through Merv to the Russian fortified railhead at Kushk, only 483 miles from the south-eastern Afghan city for which the approach was named. The Kabul line originated at Orenburg and went through Tashkent and Samarkand to Charjiu on the Amudar'ya River, alternatively called the Oxus River. Furthermore, in 1906 an extension of the railway from Samarkand to the Afghan border at Termez was under construction. A third potential line of attack through Seistan was foreseen in the planned extension of the Russian railway from the border town of Jolfa into Persia, via Mashhad.[14] 'The whole object' of this railway advance, Captain Peach suggested, was 'to show such overwhelming power in Central Asia as to force us, *without war*, to allow her [Russia] a free hand elsewhere, notably in Persia, which she no doubt wishes to have under her influence *en bloc* with its coast and ports included, just as we have India.'[15]

In addition to the extensive late nineteenth-century expansion of its Central Asian transport capabilities, Russia had an extremely large military force at its disposal in Central Asia. In contrast to the Indian Army, which consisted in 1901 of 75,000 British and 153,000 indigenous soldiers, the Russian Empire in 1897 had a conscript regular army of over one million men, with additional reserve troops numbering three million.[16] The British could not see past the sheer numerical size of the Russian standing and reserve army. Although the Russian military was spread thinly across the vast territories for which it was responsible, Britain – disregarding the obvious demands of financial constraints and existing Russian defence responsibilities – could only envisage the tremendous force that Russia might amass in any Central Asian conflict.[17]

Parallel with the growth of Russia's capabilities for further expansion in Central Asia were growing circles within Russia pushing for an advance towards India, especially as the British found themselves increasingly bogged down by the Boers in South Africa.[18] In 1898 Captain Lebedev of the Imperial Russian Grenadier Guards published a detailed 'project of a future campaign' entitled 'To India', which was circulated within the British Foreign and India Offices. Lebedev's treatise clearly advocated a Russian offensive through Central Asia against the British colony:

> We must indeed come into contact with India. ... We shall compel Great Britain to place a proper value on our friendship and to relinquish her aggressive policy in regard to Russia. The might of India will be sapped, seeing that it will become necessary to increase the armed forces of the Indian Empire; this, in its turn, would increase the taxation under which the native populations now groan, and result in an increasing feeling of discontent.

Independently of all this, a connection of the Trans-Caspian Railway with the railway system of India will give us a command of the route which the overland trade between Europe and Asia will pursue; and, finally, Russia will have found a way to emerge on an open sea.[19]

Military orders were issued from St Petersburg, strengthening the troops in Turkestan and Transcaspia in preparation for an advance in Central Asia. Instructions drawn up in early 1900 for General Dukkhovsky, the governor-general of Turkestan, called for military provisions and ammunition to be forwarded to the frontier by the end of June of that year, so that the Russian Army would be prepared to occupy Herat 'at an earlier date than [their] opponents could reckon it possible.'[20]

Similarly, in 1901, General L.N. Sobolev, basing his findings on the history of attempted conquests of India, predicted successful results for a projected Russian invasion of the subcontinent.[21] The strength of Britain's hold on India was considered by both parties to be so tenuous that it was feared that Russia would need to advance only as far as India's borders for British rule to collapse amidst a mass indigenous uprising with Russian support.[22] General MacGregor, the prominent British strategic theoretician on India, affirmed this conviction:

> The Russian army will but serve as the point of the spear with which the Russians will pierce the heart of India. The handle will be those robbers from the Caspian to the Indus, whose tough hides will permit them to join themselves to the Russians.[23]

In the eyes of the British, therefore, Russian Central Asian policy appeared clearly to be heading to the gates of India itself, if not beyond.

With the growing British economic and political involvement in India, the security of the subcontinent had become of paramount consideration in British policy formation. The steady Russian advance in Central Asia prompted the Government of India to look toward developing its northern neighbours – Afghanistan, Persia and Tibet – as buffer states in an attempt to safeguard the Indian frontier. The autonomy of these states was preferable, although this desire by necessity would be quickly sacrificed in the face of anti-British hostility within the buffer.

The strategically most important and immediately threatened member of this trio was Afghanistan; the most direct Russian challenge to British Central Asian hegemony lay in their potential to occupy Herat and become 'mistress of the Hindu Kush and Afghan mountains',[24] thus dominating the Himalayan invasion routes and perpetually posing a menace to India. For this reason, Afghanistan appeared to be at risk of absorption from both sides throughout the latter half of the century. In 1880 regional tensions increased, as Russia finally subjugated the unruly Teke Turkomans, and in 1884 the crisis reached a peak as Russia first annexed Merv and then later occupied Sarakhs on the Persian–Afghan frontier. British concerns following the annexation of Merv, popularly termed 'mervousness', prompted a push for the establishment of an Afghan boundary commission consisting of Russian and British officials, who delineated the north-western Russo-Afghan frontier over the course of the next two years. Simultaneously the Russian occupation of the oasis of Panjdeh in April 1885 resulted in an agreement between Russia and Britain to the effect that the former would retain the Panjdeh in return for relinquishing all claims to any territories within the emir's realm. In spite of this agreement, Britain felt compelled in 1885, 1887, and again in April 1888 to issue warnings to Russia that Britain would regard any advance towards Herat or any attempt to occupy Afghan territory as a declaration of war.[25]

Despite these warnings Russian 'surveyors' moved into the High Pamirs in the north-east corner of Afghanistan in 1891. These 'surveyors' were unquestionably interested in claiming the area for the tsar, and when they encountered two British officers, Captain Younghusband and Lieutenant Davidson, the Englishmen were at first detained and later driven out of the Pamirs. The Government of India protested by sending a force of Gurkhas into northern Kashmir and claiming the disputed area to be part of Afghanistan. Subsequently the Russians apologized for the detention of the officers. A direct move to annex the Pamirs, however, was made in May 1892 when 3000 Russian chausseurs and Cossacks advanced into the mountain range, defeating the local Afghan force. Although a revolt in Tashkent forced the Russians to withdraw the majority of their troops from the region, their continued manoeuvres in the Pamirs were a source of great irritation to the British. An agreement was finally reached in 1895, which delineated a tentative Pamir boundary line between the spheres of influence of Britain and Russia.[26] This agreement, combined with the 1891 Anglo-Russian agreement determining the Amudar'ya as the international boundary, marked a settlement of the Afghan border conflicts.

This settlement produced a temporary easing of tensions in the region, but the relative tranquillity was not to be long lived. As the twentieth century dawned, the threat of a succession crisis in Afghanistan threw the entire regional balance of power into disarray. In April 1900, the *St Petersburger Zeitung* predicted what they thought would be the inevitable fate of Afghanistan upon the impending death of the reigning emir, Abdur Rahman Khan: civil war, which would force Britain to interfere for the restoration of order, and ultimately result in the occupation of the southern part of Afghanistan up to the Hindu Kush by Britain, and the northern part by Russia.[27] Amid rising international concern over the Afghan succession crisis, Russia attempted to normalize relations between St Petersburg and Kabul, demanding the establishment of direct communications, which had been forbidden after the Second Anglo-Afghan War. Although during the first eight years of the 1890s trade between British India and Afghanistan had vastly diminished – which, the *Novoe Vremia* grudgingly admitted, did benefit Russian trade to an extent – the turn of the century saw Russia still forced to communicate with its southern neighbour through London.[28] On 6 February 1900 Baron de Staal, the Russian ambassador in London, submitted to the Foreign Office a memorandum demanding direct diplomatic relations with Afghanistan regarding frontier and commercial matters. Circumstances, St Petersburg argued, had completely changed since Russia had agreed that Afghanistan lay entirely beyond its sphere; the construction of the Trans-Caspian Railway and the development of commerce between Russia and Afghanistan now demanded direct relations with the emir, since the current situation created, they claimed, 'an atmosphere of mistrust and uneasiness which could not fail, in the long run, to lead to regrettable complications'.[29] Although the Russian government assured Britain that it regarded Afghanistan as 'entirely outside the sphere of Russian action and influence',[30] the fear that Britain would lose its semi-protectorate in Afghanistan and find itself with Russia on its border was a devastating blow to any previous sense of security that the Afghan buffer had provided.

The issue of direct communication between St Petersburg and Kabul had not yet been decided when, on 3 October 1901, the long-expected death of Abdur Rahman Khan transformed the internal politics of Afghanistan. But the surprisingly peaceful transition of power to his son, Habibullah, did not result in a continuation of the Anglo-Afghan relationship instituted by Abdur Rahman. Habibullah, intent on establishing his authority and prestige within his nation in his own right, suspended all relations with Britain and refused to receive his annual subsidy. Furthermore, the new emir attempted to open independent diplomatic relations with Russia, thus antagonizing his British 'protectors'. W. Lee-Warner of the Indian government had predicted these actions when in 1896 he said of the Anglo-Afghan relationship: 'We have less, I believe, to fear from Russia than from our allies the Afghans.'[31] The Russians, unsurprisingly, supported Habibullah in his efforts, and although the emir did not establish direct communication with Russia at this time, the ongoing threat of such a move alarmed both the Indian and the British governments.

Thus, as Lee-Warner reported in 1902, the British position in Afghanistan at the turn of the century was far from secure:

In Afghanistan the situation is almost as bad as it can be. ... Professing to Russia to direct the foreign policy of the Afghans, we are unable to direct or control it. ... The Amir ... is a factor in the balance of power, who can play us off against Russia and Russia against us, and the whole position is most unsatisfactory. If Russia presses us to secure satisfaction for a just demand we cannot enforce it.[32]

Simultaneously, a similar struggle for influence was under way in Persia. Persia was unfortunate enough to be placed within comfortable reach of the Russian armies in the Caucasus to the north, and easily dominated by the British navy on its Gulf shore in the south. So situated, midway between Europe and India, Persia could not avoid being drawn into the game as an unwilling pawn. Throughout the last third of the nineteenth century, Russia was working furiously to bring Persia firmly into its sphere; Russo-Persian commerce flourished, as the Russian government matched the preferential tariffs they attained from the shah's court with government bounties on the domestic side to promote trade. Russian influence in Persia was further enhanced by the construction of the Trans-Caspian Railway, which not only allowed for the development of commerce, but also created the potential to place Russian troops on the Russo-Persian border in force within a relatively short period of time.

Russia was clearly gaining the upper hand in the competition for dominance in Persia. In 1884 the boundary conflict concerning the area around Sarakhs on the north-eastern frontier of Persia was settled in Russia's favour. Then, in the spring of 1889, Prince Dolgorukii, the Russian envoy to the court of the shah, concluded a secret convention that granted Russia a monopoly over the majority of the transportation concessions in Persia. Plans were soon drawn up for the construction of a line from Teheran to Mashhad. Furthermore, Russian troops were stationed in various parts of Persia; even a Persian Cossack brigade, commanded by Russian officers, was formed. All this was creating in Persia something akin to the informal imperial relationship that Britain enjoyed with Afghanistan. As Lord Kimberley, the viceroy of India, noted with resignation in 1893: 'Russia will, without actually taking possession of the [Persian] North Eastern Provinces, control them virtually, and ... the Shah will become a vassal of the Tsar in reality tho' not in name.'[33]

Russian domination spread from being primarily commercial and diplomatic to being financially oriented when, in 1894, Count Sergei Iulievich Witte, the Russian minister of finance, took over a failing Russian private bank in Teheran and converted it into the Discount-Loan Bank of Persia. Lamsdorff later lauded the significance of this direct involvement of Russia in the economic life of Persia: 'The greatest Russian undertaking in Persia has been the establishment of the Discount-Loan Bank of Persia. ... This bank is a possible rival to the Shah's bank, established earlier with English means.'[34]

In 1896 Nasir ed-Din Shah was assassinated, and the ministers of his successor, Mozaffar ed-Din Shah, strove to reduce Persia's dependence on Russia. However, Persia was considered by the financial houses of Europe to be a serious credit risk, since funds advanced had been traditionally squandered by the court. Therefore, despite the promise of increased influence at the Persian court that would inevitably result from the extension of loans, not even the British were willing to grant the Persians the credit they desperately needed. Lord Salisbury, in his dual role as prime minister and foreign secretary, bemoaned Parliament's unwillingness to practise such loan diplomacy:

> Other nations can lend money: and we cannot. The House of Commons, which never would guarantee the debt of India, would positively refuse any advance to an impecunious Oriental Ally. Other nations will give it. It is hopeless to struggle against that disadvantage. The real friend is the friend from whom one can borrow.[35]

In contrast to Britain's financial caution, Russia was quite willing to provide Persia with the desired funds. The loan that was negotiated in early 1900 gave Persia approximately £4 million, provided that (1) all customs revenue, except that received in the Gulf, was to be offered as security for the loan; (2) Persia was to pay off all other foreign debts; (3) Persia could borrow from no other government until the loan was paid off; and (4) no other government could receive railway concessions in Persia for ten years.[36]

At the same time, Russia prepared to occupy the port of Bandar-e 'Abbas on the Persian Gulf and to construct a branch of the Trans-Caspian Railway to the port. In his pamphlet, Captain Rittich suggested the overwhelming effect such a move would have on Russia's control of Persia:

> As regards the Bunder Abbas branch, its construction will give us influence over the whole of Persia, and will exclude the question of partition of Persia into two spheres of influence; Russia in the north and England in the south.

> We can have no partition of spheres; the whole of Persia must be ours.[37]

In response to rumours of the planned occupation of Bandar-e 'Abbas, Lord Curzon, viceroy of India, argued that a Russian 'Port Arthur on the Gulf' would result in the equivalent of the Manchurian railway through the Persian state, which would turn the flank of India's land defences.[38]

For Russia, control of Persia was desirable because of the commercial advantages – a market for Russian manufactures – and the strategic – a warm water port and an alternate route towards India. In contrast, Britain's interest in Persia was solely focused around the defence of India; the Persian–Anglo-

Indian trade that correspondingly developed was merely a welcome benefit. As Lord Salisbury said in 1889, 'Were it not for our possession of India we should trouble ourselves but little about Persia.'[39] In reaction to Russia's impressive inroads in the north, Britain actively courted Persian favour. The establishment of a Russian consulate and a branch of the Discount-Loan Bank in Seistan, which bordered on the Indian frontier, was countered with the construction of a railway from Quetta to Nushi and on to Nastrabad, the chief town of Seistan province, where a British consulate was established in 1900. However, although British attempts to oppose the extension of Russia's regional hegemony produced marked results, the Russian influence in Persia was already significantly ensconced at the beginning of the twentieth century.

The compulsion for Anglo-Russian competition for dominance in the 'forbidden land' of Tibet was far less obvious. Although Tibet bordered the northeastern frontiers of Britain's protectorates of Sikkim, Bhutan and Nepal, Russia was separated from Lhasa by over 1000 miles of Chinese Turkestan. Furthermore, the Tibetans had actively discouraged the involvement of any foreigners in their affairs, meeting those who dared to cross the mountain passes into the plateau country with armed opposition when necessary. Despite these factors – which had allowed Tibet long to remain above the fray of the Anglo-Russian rivalry – Tibet became one of the focal points in the ever intensifying Great Game as the nineteenth century drew to a close.

Tibet first caught the active attention of the British in the 1870s, when they began to look towards the development of the Tibetan market for Indian and British goods in exchange for Tibetan gold and wool; they further hoped to explore a possible trade route to the Chinese interior across the Tibetan plateau. In addition, the encouragement of good Anglo-Tibetan diplomatic relations was considered by many within the Anglo-Indian establishment to be vital to the maintenance of stability within the Himalayan states of Nepal, Bhutan and Sikkim.[40] Initial British attempts to open up Tibet to Indian trade were hampered by Tibet's nebulous relationship with China; although the Tibetans refused to acknowledge China's right to dictate Tibetan policy, the British government chose to recognize Chinese suzerainty over the country. Finally, in 1876, an article of the Chefoo Agreement between China and Britain allowed for the dispatch of a British exploratory mission to Tibet; the mission was initially postponed, and when it was finally assembled in 1886 Tibetan opposition forced the Chinese to recognize the British annexation of Upper Burma in exchange for the mission's cancellation, as formalized in the Burma Convention of 1886.

The Tibetans continued their active opposition to attempted British incursions by moving against the British protectorate of Sikkim in 1888. A

Tibetan detachment set up a military post in the Sikkim village of Lingtu in an attempt to reassert their ancient claims over the land. The Chinese, although they were proving unable to persuade the Tibetans to withdraw in response to British requests, refused to surrender the illusion of suzerainty and insisted that the British continue to negotiate with Peking. The resulting two agreements – the Anglo-Chinese Convention signed at Calcutta on 17 March 1890, and the Tibet Trade Regulations signed at Darjeeling on 5 December 1893 – delineated the Sikkim–Tibetan boundary and arranged the opening of a trade mart at Yatung in the Chumbi Valley. But continued Tibetan denunciation of the agreements, supplemented by the Tibetan seizure and murder of two English subjects, ensured the ongoing instability of Anglo-Tibetan relations.[41]

As frustrating as Tibetan opposition was proving for the Government of India, affairs beyond their north-eastern frontier were of a relatively minor concern for the British when compared with the numerous other impending crises that threatened their imperial hegemony, like Fashoda, the Boxer Rebellion and the Boer War. The landscape was vastly altered at the turn of the century, however, by growing rumours of Russian activity on the Tibetan plateau. Relations between Russia and Tibet on a local and spiritual basis were unavoidable; the Buriats and the Kalmyks of the Trans-Baikalia region were culturally and religiously linked to the Tibetan Buddhists, and the Dalai Lama served as their spiritual leader.[42] Most alarming for the British was the apparent influence of Agvan Dorjiev, a Buriat subject of the tsar whose very presence within the Dalai Lama's inner circle seemed to indicate to the British the inescapable threat of Russo-Tibetan entanglement. Dorjiev, who had studied in Tibet and was an assistant tutor to the 13th Dalai Lama, had been summoned in 1898 to St Petersburg by Prince Ukhtomsky.[43] Although Lamsdorff denied in a conversation with the British ambassador on 3 July 1901 that the subsequent meeting between Dorjiev and the tsar had been of an even remotely diplomatic nature, the Buriat was continually described in the Russian press as an 'Envoy Extraordinary from the Dalai Lama of Tibet'. The idea of an official embassy from the Dalai Lama to the tsar was particularly galling to the British since, as the secretary of state for India pointed out, the Dalai Lama had refused to receive any communications from the viceroy at all.[44]

Simultaneously, rumours were circulating in China and Russia of a proposed agreement between these two countries that would place Tibet within Russia's sphere of influence in exchange for a Russian promise for the maintenance of Chinese geographic integrity. The Chinese Foreign Board quickly denied the possibility of such an agreement, and Count Benckendorff, the Russian ambassador in London, officially informed the British foreign minister, the Marquess of Lansdowne, on 8 April 1903 that Russia had no designs on Tibet. Nevertheless the rumour was sufficiently widespread to promote Anglo-Indian fears of a permanent Russian presence on the very perimeter of their possessions.[45]

George Nathaniel Curzon, who had been appointed viceroy in 1898, was convinced that this apparent Russian advantage in Tibet had to be countered with an expedition to Lhasa. But the Home Government was concerned that such an expedition would complicate both Anglo-Chinese and Anglo-Russian relations; furthermore, they feared that the establishment of a precedent allowing Tibet to conduct its own foreign affairs might inspire the Afghan emir to act similarly.[46] Despite these hesitations in London, the Anglo-Indians continued to push for action. In his 1910 monograph, *India and Tibet*, Younghusband, who followed his earlier adventures in the Pamirs by leading the Tibetan expedition that was eventually dispatched, ruminated on why it was felt that Russia's advance must be neutralized:

> Why should we trouble? What possible harm could a few Russians do in Lhasa? Russia might invade India through Afghanistan, but she could never invade India across Tibet and over the Himalayas. ... [If] we complacently, and without a protest, allowed her to establish herself in Tibet, we could hardly expect those States dependent on us and bordering Tibet to think otherwise than that this was the real Power in Asia, and this, therefore, the Power to look up to.[47]

At last, Curzon received permission from London to dispatch a mission with Younghusband at the helm; the expedition was to go as far as Khambajong, just over the Tibetan border, to force a discussion of the outstanding trade and border disputes. As Curzon had predicted, these efforts proved fruitless, and Younghusband was sent deeper into Tibet to Gyangze, which lay on the road to Lhasa. After the expeditionary force was attacked by the Tibetans at Gyangze, Younghusband moved on to the Tibetan capital itself, entering Lhasa in August 1904. The Dalai Lama had fled to Mongolia, taking Dorjiev with him, before the British entered his capital, and the monks who remained signed a convention on 7 September 1904 by which Tibet guaranteed the following: (1) Tibet would respect the Sikkim frontier (Article I); (2) markets would be opened at Gyangze and Gartok in addition to the one already pledged at Yatung (Article II); (3) Tibet would pay an indemnity of £500,000 (Article VI); (4) the Chumbi Valley would be occupied by Britain until either the indemnity had been paid or the trade marts had been opened for three years, whichever date proved later (Article VII); (5) Tibetan territory would not be alienated to any foreign power (Article IX, section a); (6) no foreign power would be allowed to intervene in Tibetan affairs or send representatives there (Article IX, sections b and c); (7) no concessions would be granted nor any Tibetan revenues pledged to any foreign power or subject (Article IX, sections d and e).[48]

Russia, for its part, viewed the dispatch of the Younghusband expedition as 'calculated to involve a grave disturbance of the Central Asian situation', as Benckendorff protested to Lansdowne in November. Lansdowne attempted to explain the extenuating circumstances by which Britain felt compelled to take this action, appending an additional admonition against too vehement a Russian reaction:

> It seemed to me beyond measure strange that these protests should be made by the Government of a Power which had all over the world never hesitated to encroach upon its neighbours when the circumstances seemed to require it. If the Russian Government had a right to complain of us for taking steps in order to obtain reparation from the Tibetans by advancing into Tibetan territory what kind of language should we not be entitled to use in regard to Russian encroachments in Manchuria, Turkestan, Persia (and elsewhere).[49]

As Younghusband progressed through Tibet, Lansdowne continued to assure Benckendorff that the British government had no intention of allowing the mission to lead to either a permanent occupation or a permanent intervention in Tibetan affairs.[50] Reaction in Russia to the publication of the terms of the Lhasa Convention was, however, extremely negative. The Russians felt the agreement violated the assurances that had been given to Benckendorff. Firstly, the indemnity had been set too high, which would result in an occupation of the Chumbi Valley for at least three years. Furthermore, Article IX was interpreted by Russia as well as by Germany and the United States as the establishment of a virtual British protectorate over the country.[51] Therefore, although the Younghusband expedition had been dispatched in the hope of stabilizing the region, the resulting dissension within the international community suggested that the regional tensions were far from pacified.

At the turn of the twentieth century, the growing tension between Britain and Russia in Central Asia appeared to be unresolvable. For a variety of reasons, however, both powers chose to come to terms with one another rather than risk armed conflict over the region. From the time of the Boer War, the British Empire was increasingly aware of the growing array of economic and military challenges it faced. Lord George Hamilton, then secretary of state for India, saw the war in South Africa as indicative of a deep-rooted problem of over-extension throughout the Empire: 'I think all my colleagues feel, as I do, that this war makes self-evident that our Empire is in excess of our armaments, or even of our power to defend it in all parts of the world.'[52] Taking into account Britain's relatively decreasing industrial growth, increasing national debt, and evident military over-extension, especially concerning the Indian subcontinent, a move towards a diplomatic resolution of potential international conflicts appeared preferable. As Hugh Arnold-Forster, secretary of state for war, wrote in his diary in 1904, 'Diplomacy, rather than preparations on the Frontier must come to our aid.'[53] The first attempt to achieve security in Asia through diplomatic means manifested itself in the Anglo-Japanese Alliance of 1902. Then, in 1904, Britain's Middle Eastern and African concerns were lessened with the conclusion of the Anglo-French Entente Cordiale.

But this Anglo-French agreement did not sufficiently relieve Britain of its colonial cares; before long the escalation of Franco-German tensions and the onset of the First Moroccan Crisis had demonstrated to Britain the fragility of Europe's tenuous balance of power and the German expectation of inclusion in any colonial settlement. The German diplomatic defeat at the Algeciras Conference, convened to settle the dispute, resulted in the crystallization of the Anglo-French relationship rather than the rupture in the nascent entente that Germany had hoped to encourage. But it was clear to the British that the loose colonial agreement they had recently achieved with France would not sufficiently free them to devote their overtaxed energies to the defence of the rest of their besieged empire; Anglo-French military and naval talks soon began with the idea of converting the entente into an outright alliance, and a rapprochement with Russia in Central Asia was contemplated. Yet, while it is true that Morocco – like the experience of the Boer War – reminded Britain just how overstretched its imperial resources were, and promoted a clarification of British security concerns throughout the Empire, the Anglo-Russian rapprochement should not be seen as a diplomatic move to counter German expansion. Rather, the awareness that the strategic landscape throughout the world could not be simplified to allow Britain to concentrate on the defence of India prompted Britain to act directly to alleviate its most pressing security concern – the Russian threat in Central Asia.

Russia had faced a similarly sobering military encounter to that which Britain endured in South Africa. On 8 February 1904 the Japanese fleet successfully attacked the unsuspecting Russian fleet in the outer harbour of Port Arthur. The ensuing war proved humiliating for the Russian giant. An unprepared, disorganized, internally troubled, diplomatically isolated Russia was defeated by a well-organized, modern Japan allied with Great Britain and favoured by world public opinion. The war strained further the already tense relations between Britain and Russia; although Britain remained neutral throughout the war, its alliance with Japan led it to deny coaling to the Russian fleet from its coasts. Then, on 21 October 1904, the *Kamchatka* of the Russian Baltic fleet, which was making its way to the Pacific, mistakenly fired on a fleet of British steam trawlers that were fishing in the Dogger Bank, sinking three ships and severely damaging one more in a shooting barrage that lasted nearly half an hour. Britain's involvement in the war was only narrowly averted through some hasty diplomatic manoeuvring and the personal intervention of the tsar.

Unable to supply its field army along the single-track Trans-Siberian Railway, hampered by a divided navy – one-third of which was trapped in the Black Sea by the hated Straits Convention – and hindered by the emphasis on administration rather than field operations within the senior command ranks, any hopes that Russia might have had of being able to fight a successful war of attrition in Manchuria were dashed by the outbreak of revolution on 22 January 1905. The events of what became known as Bloody Sunday, when a crowd of demonstrators longing to present their grievances to the tsar were fired on outside the Winter Palace in St Petersburg, plunged Russia into a domestic crisis that forced a speedy conclusion to what was proving to be a disastrous military conflict. By September 1905 the war was over.

But even the outcome of the war was not seen by the British to diminish greatly the strength of Russia's position or their desires in Central Asia. Rather, the British predicted that the thwarting of Russian expansionist aims in the Far East would lead Russia to look for fulfilment of its goals in Central Asia instead. Russia's ongoing commitment to Central Asia had been underscored by the fact that, even as defeat loomed in Manchuria, not one battalion was transferred from Turkestan to the Japanese front.[54] As Claude MacDonald, the British minister in Tokyo, suggested in May 1905: '[Russia's] next venture is much more likely to be an attack upon us through India than an attempt to wipe out old scores with [the Japanese].'[55] MacDonald also underscored Russia's ability to maintain in defeat an army of 250,000 men 3000 miles from Russia proper via the sole link of the single track of the Trans-Siberian Railway, adding ominously that India was a good deal nearer St Petersburg than Manchuria was.[56]

The Russians, on the other hand, saw the defeat by Japan as indicating a need for a critical reorientation of Russian strategy. The war in Manchuria had shown that Russia was dangerously overextended, and would be unable to commit the resources necessary to defend itself in case of a two-front war in both Europe and Asia. Where Russia would next find itself at war had long been a subject of debate between those who advocated Russia's European destiny in the Straits and those who saw its destiny in Central Asia and the Far East. But all were in agreement that a simplification of Russia's international security environment was in order, no matter where they felt the threat was most acute.[57] A rapprochement with Britain in Central Asia might alleviate regional tensions enough to allow Russia to concentrate its overstretched resources elsewhere.

In the wake of the 1905 Revolution, Russia's Manchurian defeat and the First Moroccan Crisis, both the British and Russian governments began to consider seriously a mutual rapprochement. The first official steps towards Russia were made by the Unionist foreign secretary of Great Britain, the Marquess of Lansdowne, in mid-1905. Urged on by the French government, he broached the subject of a possible agreement over Afghanistan with Tsar Nicholas II's minister in London, Count Benckendorff. S.A. Poklevsky-Kozell, then counsellor at the Russian embassy, passed on the suggestion to Witte, who was chairman of the Council of Ministers from 1905. Witte, adamantly opposed to an Anglo-Russian rapprochement, responded: 'Russia, after that incautious war with Japan, should, in order to regain her status as a Great Power, have free hands and not bind herself with agreements.'[58] Nevertheless, while Benckendorff responded to Lansdowne that the time was not auspicious for a written agreement guaranteeing that Afghanistan would remain outside Russia's sphere of influence, the groundwork was laid for further discussions.

As the Liberal government took office in Britain in December 1905, the drive towards a British settlement with Russia of their Central Asian differences was gaining momentum. The new prime minister, Sir Henry Campbell-Bannerman, made an immediate appeal for the cultivation of friendly relations with other powers, in order to 'secure for the States of Europe that immunity from the intolerable burdens of naval armaments, which can be secured by no height to which jealousies and rivalries and insane competition can carry us.'[59] The Liberals had come to power pledging a course of economy and retrenchment. Although a reconciliation with auto-cratic Russia was not necessarily in keeping with the tenets of liberalism, the economic and strategic benefits of an agreement with the tsar's government took precedence over the international championing of civil liberties.

In March 1906 the Liberal foreign secretary, Sir Edward Grey, first suggested to Benckendorff a formal entente, similar to that already in existence between Britain and France, in which the contracting parties would pledge to maintain the status quo in Asia. In response to Benckendorff's hesitation to involve his government in an agreement that might further exacerbate Russia's domestic unrest, Grey assured the ambassador 'that every arrangement of this kind must have two sides.'[60] In the meantime, Witte resigned on 2 May, followed two days later by Lamsdorff. Most significantly for Anglo-Russian relations, Aleksandr Petrovich Izvolskii, whose 31 years in the Russian diplomatic service had most recently included the post of Russian minister to Denmark, was appointed to the office of minister of foreign affairs. Izvolskii, generally pro-British and strongly influenced by his time spent with the Germanophobic Danish, was clearly in favour of an Anglo-Russian understanding.[61]

With both sides desiring an agreement, only the resolution of the outstanding issues remained. Negotiations progressed slowly. On 21 July the first Duma was dissolved, and Britain was convinced that Russia was on the verge of revolution, which greatly hampered diplomatic progress.[62] When talks at last commenced in September, Persia was the first issue to be discussed; in an effort to forestall increased German involvement in Persian affairs, Britain and Russia quickly agreed to underwrite a joint Anglo-Russian loan to Persia. The question of Tibet was also easily settled: Russia readily acknowledged that its interests in Tibet were not equivalent to Britain's – notwithstanding the Dalai Lama's spiritual authority over numerous Russian subjects – and sought primarily to keep the British from absorbing Tibet themselves. There remained, however, numerous outstanding issues. In Persia the main priority for the British lay in their need to have Russia accept that the strategically crucial Seistan province must fall within the British zone. In exchange for this concession, the Russians demanded that Britain renounce any intended railway construction in Afghanistan. Furthermore, the Russians required that all restrictions on their Afghan trade be removed, guaranteeing them access equal to that enjoyed by the British.[63] The British were willing to cede the Russians this allowance, but were quick to point out that they enjoyed no particular privileges in Afghanistan, and were at the mercy of the emir's whims just like their Russian counterparts.[64]

The final stumbling block was the seemingly unpalatable demand that Russia forgo any right of intervention in Afghanistan in exchange for a British declaration not to annex any Afghan territory. After great effort, Izvolskii was able to persuade Russian military and reactionary opinion to accept the British guarantees. He forced the Council of Ministers in August 1907 to recognize that, without a stabilization of Russia's Asian position, they risked demotion to the ranks of second-class powers, banished from a position of authority in European concerns: 'We must put our interests in Asia in proper order or else we shall ourselves become an Asiatic state, which would be a great disaster for Russia.'[65] As the finance minister Kokovtsov had conceded during the meeting of the Special Committee on the Afghan Question of 14 April 1907: 'The importance of the agreement with England is so great, that its achievement would even be worth partially forgoing strategic considerations related to the Afghan question.'[66]

The Anglo-Russian Convention that was signed at St Petersburg on 31 August 1907 incorporated a series of compromises on both sides for the sake of regional stability. The Convention consisted of three separate agreements concerning Persia, Afghanistan and Tibet, respectively. 'The Arrangement

Concerning Persia' divided that country between British and Russian spheres of influence with a no-man's land in between. The British promised not to seek:

> any Concessions of a political or commercial nature – such as Concessions for railways, banks, telegraphs, roads, transport, insurance, etc. – beyond a line starting from Kasr-i-Shirin, crossing Isfahan, Yezd, and Kakhk and ending at a point on the Persian frontier at the intersection of the Russian and Afghan frontiers.

Similarly, Russia agreed not to seek the same 'beyond a line going from the Afghan frontier by way of Gazik, Birjand, Kerman, and ending at Bunder Abbas'. Great Britain declared its lack of desire to change the political status of Afghanistan, and Russia recognized that Afghanistan was outside its sphere of influence, agreeing to conduct all dealings with Afghanistan 'through the intermediary of his Britannic Majesty's government'. In addition, both nations would enjoy equal trading opportunities in that country. And in Tibet, both the British and Russian governments agreed to recognize the suzerain rights of China over Tibet.[67] In an ancillary note, both powers pledged to forgo the mounting of scientific missions to Tibet for a period of three years.[68] For many, the Great Game appeared to have come to an end.

The agreement that Britain and Russia concluded in the late summer of 1907 was clearly designed to alleviate the Central Asian concerns of both Great Powers and to relieve the regional tension that had been building between them for decades. This was an agreement forged in and addressing Central Asia; any advantages which might accrue to either power such as a revision of the Straits Agreement or the development of a loose tripartite entente was secondary to the immediate regional considerations that motivated the agreement. The Anglo-Russian rapprochement has been seen to have been motivated by several different factors. Post-First World War historical hindsight has produced a school of thought that interprets the agreement as a calculated step by Britain and Russia to lay the groundwork for a Europe-oriented alliance system focused on countering a growing German threat. In this theory, Central Asia serves as the theatre for an agreement, while regional interests are secondary to those of the European alliance structure. But it is misguided to think that the motivating force behind British and Russian imperial strategic concerns in 1907 was subordinate to Continental manoeuvring for alignments; such a conclusion virtually ignores both the crucial role India and the rest of the Empire played in the formation of British foreign policy, and the importance of the continued growth in Russia's Asia orientation in the post-Russo-Japanese War period. The significance of the 1907

Anglo-Russian agreement was not as a precursor to the three-power Anglo-Franco-Russian concert in 1914, but as a deterrent of what was seen to be an impending Central Asian crisis. The extent to which this agreement was successful in diffusing regional tensions and alleviating mutual suspicions remained to be seen in the years leading up to the outbreak of the First World War.

CHAPTER 2

Triumph or Tribulation? The Realities of the Anglo-Russian Relationship: 1907–8

Although the treaty of rapprochement signed on 31 August 1907 normalized official relations between Britain and Russia concerning Persia, Afghanistan and Tibet, it opened up each government to attacks from both the right and the left. The Russian Ministry of Foreign Affairs (MID) had acted quickly to quell opposition within its own ranks, immediately disseminating a circular letter internally and to its embassies and legations abroad explaining Russia's motivations for reaching the agreement with Britain.[1] Such a pre-emptive strike did little to assuage the imperial traditionalists who had long advocated a forward policy in Central Asia. Ivan Alekseevich Zinoviev, a rigid Anglophobe who had served in Persia for nearly 27 years and had been director of the Asiatic Department of MID for eight more, saved the most vociferous expression of his disgust for his 1912 tirade against Izvolskii's policies entitled *Russia, England and Persia*.[2] Within private circles, however, his condemnation was even less restrained. Similarly, Witte, whose initial opposition to an Anglo-Russian rapprochement had obstructed agreement in 1905, continued to oppose the convention. In addition to his criticisms that the agreement gave Britain far more than Russia gained, especially in Persia, Witte condemned what he saw as a turn from Germany towards Britain:

> This convention signified a sharp turn from our policy of rapprochement or, otherwise, flirtation with Germany towards one of rapprochement and flirtation with England. Just like women, England and Germany appear to be fairly jealous persons, and as they are supplied with mental faculties no less highly developed than ours, we find ourselves for the time being in a duplicitous condition in which Germany believes that we, of course, love Germany above all, and are flirting with England more for appearances; to England, when

necessary, we speak the opposite. I believe that to sustain these appearances
... in the future will prove unfavourable for us.[3]

The voices of the extreme right agreed with Witte's analysis, as the
Moskovskie Vedomosti wrote on 22–23 September/5–6 October 1907:
'Friendly relations towards Germany for us are one of the principal, if not the
most important, elements of our foreign policy for the task of the internal
pacification of the state.'[4] However, the majority of the Russian press was less
concerned than Witte over the shift in Great Power inclination that the
rapprochement might represent. Rather, the hostility of the press towards the
agreement centred around what was perceived to be a sacrifice of Russian
regional interests and the potential diminution of Russian prestige among its
own Asiatic subjects. Even those newspapers like *Rech* that approved of the
convention overall complained that Britain had gained far greater advantages
than Russia.[5]

The British press, in contrast, was far more favourably inclined towards
the agreement than its Russian counterpart. No matter their individual
ideological inclinations, the press came down in support of the convention's
aims. *The Times* was fully in favour of the terms of the convention, and
upheld the agreement as the best means of freeing the world 'from the his-
toric rivalry of the two great European Powers in Asia'.[6] *The Economist*,
responding to the criticisms from those factions of British society that felt that
an agreement with Russia was inappropriate for Liberal Britain, insisted that,
'as we think fit, like all other nations, to maintain diplomatic relations with
Russia, it is not wrong in itself to conclude an arrangement with her.' Furthermore, they felt that the terms of the agreement, with the exception of a
few unfortunate phrases concerning Persia, such as 'requests for concessions'
and 'control over sources of revenue', could not be improved upon.[7]

Even the *Manchester Guardian*, whose typical stance as champion of the
left would have pointed towards an outright condemnation of the agreement,
was unpredictably generous. While finding little to commend in the terms of
the convention, they found little to criticize, either:

> The Anglo-Russian Convention seems to us to merit neither strong praise nor
> strong blame. Things in Persia, Afghanistan, and Tibet were drifting in cer-
> tain directions. The Convention in each case takes note of the drift,
> formalises it, and, as it were, legalises it. Such agreements are often worth
> making, but they seldom give sufficient cause for having the bells rung, or for
> tearing our hair either, and so it is with this one.[8]

In the opinion of the *Guardian*, the agreement would serve to protect legitimate British interests in Central Asia 'with the least possible discredit', and,
therefore, even a liberal could not in good conscience condemn it.

While the British press was remarkably sanguine in response to the convention, political factions both in and out of government were far more open in their attacks against the Anglo-Russian agreement. The British left was vehemently opposed to what they saw as an alliance with autocratic Russia, ruled by a despot who had just dissolved the Duma. Even before the details of the agreement were settled, the Independent Labour Party (ILP) had condemned the spirit of Anglo-Russian reconciliation, passing a resolution at a meeting of its National Administrative Council on 8 July 1907 protesting against any agreement with a government, 'which has used, and is using, every means of barbarism to repress the movement for Constitutional freedom ... in its violation of every principle of freedom and humanity.'[9]

While the ILP protested against the 1907 Anglo-Russian convention on social and civil grounds, the Conservative opposition attacked the letter of the agreement. Curzon, as expected, led a vociferous attack in keeping with his well-established Russophobia and pro-imperialist stance. Although he was no longer officially involved in government and was serving as chancellor of Oxford University, Britain and Russia both regarded Curzon as the foremost Anglo-Indian authority on the Anglo-Russian competition.[10] In a speech at Oxford on 2 November, and later in his maiden speech in the House of Lords on 6 February 1908, Curzon condemned on every count what he regarded as the most important treaty concluded by a British government in nearly half a century. While he supported the spirit of rapprochement that prompted the conclusion of the agreement, he could not but criticize the details of a 'bargain [that] is doubtful in respect of Afghanistan, bad in respect of Tibet, and worse in respect of Persia.'[11] The barrage of objections from the Conservative Opposition continued with a motion in the House of Commons from Earl Percy on 17 February 1908, positing 'that the terms of the Convention, while involving at several points a material sacrifice of British interests, still leave room for international misunderstandings of a kind which both the Contracting Powers desire to avoid.'[12] Although the motion was ultimately withdrawn, the harsh parliamentary debate that it sparked encompassed a point-by-point attack on every aspect of the agreement.

Well-positioned individuals in the government also questioned the wisdom of guaranteeing a status quo in which Britain found itself at a disadvantage to Russia. Sir Cecil Spring-Rice, the British minister in Teheran, took Grey to task for aligning Britain with a country intent on supporting reaction in Persia:

It would seem that there is at least a prima facie case for those who are ready to criticise you for all you do either in co-operation with an autocratic power or in opposition to the liberties of smaller nations. ... It is possible that Russia will use the agreement ... in order to carry on her old designs under a new cover. It will be more serious from the point of view of public opinion if the old policy is still carried on under the new Convention. For the breach by treachery of a formal agreement is a far more serious matter than the open prosecution of a policy of undisguised hostility.

As Spring-Rice cautioned Grey, the agreement could only weaken Britain's standing in the eyes of the Persian populace: 'We are worse off than the Russians because we are not feared as they are, and because we are regarded as having betrayed the Persian people.'[13]

Grey was left to counter the criticisms by which the agreement was being besieged from all sides. In a speech on foreign relations at the Corn Exchange at Berwick-on-Tweed on 19 December 1907, the foreign secretary stressed the decision of both countries to pursue 'peace and friendly relations' with each other as opposed to 'political distrust and friction'. He insisted that the agreement signified a renunciation by both Britain *and* Russia of a forward policy in Central Asia, and declared that such a policy had not been in the best interests of either country. Furthermore, the convention had safeguarded the Indian frontier without sacrificing any existing commercial prospects in Persia. And most significantly, the understanding between Britain and Russia had prevented the intervention of either Great Power in the state of revolutionary chaos in which Persia was increasingly enveloped.[14] Thus, he asserted, the agreement was already in many ways a proven success.

While Grey was striving to persuade the public of the merits of the agreement, the Foreign Office attempted to overcome resistance within the government. A memorandum was dispatched to the India Office in late January 1908, which sought to clarify the advantages of the agreement for those within the Anglo-Indian establishment who distrusted the current spirit of rapprochement. Like Grey's Corn Exchange speech, the memorandum maintained that the convention had prevented conflict in Persia and had allowed the two powers to achieve a level of co-operation that would have been virtually impossible had no such agreement been reached. Furthermore, the memorandum lauded the convention as having successfully obviated the sources of Anglo-Russian friction in Asia. And as a final reminder that Central Asian concerns were not the sole consideration in the formation of British policy, and that the India Office and the Government of India would have to abandon their traditional Russophobia and accept the reality of the rapprochement, the memorandum flatly stated that, 'the removal of all causes of discord in Asia will no doubt contribute to more harmonious relations between the two Powers in Europe.'[15]

In crediting the convention with 'the removal of all causes of discord in Asia', however, the Foreign Office was being overly optimistic. Almost immediately after the signing of the treaty, the Anglo-Russian relationship faced its first significant challenge. The Afghan emir, Habibullah Khan, jealously guarding his independence and completely suspicious both of his neighbours looming to the north and of his supposed protectors to the south, refused to recognize the provisions of the agreement concerning Afghanistan. Britain had anticipated that the emir might react negatively to the agreement, and had asked the Russians to delay its publication until the Government of India itself had been able to communicate it to the emir.[16] Their efforts to preclude the emir's antipathy were futile, and Russian intelligence reports from Afghanistan reported that the emir was calling his people to arms against his neighbours:

> Let all persons present render us for war with the infidel one man from every two homes, and to take upon yourself their support. Arms and cartridges will be provided from the treasury. All these new soldiers must train in the methods of war, because in a year we will begin a national war with either the British or the Russians.[17]

Despite his obligation to follow British advice concerning foreign relations, the emir chose instead to heed the convictions of members of his court who advised him not to consent to the agreement without adequate compensation from the British. As Sardar Nasrollah Khan, Habibullah's brother and principal adviser, warned: 'Allow them to open only a pin-hole; they will make it wider and wider by their skill, so that in a short time they will pass through it on elephants.'[18]

The British remained convinced that the emir would in time sign the agreement, as the Foreign Office noted at the end of January: 'In view of the time which Orientals take over correspondence, and the importance of the subject, which necessitated consultation with his advisers, it is no matter of surprise that he has not yet replied.'[19] Seven months after the signing of the agreement, however, Grey remained unable to do more than assure the Russians that the Indian government was continuing to work on obtaining the emir's consent. In March 1908 Benckendorff suggested to Izvolskii that Russia would be best served by carrying on as if the emir's agreement had been secured, but even with Russia's demonstration of good faith in overlooking the awkwardness of the situation, the strength of the agreement came into question.[20] Izvolskii subsequently assured the British chargé d'affaires, Hugh O'Beirne, that Britain's Afghan policy was not under suspicion in either official or military circles and that Russia would not take advantage of Habibullah Khan's obstinacy.[21]

Nevertheless, the British recognized that their inability to bring their semi-protectorate into line might throw the entire Anglo-Russian Central Asian relationship into disarray and take Britain's regional prestige with it. As

Sir Arthur Nicolson, British ambassador to St Petersburg and one of the
principal architects of the rapprochement, predicted in a private letter to
Grey on 19 July:

> If the Afghan Convention has to go by the board, and if the Ameer were al-
> lowed to veto an arrangement to which the Sovereigns and Govt.s of Russia
> and England had subscribed and had finally ratified, I should imagine that our
> prestige would suffer seriously throughout the Middle and Far East. Further-
> more the opponents, both in and out of Russia, to an understanding between
> the two countries would be greatly encouraged, and I do not consider that
> the unfortunate effects ensuing from our failure to secure the consent of the
> Ameer would be limited solely to the points at issue. The consequences
> would be more serious, and would flow over a wider field.[22]

Finally, at the end of August 1908, nearly a year after the original signing
of the Anglo-Russian Convention, Habibullah Khan sent the viceroy the
opinion of the Afghan State Council on the agreement. The Council were
vehemently opposed to what they considered a betrayal of Afghanistan by the
British to their former Russian rivals: 'To sacrifice for the sake of such an
enemy a friend like Afghanistan, which for years has prevented the enemy of
the Power allied to him from pushing a foot on his soil, is a thousand pities.'
Complaining that 'the words "freedom" and "independence" have no meaning
as applied to Persia,' the Council claimed that the complete absence of these
words in relation to the articles pertaining to Afghanistan suggested that
Afghanistan held a subordinate position even to the carved-up Persia. Above
all, the Council maintained that the convention destroyed the very essence of
Afghan independence.[23] Although the emir actually rejected the Council's
statement, the Council alleged that under Islamic law the emir had no power
to alienate his subjects' rights, and thus its condemnation of the convention
would have to stand.[24]

By this point, however, the consent or lack thereof of the emir was no
longer a primary concern, as Russia had assured Britain several times that it
intended to adhere to the spirit of the convention with or without the formal
agreement of Afghanistan. Britain felt strongly, though, that this demonstration of goodwill on the part of the Russians only increased Britain's duty to
obtain the emir's adhesion.[25] Anything short of complete Afghan recognition
and agreement to the terms of the convention would appear to be an evasion
of British obligations to Russia, if not a categorical act of bad faith.[26] The
British were determined that Afghan obstinacy would not force Britain into
being the first to fall short of their promises.

The Russian decision to act as if the agreement were actually in effect was
more than just an inconsequential promise to uphold a relationship that was

not being tested; in contrast, tensions along the Russo-Afghan border continued to flare up, aggravating an already difficult situation. The frontier region was a potential powder keg, as both the Afghans and Russians regularly practised with guns and rifles on their respective sides of the border.[27] Russia was extremely concerned by its inability to protect its own citizens from frequent and ferocious cross-border raids by the Afghan border patrols, and in October 1907, officials in the Transcaspian District had begun to explore the possibility of establishing some sort of order in concordance with the local Afghan authorities.[28] Izvolskii, however, preferred to avoid local relations between the Afghan and Russian border forces, choosing to adhere to the convention under which they were required to conduct all relations with their southern neighbour through British intermediaries.[29]

With the border situation already tense on account of the Afghan incursions into Russian territory, St Petersburg learned in mid-July of a flow of Jamshedi fugitive tribesmen into Russian territory. Alarmed by the potential cost to the chancellery of the Turkestan governor-generalship – estimated at an extra 15,000 roubles for every two weeks the fugitives remained in Russian territory – the Russian government turned to the British to persuade the emir to grant the Jamshedis safe passage if they returned to Afghanistan.[30] Initial reports counted the Jamshedi at close to 10,000, but the Government of India quickly discounted this Russian estimate as a gross exaggeration by Russian frontier officers calculated to bring Britain and the emir into conflict.[31] Further complicating matters, the Jamshedis, under the leadership of Saiyid Ahmad Beg, proceeded to launch raids back into Afghanistan from their base on the Russian side of the frontier. Saiyid Beg's incursions appeared to be financed and encouraged by the Russian governor of Kushk, prompting the British military attaché in Mashhad, Captain Smyth, to complain of Russian duplicity: 'Russian action in allowing the Jamshedis to make use of Russian territory as a base for attacks on Afghans, and making simultaneously complaint to us regarding Jamshedi incursions, looks as if they were playing a double game.'[32]

The Jamshedi refugee crisis became a test case for whether or not the Anglo-Russian understanding concerning Afghanistan could, in reality, work without the express agreement of the emir. The British acknowledged that if they were unable to obtain a response from the emir, they risked a Russian move to deal directly with the Afghan authorities.[33] Meanwhile, as a diplomatic solution was sought in the higher echelons of the British, Russian and Indian governments, the conflict threatened to spiral out of control. Captain Smyth reported on 19 August that a significant number of Afghan regular and irregular troops had been sent to the frontier to prevent both cross-border raids by Jamshedi already in Russia, and the further flight of more Jamshedi across the border. Smyth continued his dispatch with the news that the Russians had reinforced their Kushk garrison, bringing the total number of Russian troops available to 4500 men.[34] As H.C. Norman of the Foreign Office's Eastern (Europe) Department observed: 'This is the worst news we have yet had.'[35] Russia, however, had no desire to see an armed collision between Russian and Afghan troops at that time, and the authorities in Turkestan were instructed to take all measures to prevent this from occurring.[36]

Fortunately, armed conflict was averted by the emir's eventual response to the British query on 17 September. In his letter to the viceroy, Habibullah claimed that the Jamshedi who had fled to Russia had been misled by their leaders, Saiyid Ahmed Beg and Saiyid Mohammed. Since the general Jamshedi populace were not responsible for their actions, but had fled out of ignorance, he would allow them to return to their homes unmolested. However, the leaders of the migration and the subsequent raids across the border would not be permitted back into Afghanistan, and he demanded that they be settled in Russia far away from the Russo-Afghan frontier.[37] The Russians agreed to this proposed settlement, but they insisted that the governor of Herat was inclined to disobey orders that he might receive from Kabul; therefore, they proposed that Habibullah dispatch an officer of rank to the frontier to oversee the repatriation. The governments of Britain and India felt that this was not at all appropriate, and that the assurances given by the emir were and should be considered sufficient.[38] Russia, however, demanded a written guarantee, with the emir's own seal, that the repatriated Jamshedi refugees would not be mistreated.[39] The British government opposed this demand, and the Russians were left to draft their own written assurances of the emir's security guarantee for the sake of the returning refugees.[40]

Throughout the initial stages of the emir's non-recognition and the entire Jamshedi crisis, the British had been amazed by how 'remarkably well informed' the Russians were of events in Afghanistan.[41] Both Russia and Britain found information gathering in and about Afghanistan extremely difficult. As General F.F. Palitsyn, chief of the Russian general staff, lamented to the Russian minister of war, General A.F. Roediger: 'The seclusion of the country and the highly developed suspiciousness of not only her leaders, but of the population along the borders, as well, complicates the satisfactory organization of ongoing intelligence gathering here; this intelligence gathering is at present poorly clarifying our understanding of Afghanistan's military strength.'[42]

Nevertheless, despite the inherent difficulties in the gathering of information about Afghanistan, the Russians were still able to compile detailed monthly intelligence digests covering the military, political affairs, telegraphs and transport of the kingdom.[43] This was accomplished from the Persian town of Mashhad in the province of Khorasan, described by Palitsyn as 'the great trading and religious centre of the Middle East ... supporting lively trading relations with Afghanistan and an established point for the ebb and flow of Persian, Afghan and Indian Muslim pilgrims.' In 1905 Palitsyn had recognized the importance of Mashhad as a base for intelligence gathering in the region and assigned a consular convoy agent, Captain Skurat, to the city for the purpose of organizing a strategic intelligence network for both Afghanistan and Khorasan; at the end of 1908 Skurat's position was upgraded to that of military attaché, following the British example, and 60,000 roubles per year were budgeted for his efforts.[44]

Although in theory the British held the advantage in the intelligence competition – since Afghanistan was their semi-protectorate, and they, therefore, should have enjoyed greater access – in reality they were no better positioned than the Russians in their quest for knowledge about the emirate. The official representatives of the British Foreign Office in Afghanistan were limited to an envoy at Kabul, a news-writer at Qandahar and a news-writer at Herat. To supplement this rather meagre source of information, Major-General A.A. Pearson, the officiating adjutant-general in India, had recommended the formation of a nucleus intelligence corps in 1904. He proposed a composition of one British officer, one 'native' officer, and five 'native' non-commissioned officers, with an enlisted force of at least 30 men from the trans-border races, attached to the Queen's Own Corps of Guides on the North-West Frontier.[45] A formal division along these lines was not, however, created, but an authorized organization of permanent news-writers was established in towns like Kabul, Qandahar and the major frontier towns like Peshawar.[46] Like their Russian counterparts, Britain found the province of Khorasan to be the best alternative location to Afghanistan itself for the procurement of information about events in Central Asia. In the summer of 1905 a military attaché was temporarily established at Mashhad for the purpose of gathering intelligence primarily on Russia, and later, after the rapprochement, on Persia and Afghanistan as well. The intelligence that these British sources gathered about the region did not ever reach the scale of the more far-reaching and well-developed Russian networks.[47]

The Indian Army were not at all convinced that the convention with Russia had lessened the need for a reliable military intelligence network, and urged the government to convert the Mashhad position from a temporary appointment to a permanent one:

> If we are to continue in the future to receive exaggerated bazaar rumours, or garbled Afghan versions, wholly unchecked by reports derived from trained and reliable agents, as to what is passing in Central Asia, it seems probable that the mutual suspicion and distrust which have unfortunately obtained in

the past, and which it should now be our particular object to remove, may
continue to exist. ... From the point of view of making the recent Convention a success, it is most desirable that we should be in a position to receive
direct and impartial information as to what is really happening.[48]

In contrast, Charles Hardinge, permanent under-secretary at the Foreign
Office and former ambassador to St Petersburg, opposed the retention and
promotion of a Central Asian spy network based in Mashhad. He argued that
the Russians would view its existence as a demonstration of bad faith: 'The
retention of a net-work of native Agents (who are very unreliable and may be
in Russian pay) as spies throughout Central Asia must naturally become
known to the Russian Military Authorities, and will create suspicion as to our
intentions and bonafides.'[49]

The principal issue that needed to be determined, however, was not
whether the post should be maintained or eliminated, but who should pay for
it – India, Britain or a combination of the two. The Foreign Office insisted
that the appointment of the military attaché at Mashhad was of purely Indian
concern. The Government of India just as adamantly insisted that the duties
of the attaché were of imperial as well as Indian interest. The secretary of
state for India, Viscount Morley, asserted that, above all, the attaché in
Mashhad was well positioned to disprove the kind of exaggerated rumours
that ran rampant in the East; by that, alone, he would be performing an
invaluable service for both the Government of India and the Home Government.[50] Ultimately, the matter was referred to the Army Council, who
supported the maintenance of what they considered to be a successful source
of intelligence not just on Russia, but also on the northern frontier of Afghanistan and Central Asia.[51] Subsequently, the Treasury sanctioned the
permanent appointment of a military attaché at Mashhad in November 1908,
and authorized the payment of half the expense, with the remainder to be
made up from the Indian budget.[52]

While Mashhad was of both British and Russian concern as a vantage point
for Central Asian observation, affairs in Persia were best watched from within
the capital of Teheran itself. The course of the Persian Revolution had not
been deterred by the decision of the two Great Powers to reach an agreement
about the country. Upon the signing of the convention, both Britain and
Russia had immediately set about trying to persuade the Persian government
that the reports of a contemplated partition of Persia were entirely baseless.
Spring-Rice attempted to assuage the fears of the Persian minister of foreign
affairs, writing:

> Far from desiring to attack the independence of Persia, their object in con-
> cluding an agreement is to insure that independence for ever. Far from

desiring an excuse for intervention, their object in negotiating in a friendly way has been to prevent either one or the other power from intervening in Persia, on the pretext of protecting its own interests and forestalling the intervention of the other.

Similarly, Izvolskii assured the Persian minister in St Petersburg, Moshir ol-Molk: 'Russia makes it an absolute rule to abstain from all intervention in the internal affairs of other countries as long as her interests were not affected, and it is quite impossible to depart from this rule in the present case.'[53]

Moshir ol-Molk, however, confided to his British counterpart that he sincerely doubted the Russian legation in Teheran's willingness to 'carry out the Arrangement in its spirit as well as in its letter.' For the sake of the agreement, he felt strongly that the Russian minister in Teheran, Nikolai Genrikhovich Hartwig, needed to be replaced, since he was 'of the Zinovieff school, opposed to all liberal movements, and anxious to keep the Eastern neighbours of Russia in a backward and stationary state.' The Persian minister went on to give Nicolson his own prognosis for the success of the Anglo-Russian relationship in Persia:

> He did not himself believe that Russia had in any way changed her traditional policy, and that in a very few years it would be seen that she would be as active in Central Asia as formerly. The war with Japan and her internal troubles had checked her for the moment, but she was rapidly recovering from the effects of the former, and the Government were obtaining the mastery over the latter. In five, or at the outside ten, years she would be as strong and as enterprising as formerly, and if within that period Persia had not succeeded in becoming a prosperous and indépendent [sic] country under a constitutional régime, he considered that his country was irrevocably lost.[54]

Popular opinion in Persia was in complete alignment with Moshir ol-Molk, and there was intense disgust throughout Persia for 'the Liberal Government of Liberal England' which had abandoned Persia to Russian control and deserted the causes of freedom and liberty for which the Persian people were struggling against the shah.[55]

The outbreak of revolution in December 1905 had plunged Persia into a state of chaos from which it showed little signs of ever recovering. The growing tension was not mitigated by the shah's eventual capitulation on 5 August 1906 in granting a constitution and agreeing to summon the elected assembly, the Majles.[56] On 1 January 1907 Mozaffar ed-Din Shah signed the constitution and died one week later. His successor, Mohammad Ali Shah promised to uphold the constitution, but immediately set about plotting against the Majles and the new constitutional order.[57] In these efforts, he was supported by Hartwig, who openly opposed the Constitutionalist movement in Persia and was prepared to use Russian force to suppress the revolution.[58] As Charles Marling, the British chargé d'affaires in Teheran, observed: 'M. de Hartwig ... honestly believes that a show of force would be enough to cow the Persians.'[59]

Izvolskii, however, at a special conference in November 1907, declared his adamant opposition to Russian military intervention in Persian internal affairs. If Persia were truly on the road to disintegration, active interference in Persian affairs might some day become necessary; but, at the present time, he insisted that it was extremely undesirable to become embroiled in the Persian crisis. The foreign minister felt that Russia should take advantage of the positive diplomatic relationship they had created with Britain to strengthen its real political and economic interests in Persia without direct intervention:

> The Agreement with England opened a wide field of action for Russian en-
> terprise; on this field it is necessary to work, necessary to set in motion the
> re-evaluation there of moral capital, which has been accumulated by us, and
> not to give it up unused, so that our lack of action more than anything would
> help increase the prestige of the Russian name.[60]

The committee subsequently agreed to oppose the active intervention that the government's representative in Teheran was advocating.

Hartwig was not beyond intervention of a more private nature, however, and he urged the shah to abolish all the manifestations of a nascent democracy in Persia. At the Russian minister's instigation, Mohammad Ali forced the mildly liberal head of the Persian cabinet to resign on 14 December, had him arrested the following day, and then incited a mob to take to the streets to demonstrate against the Majles. The Persian Cossack Brigade was called out to further intimidate the Majles and its supporters.[61] Spring-Rice, who had left Persia for London in November to nurse his ill health, told Benckendorff that he feared the shah was capable of anything — even an attack on the British legation or minister — in his desire to suppress the Majles.[62] In the wake of the Persian unrest, Izvolskii and Grey insisted on the absolute necessity for complete co-operation between the Russian and British legations.[63] At the same time, Grey urged the Russians to uphold the principle of non-intervention.[64] The potential for foreign intervention became immaterial, however, as the immediate crisis waned. The shah, unsure of the strength of his position, had backed off before he had done any serious damage to the Majles, and the anti-Constitutional mob faded. Then the British and Russian representatives, under instructions from their governments, jointly advised the shah to come to terms with the Majles.[65]

In the minds of both foreign ministers, the Persian crisis was a golden opportunity to prove the fruitfulness of the agreement. In Grey's Corn Exchange speech on 19 December 1907, he asserted that the convention was all that was sparing Persia from Russian intervention. Similarly, Izvolskii, in a circular letter to the Russian embassies in Berlin, Paris, London and Constantinople insisted that the agreement with Britain allowed Russia the freedom to observe events in Persia without the need to worry about British opposition to any potential Russian actions. Russia could plan its possible response to Persian events in consideration of Russian vital interests, alone. Therefore, as Izvolskii triumphantly proclaimed to his representatives abroad: 'The Anglo-Russian Agreement passed its first trial with complete success.'[66]

It was not long, however, before the agreement was on trial in Persia once again. On 13 April 1908 a Russian frontier officer named Dvoeglazov, together with four Cossacks, crossed the Russo-Persian border at Bileh Savar in pursuit of a stray horse. Dvoeglazov and several of the Cossacks were shot and killed on Persian territory by the Shahsavan tribesmen who lived in the area. Izvolskii was outraged, and refused to be content with the usual diplomatic representations to the Persian government. He immediately ordered Count Illarion Ivanovich Vorontsov-Dashkov, the viceroy of the Caucasus, to prepare a cavalry expedition to round up the guilty Persians and to occupy several points on the Persian frontier. Hartwig was similarly instructed to inform the shah's government that Russia was preparing to exact vengeance and extract reparations for the killing of its men.[67] Hartwig lodged his protest with the Persian foreign minister, and claimed that the skirmish actually had taken place on Russian soil. Despite a Persian promise to send troops to pacify the region, Hartwig was dissatisfied with the inevitable delay and advised his government to take matters into its own hands.[68]

Russia had for some time been contemplating a more active military interference in Persian affairs, and in late March the staff of the Caucasian military forces had prepared a feasibility study for a limited action on Persian territory. The report predicted that a limited action in the north of Persia would set all the peoples of Persia, not just the regular army, against Russia in 'a stubborn struggle'. The Caucasian staff felt that a small-scale expedition would be next to impossible: 'To occupy the entirety of Persia rashly could be easily accomplished even by a comparatively weak force; but to occupy part, especially Azerbaijan, is an extremely serious matter.'[69] The Russian troops who would be operating in Persia were comprised of recruits working on a two-year schedule, and were therefore vastly unprepared for such an action. Furthermore, Russia would be unleashing a torrent of anti-Russian and revolutionary sentiment among its own Muslim populations in the Caucasus who were related to the Turko-Tatar population of Azerbaijan. Finally, the occupation of the Persian customs houses by Russian officials, which would accompany a military engagement of even a limited nature, might prompt a boycott of Russian goods and would cost Russia at least 60 million roubles in trade. Therefore, the Caucasian staff considered that such military interference should be avoided at all costs.

Despite the stated reservations of the local military experts, however, a Russian punitive expedition was dispatched under General Snarskii on 28 April, with orders to drive the brigands from the frontier district.[70] Snarskii was also instructed 'to invite' the influential personages along the frontier to pay an indemnity for the families of the dead men and for meeting the expenses of the expedition. He was further ordered to burn the villages along his line of march if the expedition met with any resistance;[71] several villages in the vicinity of Bileh Savar and the Persian customs house were subsequently burned.[72] Although the Majles decided not to protest against the dispatch of the punitive expedition, they felt that the behaviour of some of the Russian Cossacks was excessive. Therefore, the Persian minister of foreign affairs complained to Hartwig of the thievery and the killing of women and children that the Cossacks were committing. Hartwig, however, refused to apologize for the actions of the troops, responding that Persia had itself done nothing in response to two years' worth of Russian complaints about unrest in the border provinces. Therefore, in Hartwig's opinion, the actions of the Russian troops were more than justified.[73]

Before Snarskii's expedition withdrew to Russia, the general addressed an ultimatum to the governor-general of Azerbaijan demanding an indemnity for the Dvoeglazov incident.[74] In addition, Snarskii gave Persia 20 days to produce those responsible for the Russians' deaths for punishment. Furthermore, he demanded reparations for cattle stolen in 1907 and 1908 from the Russian side of the border. Finally, he required that all Russian deserters hiding in Persia be turned over to the Russian authorities immediately.[75] The Persian government, wanting to avoid the punitive cavalry expedition that Snarskii threatened if his demands were not met, agreed to the terms of the ultimatum.[76]

While Persia was struggling to find a way to acquiesce to the Russian demands, Hartwig at last admitted to Marling that Dvoeglazov had himself crossed the frontier and had actually been killed on Persian, not Russian, soil.[77] In addition, despite Vorontsov-Dashkov's instructions to General Snarskii, which were, in the viceroy's words: 'always fully humanist in relation to the innocent, especially women and children',[78] Persian official accounts continued to report Russian offences against the Persian population. As Marling observed: 'That Russia should demand compensation for injuries which are insignificant as compared with the murders and damage committed on Persians by her own troops has consequently aroused great indignation here.'[79] Despite these altered circumstances, Hartwig continued to insist on the general acceptance of all the Russian terms. Marling, while acknowledging that Russia's response may have been a bit 'over the top', advised the Persian government to do its best to conciliate Russia; the Persians therefore made every effort at appeasement.[80] Finally, on 11 June, Hartwig reported that the Persians had fulfilled the principal conditions of the ultimatum, and recommended that Snarskii not re-cross the border.[81] Vorontsov-Dashkov withdrew the detachment from the border on the 15th.[82]

As the Russian newspaper *Slova* had observed, the Anglo-Russian agreement was 'receiving a baptism by fire in Asia in two places at once: on the Russo-Persian and on the Indo-Afghan borders, the north and south of the Iranian plateau.'[83] *The Times* had similarly equated the situation on India's North-West Frontier with Russia's southern flank, describing the Bileh Savar skirmishes as 'curiously reminiscent of our incessant experiences on the Indian borderland'.[84] *Slova* had gone on to predict that the problems on Russia's southern frontier could potentially complicate Russian relations with Britain in Europe.[85] The British and Russian governments were determined, however, not to let that happen, and with the aim of preserving the relative accord that the 1907 agreement had solidified, a visit of the king of England to his nephew-in-law, the tsar, was planned. The Russian press was almost entirely in favour of the proposed meeting at Reval (Tallinn), and considered it to be 'setting the seal' on the convention.[86] British public opinion was far less favourably inclined. The liberal press published numerous articles objecting to Edward VII's meeting with the autocratic head of the Russian Empire, and a vehement debate ensued in Parliament. Nevertheless, when it came to a vote, the totals showed 225 for and only 59 against the visit.[87]

Thus, in early June, the king and queen of England set sail for the Baltic on the *Victoria & Albert*, where they were welcomed by Nicholas aboard his yacht, *Shtandart*. The tsar was accompanied by Izvolskii and Petr Arkadiavich Stolypin, chairman of the Council of Ministers; Edward brought with him Charles Hardinge, and they were joined by Nicolson from St Petersburg. Hardinge and Izvolskii had several lengthy conversations, during the course of which the situation in Persia was discussed. In response to Izvolskii's concerns that the extended deadline for the Persians to satisfy the ultimatum would soon expire, forcing Russia to exact compensation directly from the tribes, Hardinge assured the Russian foreign minister that Britain had no intention of interfering in the matter.[88]

After a brief discussion of a possible joint British and Russian railway construction policy in Persia, the subject shifted to that of Afghanistan. Izvolskii enquired as to the situation along the Indo-Afghan border. In late

April, just as the Dvoeglazov affair was heating up, a large force of Mohmands
– a tribe of the Pushtun ethnic group – had massed along the Indian side of
the frontier, taking occasional pot-shots at the British soldiers defending the
border. Their numbers were reinforced by numerous kindred tribesmen
from the Afghan side of the border, who crossed the frontier to join with
their Muslim brethren. When more Afghan Mohmands congregated near the
border, ready to join their fellow tribesmen and commit 'acts of wanton
hostility against the British Government', the Government of India asked the
emir to intervene and force their withdrawal from the frontier.[89]

Simultaneously, a dispute arose over the boundary point for British jurisdiction in the Khyber Pass. Letters exchanged in 1898 had established the
headwaters at Landi Khana as the furthest point British caravan escorts were
allowed to travel, but in practice British escorts went as far as Tor Kham,
well within Afghan territory. The Government of India felt strongly that
Britain must deal firmly with the sudden Afghan opposition to established
practice by petitioning the emir:

> The aggressive attitude of Afghans may very soon assume a most serious ap-
> pearance, unless the true position is put plainly and forcibly to the Ameer.
> Any mildness on this occasion would, we are convinced, be misunderstood,
> and influences at Cabul hostile to ourselves would be greatly strengthened.[90]

They did not, however, feel that the issue should be forced by the dispatch of
escorts all the way to Tor Kham; this would, they predicted, almost certainly
bring bloodshed and would raise the frontier question to an acute level.

Secretary of State for India Morley promptly chastised the Government of
India for what he considered to be a blatant overreaction. The Government of
India was threatening a semi-hostile ultimatum for the emir when what was
needed was handling of an even friendlier nature than ever. Above all, Morley reminded the government that a border controversy at that moment
would be particularly ill timed; there were thousands of Afghan lashkars, or
tribal militia, convening along the frontier, and Britain was already preparing
a punitive expedition against the Pushtun Afridis tribe residing north-west of
Peshawar near the border with Afghanistan.[91] Nevertheless, the Government
of India refused to have its alarm brushed aside by Morley's admonitions, and
reported on 2 May the threat of an imminent attack on Landi Khana and the
fort at Chura by a lashkar force, whose numbers were estimated at anywhere
from 13,000 to 20,000 men. The political agent at Khyber, Colonel Roos-
Keppel, explained the sudden anti-British uprising in Afghanistan as stemming
from two motives: (1) a belief that the movement of 600 Indian soldiers to
the Mohmand border was a precursor for the invasion and annexation of
Afghan territory; and (2) to prove to the British the unity of Islam and the

power of Afghanistan. Roos-Keppel noted that Habibullah had done nothing to stop the rising tension because 'he considers himself grossly offended by the Anglo-Russian Convention, which he regards as derogatory to him as an independent Sovereign.'[92]

It was not true, however, that the emir had done nothing to quell the unrest. On 10 May, the Government of India reported that the emir had issued strict and, it believed, sincere orders to prevent his subjects from joining the Mohmands on the Indian side of the frontier.[93] Yet his orders did little to stem the flow of Mohmands from Afghan territory. Four hundred Afghan Mohmands had crossed the border by 18 May.[94] However, by the time Izvolskii had asked Hardinge whether or not order had been restored along the Indo-Afghan border, the excitement had died down. With the onset of the summer months, the desire to go into battle in support of their fellow Mohmands was offset by the need to plant, tend and harvest crops. Therefore, the tribesmen who had been massing along both sides of the frontier headed home in early June.[95]

Hardinge credited the peaceful settlement of the crisis to the Anglo-Russian convention. As he told Izvolskii:

> There had ... been no rumours, as was usual formerly in similar circumstances, of encouragement by Russian emissaries and intrigues with the tribes. These were the best proofs of a real improvement in Anglo-Russian relations ... and the loyalty of the Russian Government in observing that part of the Agreement relating to Afghanistan which had so far not been confirmed had been much appreciated by HMG.[96]

With these sentiments, the Russian foreign minister was in wholehearted agreement, and he expressed his satisfaction that the matter had been resolved without a British expedition to Kabul, which might have reopened the Afghan question and rendered the agreement worthless.

Britain's conflict with Afghanistan had not, however, been fully resolved, and relations between the Government of India and the emir remained extremely strained. As the Russians noted at the end of July:

> The English constantly accuse the Emir of aiding the belligerent border tribes. The Emir continues to swear to them, giving more or less successful responses by which the English become contented, although they perfectly understand these are the Emir's stock excuses. For example ... when the English demanded that the Emir return the 12,000 rifles with cartridges, which he had earlier received as a gift from the British, he immediately ordered the dispatch of these rifles by transport. However, he gave notice to the border tribes beforehand, who quickly attacked the transport and took the rifles for themselves.[97]

The Turkestan general staff considered British policy towards Afghanistan to be bordering on diplomatic failure, and many in Britain and India were inclined to agree. The ongoing raids in the North-West Frontier were, in the opinion of the Government of India, made even more 'disquieting' by the continued presence of Afghan Mohmands and Safis among the brigands. The British political agent at Khyber was convinced that Habibullah planned to incite the tribes on the North-West Frontier to rebel, hoping that the sedicious parties within the rest of India would rise up as well; he would then join openly with them against Britain in an anti-European war combining both Muslims and Hindus against the British oppressors.[98] With rumours of impending war and frequent cross-border raids by belligerent tribesmen, the Afghan situation was far from stable.

As Britain's troubles along its frontier with Afghanistan were intensifying, the turmoil in Persia, only slightly dissipated by the Persian capitulation to the Snarskii ultimatum, took a decided turn for the worse. The shah, goaded on by Hartwig and by the similarly reactionary Russian commander of the Persian Cossack Brigade, Colonel Vladimir Platonovich Liakhov, demanded that the press and the members of the *anjomans*, or nationalist political clubs, cease their verbal attacks against him. The Majles countered with a call for the dismissal of several extreme reactionaries within the shah's inner circle. Mohammad Ali's demands then escalated, and he called for the expulsion and exile of eight deputies of the Majles whom he considered to be particularly offensive. It seemed that only force would break the deadlock that had developed between the rival factions in Persia.

On 22 June the shah proclaimed martial law and appointed Liakhov military governor of Teheran. Fighting broke out on 23 June, and Liakhov unleashed artillery on the Majles building and the adjoining mosque. Several hundred Persians were killed in the melee and the Constitutionalist uprising seemed on the point of collapse. As the forces of the autocracy appeared on the verge of stamping out the revolution, a number of Constitutionalists took sanctuary, or *bast*, in the British legation. It was at this point that the situation degenerated and the Anglo-Russian relationship suffered an ominous blow. Liakhov and Hartwig conspired to prevent any more nationalists from escaping to the safety of the British legation and surrounded it with Persian Cossacks, cutting it off from the remainder of the city. This flagrant violation of the traditional sanctity of the concepts of both *bast* and diplomatic immunity by a military force under the command of a Russian officer was greeted by vehement outrage from the legation and the British government, who demanded that the blockade be lifted, that the shah's government apologize for the action of the troops, and that the lives and welfare of the refugees within the British legation be guaranteed.[99]

Izvolskii quickly attempted to convince the British that Liakhov's orders to the Persian Cossacks were issued in his role as commandant of the brigade, not as a Russian officer, and without the knowledge and complicity of the Russian legation. He also attempted to shift some of the responsibility for the chaos in Teheran on to the shoulders of the British legation, pointing out that, were he so inclined, he could accuse the British of direct interference by opening up their legation for *bast*.[100] In a telegram to Hartwig, however, Izvolskii did feel it necessary to sternly remind the Russian minister that he was under strict instructions not to interfere in the internal affairs of Persia and to work amicably with his British counterpart.[101]

The British government was not even remotely persuaded by Izvolskii's pledges of Russian innocence, as Grey confided to O'Beirne:

> I cannot help thinking that this sudden and violent action by Russians at Teheran on behalf of the Shah must be due to their belief that we were intriguing to change the Persian Government to our advantage and to the prejudice of the Russians. If we had ever had any such design it should be obvious that we should have acted upon it in the winter, when the Constitutional party had the upper hand, and not now when the Shah was much stronger. It is deplorable if the Minister for Foreign Affairs has allowed his confidence in our good faith to be upset by the suspicions of his Agents at Teheran.[102]

Hardinge similarly protested to Benckendorff: 'Hartwig and Liakhov, the first for having exaggerated the significance of a secondary custom and the second for motives which [Benckendorff himself] did not understand, were in the process of tearing to pieces the convention which had cost years of work.'[103]

Benckendorff, in turn, voiced his disgust at Hartwig's complicity in the encircling of the legation, in a flurry of confidential telegrams to his superior. The Russian ambassador questioned Hartwig's judgement in considering the prevention of *bast* more important than the entente with Britain.[104] He had learned of Hartwig's statement to Marling that their mission was to save the throne of the shah rather than to abide with the principle of non-interference – a direct violation of what Benckendorff considered to be established Russian policy. Benckendorff exclaimed his frustrations:

> Where the intervention becomes, in my opinion, flagrant and manifest is when without protest from our Legation, an active Russian officer becomes Governor of Teheran with extended powers and he attacks, on his own authority, the custom of *bast*, an international custom which can only, in my opinion, be abolished by the agreement of the Powers that exercise it and which, consequently, not even the Shah has the right to abolish by himself.[105]

Benckendorff reported that Britain had no intention of refusing *bast* to Persians who sought it, reaching the conclusion that 'if the application of *bast* constitutes an infraction of the entente, then it is evidently in danger.'[106] The Russian ambassador was convinced that the Anglo-Russian relationship was in genuine peril, and urged his government to do all that was possible to clear Russia's name post-haste.[107] He advised Izvolskii publicly to disavow the measures taken by Liakhov and to recall him to Russia. Nothing less could allow the fragile rapport between the Russian and British legations to be re-established.[108]

Hartwig, for his part, not only continued to protest his complete innocence in the actions of the Cossack brigade, he also tried to convince Marling that not one Cossack detachment had actually been involved in the pickets and protests outside the legation, nor had they even been out on the adjoining streets.[109] He claimed that the British were making outrageous assertions with no basis in reality, for example the detention of diplomatic bags, the harassment of members of the mission by Liakhov and the Cossacks, and the placement of Cossacks in the trees in order to observe the interior of the legation.[110] By Hartwig's account, when he described these reported offences to his English colleague, Marling 'repeatedly interrupted my reading with the exclamation: "I wrote nothing of the sort in my telegram." He expressed to me regret concerning this strange "misunderstanding" and left me quickly to telegraph London and put forth the truth.'[111]

Despite Hartwig's continued protestations of innocence, the British Foreign Office clearly recognized his complicity in the affair and his devotion to the Persian autocracy, as noted in the Foreign Office's 1908 annual report for Persia:

> [Hartwig] was one of those who considered at the time of the signature of the Convention, that his country was being deprived of the ripe fruit which was ready to fall into her lap, and he seems to have thought that the only way in which the results of Russian diplomacy of past years were to be secured was in the retention, at all costs, on the throne of Mohammed Ali Shah.

When Hartwig's plans to crush the opposition with the destruction of the Majles were frustrated, the British watched him vent his disappointment on the British legation. It was only the 'categorical orders' sent from St Petersburg, commanding Hartwig to support Marling's demands for the removal of the Cossacks, which lessened the tension between the two legations.[112] His refusal in his conversations with Marling to express any censure of the actions taken by the Cossacks was duly noted; Izvolskii was informed that both the legation and the government at home were extremely offended.[113] Therefore, as the British remained fully cognizant of the unabashed support Hartwig had given to the shah in opposition to the agreed principles of the convention, his position became increasingly tenuous.

The British government was more prepared to forgive the Russian government in St Petersburg than they were the Russian minister in Teheran. St Petersburg had been, Britain concluded, 'to a certain extent, influenced by the reports which they received from their agents in Persia.'[114] Hartwig, on the other hand, the agent who was responsible for misleading his government in his devotion to the principles that had governed the pre-agreement Asiatic Department of MID, clearly had to go. As Marling confided to Grey, 'frank discussion and loyal co-operation with Hartwig in Persian questions is almost impossible. ... so long as he remains as the Russian representative in Persia there is little hope that the good result aimed at by the conclusion of the Convention of 1907 will be realised.'[115] King Edward himself told Benckendorff that both ministers in Teheran should be changed. The post, he said, demanded men who understood that Anglo-Russian co-operation was the ultimate objective of the position.[116] Since Spring-Rice was already in the process of being replaced, this observation was clearly directed at Hartwig. Izvolskii saw the writing on the wall, and by the beginning of September was ready to consider Hartwig's replacement, as long as the British were prepared to shift their people around as well.[117] For the sake of Anglo-Russian amity, this seemed a small measure to ask.

The resolution of the diplomatic crisis that had been precipitated by the encirclement of the British legation was not, however, accompanied by a corresponding pacification of the unrest throughout Persia. Although Liakhov's Cossacks had succeeded in bringing Teheran back under the shah's control, nationalist uprisings were erupting steadily throughout the rest of the country. In the British and neutral spheres, the Bakhtiari tribes were threatening to revolt against Mohammad Ali's rule, and the Russian sphere was littered with numerous revolutionary strongholds. Tabriz, the principal town of Azerbaijan and a hotbed of revolutionary discontent and disorder since the outbreak of hostilities in 1905, fell to the nationalists, and Rasht, the principal city of the Gilan province, followed soon after.

The Russians were disturbed by the revolutionary unrest in their sphere, particularly in Azerbaijan. The disorder there had for some time been threatening Russian trade and the safety of its subjects.[118] Furthermore, the proximity of Azerbaijan to the Caucasian frontier and the close ties between the revolutionary movements in the Caucasus and the Persian nationalists were considered to be quite alarming.[119] Hartwig frequently urged his government to do more to prevent the movement of Transcaucasian revolutionaries across the Persian frontier;[120] these revolutionaries, by Hartwig's description, were 'the scum of Transcaucasia', and the anarchy in Azerbaijan was, in his opinion, solely promoted through Caucasian means with the aim of establishing an independent Azerbaijani socialist republic.[121]

Since the shah seemed incapable of establishing and maintaining order and peace in the region, the Russians themselves felt compelled to take measures to stabilize the border region.[122] In February, the Council of Ministers had agreed to set aside 500–800 roubles per month to secure the Jolfa–Tabriz Road in an attempt to safeguard Russian prestige and trade in the region.[123] This decision was followed by a similar Russian-funded assignment of Persian Cossacks to the Qazvin–Hamadan Road in July.[124]

Finally, in mid-October, the Council of Ministers agreed to take the following measures to pacify Azerbaijan: (1) to strengthen temporarily the consular convoy in Tabriz to 100 men and to order the Cossacks to Jolfa to increase border security; (2) to supervise the contraband export of arms from the Caucasus to Persia; and (3) to increase police supervision of the Caucasian revolutionary committees. They agreed, however, to the recommendation of the military department, not to occupy the post-houses along the Jolfa–Tabriz Road.[125] Above all, the Russian government insisted that it had no intention of occupying the region, as demonstrated by the small number of troops they were sending to reinforce the consular guards. Russia was concerned only with the protection of Russian lives and property, not the interference in Persian domestic affairs.[126]

Hartwig, although officially on his way out of Persia, could not help but interfere. He vociferously insisted that the measures set forth by the government in St Petersburg were insufficient. The unrest in Tabriz, in particular, demanded direct Russian action in defence of their interests. Intervention in the internal affairs of Persia was unavoidable, and could not, in his opinion, be considered a breach of the Anglo-Russian agreement since each party was guaranteed the right to protect its interests in its individual sphere.[127] St Petersburg, however, had been informed that the British consul in Tabriz was insisting that the lives and property of foreigners in the city were completely safe.[128] Since Russia was determined to work in concert with its British counterparts, Hartwig was told that the measures decided on by the Council of Ministers would have to suffice.[129] His last attempt to prompt active Russian interference in Persia had come to naught, and at the end of October Hartwig was replaced temporarily by the first secretary to the Russian legation in Teheran, Evgenii Vasilevich Sablin, until the new minister, the former counsellor of the embassy in London, Stanislaw Alfonsovich Poklevsky-Kozell, could be installed in his post.[130]

Therefore, despite the Russian legation's lingering adherence throughout 1907 and 1908 to the principles of mistrust and antagonism that had governed pre-rapprochement Anglo-Russian relations, the convention survived its first full year in Persia intact. Nicolson, ever a champion of the agreement he had worked so hard to bring about, triumphantly declared in his annual report for

1908 that the convention had 'led to more beneficial results than the most
sanguine could have anticipated.' While making allowances for the deep-
seated 'traditions, habits, and methods of Russian bureaucracy and diplomacy' that had led 'certain local Russian agents ... [to] have perhaps pursued
a line of action which is not in accordance with the wishes and aims of their
Government,' Nicolson credited the new-found Anglo-Russian accord and
Izvolskii's loyal adherence to the agreement with limiting the extent of the
Persian domestic crisis. As Nicolson admitted, 'it would have required the
wand of a magician to have swept away in so short a period the clouds of
suspicion, rivalry, and distrust which for so many generations have obscured
the relations between the two countries,' and he found it 'remarkable and
satisfactory that the co-operation of Russia has been so cordial and of so
liberal a character.'[131]

Although Nicolson's acclaim for the agreement's success was clearly
tinged by his self-interested desire to keep alive the spirit of his greatest
diplomatic success – one for which he had been awarded the Knight Grand
Cross of the Order of the Bath – in many ways his optimism about the Anglo-
Russian relationship appeared well grounded. The convention's first year in
Afghanistan had been rather rocky; the emir's obstinacy had threatened to
nullify the agreement concerning Afghanistan. Yet Russia's willingness to
carry on as if the agreement were technically in effect was heartening both for
the practical manifestations of British and Russian relations with and concerning Afghanistan and as a sign of the true depth of the rapprochement.
Similarly, the ongoing revolution in Persia had created an atmosphere that
was so unstable that the two powers continually risked being sucked into the
fray, willingly or otherwise. Yet, to date, both had managed to avoid active
military interference on a grand scale in the country, which in all likelihood
would have plunged Persia into even further chaos.

Even in Tibet, from whose affairs Russia and Britain had mutually sworn
to exclude themselves, there were growing signs that it might be impossible
for the two powers to limit their involvement in adherence to the agreement.
Elements of ambiguity existed in both Britain's and Russia's relationships
with the Tibetan plateau and the Dalai Lama's government in exile. The
Russian government had, from the outset of the Dalai Lama's Mongolian
exile, sought to facilitate his reinstallation in Lhasa. However, by early 1908
its attitude towards him seemed to have cooled. As Nicolson recorded, 'the
Russian Ministry stated that it took but little interest in [the Dalai Lama], and
that he was not a personage of whom much account need be taken.' The
British ambassador in St Petersburg considered this fundamental departure
from Russia's established orientation towards the Tibetan spiritual leader to
indicate an increased attitude of prudent caution; Russia, he presumed,

longed to avoid any relations with the Dalai Lama that might later prove embarrassing or involve them in any intercourse that might be considered to be discordant with the provisions of the 1907 convention.[132] Britain was convinced that Russia was content to remain aloof from Tibetan affairs in general, and from the exiled Dalai Lama in particular. By the end of 1908 Nicolson considered that Russia had 'for the time turned her back on the Far East.'[133]

Yet Nicolson's observation that Russia was determined to remain actively detached from the Dalai Lama's affairs was far from accurate. In July 1908 the Dalai Lama petitioned the Russian government through its chargé d'affaires in Peking for a substantial loan to support his forthcoming stay in Peking. Izvolskii, hoping to maintain what he regarded as a special advisory relationship between the Russian government and the Dalai Lama that had existed since the beginning of the latter's exile in Mongolia, urged the Council of Ministers to guarantee the loan from the Russo-Chinese Bank as quickly as possible. Rather than seeking to distance Russia from Tibet and its leader, Izvolskii actively attempted to solidify Russia's position vis-à-vis the Dalai Lama in the hope that continued good relations could be expected upon his ultimate return to Lhasa. Russian policy was, therefore, far more committed to and concerned with Tibet than the British government imagined was possible in the post-agreement political climate.

Izvolskii saw no contradiction between his stated commitment to steer clear of Tibet and a policy of providing financial support for the exiled Tibetan leader. Continued involvement in Tibetan affairs seemed an unavoidable aspect of Russian Far Eastern policy, especially in consideration of the ongoing Russian interests in Mongolia.[134] Similarly, the British found themselves unable and unwilling to immediately disentangle themselves from their Tibetan engagements. The annexe to the Anglo-Russian Tibet agreement had reiterated Britain's declared intention to withdraw from the Chumbi Valley in early 1908. However, this withdrawal was dependent on the functional operation of the trade marts at Gartok, Gyangze and Yatung. The Tibetans, having quickly realized that Britain had no intention of sending anything along the lines of the Younghusband expedition again to enforce the 1904 Lhasa Convention, had been far from co-operative in their commitments under the terms of the convention and had done little to facilitate and much to obstruct Anglo-Indian trade with Tibet.[135] Furthermore, the signing of the Anglo-Chinese Adhesion Convention on 27 April 1906, by which Britain reformalized its commitment to Chinese sovereignty over Tibet and undertook not to interfere in the administration of Tibet, had complicated the issue by reintroducing China as a determining factor in Anglo-Tibetan relations. British withdrawal from the Chumbi Valley and the firm establishment of Anglo-Tibetan trade relations were not proving as simple as the Home Government would have liked.

At the end of August 1907, as the details of the Anglo-Russian agreement were being finalized in St Petersburg, talks opened in Simla between Britain, China and Tibet to amend the Tibet Trade Regulations of 1893, with which Britain had never been satisfied.[136] It was clear that China was motivated in its push for a renegotiation of the 1893 agreement by a desire to assert its sovereignty in Tibet and to replace the Tibetan officials in all dealings with the British government.[137] In early January 1908 the Chinese demanded that all communications to the Tibetans be addressed through an official Chinese intermediary.[138] Opposing this requirement, the Government of India and the India Office insisted that under Article III of the Lhasa Convention, with which the Chinese had agreed to comply in the 1906 Anglo-Chinese Convention, Britain retained the right to deal directly with Tibetan authorities concerning trade, to the exclusion of the Chinese authorities.[139]

Britain was not, however, in a very strong bargaining position. The two means through which Britain might possibly exert pressure on Tibet – the obligations of the remaining unpaid instalment of the indemnity and the continued British occupation of Chumbi – became nullified in late January when the Chinese government provided the money for the indemnity. Once the indemnity had been paid in full, and in consideration of the fact that Britain had promised Russia that the occupation of the Chumbi Valley would not be extended beyond the settlement of the debt without consultation with the Russian government, there was little Britain could do but withdraw its troops. As Morley warned Minto while urging him to see to the evacuation of the troops, Russia must not be given any excuse to get 'a finger in the Tibetan pie'.[140] Even though the trade marts at Gyangze, Gartok and Yatung had not been fully functioning for the requisite three years, it was feared that a prolongation of the British occupation would be seen by Russia as an act of bad faith concerning Tibet. Therefore, early in February, the Russians were officially informed that the evacuation of the Chumbi Valley would soon commence, and on 8 February 1908 the British garrison in Chumbi withdrew across the Tibetan–Sikkim frontier.[141]

Finally, on 20 April 1908, the three signatory parties agreed to the Tibet Trade Regulations.[142] Britain attained the clarification it had sought of the terms by which Anglo-Tibetan trade would be conducted. China, however, achieved what it had sought as well: virtual recognition that it was the ultimate authority in Tibet, and a practical elimination of even the illusion of Tibetan autonomy. Russia was promptly informed of the conclusion of the negotiations and the agreement. Furthermore, the British assured the Russian government that they recognized that Articles 6 and 8 of the Trade Regulations were potentially in conflict with the stipulations of the Anglo-Russian Convention; these articles allowed for the continued presence of resident British telegraph officials along the routes leading from Gyangze to the Indian frontier and the uninterrupted right of free passage for British trade agents' couriers between the trading posts and the frontier. The British government thereby promised not to exercise the powers that it had obtained by these articles without first reaching an understanding with the Russians on the subject.[143]

Therefore, despite Russia's ongoing relations with the Dalai Lama and Britain's anticipated role in Tibetan trading affairs, both countries remained outwardly committed to the terms to which they had agreed in the 1907 agreement. Similarly, the Anglo-Russian rapprochement had also weathered the obstacles it had faced in Persia and Afghanistan. This evident dedication to a relationship whose first full year had been rather tumultuous was promoted not only by the diplomats and bureaucrats who had pledged themselves to the ideals of a rapprochement, but also by the Russian, British and Anglo-Indian press. The Russian consul-general in Bombay, Baron Heyking, noted a distinct improvement in the tone of Russia's treatment in the Anglo-Indian press; the 'jingoist-imperial organs of the Anglo-Indian press' had ceased their 'critical animosity' in relation to Russia and replaced it with a trend towards a much more positive treatment of Russia's constitutional development and political order.[144] Correspondingly, the British embassy in St Petersburg was pleased to report *Novoe Vremia's* consistent reminders to its readers of the importance of cementing and maintaining Russia's friendship with England.[145]

The ongoing benefit of the outward maintenance of amicable relations between these Great Powers was not, however, always immediately apparent. For Russia, a strong working relationship with Britain in Central Asia had done little to alleviate the difficulties Russian policies faced in the Near East, a region where Russian aims and aspirations were paramount. Although it had been hoped that a rapprochement with Britain might engender British support for Russian Near Eastern goals, a revision of the Straits Convention, which prohibited the passage of Russian warships through the Bosphorus and Dardanelles, seemed no closer to being a reality than it had been before the 1907 agreement. This was especially apparent in the wake of the Austrian annexation of Bosnia and Herzegovina on 6 October 1908.[146]

Having received little encouragement from Britain that Russia's aspirations in the Straits would be achieved, the Russian minister of foreign affairs had turned to Austria-Hungary for a diplomatic solution of a more regional origin. Izvolskii reached an informal agreement with the Austrian foreign minister, Baron Alois Lexa Aehrenthal, at Buchlau in Moravia on 16 September, securing Austrian support for a revised Straits Convention in return for

Russian approval of an Austro-Hungarian annexation of Bosnia and Herzego-vina. However, Aehrenthal acted without waiting for Izvolskii to obtain the approval of the other European powers, unleashing what became known as the Bosnian crisis. The rest of Europe was outraged, Russia's client-state, Serbia, vociferously protested against the blow to its ambitions for a southern Slav state, and Izvolskii felt betrayed. In an attempt to head off the inevitable international criticisms that would come when his role in the Buchlau deal became known, Izvolskii denounced the Austrian action and demanded that the Bosnian-Straits issue be put before an international conference, claiming that Aehrenthal had promised to do so during their meeting at Buchlau. Since there was no formal record of the Buchlau negotiations, Izvolskii's claim gained recognition, and Russia appeared as the defender of Slav rights and the champion of Serbia. As was expected, Britain and France supported the call for an international conference to solve the Bosnian crisis, and it was in light of this support that *Novoe Vremia* referred to Britain as 'the one Power disinterestedly sympathetic towards Slav interests'.[147] However, offers of more material support were not forthcoming, and as 1908 drew to a close Russia was waiting to see whether or not the rapprochement in Central Asia would translate into meaningful participation in Russia's Near Eastern poli-cies.

While Russia looked to the Central Asian rapprochement to provide succour for its concerns in the Straits, the British were hoping that the 1907 agreement would provide relief for the ongoing demands of the defence of India. One of the primary motivating factors behind British participation in the 1907 agreement was the acknowledged need to lighten the defence requirements of India in particular and Britain's global military commitments in general. In the immediate aftermath of the conclusion of the agreement, Lord Kitchener, the commander-in-chief of the Indian Army, prepared a memorandum considering the convention's effect on the strength of the Indian Army. The current size of the Indian Army, Kitchener asserted, was not based on any consideration of a recent Russian threat, since the army's strength had not been altered in the preceding 25 years, with the exception of an increase in 1885, which had been immediately absorbed by the annexation of Burma the following year. Rather, the strength of the army was calculated to meet what Kitchener delineated as its four primary purposes: '(1) to safeguard India from external attack; (2) to maintain order amongst the independent tribes on our border; (3) to enable us to fulfil our obligations and responsibilities regarding Afghanistan; and (4) to ensure the impossibility of internal revolution.'[148] To these basic obligations, Kitchener appended the Indian Army's responsibilities for contributing to imperial defence beyond India's borders.

In Kitchener's view, therefore, the threat that Russian Central Asian expansion had posed had been only one of numerous contributing factors in the determination of the army's strength. The North-West Frontier had been 'in a blaze of fanatical excitement' only ten years before, and it remained unstable. Beyond the frontier, Afghanistan continually threatened either to rise up against the British or to collapse upon itself in a torrent of dynastic chaos, dragging the North-West Frontier along into the abyss through their religious and ethnic ties. Throughout Asia, the emergence of pan-Islamism and Asian nationalism stemming from the Japanese victory in Manchuria had 'set in motion a train which must be reckoned with in the approaching future'. Therefore, the conclusion of the agreement, while relieving Britain for the time being of concerns of a direct Russian advance on India, did not significantly lessen the army's requirements for the defence of India. The Indian Army, already stretched to the limit, could ill afford a re-organization that would further diminish its relative regional strength. Rather, what the commander-in-chief felt was truly necessary was actually a significant increase of the force of the army in India.[149]

The Home Government was convinced that Kitchener and the Government of India were falling prey to their usual penchant for undue alarmism. Although H.H. Asquith, then Chancellor of the Exchequer, warned the House of Commons not to expect an immediate reduction of the numbers of the Indian Army, he simultaneously alluded to the government's sincere desire to see the agreement have a direct influence on military affairs.[150] Morley, directly responding to Kitchener's report, admonished the Government of India for its intransigence and trepidation, writing, 'Risks ... are not to be overstated. Nor is it possible for any Government to prepare against the hypothetical contingency that may be conjured up by vivid and ingenious imagination.'[151] One by one, Morley struck down the potential threats that Kitchener had foreseen, ultimately returning to the premise that the defence requirements for India must not, under any circumstances, be increased.

However, factions in London were soon coming round to the position of the Government in India. At the beginning of June, Lionel Abrahams of the India Office submitted a confidential minute discussing the numbers the British Army should be prepared to provide for use in India in case of emergency. Abrahams acknowledged that, in principle, the conclusion of the Anglo-Russian agreement should have allowed for a reduction in the size of the British Army's provision for India and, thus, the size of the army in peacetime should be correspondingly reduced. Nevertheless, the force of the British Army had actually been previously insufficient to meet the needs of a great war on the Indian frontier, and the signing of the agreement did not eliminate the risk of an Indian war. As Abrahams wrote:

The Agreement has not diminished the numbers that will be required for a war in Asia; but it may be hoped that it has reduced the likelihood of such a war, and has, in particular, lessened the risk that it may break out when the British Empire is embroiled elsewhere. ... But, if we now proceed to reduce our resources, we shall be in a worse position than ever. Our weakness will invite attack.[152]

It was not only those directly concerned with the governance of India who failed to see any mitigation of India's defence concerns resulting from the agreement with Russia. Winston Churchill, who had succeeded David Lloyd George as President of the Board of Trade upon the latter's appointment as Chancellor of the Exchequer in April 1908, similarly threw his weight against any reduction of either the home or Indian forces, condemning any such proposals as being 'fixed not with reference to Indian needs, but to British resources.' He urged the cabinet to consider the 'appalling possibilities' were Central Asia to explode and Britain to find herself immersed in a sea of international unrest:

> We are to encounter Russia in Afghanistan, to stamp out the flames of 'a re-
> ligious war' in India (and I gather simultaneously in Egypt too), and at the
> same time to be prepared with sufficient forces either to resist the German
> invader at home, or (perhaps even and) to co-operate effectually with some
> other great Power upon the continent. ... It is submitted that skilful diplo-
> macy and wise administration should be able to prevent in the future, as in
> the past, such a formidable and sinister conjunction of dangers. But if diplo-
> macy and administration should unhappily fail, it is then obvious that our
> existing army, whether doubled or halved, will be equally incompetent to
> cope with them.[153]

Clearly, in Churchill's eyes, as in the opinion of a significant portion of the British government, the 1907 Anglo-Russian agreement had done little to alleviate the growing crisis of strategic over-commitment that Britain was facing.

Therefore, as 1908 drew to a close, the relative success of the Anglo-Russian accord remained nebulous. Both powers were openly committed to the continuation of the relationship in Central Asia and vociferously adver-tised any achievements that might possibly be attributed to the agreement. Nevertheless, the immediate actual benefits gained from the 1907 convention fell far short of either government's hopes or expectations. Although the threat of an Anglo-Russian war for hegemony in Central Asia had been vastly diminished by the conclusion of the agreement, significant policy concerns of both governments had yet to show any signs of a return on their respective diplomatic investments. Furthermore, the historically unstable region continued to be a source of great concern to Britain and Russia; the buffer region between Russian Central Asia and British India persistently proved both a constant challenge to the maintenance of amicable relations between the two powers and a stumbling block to either country's efforts to simplify its individual strategic landscapes. The agreement had clearly forestalled an Anglo-Russian conflict in Central Asia, but the practical longevity of an accord barraged by Persian revolutionary unrest, Afghan obstinacy and Tibet's power vacuum remained to be seen.

CHAPTER 3

'Old Designs under a New Cover'?: 1909

At the beginning of 1909, international governmental and public interest remained focused on the crisis that had arisen from the Austro-Hungarian annexation of Bosnia and Herzegovina. Britain and France were unwilling to assure Russia of military support should the Austro-Hungarian demand that Serbia recognize the annexation escalate into armed conflict in the Balkans. As a result, Russia was forced to inform Serbia that no Russian military intervention would be forthcoming on its behalf. At the same time, Izvolskii appealed to Germany to convince its ally to reach a settlement of the crisis with which all the Great Powers could be satisfied. Instead Germany sent Russia a dispatch on 21 March 1909, which could only be interpreted as a call for Russia's complete surrender on the Bosnian question. Germany expected Russia definitively to accept or reject the annexation; anything other than a clear yes or no would be considered a refusal, and Germany would be forced to 'draw back and let events take their course'.[1] Given Russia's inability and unwillingness to face the prospect of a war with Austria-Hungary and possibly Germany, Izvolskii had no choice but to yield to Germany's demands and accept the annexation.

In the face of thwarted Russian aspirations in the Balkans and the Straits, opinion in the Russian and international press looked for Russia to seek compensation for its disappointments in the Near East through territorial acquisitions in Azerbaijan.[2] Although the imperial government maintained that any reports connecting Bosnia and Herzegovina with Azerbaijan were entirely unfounded and fictitious, persisting in its claims of 'accustomary and sincere feelings of friendship towards Persia',[3] the situation in the northern provinces of Persia was so unstable that a more active Russian involvement in the region was increasingly likely.[4] At a special conference on the Persian question at the end of December 1908, Izvolskii acknowledged that the direct damages to Russian interests resulting from the uncertainty in Azerbaijan were growing out of control. However, he warned against such active measures as those which had produced the French absorption of Algeria and part of

51

Morocco; active military involvement in Persia might escalate beyond anyone's expectations, and should be avoided. Rather, he urged Russia and
Britain to grant a joint loan of five million francs to bolster the shah's regime
against the revolutionary activity of the Majles.

In contrast, Vladimir Nikolaevich Kokovtsov, the minister of finance,
protested that such a significant monetary sacrifice was not only uncalled for
by the current state of affairs in Persia, but should have been obviated by the
agreement with Great Britain. He insisted that Russia and Britain should aim
to restore order in Persia, not to preserve a decrepit dynasty. Furthermore,
he presented two principal objections to such a loan: (1) the Russian Treasury
did not have 2.5 million francs at its disposal for such a purpose, and the State
Duma was unlikely to approve an advance of that kind to Persia; (2) it was
unlikely that 2.5 million francs would be even remotely sufficient to produce
order in Persia in the long term; such an insignificant sum would only result
in future requests from the shah for additional monetary assistance. The
minister of war, General Roediger, shared Kokovtsov's opposition, considering such attempts at 'bribery' senseless.[5]

That Russia's interests in Persia were sufficiently abundant to merit their
active defence, however, was without question in the minds of policy analysts
at home and on the spot. In his 1909 study of the Anglo-Russian rivalry in
Central Asia, M. Grulev, an agent of the Institute of Military Studies in St
Petersburg, noted that Russia's future influence in Asia was intricately linked
to the fate of Persia.[6] Russian merchants sailing down the Volga and across
the Caspian Sea had established Russia as a significant player in the Persian
trade by the middle of the nineteenth century. Russo-Persian trade naturally
moved across four principal routes: (1) by the Caucasian-Persian land route;
(2) via the Caspian; (3) through Astrakhan; and (4) by the Central Asian land
route.[7] It was not until the beginning of the twentieth century, however, that
Russo-Persian trade began to flourish.[8] By the end of 1906 Russia was responsible for 50.3 per cent of Iran's imports and absorbed 67.3 per cent of Iran's
export trade.[9] However, the Persian market's importance for Russia was not
on a quantitative level; rather, it was Persia's role as an outlet for Russian
manufactures incapable of competing on the European market that made the
development of the Persian trade a vital Russian economic interest.[10]

In light of Russia's commitment to the preservation and development of
its trade with Persia, the threat posed by the extreme unrest in northern
Persia was bound to produce considerable alarm. At the end of 1908 Kokovtsov acknowledged that the situation in the north had deteriorated to such a
degree that urgent measures were demanded to secure the roads and protect
Russian interests in the region. But the Ministry of War adamantly opposed
assigning Russian troops to secure these roads. Nevertheless, Russia consid-

ered the pacification of the north and the stabilization of Russian trade and interests sufficiently essential that the minister of finance authorized supporting the organization of an independent guard of 40 additional men for the Tabriz Road company, at a cost to the government of 23,000 roubles per year.[11]

It soon became apparent, however, that an increase in the private guard on the Tabriz Road would be far from sufficient to pacify the region. In mid-February, Colonel Liakhov, who was still commanding the Persian Cossack Brigade, predicted that if the revolutionary agitation in Persia continued on its present course, the routes to the interior of Persia would be closed to Russian subjects and Russian trade.[12] Liakhov's call for active measures to support Russian prestige in Persia was matched by the first secretary to the Russian legation in Teheran, E.V. Sablin, who urged his government to do more to offset the serious blows being suffered by Russian interests throughout the north.[13] In response to the pleas of Liakhov, Sablin and the Russian consul-general in Tabriz, Aleksandr Iakovlevich Miller, the Russian government decided to dispatch troops to Persia to maintain the freedom of movement on the Tabriz–Jolfa Road and defend Russian and foreign institutions and subjects.[14] On 9/22 April 1909 Kokovtsov, Izvolskii and General Vladimir A. Sukhomlinov, who had recently replaced Roediger as minister of war, ordered Russian troops to Tabriz under the command of General Snarskii.[15]

Once the order had been given for the dispatch of Russian troops into Persian territory, it remained to be determined if the troops' mandate would be solely to restore order along the trade route, or to re-establish the shah's authority in the region as well.[16] The Tabriz detachment was subsequently instructed not to interfere in the local administration in Azerbaijan, except on issues that directly affected the security of the roads. However, on questions concerning the roads, the detachment was instructed to act independently of the Persian authorities to stabilize the roads. They were, above all, reminded to conduct themselves 'with firmness and energy, and like peaceful inhabitants of a friendly power', and 'to carefully observe the inviolability of the Muslim women'.[17] By 16/29 April, 120 Cossacks, 65 riflemen and 24 machine gunners with two machine guns had arrived at the gates of Tabriz.[18]

As might have been expected, the British were extremely displeased by the dispatch of Russian troops to Tabriz. In March, Grey had once again found himself forced to respond in Parliament to harsh criticisms of Russian policies in northern Persia. The foreign secretary insisted that the British government could not possibly be held responsible for the actions of Russia or the Russian officers in Persia: 'There is nothing in the Convention which makes it responsible upon the British Minister to explain, account for, or defend the action of the Russian Government, which was taken on its own initiative and responsibility, and to which we are in no way party.' Despite this vociferous disavowal of accountability, Grey still rose with mordant wit to Russia's defence against the attacks of British parliamentarians:

> I understand that the hon. Member for Mayo [John Dillon] said that the action of the Russian officers in interfering with constitutional struggles in Persia was the sole cause of the anarchy there, and that he had an absolute conviction on the point. I notice it is very much easier to have an absolute conviction about the state of affairs in a foreign country when one is outside the Foreign Office than when one is inside of it.[19]

Although Grey was prepared to support Russian policy and, by extension, his own in entering into the 1907 agreement, he was firmly committed to the limitation of Russian involvement in Persia. As it appeared that Russian interests and property in northern Persia were not as damaged as the Russians claimed, the foreign secretary felt he had the grounds to protest against any expansion of Russian interference in Persian domestic affairs. Sir George Barclay, who had replaced Spring-Rice as minister in Teheran, had quickly responded to Russian complaints by informing Grey that trade in the Russian zone had not suffered from the Persian unrest nearly as much as in the neutral and British zones: only an 8.4 per cent decrease in customs receipts had occurred in the Russian zone for the year 1908–9, as opposed to 23.3 per cent in the British and Indian commercial zone.[20]

At the same time, Russian involvement in Azerbaijan was escalating quickly. Vorontsov-Dashkov commented in early May that the dispersal of Russian troops already resembled an occupation of the province, and the governor-general recommended that the detachment be strengthened.[21] Similarly, there were simultaneous calls for the further dispatch of Russian troops to other principal trade routes besides the Tabriz–Jolfa Road.[22] While the Russian government feared that the movement of its troops along the roads leading to Teheran might lead to an undesirable occupation of the Persian capital, it did decide to prepare four *sotnia* – military units of approximately 100 men – of Cossacks at Baku for immediate transfer, if necessary, to Anzeli and Rasht.[23] Grey, displeased at the prospect of further Russian involvement in northern Persia, instructed his ambassador in St Petersburg to counsel Russia that it would be inadvisable to proceed beyond merely the threat of such a troop transfer, since the further dispatch of troops 'would create the impression of intervention.'[24]

The Russians were well aware that any action taken by their troops risked being interpreted as direct interference in Persian affairs.[25] Thus they were not surprised when the British voiced their concern that the Russian military authorities in Tabriz were exceeding their mandate and were taking active measures against the nationalists. The Russians were warned that should this direct interference by Russian troops prove to be the case, Britain might be forced to intervene on behalf of those struggling against the shah; both countries would then be supporting different sides, and the benefits that had already accrued from the 1907 agreement would quickly be obliterated. Therefore, the British government urged the Russians either to withdraw a portion of their troops or, if that was considered impossible, at the very least to remind their commanders in Azerbaijan to abstain from all intervention in internal affairs.[26] In response, Izvolskii reassured Nicolson that the Russian troops had no intention of taking action against the nationalists, and were only doing the minimum necessary to protect Russian subjects and interests.[27]

It was not only Russian trade that was disrupted by the revolutionary unrest gripping Persia. British trade through the Persian Gulf ports and the British sphere up into the neutral zone was considerable. Even within the northern sphere, where Russian trade was favoured by geographical proximity and was consequently predominant, the British managed to maintain a significant trading presence after the conclusion of the 1907 agreement.[28] In fact, the bulk of British and Indian trade actually entered Persia not from the Gulf but via Baghdad to Kermanshah in the Russian sphere.[29] The development and defence of this trade in the face of Russia's advantageous position was considered a priority for the British Board of Trade and the Foreign Office.[30] The desire to counter Russian competition was especially intense within the ranks of the men-on-the-spot in Persia, who felt, in the words of Captain Lionel Berkeley Holt Haworth, the Indian Army officer who was consul at Kermanshah, that 'with the Russians political influence and commerce are, in Persia, interchangeable terms.'[31]

The British consuls were not alone in seeing a direct correlation between commercial success and political influence. In early 1909 the Russian vice-consul at Ardebil, Ivan Ivanovich Reshetov, warned his government to be wary of the appearance of British manufactures in the northern markets, 'since the propaganda accompanying these goods carries an especial character and without a word pushes Russian products out from the local markets.' According to Reshetov, British goods – principally chintz and cheap cotton – were being marketed by 'Hamadan Jews' who had entered into an agreement with the British to sell their goods at such reduced prices that there could be no profit from the sale; this price manipulation was clearly an attempt to open up the north to British trade and influence and force Russian goods from this market. Reshetov insisted that Russia needed to meet this challenge from the British by lowering their own prices, tailoring their products to suit 'the Oriental's tastes' and by securing the roads.[32]

Britain's actual ability to compete with Russia for commercial predominance in northern Persia was, however, not nearly as great as Reshetov feared. Nor was its control over the trade in the south at all incontrovertible, as the Foreign Office had noted in 1908:

> Although Great Britain has occupied a predominant position in Southern Persia for more than 100 years, British trade and enterprise have so far failed to obtain any permanent results beyond a concession for the navigation of the Karun, the construction of a road from Ahwaz to Ispahan and Teheran, and certain telegraph lines.[33]

Furthermore, not only was British trade in the north subject to the same levels of disruption as Russian trade, the trade in the south and along the Persian Gulf, where Britain had enjoyed commercial supremacy, noticeably declined between 1907–8 and 1908–9.[34]

The British believed that the instability in the south, which was producing this decrease in trade, resulted in opportunities for Russian trade to descend from the north and displace goods of British origin. Since the Russians were taking active steps to stabilize the roads and pacify the northern sphere, Russian trade was able to flow much more freely throughout the country. Therefore, H.G. Chick, the British vice-consul at Bushire, called for the British themselves to institute a security regime in their sphere;[35] a similar insistence on the pressing need to police the southern roads was transmitted by Barclay to Grey in mid-June.[36] The British government, however, remained determined to uphold its commitment, which it had reiterated to Russia in early February 1909, 'to stand aloof from the internal affairs of Persia' no matter the cost to British commercial interests.[37]

With the spreading disorder in the north, particularly around Teheran, Russia was finding it increasingly difficult to hold itself to the same standard. Nationalist *fedaiyan*, or popular forces fighting for Iranian constitutionalism, from the north and Bakhtiari tribesmen from the south were marching on Teheran, threatening to take the city. The capital was endangered, the lives of the shah and his family at risk, and Russia was forced to confront the question of what role Colonel Liakhov and the other Russian officers in command of the Persian Cossack Brigade should and could take in the defence of the shah and his regime.[38] For several months, Sablin had been striving to establish the official limits of the Russian officers' freedom of action in the event of an uprising in the capital. The Russian chargé d'affaires feared that if the Cossack Brigade, commanded by Russian officers, were to take an active part in the suppression of disorder against the people, they risked inspiring the enmity of the masses against Russia.[39] Izvolskii had answered Sablin that the Russian officers should do everything possible to protect the shah's individual security if he were attacked, but if the shah were to order the brigade to march against the revolutionaries, Liakhov should pass on the command of the brigade to Persian officers. But Izvolskii retained for Liakhov and his colleagues the option for military action 'against thievery and marauding ... to support order and discipline', thus allowing for the possibility of continued involvement by the Russian officers in the defence of the capital.[40] With such an indeterminate mandate, the position of the Russian Cossack officers was bound to inspire an element of distrust in the British, as Nicolson noted in May: 'They are, I am told, no longer on the active list of the Russian army, and are supposed to be entirely in the Persian service. At the same time on certain occasions they receive and act upon orders from the Russian authorities.' While Nicolson acknowledged that the Russian government did desire that the officers abstain from active interference in the internal Persian conflict, he noted with regret that such abstention 'must on occasions be difficult to observe'.[41]

Thus, when the shah was directly threatened in late June, the potential involvement of Liakhov and the Russian officers remained ambiguous. The Council of Ministers, after careful consideration, concluded that the Russian officers should be instructed 'to take all obligatory measures to defend His Highness and His family', and should not avoid command in the event of a revolutionary attack on Teheran.[42] Yet, as panic in the capital grew, it soon became apparent that the strength of the Cossack Brigade would be far from sufficient to offset the revolutionaries, and Sablin entreated St Petersburg to dispatch a cavalry detachment from Baku.[43] Grey urged Russia to avoid at all costs a Russian armed intervention in Teheran, apprehensively predicting that any remaining loyalty that the Persian government could muster would be destroyed by the appearance of foreign control of the shah's regime, leading to an anti-Russian and anti-European backlash and the possible break up of the country.[44] Furthermore, Grey warned Russia that the intervention of Russian troops in Teheran might necessitate a 'serious change' of Britain's entire Persian policy.[45]

In response, Izvolskii insisted that Russia's interests in northern Persia were far greater than Britain's, and required the kind of protection that he had already been severely criticized for not furnishing sooner.[46] Therefore, Russia decided partially to heed Sablin's call, and dispatched a Cossack detachment from Baku to Anzeli to maintain order on the Anzeli–Teheran Road. These troops were categorically instructed not to interfere in Persian politics, but only to protect the foreign legations, enterprises and subjects.[47] When at last the Bakhtiari and the nationalists joined forces and took the capital on 13 July, the city was surprisingly calm, and Sablin recommended that no Russian troops should be sent at that time.[48] The presence of Russian troops in Anzeli and Qazvin, apparently poised to march on Teheran, however, seemed to point towards a Russian action to free the capital from revolutionary hands.[49] The Russian director of the Discount-Loan Bank of Persia complained that the bank and its employees were in danger and called for the immediate dispatch of Russian troops to Teheran: 'The shooting is terrible. Bullets are smacking against the walls and the doors of the Bank.'[50] But his demand was waved off by Sablin, who continued to advise St Petersburg against the dispatch of troops until there was a real danger to foreigners and the bank; Cossacks might eventually be summoned from Qazvin to guard the bank, but only under extreme circumstances.[51] At this rebuff, the bank director took matters into his own hands and telegrammed the Ministry of Finance in St Petersburg to insist that the bank's security could not be trusted to the *fedaiyan*.[52] Sablin, infuriated by this attempt to go over his head, assured St Petersburg that Teheran was completely peaceful and suggested in no uncertain terms that the alarmist bank director should be dismissed.[53]

While the dispatch of Russian troops to Teheran continued to be both expected and debated, the royalist troops were outmanoeuvred by the nationalists, and the shah took *bast* in the summer residence of the Russian legation at Zargandeh on the morning of 16 July;[54] he was formally deposed in favour of his 12-year-old son, Ahmad Mirza, later in the day. After careful deliberation the British flag was also raised over the residence, and Mohammad Ali came under the joint protection of both Russia and Britain. The fate of the Cossack Brigade – charged with protecting the personage of the shah and his family – and its Russian officers was in question now that its raison d'être was no longer valid. The Russian legation, anxious to prevent a backlash against its officers and their protégés for their role in defending the now deposed shah, immediately set about trying to secure amnesty for the Cossacks and their officers from the provisional government that had replaced Mohammad Ali.[55] The legation further wished to guarantee the continued employment of Russians at the head of the brigade, since it was a source of such tremendous potential influence and prestige in the country. Complicating the matter, Liakhov refused to subordinate himself to the new Persian minister of war, and continued to urge Sablin to arrange for the attachment of Russian troops to the Persian Cossack Brigade to assist in the defence of the foreign missions and of the brigade itself. Sablin, concerned that any official support of Liakhov's somewhat reactionary stance might further alienate the new Persian government, who were, in his opinion, 'already wary of foreigners and above all are concerned about protecting themselves from foreign invasion', told Liakhov to cease attempting to drag the Russian government into a conflict that it would be 'extremely desirable' to avoid.[56]

Throughout the crisis, Sablin had consistently recommended caution and restraint in the Russian response to the seizure of the capital and Mohammad Ali's abdication.[57] He stressed the complete lack of anti-Russian hostility being demonstrated by the new Persian government, and commended the 'sincere and most active support' he had received from his British colleagues.[58] Rather than conforming to expectations and yielding to the temptation to safeguard Russian property and prestige through the further dispatch of troops into northern Persia and on to Teheran, the chargé d'affaires, Russia's man-on-the-spot after Hartwig's departure, had beseeched his superiors not to increase their presence in the region and further embroil themselves in the internal affairs of their southern neighbour. As Sablin proudly informed St Petersburg: 'By not sending our troops to Teheran we crushed the widespread legend, not without some foundation ... [sic] to support reaction in Persia and to stand on the side of the shah in his struggle with the nationalists.'[59]

The British were pleasantly surprised that Russia did not react to the fall of the Shah with armed intervention to defend its protégé. Britain had been vociferously urging Russia to avoid an increased military involvement in Persia at all costs. Just how much self-control was demanded by the exercise of this restraint was fully recognized by Grey, who openly acknowledged in a conversation with Poklevsky-Kozell how great the difficulties created by the Persian unrest were for Russia:

> I could not even say with certainty that, had there been a precisely similar state of things close to the Indian frontier, we ourselves would not have sent troops. I realised that if, for instance, our Officers had for years been instructing the Ameer's forces at Kabul; if we had used Indian Government money to make into Afghanistan a road on which British trade depended; if we had a Bank in Kabul with a large deposit; and if a large number of disaffected and very hostile people from India had gone into Afghanistan and were endeavouring to bring about a revolution there: it was quite certain that great pressure would be brought upon us to act in the same way as the Russians were acting in the case of Persia.

Grey concluded, however, by reminding Poklevsky-Kozell that no matter how intense the pressure, it would still not be a wise step to send troops to Persia. Once there, Russia might find it impossible to withdraw. The British foreign secretary advised Russia to take as a cautionary tale his own empire's experience, and not to think it would be easy to withdraw in two or three months: 'Mr. Gladstone's intention [for a brief occupation] had been precisely the same with regard to Egypt; but ... it had been impossible to carry it out, and we had drifted into an occupation of Egypt.'[60] Grey earnestly hoped that Russia would not fall into the same trap.

It was true that, as Grey had implied, Britain's position in Afghanistan was far less precarious than Russia's in Persia. Nevertheless, Britain's official relations with its semi-protectorate were, in the words of Lithuanian Life Guards Captain Gias, the commander of the Russian Pamir Detachment, characterized by 'restraint and extreme caution, through which shined a poorly concealed ill-nature'. Gias's summary digest of the intelligence gathered by Russian agents in Afghanistan in March 1909 further documented the anti-British agitation that dominated the country. One high-ranking Afghan official in Feyzabad was quoted as saying, 'The English don't worry us at all. If Russia doesn't help them, we will always defeat them.'[61]

The British were as aware as the Russians of the ill will with which they were regarded in Afghanistan and the tenuous nature of their relationship with the Afghan ruler, especially in light of the instability of Habibullah Khan's own position. Reports of continued unrest and anti-Habibullah agitation in Afghanistan had been spreading since the emir's modest attempts to punish those who had participated in the frontier rising against the British in 1908.[62] By October 1908 the treasury in Kabul was nearly empty, and much state control rested in the hands of Sardar Nasrollah Khan, Habibullah's brother and chief rival.[63] In March 1909 a conspiracy to assassinate the emir and two of his sons was uncovered, the responsibility for which appeared to rest in Nasrollah's hands.[64] Furthermore, rumours ran rampant throughout Afghanistan, where any conduct that might possibly have been interpreted as in keeping with the emir's obligations to the British was met with loud declarations that he could easily be replaced by 'another more suitable leader' who would do more to preserve Afghan interests.[65] The extreme state of domestic disorder could only adversely affect Britain's relations with Afghanistan. As the Government of India's A.H. McMahon noted at the end of May:

> The weaker the Amir realises his position in the country to be, and this conspiracy must naturally have alarmed him on this point, the more he will have to play to the gallery, and this generally means renewal of the familiar policy of impressing the people by high-handedness towards us. On the other hand thanks to the religious fanaticism which Nasrulla Khan has been so zealously fanning, the more numerous our complaints to the Amir are likely to be and the more trying his position will become between his people on the one side and ourselves on the other.[66]

With the emir so negatively disposed towards good relations with Britain, there was little chance that he might change his position and agree to sign on to the 1907 agreement. International Muslim opinion appeared to support his obstinacy; as the Young Turk party reportedly advised the emir:

> Do not at all agree to the Anglo-Russian Convention which has been sent to you. The Sultan and the musulmans in Egypt are all with you. Do not at all be afraid of the English. Reject the Convention and have no anxiety on the subject. The English cannot fight with you. Should they do so, from this direction we shall get war declared against the English. ... If you sign the Convention, your country will be taken possession of by the English in a short time.[67]

Thus, like Britain, Russia could not realistically hope to improve its official relations with Afghanistan at any point in the near future. As the Government of India noted in late 1908, the Afghan Council regarded Russia with deep and unwavering distrust.[68] Nevertheless, Russia continued to seek a normalization of its relations with Afghanistan. Although the emir refused in February to approve the direct correspondence between the governor of Herat and a local Russian border official concerning the still vexatious Jamshedi issue,[69] the realities of Russo-Afghan border relations included frequent interaction between the local officials of both states. For example, when a number of Russian oxen and horses were stolen by a cross-border Afghan raid in November 1908, Captain Gias used the incident as an excuse to send a courier to the Afghan official in Feyzabad, not only with a letter documenting the affair, but with a number of gifts sent 'in the name of friendship and with the sincere wish that these gifts would support the improvement of relations'. The courier was so welcomed by the local Afghan official that he was freed of all tolls and taxes along his route to Feyzabad and, once there, was treated as a guest of the local authorities. In response to Gias's letter, the substance of which was transmitted to Kabul, the Afghan official sent his thanks for the goodwill expressed by the Russian, and informed Gias that he was gladly prepared to support future correspondence of such a 'friendly and completely pure character'.[70] Gias concluded from this interchange that it might, in fact, be possible to develop friendly relations with Afghanistan, although he feared that it might not be achievable without aggravating the British.

Nicolson meanwhile, ever the advocate of greater accommodation towards Russia, expressed his fears that the emir's refusal to condone the direct interaction between Russian and Afghan frontier authorities along the lines concluded in the 1907 agreement would unquestionably aggravate the Russians. As the ambassador wrote to Grey in early February:

> I know well the difficulties in the way of inducing the Ameer to be amenable in any matter in which the Russian authorities are concerned, but it is unfortunate that he does not see that in his own interests it would be preferable

that correspondence with the frontier authorities should be recognized and regularized than that it should continue as I believe there is little doubt that it does continue, in an irregular and unrecognized manner. I am much afraid that when the Russian Government are informed that the Ameer does not agree to their proposal, and that His Majesty's Government are unable to assist them in the way which they proposed, they may reconsider their present attitude towards the Convention.[71]

In contrast, Russia appeared outwardly more committed to the agreement than ever before. In May, Nicholas II confided to the French ambassador, Admiral Touchard, that he longed for the word 'cordiale' to be added to the 'Triple Entente'. As Nicolson reported, 'Great Britain, whom he had heard spoken of as "perfide Albion", had, in his experience, proved particularly straightforward and loyal.'[72] The tsar pointed to the co-operation between Russia and Great Britain in Persia as exemplary of the benefits of a good understanding between the two powers.

Although Nicholas was, in part, correct in attributing the relative containment of the Persian crisis to the Anglo-Russian rapprochement, the 'good understanding' that he perceived as existing between the two countries was far from universally acknowledged. At every turn, Russia saw its actions in Persia criticized most vehemently not by the Persians who were affected, but by foreigners. Most notable in the campaign against the continued presence of Russian troops in northern Persia was the Persia Society, a London-based independent group of British citizens concerned with the fate of Persia and its revolution.[73]

On 14 July the most prominent members of this group – the Cambridge orientalist and Persia specialist, E.G. Browne; H.F.B. Lynch, whose firm, Lynch Brothers, had a significant trading concern throughout the south of Persia and ran the steamers on the Karun River; James O'Grady, the Labour MP; and Lord Lamington, the governor of Bombay and president of the Society – wrote a scathing letter to the editor of *The Times*, in which they condemned the Russian troops and their officers for prolonging the current state of unrest in Persia. Although they had long sought to give the Russian government the benefit of the doubt, and credit it with good faith concerning its obligations under the 1907 agreement, the Society had reached the conclusion that there could be only two explanations for the recent behaviour of the Russians-on-the-spot in Persia in favour of the shah's regime:

Either the Government of St Petersburg are not masters in their own house, in which case any agreement with them is not worth the paper upon which it is written, or that they have connived at the doings of their representatives and agents in Persia and must take the full responsibility for the actions of these personages, including the use which they may make of the Russian expeditionary force.

In the eyes of the Society, all the signs indicated that the Russian government was intent on occupying northern Persia, and they urged the British government to stop aiding Russia in its steady progression towards the Indian frontier:

> At present we are concurring with Russia in the destruction of the independence of an ancient nation just at the moment when that nation is making strenuous endeavours to rise to the level of her past. And we are preparing for our own people the defence of a long land frontier in Asia against one of the first-class military Empires of Europe. If that is to be the result of our entente with Russia, the sooner it comes to an end the better it will be for us.[74]

That Russia was preparing to occupy Persia was an opinion not unique to the Persia Society. In May 1909 the Intelligence Branch of the Indian Army recovered a strategical fragment outlining a plan for such an occupation. As Colonel W. Malleson, the assistant quartermaster-general, Intelligence Branch, described in his preface to the plan:

> The fragment which follows was secretly obtained from Russian sources in Persia. It would appear to form part of a scheme drawn up by the Russian General Staff for future military action in Persia. ... It is significant to note ... that the scheme appears to contemplate a Russian occupation, not only of the Karun Basin, in which we are now pegging out very considerable claims, but of places as far south as Bushire and Bandar Abbas which, for generations past, have been peculiarly under British influence.[75]

Whether or not the fragment was an authentic plan for a possible military operation was irrelevant; the Indian Army and subsequently the Government of India were convinced that it was – a fact that only served to bolster their inherent Russophobia.

Despite the indications that Russia planned to expand the scope of its involvement in northern Persia, there was great division between the various factions within the Russian government and military establishment over the prolongation and extension of the Russian troop presence in the region. General Snarskii, the commander of the Russian troop detachment, was convinced that the Russian presence was excessive, and had no correlation to the character of the local opposition and the rudimentary nature of the armed resistance faced by the Russians. Snarskii therefore strongly recommended a significant decrease in the size of the detachment in mid-June and was supported in this position by Vorontsov-Dashkov. From Tabriz, however, an alarmed Miller circumvented the legation in Teheran and wrote directly to St Petersburg to promote the desired level of intervention that had come to be expected from Russia's consular staff. He contradicted Snarskii's opinion, suggesting that the Russian presence should be augmented rather than decreased.[76]

While the composition of the Russian troops remained in question, the unrest in the north continued to increase. Sablin described the steady deterioration of conditions for Europeans throughout the north and especially in Mashhad.[77] Reported raids by the border tribes against Russian frontier posts were severely disrupting Russian commercial interests. At stake for Russia was not only the security of the flocks and herds of Russian subjects that grazed along the border, but the prestige of the Russian government among their own Caucasian population.[78] Furthermore, Russian prestige within Persia itself seemed under attack, as the Constitutionalists who had overthrown Mohammad Ali sought to extricate Ahmad Mirza Shah from the excessive influence of his Russian doctor, Sadovskii. Complicating matters, the Persians sought to replace Sadovskii with an Englishman, Dr Lindley, and eventually to get rid of the shah's Russian tutor, Captain Smirnov, as well. Barclay was extremely concerned that Lindley's appointment would weaken Russian influence at court, and would therefore be adamantly opposed by St Petersburg. At the same time, he feared that if Britain did not support the plan, Persia would look beyond either Russia or Britain to a third power for men to fill these influential slots.[79]

Fortunately for the continuation of Anglo-Russian co-operation in Persia, Sablin was similarly concerned that, were Lindley not to be engaged, the position would go to a German. But the Russian chargé d'affaires put forward a compromise: Russia would not oppose Dr Lindley's appointment so long as Smirnov, whose contract had four years to run, was retained in his post as tutor.[80] The Persians refused to co-operate, however, and not only was Lindley officially appointed first European doctor, but Smirnov was discharged without warning at the end of August.[81] Sablin was extremely disappointed that Russia's wishes had been so blatantly disregarded by the new government. He had, as he wrote to St Petersburg, been extremely patient:

> I had a multitude of pretexts to summon the troops here; I didn't do this out of respect for the nationalist movement, who have taken upon themselves a tremendous responsibility, in the hope that the new people would understand and appreciate Russia's policies. They have neither understood nor appreciated them.

In contrast, the slights against Russia had been numerous: in the provinces adjacent to Russia, useless governors had been appointed; Smirnov and Sadovskii were removed from their positions; the Russian bank received no co-operation in its suits against its Persian debtors; the right of *bast* had been disrespected; no peace had been established along the Russo-Persian frontier. In short, it appeared as though the new Persian government was doing everything possible to create difficulties for Russia, to infringe upon the obligations that had been incurred towards Russia by the previous government, and to exclude Russians from positions of influence and authority within the country with impunity.[82]

Ultimately, at the insistence of the two legations, Sadovskii and Smirnov's appointments were renewed.[83] But the lingering effects of what Sablin considered to be a blatant attack on Russian influence and prestige in Persia contributed to the end of discussions on the reduction of the Russian detachment in Tabriz. In the middle of September, the Ministry of Foreign Affairs had begun exploring the gradual decrease of this detachment in conjunction with the Ministries of Finance and War.[84] Simultaneously, Snarskii was continuing to urge a reduction of these troops to a maximum of two companies.[85] Yet by the end of September, a special committee of the Council of Ministers had concluded that it was not desirable to decrease the detachment at that time.[86] Poklevsky-Kozell, who had at last arrived in Teheran to assume his post as Russian minister, urged his government to rethink its position in light of the significant tranquillity that had overtaken Tabriz, but to no avail.[87] The Russian military presence in Azerbaijan would continue.

While the Russians were failing to acquiesce to Britain's clearly stated wishes that they withdraw their troops from northern Persia, they simultaneously endeavoured to persuade their British counterparts actively to support one of the principal projects of Russian Central Asian policy – regional railway construction. From the signing of the agreement, the Russians had sought to take advantage of Anglo-Russian co-operation in Persia by pushing for the construction of a trans-Persian railway project that would connect the Russian Central Asian railway system with the Persian Gulf and, ultimately, the railways and markets of India. Soon after the agreement was published, *Novoe Vremia* proclaimed the possible connection of Europe and India by an uninterrupted railway line through Persia as 'one of the most important results of the Agreement concluded'.[88] The Russian daily was supported in its call for such a railway by the *Daily Telegraph*, which wrote: 'Railroads ... can serve as better means for the preservation of peace, than protocols of conferences. Their influence is more concrete and enduring.'[89] Furthermore, within both the British and Russian camps, the imperative to construct a railway system through Persia was greatly intensified by the growing sense of commercial threat and challenge of influence from the developing German-backed Baghdad Railway.[90]

In addition to a wish to offset any potential German challenges to Russian ascendancy in the north – for which Russia strongly desired German official recognition of the Russian sphere of influence – there were several other strong motivating factors behind the Russian aspiration for the extensive development of railways both within their sphere in Persia and connecting to the rest of the country.[91] Hartwig, in May 1908, had pushed for the construction of a number of lines – not merely a north–south trans-Persian trunk line – that he considered would be advantageous for Russian trade and its military strategic position.[92] Izvolskii endorsed Hartwig's position, urging his colleagues to take advantage of Russia's exclusive right to build railways in Persia until 1910 under the concession they had been granted in the Russo-Persian Railway Agreement of 12 November 1890, which had been renewed in 1900. He was convinced that such railway development could only serve to support all of Russia's vital interests: 'The construction of railroads in Persia is important not only from the point of view of economics, as a means to quickly spread in Persia the products of our industry; it has paramount significance in relation to both our political and our strategic interests.'[93] With the aim of promoting the Russian construction of railways in Persia, the minister of foreign affairs assembled a committee composed of representatives from all the relevant departments to examine the Persian railway question.

The first meeting of this special committee, on 11/24 July 1908, reached mixed conclusions over whether or not the construction of railways by Russia in northern Persia was desirable or possible. While the assistant minister of foreign affairs, N.V. Charikov, reiterated Izvolskii's conviction that a railway scheme was crucial for Russian political, strategic and economic concerns in Persia, Kokovtsov was gloomy in his typically austere attitude towards the actual realization of any Russian-financed construction in Persia; he insisted that the Duma would not possibly vote to finance Persian railways 'when so many urgent needs in Russia await satisfaction'. Furthermore, the minister of finance disputed the prospect of any return on further Russian material investment in a country that had thus far, in his opinion, proven no more than a drain on Russian resources: 'We need to take into account that all our former undertakings in Persia have had little success and lots of disadvantages. ... In general, we have spent more in Persia than in other countries, and the results which we have received are nothing.'[94]

Kokovtsov was, however, alone in his adamant opposition to Persian railway construction. Charikov assured his colleagues that the money for the railway would not have to come out of the Russian treasury; rather, a combination of railway-assisted Persian trade and foreign capital – principally British and French – would pay for the Russian-sponsored project. The Ministry of Trade and Industry agreed with the Ministry of Foreign Affairs' prediction that the Persian market was growing, and that future Persian prosperity would make an Anglo-Russian railway project advantageous for both countries. In addition, all those Russians even remotely in favour of the project felt that Britain would find the opportunity to participate in railway construction in Persia too great to pass up.

The British were less convinced than their Russian counterparts that an extensive British commitment to Persian railway construction was in order. Shortly after the conclusion of the 1907 agreement, Morley had privately warned Grey that he would, in the future, be invariably opposed to any financial participation by the Government of India in Persian railway construction; as the secretary of state for India reminded Grey, one of the principal motivations behind his support of the convention had been the promise that an Anglo-Russian agreement would free the Government of India from the bulk, if not all, of expenditures in Persia.[95] In September 1908, when the issue of Persian railway construction had become more pressing, Morley reminded the Foreign Office of his extreme opposition to contributing Indian revenues to pay for British political and commercial enterprises in Persia; if a line were to be built, it would need to be financed by the Home Government, not by the Government of India.[96]

Not everyone in the British government was opposed to Persian railway construction, however. In 1908 a memorandum by Percy L. Loraine, the third secretary, in charge of commercial matters at the British legation in Teheran, had outlined the advantages to Persia of an extensive communications network. Loraine predicted that co-operation between Britain and Russia in the spirit of the 1907 agreement would allow southern and south-western Persia to experience the same level of agricultural and commercial development that had, to that time, only been enjoyed by the north.[97] The Foreign Office and its representatives in Persia recognized that if Britain did not participate in the railway development of Persia, it would nevertheless be undertaken by Russia or, of even greater concern, a third power, with no consideration given to British strategic and economic needs.[98] Thus, in August 1908, Britain and Russia exchanged notes establishing the principle of Anglo-Russian co-operation in railway construction in Persia.[99]

For Britain, the chief concern was that any railway agreement must be protective in character, with the sole aim of excluding all third parties from future Persian railway construction; the British were not prepared even to contemplate actual construction at that time. Above all, while Russia hoped to secure British finance for the construction of railways in the north, the

Foreign Office recognized that public opinion would find the idea of Britain paying entirely for a railway that would be almost two-thirds within the Russian sphere laughable.[100] Therefore, Britain responded to the initial Russian proposal for railway co-operation with a suggestion that the two powers agree to obtain the necessary concessions from the Persian government for railway construction while acknowledging that, at the present time, any definite plan for railway development in Persia would be impracticable. The British were insistent that railways could not be built before a semblance of financial equilibrium had been established in Persia. Above all, they were unwilling to commit to the scheme the capital Russia required.[101]

One of the great stumbling blocks to British participation in the Russian railway plans was a strong sense within the British government that the rail lines that Russia intended to build would virtually destroy all chances for British trade to prosper within the Russian sphere. This predicted 'disastrous effect on British trade in Persia'[102] would be the result of two distinct characteristics of the Russian proposals: (1) Russia planned to begin building the north–south line within its sphere at the earliest possible date, while Britain remained unwilling to commence construction immediately on the lines lying within its sphere; and (2) Russia intended to impose a differential rate for goods travelling on the railway within its sphere. Barclay gloomily informed Grey that the Russian proposals were far from encouraging; they would produce a situation in which British capital would be paying for, and the British government would be guaranteeing, the interest of a railway that, under Russia's proposed conditions, would destroy British trade in the Russian sphere. As Barclay summarized, 'In short, we should gain nothing at Russia's expense, whereas she would gain much at ours.'[103]

While Britain predicted that Russia would enjoy considerable trading advantages in Persia were the trans-Persian railway to be constructed according to the Russian proposals, in Afghanistan Russian trade continued to be far from privileged. Growing frustration over the inflexibility of the Afghan government towards its neighbours permeated the correspondence of MID's Central Asia Desk and the Russian districts bordering Afghanistan. Russian officials in the Transcaspian province harshly criticized a situation in which 'Afghanistan is getting rich at our expense.'[104] They suggested that Russia should close its borders to Afghans, in order to force Afghanistan to admit Russian merchants to its markets.

The Central Asia Desk, however, disagreed with this proposal. In late September a departmental report was circulated that examined Russia's options in the pursuit of the Afghan trade. While bemoaning the difficulties of dealing with a country whose trade policy was overwhelmingly driven by a fear that foreign goods would be quickly followed by foreign political influence, the report concluded that there was little that Russia could do to alter the state of affairs:

> Reprisals, such as closing our borders to Afghan goods, as the commander of our Transcaspian province recommends, will hardly influence the Emir to change his policies. The result of such a step will be, in all truth, that border relations with Afghanistan will conclusively wall up and our direct trade with this khanate, which is gradually growing, albeit very slowly, would completely cease and will entirely be transported through Persia. Such a result would hardly correspond with our interests. We are only playing into the arms of the Emir's Government and are losing the sympathies of the Afghan border population, which would be hugely disadvantageous.

Rather than sealing off the border, the report recommended the encouragement 'by every means possible' of what direct trade already existed between the ethnically and economically linked peoples who lived along both sides of the Russo-Afghan border. Through these means, both Russian goods and Russian influence would be disseminated through northern Afghanistan. As the Central Asia Desk concluded: 'Sooner or later, the Afghan Government itself will realize the necessity of renouncing its seclusion, and reprisal, like every other hostile action, can only delay this moment.'[105]

Of course, the penetration of the Afghan border by Russian merchants would not serve only to promote Russian trade. The free movement of Russian subjects back and forth across the frontier would provide Russia with a vast and much needed source of intelligence on a country about which alarmingly little was known. As the Transcaspian provincial government observed:

> Information about the condition of affairs in Afghanistan, which remains completely closed to us, is delivered to us only by native intelligence agents and is marked by its incomplete and fragmentary nature. ... We could have more exact information about Afghanistan if our traders could enter there with the rights under which Afghan merchants and workers come to our territory.[106]

The unsteadiness of Habibullah Khan's hold on the throne made such information vital for Russian regional stability. The governor-general of Turkestan, Aleksandr Vasilevich Samsonov, predicted that the unrest might very well result in Habibullah's overthrow in favour of his brother, Sardar Nasrollah Khan; a tangential effect, in all likelihood, would be a call by Nasrollah for a holy war against Europeans to unite the Afghan people in a common cause. Samsonov feared that if the Afghans were to rise up in an anti-European fervour, they would choose what he called 'the path of least resistance' and would massacre the Russians stationed in the garrisons and detachments along the Bukharan side of the Amudar'ya. The Afghans would most likely not attack the Indian frontier, since it was much more heavily defended by the British than the weakly guarded border to the north – a fact of which Afghanistan would be well informed by the numerous Afghan subjects living and working in Russian territory. To make matters worse, Russia would be unable to mount a significant counter-attack across the Afghan frontier for fear that it might be interpreted by the British as the first stage of a march on India.

Samsonov was extremely concerned by the prospect of an independent attack by Afghanistan against Russia. Although he credited the 1907 agreement with freeing Russia from the threat of a combined Anglo-Afghan military opposition, he was convinced that Britain would be able to do nothing to protect Russia from 'the possibility of independent hostile Afghan action in the current political state of religious fanaticism.'[107] As a 1908 general staff report had noted, of great concern for Russia was the strong possibility that a war with Afghanistan would not be contained, and would spread to include the 'adjoining Asiatic powers, with whom political relations are extremely uncertain and flimsy in the system of our diplomatic relations in Asia.'[108] Samsonov therefore insisted that Russia must be prepared to meet this threat, which was part of the growing trend of pan-Islamism sweeping the region:

> It seems to me that we were wrong when we considered Afghanistan to be a submissive follower and almost a vassal of England. ... Possibly the conflagration, which is partially affecting Turkey and Persia, will be spreading in the near future into the possessions of the Emir of Afghanistan. If this happens, don't look to the Agreement with England, which will be ultimately without any strength to help extinguish it. The sparks of this fire can hurt us, and we must prepare ourselves in every possible way.[109]

Russian preparations for an armed conflict with Afghanistan had been going on for quite some time. Between 1903 and 1904, a plan for military operations on the Turkestan–Afghan front was laid out under the direction of then minister of war, General Kuropatkin, which the Turkestan general staff saw fit to refine in 1909.[110] By 1909 the 1904 plan was obviously outdated, for three principal reasons: (1) the plan was based upon 'the dream of a campaign to India ... based more on romantic aspirations towards this legendary country of sun and blue skies, than any element of real policy'; (2) Russia's ruinous experiences in the Far East during the Russo-Japanese war should have prevented any 'further fantasies' in Central Asia; and (3) the construction of the Orenburg–Tashkent railway and the reorganization of the

Turkestani infantry had made the previous choices of Herat and Qandahar as the principal operational objectives obsolete. This altered strategic landscape could only convince Russia, 'that even Great Powers must necessarily conform their political objectives with an understanding of available means and the present situation.'[111]

In response, the Turkestani military staff proposed a number of revisions of the general Russian military orientation towards Afghanistan: (1) the delineation of Kabul as the primary and Herat as the secondary strategic objectives in an Afghan campaign; (2) the open renunciation of aggressive designs on Afghanistan and of the even more unreasonable plan for a campaign to India; (3) a regrouping of the existing Russian military presence along the Afghan frontier; and (4) the reinforcement of those troops with the addition of five Armenian corps from European Russia.[112] This call for reinforcements and a strategic realignment indicates a surprisingly intense sense of vulnerability along the Turkestani front. As the Turkestan general staff described the importance of the Afghan military theatre for Russian state security:

> Under the influence of our failures in the Far East, we are now inclined to exaggerate the military significance of our Asian outskirts, to design in our imaginations formidable images of a great war in Persia, in Afghanistan, and even in Mongolia! In Central Asia we do not, at this time, have enemies who, in accordance with the constitution of our military strength and our geographic position, would offer us peace.[113]

Although serious apprehensions over the instability of the Russo-Afghan border challenged Russian strategic planning, Russia in 1909 was no longer concerned about the inevitability of a joint Anglo-Afghan military response to Russian action along the frontier.[114] This alleviation of security threats in the Afghan theatre was not only an outgrowth of the Anglo-Russian rapprochement; it resulted from the steady deterioration of relations between the emir and the people of Afghanistan on one side, and the Government of India and Great Britain on the other. Habibullah, intent upon defending his throne and his reputation from accusations of being a British pawn, openly disdained British attempts to conduct normal relations between Afghanistan and India.[115] All along the Indo-Afghan frontier, harsh measures were being taken against unlicensed Anglo-Indians, and the Afghan government reinforced its surveillance of all its subjects who had relations with India.[116] There were further rumours of Afghan agents operating throughout India, especially in the north, with the aim of stirring up Muslim sentiment against the British. As the Russian intelligence agents operating in the region reported, it was Habibullah's aim to unite the Muslim states under his leadership, making him, after the sultan in Constantinople, the most important defender of Islam. At the same time, Britain refused to retreat from its pursuit of the relations with Afghanistan to which it felt entitled by precedent and by the terms that ended the Second Anglo-Afghan War; the British insisted that the emir establish two new British tribal and political agents and a regular convoy from India to Kabul.[117]

While the Russians were pleased that Britain's own problems with Afghanistan offered a modicum of relief for Russia's security concerns in Central Asia, they were alarmed by the precedent being set along the Indo-Afghan frontier. They actively feared that the anti-British reprisals and active surveillance that had become standard practice in southern Afghanistan would be similarly established along the Afghan border with Russia. In March 1909 the Russian political agent in Bukhara had warned MID that Russia could not possibly decrease the number of intelligence agents they had stationed along the Bukharan–Afghan frontier. Yet despite the obvious need for information, Russia's agents in place were dwindling. The Russians had lost their agents in a number of towns, their agent in Herat had died, and the Armenian traders who had previously acted as controllers for spies within the Afghan government were refusing to continue service after a number of Armenians were executed for espionage.[118] In short, just as the Afghan situation was becoming increasingly destabilized, rendering accurate intelligence an ever more vital necessity, Russia found the possibilities for gathering such intelligence to be shrinking.

The acquisition of intelligence about Persia was a far less troublesome task. Most obviously, the very significant Russian presence in the north made the gleaning of information a much simpler exercise, as it was also for the British in the south. In addition to the standard methods of intelligence gathering by the consulates and military staffs, Russia sent a number of officers to Persia with the primary mission of improving their language skills after the completion of a course of Eastern language study in Tashkent; the secondary and almost equally significant aim of their tours, however, was the execution of extensive reconnaissance along their routes. Not only were these officers dispatched within the Russian sphere, they were sent to the neutral and British zones as well.[119] One such officer, Second Lieutenant Fedorov of the 2nd Transcaspian Rifle Battalion, returned from his mission to eastern Persia to call for an increased Russian intelligence presence in the regions of Persia not under Russian influence. He urged his government to go beyond the haphazard and occasional dispatch of officers to tour the south; in his opinion, the permanent establishment of covert intelligence networks within the British sphere was not only desirable, it was required by the realities of conditions throughout Persia.[120]

Like the Russian sphere, the British and neutral spheres were extremely unsettled. The brigandry along the principal trade routes of the south had reached such alarming proportions that the British proposed the creation of a native road guard, numbering 600 men, to police the roads; the guard would be financed by a surcharge of 10 per cent on the import and export duties collected in the Persian Gulf ports.[121] Although the British would have preferred that this guard be commanded by British officers, they recognized that the Russians would have found that offensive. Therefore, Barclay proposed that the officers be lent from the Indo-European Telegraph Department. This proposal was communicated to Izvolskii on 2/15 November 1909, who immediately questioned the actual independence of the telegraph officers and proposed a joint Russo-British command of the proposed road guard.[122]

While the two powers considered the various options for a security force, an attack on the Bushire–Shiraz Road underscored the critical state of unrest that characterized the region. The caravan of the Russian consul-general at Bushire, N.P. Passek, and the late acting consul-general at Bushire, V.M. Kadlubovskii, was attacked by members of the Boramadi tribe as the Russians travelled from Shiraz to Bushire. One Russian Cossack was killed and several members of the escort were wounded.[123] Understandably, the Russians were incensed by this attack on their officials, and public opinion at home demanded justice. *Novoe Vremia* insisted that the outrage proved that the only safe places in Persia were the areas where there were sufficient numbers of Russian troops stationed, and called on Poklevsky-Kozell to take independent measures to right the egregious wrong that had been committed: 'If the Russian Minister feels that he is indeed the representative of a Great Power and not merely a diplomatic clerk, he should take other steps on his own responsibility.'[124] *Birzhevye Vedomosti* railed against a situation in which they felt they were dependent on the British for Russian security and the fulfilment of their rights to pacify the country:

> Our diplomacy, if it really values the prestige of Russia, will be obliged to make demands for satisfaction from the impotent Persian Government, and this will call forth fresh protests against Russian claims. A vicious circle is thus formed from which there is no escape; only when it is acknowledged by England and Russia alike that the geographical position of the latter gives her an undisputed right to restore order and pacify the country when the Persian Government is unable to do so will this circle be broken.[125]

The British, for their part, used the attack on the Russians as an opportunity to push for their gendarmerie proposal.[126] Furthermore, the British acting consul at Shiraz, Walter Smart, called for active British intervention to pacify the region and for the dispatch of a punitive expedition against the tribe responsible. While Barclay felt that such measures were not yet necessary, he did anticipate a not-so-distant date when Britain's policy of non-intervention would have to be reconsidered.[127] For Russia, the British plan had numerous acknowledged advantages. As Kokovtsov advised Izvolskii, not only would the instalment of a security force along the trade routes of the southern and neutral zones secure Russian interests in those regions in the process, a public relations triumph would be scored as well; were Britain to impose its own security regime in the south, Russia could no longer be condemned for the continuing presence of its troops in the north.[128] Therefore, at the beginning of 1910, the Russian government committed itself to a serious discussion of the British proposals.[129]

Russia had been waiting for the British to admit that their policy of non-intervention in Persia was not working. The Russians were convinced that the growing chaos in Persia posed an even greater challenge to British regional security than to Russia. As Poklevsky-Kozell noted at the end of 1909:

> The British Government, much more than we, fears the re-establishment of anarchy in Persia, which could compel both Powers to undertake active intervention or the establishment of a condominium. In both instances, the spheres of action of Russia and Britain would draw nearer, Persia would become the buffer state, and for Britain, danger for India and Afghanistan could arise again.[130]

Fears that India was still threatened by the lingering spectre of a Russian invasion continued to influence factions within the British Empire despite Russian professions, both domestically and internationally, that they no longer harboured any hostile inclinations towards British India.[131] In his 1909 study of the Anglo-Russian Central Asian rivalry, M. Grulev of the Institute of Military Studies in St Petersburg insisted that Russia could and should no longer entertain thoughts of a march on India, writing: 'We all know that we don't need India, that the inclusion of three-hundred million new polyglot, heterodox subjects located far from the centre of the state, would draw Russia from her vital roots.' Grulev urged his country to concentrate on the goal of achieving free passage through the Straits, and not to concentrate any more effort on the dream of using a threat to India as a means to strong-arm Britain into supporting Russian Near Eastern aims:

> The road to Constantinople we have already known for 1000 years; our victorious troops have never once gone up to it, and the road to India we only know according to extremely meagre books based on English sources. Is it possible to allow oneself on such a grandiose diversion, demanding in every instance enormous means? Would it not be better, when the time arrives, to

direct these means towards the straight route to the achievement of the well known, sworn aim, long close to the Russian heart?[132]

Yet, despite Grulev's affirmations and what Grey described to Benckendorff as 'irrefutable proof of [Russian] disinterest',[133] there remained strong factions, most notably within the Anglo-Indian press and governing communities, who persisted in disbelieving existing limits on Russian expansion in Central Asia. The latest disappointment of Russian Near Eastern goals after the retreat in the face of Austro-Hungarian–German unity during the Bosnian crisis seemed to push Russian attention once again eastward from the Straits. In Central Asia, the greatest stumbling block for the Russo-British understanding continued to be Persia, where the revolutionary unrest and growing Russian presence threatened to undermine the earnest efforts of the two Great Powers towards regional co-operation. Both governments openly attested to their sincere satisfaction at the ways in which the convention had, as the tsar told Grey when they met at Cowes in early August, 'stood so well the test of the difficulties in Persia'.[134] But it was clear that the ongoing difficulties in Persia, coupled with the stubborn refusal of the Afghan emir to heed the wishes of his Great Power neighbours and normalize relations on both his southern and northern frontiers, were posing challenges to the rapprochement that, if not resolved, could force Britain and Russia to re-evaluate their commitment to the agreement.

CHAPTER 4

Conflicting Motivations and the Drift towards Discord: 1910

As 1910 commenced, the Anglo-Russian rapprochement in Central Asia appeared stable in the face of considerable regional challenges. *Novoe Vremia* had remarked on the manifest harmony between the two Great Powers during the tsar's visit to Cowes: 'The change in our relations with England has already produced its results. Our rapprochement has cleared the air in the Far East, has very much lightened the difficulties of our diplomacy created by the situation in Persia, and contributed towards consolidating the political balance of power in Europe.'[1] Although 1909 had been a year dominated by Persian unrest and Afghan intransigence, the relationship remained intact. While the two buffer states directly separating Russian Central Asia and British India had proven, at times, to be extremely troublesome for Anglo-Russian co-operation, relations between the two Great Powers and the third country governed by the 1907 agreement, Tibet, had been relatively uneventful. The primary point of consideration for Britain and Russia had been the unauthorized entry into Tibet of an exploratory scientific expedition from the Russian Geographical Society in March.[2] At the end of 1909, however, with 2000 Chinese troops poised to enter Lhasa, the mountain kingdom and its Buddhist inhabitants promised to return to the arena of Anglo-Russian concerns.

China had been steadily advancing into eastern Tibet throughout 1909 in an attempt to solidify its hold over the country.[3] Soon after the Dalai Lama had at last returned to Lhasa on 25 December from his self-imposed Mongolian exile following the Younghusband Expedition, the Chinese Amban, Lien Yü, assured the Dalai Lama that only 1000 Chinese soldiers were on their way to the Tibetan capital; their purpose, he promised, was to provide police protection for the trade marts in an effort to persuade the British to withdraw the Gyangze trade agents' escort according to the provisions of the 1908 Trade Regulations. When the Dalai Lama realized in early February 1910 that he had been duped into false complacency by the Chinese, he hoped to organize an effective resistance to the invasion.[4] Unfortunately the British trade agents at Gyangze, Captain R.S. Kennedy and Lieutenant J.L.R. Weir, had already informed the Tibetans that the Indian government would do nothing to interfere with what it felt 'was purely a matter between the Tibetans and Chinese'.[5] Therefore the Dalai Lama, resolving to avoid surrender to the Chinese, fled through one of Lhasa's city gates just as the Chinese vanguard entered through another. With the Chinese close on his heels, he narrowly escaped across the border into British territory and presented himself to the telegraph office at Gnatong in Sikkim. Alastair Lamb describes the event in his study of Anglo-Chinese-Tibetan relations, *The McMahon Line*: 'Two very surprised British telegraphists invited the "Dally Larmer" in for a cup of tea, thus ushering in a new era of Anglo-Tibetan relations.'[6]

While Britain had insisted to the Tibetans that it could not interfere in what it considered to be Chinese internal policy, the abolition of Tibetan autonomy and the subsequent imposition of revolutionary anarchy in the country posed a considerable threat to Britain's sense of security – both strategic and mercantile – along its north-eastern frontier. As Minto telegraphed to London: 'There can be no doubt that a state of anarchy in Tibet would be a very serious factor on the Indian frontier, in view particularly of the complications which might arise from the racial sympathy existing between the Tibetans & the Nepalese, Sikkimese & Bhutanese, & the paralysis of trade which would be inevitable.'[7] Of greatest concern for the British was the effect that Chinese actions in Tibet might have on their own protectorate of Nepal, the source of the Gurkha recruits for the Indian Army and police forces so vital for Indian external and internal security.[8]

Nepal had good reason to feel worried by the Chinese efforts to exercise their suzerain rights over Tibet. Although Nepal was linked by treaty obligations to British India, an earlier admission of allegiance to the emperor of China, however unrecognized by Britain, could complicate matters were the Chinese to push their advance to the Tibetan–Nepalese frontier.[9] In an indication of the extent to which the Nepalese felt menaced by Chinese troops so near their border, the prime minister of Nepal threatened to launch his own armed opposition to the violation of Tibetan territorial sovereignty.[10]

Whether the threat were to come from China or Nepal, Russia had no intention of unilateral intervention in Tibet. Although the Russian chargé d'affaires in Peking, Ivan Iakovlevich Korostovets, informed the Chinese government that, 'the fact that Russia has millions of Lamaist subjects of her own made it impossible for her to ignore developments in Thibet',[11] observing developments was a far cry from active interference. In response to the appeals of the Dalai Lama for assistance, Izvolskii replied that, while his government sympathized with the Tibetan's misfortunes, it would do nothing without consultation and agreement with Great Britain.[12] Britain, so long as

China did not renege on its promises to fulfil scrupulously all treaty obligations concerning Tibet, was content to wait and see how the change in
administration in Lhasa would affect British-Indian relations with Tibet.
Britain was even prepared to accept Nepalese intervention, although
Hardinge voiced fears that it would be difficult to persuade Russia that the
Government of India was not behind Nepal's actions.[13] The British were,
however, adamant that China be made to see that they would not tolerate any
interference in Nepal or the two smaller states of Bhutan and Sikkim.[14]

Veterans of the Younghusband Expedition and old Tibet hands such as
Major W.F. O'Connor, the first British trade agent at Gyangze and now the
consul for Seistan and Qaen, and Charles Bell, the political officer in Sikkim,
clamoured for active British support for the Dalai Lama's cause and the
dispatch of a British agent to Lhasa – if only to prevent his turn to other
powers with an offer of a protectorate over Tibet in exchange for assistance
against the Chinese. The British government, however, was resolutely determined to avoid entanglement in the Tibetan morass.[15] Bell, in the face of
London's insistence that it would not intervene on the Dalai Lama's behalf,
warned his superiors that isolated attacks against the British agencies at
Yatung and Gyangze would most likely result from the inevitable Tibetan
resentment of the British restraint. The Government of India agreed with
Bell's assessment that the trade agents' escorts should be increased considerably; Grey and Hardinge acquiesced, as long as the Russians would be duly
informed of the troop increase.[16] However, the Secretary of State for India,
Viscount Morley, feared that the movement of British troops into Tibet, even
if only to protect the existing British presence, would give rise to 'embarrassing consequences politically', such as a Chinese demand for the complete
withdrawal of the escort under Article 12 of the 1908 Trade Regulations.[17] At
the end of June, Morley elaborated on his vision of the 'embarrassing consequences' Britain might face from an increased British military presence in
Tibet:

> Are troops to stand by while Thibetans are punished by Chinese, or while
> Chinese and Thibetans fight it out? Is it not inevitable that we shall be driven
> to take the part of the weaker side, with results that, whichever side it may
> be, will be equally embarrassing? Will it be possible, again, without loss of
> prestige in Nepal and border States, to withdraw when order is re-
> established? ... it is likely that massing of troops on frontier, by encouraging
> Thibetans to believe that we are going to help them, will even provoke dis-
> turbance.[18]

The Tibet lobby was thus overruled, as the government at home and in
India were determined to avoid armed intervention in Tibet unless there was

a direct attack on the British agencies. The Government of India, however, pressed for the preparation in Sikkim of troops to be held ready in the event of a threat to the trade agencies.[19] The British government instead proposed the withdrawal of the trade agencies in the face of the growing security threat, a proposal to which the Government of India was adamantly opposed. Grey, noting the Anglo-Indian tendency to vacillate in their appraisal of the situation in Tibet, commented, 'It is interesting to see how the danger to this post [the Gyangze trade agency] is thought to be great when there is a question of strengthening it and slight when there is a question of withdrawing it.'[20] Despite Grey's scepticism, however, the troop preparations were agreed on, and *The Times* broadcast the defensive measure at the end of July.[21]

Izvolskii was disappointed to learn first of the British troop preparations along the Tibetan border from the published press reports, rather than directly from the very government with whom Russia had signed a convention guaranteeing mutual non-interference in Tibet less than three years before.[22] *Russkoe Slovo* soon predicted that Britain was most likely planning to propose a re-examination of the 1907 agreement concerning Tibet.[23] Grey urged Nicolson to assure the Russians that they considered an advance of these troops into Tibet to be improbable at most; the troops would only cross the border if British lives were endangered and would, under no circumstances, intervene between the Chinese and the Tibetans. Above all, the Russians were to be convinced that, had there been even the slightest possibility of a violation of the 1907 agreement, they would have been duly consulted.[24]

The Chinese quickly noticed the concentration of British troops along the Tibet–Sikkim border, and informed the British that they considered the protection of the British escorts in Tibet to be Chinese duty under the existing trade regulations; they were prepared to guarantee the safety of the British agents if the British would withdraw the reinforcements that had already been dispatched to garrison the trade agencies.[25] Although the British were unwilling to withdraw their reinforcements, the decreased threat to the British agencies and the growth of regional stability produced by this promise of protection was duly noted. Morley vetoed the suggestions of the Government of India, which felt that the positive political effect that the troop mobilizations in Sikkim had had on the situation in Tibet warranted the continuation of these preparations despite the elimination of the threat against which they had been initiated.[26] On 3 September the mobilization was discontinued. After regretting to inform their Russian counterparts of the decision to mobilize the troops in the first place, the British did not hesitate to publicize the demobilization in an official memorandum to the Russian embassy: 'His Majesty's Government have accordingly authorized this step which in their opinion has the additional advantage of clearly demonstrating to the Chinese Government that British policy as regards Tibet is actuated by no selfish political ambitions.'[27] The resoluteness of this proclamation suggests a zealous concern to demonstrate the absence of British ambitions to the Russian government as well.

While the north-east frontier with Tibet had continued to pose a considerable challenge to British Indian security, the situation in Afghanistan appeared equally troublesome for both Great Powers. Late in 1909 a proclamation of dubious origin had been read in all the primary market towns throughout the country, claiming the existence of a secret agreement between Britain and Russia to divide Afghanistan between themselves. The Afghans were warned, 'if you will sleep, you will perish.'[28] Similarly, in June 1910, the emir warned his people that Afghanistan's adversaries in a future conflict could be *either* Russia or Britain. Habibullah, however, officially discounted the threat from Britain, relying on the mutual pledges that had been made during the reign of the late Abdur Rahman Khan in which both states swore to support reciprocal peace.[29]

In stark contrast, he made no such claims to dismiss the possibility of a conflict with his neighbours to the north. What existed of relations between Russia and Afghanistan in 1910 remained strained. In addition to the ongoing tensions engendered by the lack of direct communications between the two governments, the lingering Jamshedi refugee crisis was a continued mutual aggravation. Just as the Russians were annoyed by the emir's unwillingness to pacify his people and prevent their trans-border flight, Habibullah had been irritated by Russia's refusal to resettle the ringleaders of the Jamshedi uprising and mass exodus, who had remained in Russian territory, anywhere but directly along the Russo-Afghan frontier, because of what Russia claimed was 'the entire absence of free land, water, and pasturage for cattle, which could be granted to those Jamshedis now within Russian limits.'[30] As the emir incredulously asked the viceroy of India, 'how is it possible that such a great Power should not have land enough for the settlement of a few refugees?'[31] The Jamshedi issue, Habibullah warned, might very well blow up into a Russo-Afghan conflict.

Of course, the Jamshedi were not the only source of regional tension. Afghan trans-border horse thievery continued to irritate the local Russian officials, leading Russia to ask Britain once again to restrain its semi-protectorate.[32] The British and Afghans, on the other hand, were being bombarded by rumours reported in the Anglo-Indian papers of extensive Russian activity in Central Asia, which seemed to point towards plans for a Russian advance on Afghanistan. *The Advocate of India* insisted that Russia was preparing to build a bridge across the Amudar'ya at Kelif; this bridge would ostensibly be to facilitate commerce, since Kelif was a trading point, not a strategic point.[33] More alarming for the British were reports in *The Pioneer* of Russian plans to construct a cotton mill at Termez, across the Amudar'ya from the Afghan post of Patta Hissar. This spot, far from the existing branches of the Central Asian Railway, could, in British opinion, only have been chosen for its strategic advantages, not its agricultural or industrial ones; advocates of a Russian forward policy in the region had long pushed for an extension of the railway from Samarkand to Termez, thus providing Russia with a secondary route of military advance on Afghanistan. As *The Pioneer* pointed out, 'It looks as if the hands of the Ministry for Railways are to be forced into the construction of the Termez railway through the creation of a bogus industrial activity.'[34]

Although the validity of these fears was dubious, Russia had been working to consolidate its strategic position along the Russo-Afghan frontier, most significantly in the area of military border reconnaissance. From 1908 on, special attention had been given to regional staffing issues concerning the officers, agents and commanders of the reconnaissance points, and active recognition was given to the general difficulties of mounting reconnaissance operations directed against the Afghan border fortresses. By the beginning of 1910, all the careful attention paid to the region was rewarded by the Russian acquisition of the plans to the Afghan fortress at Daidad. This coup was, according to the chief of staff of the Turkestan Military District, exemplary of the tremendous success that Russia had experienced in its Afghan-oriented intelligence efforts.[35] The Russians had detailed reports from various sources of Afghan defences, troop deployments and fighting methods.[36] Similarly, frequent rumours of numerous Russian agents in Kabul were supported by the observations of a British technical expert employed by the emir named Miller, who reported that there were a significant number of Russians living in Kabul 'on the Amir's bounty'; they all claimed to be Muslim refugees from Russian oppression, but 'the depth of their Muhammadan convictions' was certainly open to question.[37]

The extent of ongoing Anglo-Indian fears of Russian Central Asian advances seemed to many within both the British and Russian governments to be reactionary alarmism, hearkening back to the era before the rapprochement. The Russian consul-general in Bombay, Boris Konstantinovich Arseniev, lamented openly to the secretary of state for foreign affairs of the Government of India that nothing had changed in Russo-Indian relations despite the completely altered geostrategic landscape:

Fear has so profoundly taken root in the English in India of an alleged Russian
political offensive in Central Asia, that to this time they cannot waver, not in
response to the alteration of the course of our politics following the misfor-
tune which befell us during the time of the last war, nor the Anglo-Russian
Agreement of 1907, nor even logic, which, when properly acknowledged,
demands that we work amicably, hand in hand, in the name of the preservation of influence and prestige of the white races in Asia.[38]

While Arseniev insisted to the Government of India that it had nothing to
fear from his empire, he did recognize that, even if Russia was not intending
to pose a direct threat in Central Asia, the British position in India was far
from secure:

The fateful day for England is still to come. If, having been dragged into a
European war, serious events in Afghanistan or Tibet forced the Indian Government to transfer all or a large part of their army to the borders of the
Empire, in the end, dissemination amongst the native soldiers of anti-
government propaganda could accelerate the offensive of the critical moment. ... But this critical moment for England will come sooner or later.[39]

The British experience in Asia might have been, as Arkadiy Petrov announced in his 1910 treatise, *How England and Russia Defend their Interests
in Asia*, a model for formal and informal imperial expansion, but the slogans
of nineteenth-century European colonialism upon which such expansion was
based – 'winning markets for free trade', 'open doors in the East', 'railways
to the East' – were no longer applicable in an age in which nationalist feeling
was spreading among the peoples of Asia.[40] While Petrov insisted that Russia
needed to follow Britain's example and base its relations with the East upon
'the politics of economic agreement', other influential persons within the
Russian Foreign Ministry considered the British difficulties in controlling an
unruly and independent Afghanistan and the challenges faced in pacifying an
increasingly disquieted and divided India to be unexemplary.

The rising pan-Islamism that undermined British authority and prestige in
Afghanistan and India was showing clear signs of spilling over into Persia as
well. At the end of 1910, a letter from a highly placed Afghan was published
in a Persian national newspaper alerting the Persians to the danger of trusting
either the British or the Russians:

We, the people of Afghanistan, forgot the history of the last war, and showed
the British government complete trust, which gradually is being annihilated
by the Anglo-Russian agreement. 'Why?' he asked; Because Persia at this
time represents the centre of Islam and, if the English are helping the Russians in the annihilation of this centre, in order to have the possibility

themselves to build on its ruins, then how can we, the Afghans, trust Britain?[41]

Elements of the Russian press were less convinced than the Afghans that Britain and Russia were working in concert to dismantle the remnants of Persian sovereignty and integrity. In February, *Golos Pravdy*, in an article entitled, 'An Old but not Harmless Delusion', condemned the 1907 agreement as 'almost a myth, a flight of the imagination' as it concerned Afghanistan and Tibet. In Persia, however, the only country in which the convention was even remotely applicable, the agreement had brought the Russians nothing but degradation:

> Russian trade has fallen 30 or 40 per cent. British trade has increased. Russians are now hated in Persia; we have lost all influence in that country. We no longer control the Cossack Brigade. We have dispatched a few punitive expeditions, which, beyond costing us a lot of money and increasing Persian hatred of us, have led to no result. Russian subjects are not only insulted in Persia, they are murdered. Can we in face of all this declare truthfully that we have reaped any benefits from the Anglo-Russian Agreement as far as Persia is concerned?[42]

The claims of the *Golos Pravdy* were not, however, supported by the evidence. For example, the volume of trade between Russia and Persia continually grew, while the Anglo-Persian trade volume fell.[43] Moreover, the gross Persian customs receipts showed that, while the general imports to Persia grew 96,300 tomans (£19,260) for 21 March to 21 September 1909 over the receipts for the same period the year before, the Russian share of that trade increased more than 200,000 tomans (£40,000). This disproportionate growth came at the expense of British imports in the south, especially through the ports of Bushire and Lingah, which accounted for a loss of over 100,000 tomans (£20,000).[44] In light of the difficulty that British trade in Persia was facing, *The Times* called on the British government to shift its Persian policy towards the active protection of British commerce rather than one motivated by outdated strategic considerations. As the newspaper insisted:

> The arrangement with Russia, in fact, has completely changed the situation, and where we have hitherto abstained from demanding fair treatment of our commerce from Persia for fear that coercion on our part would be used as an excuse by Russia to forward her own aggressive designs, we can now insist on obtaining justice, assured that Russia will not stand in the way nor take advantage of the situation.[45]

The Russian mercantile community, however, was not inclined to sacrifice any portion of its control of Persian trade to the British. Despite the relative success that Russian trade was experiencing in northern Persia, there were vociferous calls for proactive measures to promote and protect this trade. The Tbilisi Stock Exchange Committee urged the Russian Ministry of Trade and Industry to work not only to increase the trade in sugar and fabric, which together comprised 80 per cent of Russian exports to Persia, but to promote the trade in all the goods that Russia and Persia exchanged and that were threatened by competition from western European goods. Furthermore, the Committee adamantly protested against the construction of roads in northern Persia, such as the Qazvin–Hamadan Road, which attracted competition from English manufactures; they greatly feared the railway routes under proposal – most notably the plans for a Great Indian Railway, connecting India and Russian Central Asia through Persia – as posing far too great a threat to Russian commercial hegemony.[46] As *The Caucasian Press* warned at the end of 1909, 'Competition for the construction of railways in Persia – a country which is adjacent to our own – is indeed a struggle for international supremacy.'[47]

This concerted opposition to the trans-Persian line was an unusual position for Russia's merchants to take, the majority of whom were less concerned about Indian competition than German; a significant portion of the Indian–Persian trade – much of which already travelled the roundabout route to Persia through Transcaucasia – was exclusively in goods that Russia did not produce: cardamom, chicken, ginger, cloves, peppers, nutmeg and coffee.[48] The growing threat from the German-sponsored Baghdad Railway, on the other hand, appeared to pose a far more immediate challenge.[49] The Russian government was equally alarmed by the steady advance of the Baghdad Railway on Russian interests in Persia, particularly in light of German attempts to win British support with the promise of increased ease in inserting competitive manufactures into northern Persia from Alexandretta and Khanaqin.[50] As the *Daily Telegraph* noted in late April, the German government had embarked upon a persistent campaign of official encroachment along the western border of Persia; although the region harboured no direct German interests, German officials and compounds were becoming more and more ubiquitous along this frontier. Most significantly, in the eyes of the *Telegraph*, the proposed branch of the Baghdad Railway from Khanaqin to Teheran, which would cut directly across every one of Russia's most profitable Persian trade routes, was a direct challenge to Russian political and economic influence.[51] Minister of Finance Kokovtsov fully recognized the threat to Russian economic and political influence in Persia that Germany was mounting through its railway. He strongly urged his colleagues to exert all possible pressure on

Persia to prevent it from granting Germany railway concessions from Kha-naqin to Teheran in exchange for monetary assistance, since the ten-year Russian monopoly on Persian railway construction had now expired. Kokovt-sov proposed that Russia threaten to call in the outstanding loans from 1900 and 1902 as coercion for Persian compliance.[52]

The British, in contrast, continued to be more concerned about the potential Russian strategic threat to India that a trans-Persian railway would pose than the potential German commercial threat that the Baghdad Railway offered. In mid-June, the general staff submitted a study of the Persian rail-way projects, a question that they recognized was 'one of supreme importance ... [which] must vitally affect the defence of our Indian Empire and possibly the entire situation in Asia.' From a strategic standpoint, the general staff considered any improvement of land communications towards India, particularly the construction of railways in Persia, to be extremely detrimental to Britain's position:

> Geographically, Persia lies between India and Russia. So long as it remains devoid of the means of rapid communication, the country interposes a practi-cally insuperable military obstacle between the two great neighbouring States. The introduction of railways will at once remove the barrier and ren-der possible, if not actually provoke an aggressive policy on the part of one or other or both Powers.[53]

The report recognized that, no matter how desirable, it would be impossible to prevent Russia indefinitely from constructing railways in Persia; therefore, it was Britain's responsibility to strike a balance and do all that could be done to ensure that the alignment of the constructed rail lines posed as little threat to Indian security as possible. As the Government of India's Lieutenant-Colonel Sir H. McMahon warned, 'We must, however, endeavour, when steering wide of the Scylla of unreasonable opposition, not to shipwreck on the Charybdis of blind acceptance.'[54]

Both the War Office and the Government of India urged the British government to remember that, notwithstanding the present state of amicable Anglo-Russian relations, Britain could not ignore the strategic possibility of future regional antagonism.[55] As Major-General Grulev of the Russian general staff had written as recently as 1909, 'the struggle between Russia and Britain for political supremacy in Persia has been postponed but not concluded.' Britain must therefore take all 'sane and vigilant precautions'. General Douglas Haig, the Indian Army chief of staff, cautioned that the construction of railways in Persia would demand a corresponding growth in the size of Britain's standing army to that which the empire could neither contemplate nor support. He emphasized the great strategic advantage Russia already possessed in the region, even without further railway construction in Persia that would vastly augment Russia's troop movement capabilities along the Kabul and the Kandahar lines towards the Indian frontier. If Britain were not to prepare responsibly for all possibilities, Haig predicted dire consequences: 'We shall be throwing upon our children, if not upon ourselves, the greatest military problem that has ever confronted the Government of this country.'[56]

While the British military pointed out the potential dangers that would ensue from the construction of a trans-Persian railway link with the Indian railway system, others in the government debated the commercial advantages and disadvantages for British trade. The India Office, in late December 1909, had postulated that the construction of railways in southern Persia would not benefit British trade at all; it predicted that the existence of cheap rates for goods travelling along British railways in the south would be a strong inducement to Russia and Germany to transport their goods in subsidized steamers to the Gulf ports instead of on the British lines.[57] Grey, in response, proposed that India, geographically closer to the Persian Gulf than either Russia or Germany, would be able to benefit most of all from any increase in Persian Gulf steamer traffic consequent upon an extension of the Persian railway system down to the Gulf.[58] The director-general of Commercial Intelligence, F. Noël Paton, late in 1910, agreed with Grey, insisting that both Indian commerce and British regional influence could only benefit from improved transportation in Persia:

> No doubt the new railway will serve [Russia] better than it will us, but it will serve us too, and on the whole it would, I think, create a greater likelihood of our getting even with Russia than can be said to exist at present. ... It is almost incredible that the more intimate 'commerce', mercantile and social, that would attend the creation of a railway could fail to bring about some sort of assimilation of that part of Persia which is nearest our borders. I should imagine that, from a political point of view, this would be worth something, even if the railway did not pay for a good many years.[59]

For the Russians, the advantages of connecting their railway system with that of India were so obvious as to be not worthy of debate.[60] As Sergei Dmitrievich Sazonov, who had replaced Izvolskii as foreign minister after the latter had chosen in the autumn of 1910 to trade the burdens of MID for the embassy in Paris,[61] wrote to Kokovtsov in December:

> It is unquestionable that a country with 300 million people and extremely significant natural riches, like India, needs or, ultimately, will absolutely require direct land communications with the neighbouring countries of the world, more convenient and quicker than boats along the circular route through the Suez Canal. India at this time is already gradually joining with

European culture, and there is a noticeable aspiration of the local cultural elements for interaction with European countries. The construction of a transit railway from Europe to India undoubtedly would give a significant push to this aspiration. ... For Russia, like for all the near neighbours of India, it is, of course, of the highest importance that this intercourse not pass her by.[62]

Russia, Sazonov admitted, could not attempt to prevent an influx of British goods from the south into the Russian zone: such economic penetration and the construction of railways that would facilitate it was inevitable. Instead, Russia needed to ensure that the transit roads that would be developed within Persian borders should rest in Russian control and should be so oriented as to favour Russian commercial interests.

Thus, while British concern for controlling the orientation of Persian rail lines was predominantly focused on strategic considerations, Russian interest in the issue concentrated on questions of the expansion of trade. For the British, the entire regional landscape was dominated by Indian security requirements: theirs was a defensive position, and until the development of oil as a vital commodity, all of their policies in Central Asia in general and Persia in particular revolved around the ultimate question of how they would affect India. Russia's Persian policies, in contrast, were directed towards the expansion of Russian trade and regional influence; theirs was a forward policy, although the methods and goals during this period were clearly those of informal empire rather than the formal absorption of Persia into the Russian Empire.

The promotion of trade in northern Persia continued to be greatly hindered by the ongoing unrest in the areas closest to the Russo-Persian frontier.[63] The Russian troops in Tabriz, numbering 500 men, were under constant assault from the more than 2500 *fedaiyan* troops in the region, and in February Stolypin ordered the provincial governor in the Caucasus to prepare to cross the border with a battalion of riflemen and 100 Cossacks if the Persian government could do nothing to pacify the region.[64] Russia had long been promising both the Persians and the British that it was planning to withdraw its troops from Persia as soon as the situation became less agitated.[65] The dispatch of troop reinforcements, therefore, was in direct contradiction to the pledged Russian withdrawal.

While Russian troops once again advanced towards Tabriz, Benckendorff, from London, urged moderation. Above all, he felt it vital that Russia should not embark upon an occupation of Teheran. He feared it would be looked on as an act of war, rather than an attempt to assist the government of Persia in the maintenance of order, as Russia was attempting in Tabriz and Qazvin. As Benckendorff warned, with the entrance of Russian troops into Teheran, '[the situation] would become infinitely more serious and transform categorically a difficulty between Russia and Persia into a European question.[66] Similarly, Poklevsky-Kozell lobbied against the dispatch of new soldiers and Cossacks to Tabriz at a time when the government was preparing to withdraw troops from Persia.[67] If the principal purpose of the troop presence in Tabriz was to protect Russian citizens, this requirement could be better met with a strengthened centralized Persian authority that was capable of establishing and preserving order throughout the country. In Poklevsky-Kozell's opinion, the continued presence of Russian troops in Tabriz and the clashes with the local population that seemed to be the unavoidable result only postponed the development of the necessary Persian governmental authority.[68]

The restrained stances of the Russian ministers in London and Teheran were justified by the support that they were receiving from their British colleagues. In July, Charles Marling, the British chargé d'affaires, in response to Benckendorff's demand for a strong showing of Anglo-Russian solidarity in Teheran,[69] reprimanded the Persian minister of war for his country's malicious conduct towards Russia:

> As for myself, I could not understand the extraordinary folly of these people. Could they not realise that as Persia must have relations with Russia it was well that those relations should be good and friendly, and were they so insensate as to imagine that they could struggle against a Power whose armed forces alone were equal to one-third of the entire-population of Persia?[70]

Just as the British supported the Russians in their clashes with the Persians in the north, so Russia upheld British security policies in the south. The state of the roads in the British and neutral zones had reached a point of such overwhelming insecurity by mid-summer that the British again proposed the installation of a gendarmerie along the Bushire–Esfahan Road, commanded by eight to ten Indian Army officers loaned for the purpose.[71] Like the plan under discussion in 1909, the troops would be paid for by a surcharge of 10 per cent on the customs duties on all goods imported through the southern ports.[72] Barclay accordingly told the Persian government that if order was not restored in the south by the end of September, the plan would be put into effect.[73] Poklevsky-Kozell, when asked for his opinion by St Petersburg, stated that he had no objection to the British plan for road security, as long as the troops did not operate in the environs of Esfahan. The institution of a security force in the south under British officers could, in his opinion, only help to pacify the unruly land.[74]

Unfortunately Persia did not agree with either the British ultimatum or its Russian supporters. There was almost universal agreement in Persia that the British had only decided on this course of action at Russia's instigation. As one Persian newspaper, *Istikliali-Iran*, observed, 'The British want to become Russian.'[75] The Persians were supported in their opposition by prominent members of the Persian lobby in Britain. Professor Edward G. Browne, whose monumental study, *The Persian Revolution of 1905–1909*, was published in 1910, wrote a scathing piece for the liberal-radical paper, *The Daily Chronicle*, at the end of October. He insisted that the ultimatum was nothing less than the announcement of a military occupation of southern Persia. He felt that it would be impossible for the British to limit their involvement, which would ultimately result in the partition of Persia and the official absorption of the southern and neutral zones into the Empire:

> In the end, after a certain number of English officers and Indian soldiers, and a very much larger number of Persians had been killed, and a distribution of medals, V.C.'s and D.S.O.'s had taken place we should be left with a long and indefensible Anglo-Russian frontier, a large acquisition of new territory, and a sullen population robbed of their independence and cherishing bitter memories of burned homesteads and slain kinsmen, a new 'problem' of 'unrest' far worse than India or Egypt, and a new argument for conscription.

All this would be an unfortunate legacy for 'a Liberal Government whose watchwords are supposed to be "Peace, Retrenchment, and Reform"!'[76]

The Persian government, in correspondence with this British and Persian public opposition, insisted that the plan was incompatible with Persian independence and refused to agree to it. Instead they requested that the 10 per cent surcharge be allocated to Persia for the pacification of the southern roads.[77] The British, however, were extremely unwilling to allow for a 10 per cent customs surcharge if the troops would be commanded by Persian officers.[78] Grey nevertheless felt it vital that something – short of a British occupation – be done to restore order in southern Persia.[79] Russia, unsurprisingly, fully supported the British security plan as completely in accord with Russia's own policies in the north, although Sazonov did feel that, in the neutral zone, the officers should be both British and Russian, with the control over the troops resting in the hands of the local Russian and British consulates together.[80] Therefore, while the Persian government and public opinion were harshly critical of the British ultimatum and the insistence on the creation of a British-led southern road guard, the controversy had produced a strong demonstration of Anglo-Russian agreement.

There was, however, one seemingly irreconcilable difference between the two governments that threatened to undermine the spirit of co-operation – the question of a Persian loan. At the end of July, Grey had informed the Russians that he feared the only way to restore order in Persia and to avoid large-scale Anglo-Russian intervention was to furnish the Persian government immediately with both men and money. Furthermore, he felt that were Russia and Britain not to offer a significant loan to Persia, except under 'onerous conditions', Persia might very well turn to an unnamed third power for monetary assistance. The foreign secretary therefore proposed that Russia and Britain jointly offer the Persian government an advance of £400,000 on the sole condition that it would eventually be repaid.[81]

Izvolskii agreed with Grey that Persia would soon be in complete anarchy without foreign assistance.[82] Russia, however, had long been insisting that no loans should be advanced to the Persian government without the exaction of significant retribution for what it considered to be long-standing and substantial offences.[83] Despite remonstrances from both Britain and Russia for increased Persian governmental efforts towards the establishment of order, what the Russians considered to be the 'malevolence' of the Persian cabinet towards Russia continued. The Russians claimed that the Persian government encouraged anti-Russian movements in the country and actively paralysed all attempts to establish normal Russo-Persian relations. Therefore they were unwilling to come to the aid of the present Persian government without what they called 'a guaranty of its intention to observe a more correct attitude regarding Russia'.[84] The two powers had reached a deadlock.

While Russia and Britain were vehemently disagreeing about the course of action to take concerning the Persian loan, Russia began inching towards a rapprochement with Germany. Throughout the year, Germany had been attempting to entice Russia into two-party negotiations on the Baghdad Railway question.[85] The replacement of the Anglophile and Francophile Izvolskii, who had never recovered from the humiliation of the Bosnian crisis, was the first clear step towards a Russo-German détente. Public opinion in Russia and in Europe immediately expected the new foreign minister, S.D. Sazonov, to be much less conciliatory in his attitude towards Great Britain than his predecessor had been perceived to have been. *Zemschina*, an extremely reactionary newspaper, predicted that Sazonov could be expected to conduct a far more independent Russian foreign policy, in accordance with the promotion of Russian 'interests and dignity'.[86] Sazonov, in agreement with his brother-in-law, Stolypin,[87] was convinced that the only path open to Russia was the maintenance of the existing entente in concurrence with the cultivation of improved Russo-German relations.[88] Sazonov's first foreign endeavour after his appointment, a meeting of the tsar and the kaiser at Potsdam, promised to afford Izvolskii's heir apparent the opportunity to attempt just such a rapprochement.[89]

Shortly before joining the imperial family at Darmstadt, from where he would accompany them on the journey to Potsdam, Sazonov met with a special session of the Council of Ministers to discuss Persian affairs. Sazonov proposed that Russia seek to neutralize the potential disadvantages that might ensue from the construction of the branch line of the Baghdad Railway from Khanaqin to Teheran. He recommended that it should be Russia, not Germany, that constructed and, therefore, controlled this line. Furthermore, he thought that Russia might be able to promise to construct the line at a future date, but delay the construction until such time as the penetration of Russian goods from the north had so saturated the market that Russian manufactures would be able to compete successfully with German products. In the meantime Russia should construct two lines – Jolfa–Tabriz and Anzeli–Qazvin–Teheran – which would connect southern Russia with northern Persia to facilitate this trade. Although the minister of trade and industry, S.I. Timashev, criticized the plan for the construction of *any* connection from Khanaqin to Teheran as exclusively serving the interests of German trade, he was alone in his opposition, and Sazonov left the meeting prepared to effect improved relations between Germany and Russia through the upcoming Potsdam discussions.[90]

Two and a half weeks before the meeting, the British were informed that Sazonov would be going to Potsdam. O'Beirne urged the Russian minister to conclude nothing concerning Persia without consulting the British and, regarding the Baghdad Railway, France as well.[91] Sazonov subsequently assured O'Beirne that 'nothing will be signed at Potsdam'; he promised to 'inform [O'Beirne] of "every syllable" exchanged at interview.'[92] The meeting between the German and Russian emperors and their ministers that took place at Potsdam on 4–6 November 1910, however, achieved far greater Russo-German accord than Britain had thought possible. Russian opposition to the Baghdad Railway was formally ended, and the two foreign ministers discussed the construction of the Khanaqin–Teheran line, which Russia pledged eventually to build. Furthermore, Russia promised not to restrict the transport of German goods along this line. In exchange, Germany would seek neither railway, telegraph, nor territorial concessions in northern Persia.[93] Although Sazonov had kept his promise and did not commit anything to a written agreement, his verbal assurances to Germany concerning the Baghdad Railway question infuriated his French and British counterparts who felt that anything other than discussions à *quatre* were entirely inappropriate. Exclusive Russo-German discussions on the Baghdad Railway were especially galling to the British, who had suffered Izvolskii's anger at British consideration of a German offer for discussions à *deux* at the end of 1909.[94]

Soon after the Potsdam meeting, Alfred von Kiderlen-Wächter, the German foreign minister, had expressed to the British ambassador in Berlin, Sir W.E. Goschen, the opinion that, unlike Izvolskii, of whom the Germans were not particularly fond, Sazonov was a man to be trusted: 'He had found him open and frank, and devoid of personal vanity, a man with whom one could talk freely, and who, moreover, seemed little likely to spring surprises upon Europe as other people had been in the habit of doing.'[95] As the details of the Potsdam discussions became clarified, the British became less and less convinced of the accuracy of Kiderlen-Wächter's opinion. Sir George Buchanan, who had replaced Nicolson in St Petersburg in November when the latter returned to the Foreign Office to become permanent under-secretary, commented in a private note to his predecessor that the entire trend of Sazonov's negotiations with the German ambassador, Pourtalès, left him feeling extremely nervous. On several issues, Buchanan felt that the Russian minister of foreign affairs was being far from forthright. Sazonov had told Buchanan that the first article of the draft Russo-German agreement had no practical political significance, yet the British ambassador felt strongly that the article was a direct effort by Germany to stop Russia from demonstrating any support for British efforts to prevent the Gulf section of the Baghdad Railway falling under Germany's exclusive control. Furthermore, the British ambassador found it curious that the draft agreement contained no references to the Baghdad–Khanaqin branch, the construction of which Sazonov had previously implied had been agreed to as Russia's right and responsibility. It was possible, in Buchanan's opinion, that Sazonov might be holding back additional articles from the British. In short, Buchanan was convinced that Sazonov was not 'acting quite loyally by [Britain]'.[96]

After further discussion with Sazonov, Buchanan altered his opinion: the Russian was not underhanded, just inexperienced and habitually hasty in his decisions.[97] This did not mean, however, that the British could expect Sazonov to conclude no arrangement with Germany without first consulting their entente partners;[98] they could not rely upon the minister of foreign affairs' discernible appreciation for and professed devotion to a close understanding with Great Britain. As Buchanan later observed, '[Sazonov] is not, however, a match for Kiderlen and there is always a danger that, now that these intimate conversations have been opened between Petersburg and Berlin, he may be carried further than he intends to go.' Furthermore, any Russo-German détente threatened an adverse effect on Anglo-Russian relations. Buchanan noted, 'It was the tension existing between her and Austria and Germany that threw Russia into our arms; and should that tension be replaced by intimate relations with the two neighbouring Empires, our interests are bound to suffer.'[99]

Britain's opposition to the Baghdad Railway encompassed not only its concern for the entente and fears of increased German regional involvement and the threat to British supremacy in the Gulf that a German controlled through-route would produce; in mid-December, Grey expressed to

Benckendorff the opinion that the Baghdad Railway was a direct security threat to British India. If the Baghdad Railway was to be linked with the proposed trans-Persian railway, Turkish Muslim troops would be able to mass with ease along the Indian frontier in the event of any pan-Islamic unrest on the subcontinent.[100] Like the British, the Russians were greatly concerned about the spread of pan-Islamism through Asia; the Young Turks were taking active measures to conduct a propaganda campaign throughout southern Russia and Turkestan.[101] Events in Persia, in particular, were being closely watched by all its neighbours. As E.G. Browne observed:

> Persia is the vital spot of Islam, and that her absorption by Russia and England, or either, means the political death of Islam and the speedy destruction of Turkey and Afghanistan. ... The Turks ... know very well that if Persia is eaten for breakfast they will be eaten for supper.[102]

Turkish troops were deployed on Persian territory, and Afghanistan was taking a careful interest in Persian affairs. As the Russians noted in late December, 'Every new direction of politics in Persia should be considered in light of the present solidarity between the people of Islam.'[103]

The hostility of Afghanistan towards Russia was becoming a matter of increasing concern for the Russian government. In May 1910 Russia became aware that the Afghan government had undertaken a systematic intelligence operation against Russia. Afghan agents were regularly sent disguised as traders to Kushk, Pendeh, Bukhara, Tashkent, Samarkand and Merv; since these trading centres were populated by all sorts of different nationalities, it was impossible to uncover the Afghan spies. Although Captain Skurat, the military attaché in Mashhad, did not think the agents posed a significant threat from a military standpoint, he saw their often alarmist reports – including tales of active Russian preparations at Kushk for a war against Afghanistan within the year – to be a worrying contribution to the spread of anti-Russian sentiment in Afghanistan and in Russian Central Asia.[104]

Although Russian intelligence on the state of the Afghan Army suggested that Afghanistan would be unable to present a solid obstacle in the event of a Russian move, Afghan military preparations, including the periodic arrival of new foreign (mainly Turkish) military instructors, were closely watched.[105] The extreme hostility with which Afghanistan faced its northern neighbour was well noted by both the Russians and the British.[106] Rumours about Afghan military preparations were perpetually pursued by the Russian border authorities.[107] In December Skurat once again asked why the Afghan government was paying such a significant sum to support agents within Russian borders; his report further examined the issue of pan-Islamism, proposing the movement as the principal explanation for the heightened Afghan interest in

Russia.[108] It was clear that Russia found the considerable presence of Afghan agents in Bukhara and Turkestan to be more than just a nuisance. As the year ended, the Russians became aware that Habibullah Khan was preparing his country, especially along the border, for a possible war with Russia. Towards that end, the emir was also looking to mobilize pan-Islamic enthusiasm in Turkestan, Khiva and Bukhara, which would foster local support for Afghanistan's upcoming fight with Russia.[109]

Russo-Afghan tension had been exacerbated in mid-November when the Russians reported the trans-border flight of 12,000 Hazarahs into Russia near Kerki in an exodus from alleged Afghan oppression that soon brought back memories of the relatively recent Jamshedi crisis.[110] The Russians quickly asked the British to convince the emir through the Indian government of the need to prevent a massive flow of Hazarahs into Bukhara.[111] Turkestani governor-general Samsonov was extremely concerned that the huge influx of refugees into Old Bukhara, most of whom were members of the Afghan Army, would greatly destabilize a city that was already the centre of pan-Islamism in Turkestan and Bukhara.[112] The 'Hazarin riffraff' were quick to establish a pattern of quiet and steady thievery and robbery in Russia, and the local authorities vociferously called for their expulsion.[113] The Hazarah flight, combined with the existing Russo-Afghan tension, therefore produced a year-end regional situation that was far from stable.

Thus, as 1910 drew to a close, the Anglo-Russian relationship was under attack on the local, regional and international levels. The unrest in Tibet, the ongoing refugee problem on the Russo-Afghan frontier, and the continuing chaos in Persia were each individual challenges that had to be faced within the context of the agreement. The rise and dissemination of pan-Islamism throughout Asia threatened the position of both powers within their own territories and in their spheres of influence, and forced Britain and Russia to re-evaluate the state of their regional security. And the introduction of German interference in Persian affairs under the guise of the Baghdad Railway scheme appeared to be a strike at the very foundations of Anglo-Russian co-operation and entente relations. Furthermore, the developing disagreements over the trans-Persian railway were demonstrating the mutual incompatibility between British and Russian regional motivations; it appeared increasingly likely that the British, concerned above all with the defence of India, and the Russians, looking to expand their trade and influence, could not hope to see their conflicting goals co-exist indefinitely. The year 1910 had seen Anglo-Russian relations in Central Asia take a turn away from the more mutually accordant regional relations that had been evident in the past. Whether, in the year to come, the Anglo-Russian relationship would continue on this new path towards division and disagreement was extremely unclear.

CHAPTER 5

The Strangling of Anglo-Russian
Foreign Policy: 1911

As 1911 began, the structural flaws of the Anglo-Russian Central Asian relationship were becoming increasingly apparent. The flight of the Hazarahs across the Russo-Afghan border in late 1910 had once again emphasized the difficulty of resolving local crises without officially sanctioned direct communication between the Russian government and the emir, and the problems that manifested themselves showed no signs of abating. Although the India Office insisted that the Hazarah exodus had been a Russian invention, which had not been confirmed by any other source, the Russians reported an ongoing flow of Hazarah families from Afghan Turkestan into Russian territory.[1] Further complicating the matter, at the end of February, another flood of refugees was reported crossing the frontier. The commander of the Russian fortress at Kushk frantically telegraphed the governor-general in Turkestan, A.V. Samsonov, to alert him to the fact that 80 members of the 'Mishmez' – a tribe numbering at least 10,000 in Afghanistan – had fled across the border.[2] Samsonov in turn warned St Petersburg that if this flight were merely the first wave of a mass Mishmez exodus, the result would be disastrous.[3] In early April more than 1000 Mishmez with tilt carts were said to be moving towards the frontier, an assemblage that bore a striking resemblance to an 'avant garde' for a major move across the border.[4] The Russians again found themselves asking the British to intercede.[5]

There remained little chance that Britain would be able to achieve any gratification on Russia's behalf in its dealings with the emir. Habibullah Khan, secure in his understanding that Britain would forever rely on Afghanistan to serve as a natural barrier against a possible Russian invasion – no matter how remote the present possibility of such an invasion – was extremely cocky in his relations with the British government. As the British agent at Kabul had observed late in 1910, the Afghan government was actively stirring up unrest along both sides of the Afghan–Indian frontier:

The unremitting zeal of the British Political officers, and their untiring efforts, however, can never succeed in checking the ever-increasing influence
of the Afghan Court over the frontier tribes for the obvious reason that the
former have recourse only to stratagems, and the spending of money, which
produce a temporary effect only so long as the hands of the tribesmen are
warm with money or utterances are fresh in their ears, while the latter are
united with them under the strong tie of a common religion, and in consequence exercise successful persuasions through the agency of spiritual
leaders.[6]

This border unrest might prove to be a considerable cause of concern for the
British, especially in light of the emir's toleration of arms smuggling from the
Makran coast of the Gulf of Oman up through Persia to Afghanistan. These
contraband arms provided both the Afghan Army and the general population
along the Indo-Afghan border with a steady supply of weaponry, further
destabilizing an already shaky frontier.[7]

Despite the difficulties Britain was having in its own relations with its
semi-protectorate, the actual interaction of the local Russian officials with
their Afghan counterparts on issues of regional importance was far more
productive. In mid-April, when the Russians complained to the British of the
blatant ill will with which the Afghan frontier officials treated the Russians-
on-the-spot concerning a matter of stolen horses, the India Office challenged
the allegation of malevolence.[8] Rather, as Grey informed the Russian ambassador, 'frontier cases are constantly adjusted locally', and he cited two
examples of just such amicable resolutions of local problems.[9]

While conflicts along the Russo-Afghan frontier underscored the continued structural problems inherent in the 1907 agreement, ongoing
disagreements over Russia's shifting relationship with Germany as a result of
the recent meeting at Potsdam posed a serious threat to Anglo-Russian
understanding and co-operation as a whole. In mid-January, British examination of the terms of the draft Russo-German agreement uncovered a
reference excluding Germany from seeking concessions to a portion of the
neutral zone along the Afghan frontier – an area that Sazonov had promised
the British had not even been considered in the Potsdam discussions. Sazonov
assured Buchanan that the reference had only been made in order to prevent
Germany from seeking concessions for railways in this district, and was not a
Russian attempt to assert its own control over the region.[10] The British,
however, remained suspicious, especially in light of the ongoing indications
that the Teheran–Khanaqin branch would be constructed and controlled by
Germany. Furthermore, Britain was concerned that, having been specifically
excluded from concessions in one portion of the neutral zone, Germany

would feel free to seek them in the remainder of the neutral zone not mentioned in the treaty.[11]

For both the British and the Russians, preventing the Teheran–Khanaqin branch from falling into German hands was considered to be crucial. Were Germany to control the line, German goods would have unrestricted access to the Persian market. In addition, there would be nothing to prevent the unimpeded passage of Turkish troops into Persia and on towards the Indian frontier were a conflict to ensue. Sazonov was therefore committed to maintaining Russian control over this vital branch. He recognized that unfortunately this plan would be far from easily realized. Russian public opinion would be vociferously opposed to the commitment of Russian capital to a project that would promote German trade and economic interests; the Duma would not vote for the capital necessary to construct railways in Persia while there was so much railway construction to be undertaken in the Russian interior itself. It seemed clear that foreign financial support for the Russian plan – kept secret, to prevent Germany from insisting on its own share of the scheme – would need to be forthcoming from Paris and London.[12]

Britain, however, was not prepared to provide financial backing for the construction of a line into northern Persia that would give German goods easy access to the region without a quid pro quo providing for the continued health of its own regional trade.[13] The German line from Baghdad to Khanaqin alone would introduce considerable foreign competition in the area around Hamadan, which had been an almost exclusively British market.[14] Britain therefore proposed to apply to the Persian government for a concession for a line through the neutral zone from Mohammareh on the Karun River to Khorramabad, bordering the Russian sphere of influence.[15] This route would allow the nearly £1 million per year in British goods – currently travelling to the neutral zone by ship via the Persian Gulf, up the Tigris River to Baghdad, and then overland by caravan to Kermanshah – to travel more directly and avoid the German-controlled route under development.[16] Sazonov quickly informed Buchanan that the construction of such a line, which so obviously would threaten Russian economic interests, would make his country 'very uneasy'.[17] Stolypin, in concert with his brother-in-law, also predicted to the British ambassador the inevitable protests that would be lodged by the merchants of Moscow against any railway scheme allowing seaborne goods to be brought by rail to the Russian sphere.[18] Nevertheless, the British held firm to their supposition that such a line was vital for the preservation of British trade in the face of the unfair competition that would result from the construction of a German-controlled route from the west.[19]

The Russians recognized that Article 3 of the 1907 convention denied them the right to oppose formally Britain's application for the concession for this railway, since it lay completely within the neutral zone. This did not mean, however, that they were not concerned about the inevitable prejudicial effect that the construction of such a line would have on Russia's economic interests in northern Persia and the subsequent displeasure of Russian public opinion that would ensue.[20] Anatolii Anatolievich Neratov, who served as acting minister of foreign affairs during Sazonov's prolonged illness from March 1911 until the end of that year, made a personal suggestion to Buchanan that the terminus of the line be placed further south than Khorramabad, so as not to lie directly alongside the Russian zone. Buchanan responded by questioning the justice of allowing German goods into the very heart of the Russian zone while preventing British goods from even making it as far as its borders.[21] At last the Russians agreed not to oppose British acquisition of the concession, as long as the British promised not to construct the railway without first securing Russia's agreement.[22] The point became moot, however, when the Persian government refused the British application for the concession on the grounds that a request made on behalf of a government, not a commercial venture, which referred expressly to railways 'in the south', made the project look like yet another strategic undertaking with the intention of carving up the country into spheres of influence.[23]

During the Anglo-Russian debates over the projected Mohammareh–Khorramabad line, the British had considered dangling the carrot of decreased British opposition towards the trans-Persian railway scheme linking India with Russia in return for Russian acquiescence on the Mohammareh–Khorramabad railway.[24] At the end of January it became clear that, while the Russian government officially favoured the trans-Persian project, financial support would not be forthcoming from the Russian treasury.[25] The project was, however, supported by a significant and influential consortium of Russian banks and businessmen led by N.A. Khomiakov, the former president of the Duma. The Council of Ministers ultimately agreed to recognize this group as a Société d'Études for a trans-Persian railway. Included in the Société d'Études were a number of leading Russian merchants, the directors or chairmen of the Volga-Kama Bank, the Russian Bank for Foreign Trade, the Russian Bank for Commerce and Industry, the Anglo-Russian Bank and the Russo-Asiatic Bank, the mayor of Moscow and several members of the Council of Empire.[26] The backing of this powerful group ensured that the Russian government would not be able to allow the project to be sidelined indefinitely, despite the opposition from Britain. Sazonov's illness and six-month absence from his post until December 1911, however, resulted in a temporary suspension of the government's concerted efforts on behalf of the scheme, since Neratov was far less enamoured of the project than his superior.[27]

Despite Britain's growing acceptance of the idea, if not the reality, of a trans-Persian route, the project was continually subjected to intense criticism at home, from both official and public elements, concerning the railway's potential threat to imperial defence. A War Office analysis of the trans-Persian railway project in late April questioned the advantages for Britain of any railway construction in southern Persia. As the memorandum, written by chief of the British Imperial General Staff Field-Marshal Sir William Nicholson, maintained, the cost of constructing, running and securing railways in that region of Persia would far outweigh any commercial value that might accrue from the 'comparatively trivial aggregate' British trade that passed through the region. Furthermore, vast stretches of the line would be indefensible without a considerable increase in Britain's naval presence in the Persian Gulf and a corresponding augmentation of Britain's regional land forces, expenditures that would far exceed Britain's defensive capabilities:

> We should have to pay heavily for these precautions, and it has to be considered how the ships and troops are to be provided. We have no spare men-of-war outside home waters and the British and native garrison of India is not in excess of local requirements. ... It is submitted that, from a naval and military point of view, our responsibilities for the defence of the Empire are so extensive at present that it would be folly to add to them with the object of benefiting and tranquilising Southern Persia.

Nicholson concluded with a scathing attack on what he considered to be a plan concocted with complete disregard for Britain's policy of retrenchment in light of its growing sense of imperial overstretch:

> No country is rich enough to incur large unproductive expenditure except for its own safety or in furtherance of its own interests. In proportion, as we spend British capital on the railway under reference and employ naval and military force for its protection we shall weaken ourselves in other and more important directions.[28]

Grey was extremely displeased by Nicholson's memorandum. As well as feeling that the field-marshal had underrated the commercial value of a line running north from the Persian Gulf at Bander-e 'Abbas, he reproved Nicholson for criticizing the defence requirements of a line that had already been approved in principle by the Government of India.[29] Nevertheless, the approval of the Government of India and, by extension, His Majesty's government was not unconditional. In mid-May, Britain insisted to the Russians that it would only support the scheme for a trans-Persian railway if a number of its demands were met, most notably that: (1) the line should enter the British sphere at Bandar-e 'Abbas on the Persian Gulf, not Kerman, much further to the north. Similarly, the line would join with the Indian railway system at Karachi, not at Nushki, as the Russians had proposed. This would make the line defensible by the Royal Navy from the Persian Gulf and the Gulf of Oman; (2) A break of gauge would be necessary where the railway entered the British sphere; (3) No Russian lines would approach the Persian–Afghan frontier.[30]

In response to the British conditions, Neratov predicted that Russia would return with conditions of its own, although he wanted to withhold judgement until the Société d'Études had presented their conclusions.[31] In correspondence with Benckendorff, however, he admitted that, although Karachi was unobjectionable as a terminus of the railway, Bandar-e 'Abbas was entirely unacceptable; a line running from the Persian Gulf up to northern Persia would pose too great a commercial threat to Russian trade for the Russian government to grant approval without irritating the Russian trade and industry lobbies. Furthermore, a line via Bander-e 'Abbas would necessarily lie far too close to the Baghdad Railway, and would therefore also assist German goods in threatening Russian commercial hegemony.[32]

For the time being, however, Russian trade with Persia was not threatened by British or German competition, but by the state of anarchy that ruled in the country and the increasing Russo-Persian friction that was exacerbated by the continued presence of Russian troops in northern Persia.[33] An attack on some Russian Cossacks near Astara in February, resulting in one Russian death and two or three wounded, led to the dispatch of yet another Russian battalion across the frontier into Persia.[34] Russia had long been promising to withdraw a significant portion of its troops from the region; the attack on the Cossacks, together with pockets of unrest scattered throughout the north, however, threatened to derail these plans. Although by mid-March the Russian troops had at last withdrawn from Qazvin, by mid-April the usually unruffled Poklevsky-Kozell was calling for the reinforcement of either Rasht or Anzeli by another *sotnia* of consular guards.[35]

The Russian minister, however, soon assumed a more typically moderate stance. By mid-July, he was once again assuring St Petersburg that the further dispatch of Russian troops to Persia was neither necessary nor advisable in respect to Persian and European public opinion.[36] Similarly, he advised that the Cossack guard on the Hamadan Road did not need to be increased.[37] Poklevsky-Kozell also called for the dismissal of the officer who had responded to the February attack on the Cossacks near Astara with the sacking of the village from which the men responsible for the assault had come, resulting in the accidental deaths of a number of women and children.[38] Above all, he was concerned that the unfortunate actions of this officer, which far exceeded his instructions, looked alarmingly like official Russian support for Mohammad Ali, who was once again making a play for power in northern Persia.[39]

That Russia was considering support for the deposed shah, despite Britain's open favour for the Persian Constitutionalist movement, was very much a reality. At the end of June, Neratov sent Poklevsky-Kozell top-secret instructions on Russia's position on the shah's return. The acting minister of foreign affairs thought it very likely that the ex-shah might re-ascend the throne, and Neratov was determined that Mohammad Ali should consider Russia his friend and ally if he were to do so. MID was completely in favour of the re-establishment of a strong central government in Persia, especially if that government were favourably inclined towards Russia. Nevertheless, Russia could not risk openly supporting Mohammad Ali in the face of British opposition and the possibility that his efforts to regain power might fail. Therefore, Poklevsky-Kozell was instructed to observe cautiously the course of events in Persia, all the while preparing to embrace the deposed shah upon his return.[40]

From London, Benckendorff protested strongly against any Russian support for Mohammad Ali's cause. As the Russian ambassador pointed out, Mohammad Ali's reign had been marked by weakness and incompetence; he was not a man who was capable of restoring the order and stability that Russian interests so distinctly demanded.[41] Ultimately, Neratov was brought round to Benckendorff's reasoned position, and Russia withdrew from Mohammad Ali even the permission to enter his former territory across the Russo-Persian frontier.[42] The ex-shah was not deterred, however, and he secretly travelled from Austria to the Turkmen steppes, and from there on into Persia.[43]

The British immediately stated their intention to remain absolutely neutral in the struggle once again being waged in Persia.[44] The Persian government, surprised by the lack of support from Liberal Britain for its fledgling constitutionalism, made an unlikely turn towards Russia for assistance in defending the existing government structures in Persia.[45] This reliance on the protection of Russia was particularly remarkable in light of the Persian foreign minister's recent exclamation that he, his ministry and his government had all concluded that Russian policies were directed not only towards the downfall of the current Persian regime, but towards the complete destruction of the entire independent nation. In response to this accusation, Poklevsky-Kozell defended his government, insisting that they were not at all hostile towards Persia. Rather, their Persian orientation could be easily summed up by a few basic demands: demonstrated friendship towards Russia by the Persian government and complete agreement with both the letter and the spirit of the 1907 Anglo-Russian agreement. If the Persian cabinet were to abide by these very simple guidelines, the present dangers facing Russo-Persian relations could be avoided.[46]

The most obvious 'danger' to which the Russian minister was alluding was the controversy brewing around the spreading influence of the recently appointed treasurer-general, the American, W. Morgan Shuster.[47] In August 1910 the Persian government had informed the British and the Russians that it intended to retain a number of foreign advisers for its financial regime and civil service. Both Russia and Britain immediately agreed that Persia should not look for advisers among the other Great Powers; rather, if Persia insisted on looking for advice from quarters other than Russia or Britain, only citizens from minor states, like Holland or Belgium, would be acceptable to the two most interested international parties.[48] The Majles, however, chose to invite Americans rather than the subjects of any minor European power acceptable to Britain and Russia. Sazonov, who was then serving as acting foreign minister, was extremely opposed to the employment of Americans as financial advisers:

> The invitation to a subject of a Great Power shows that the Persians don't wish to follow the advice of Russia and England. In addition, the invitation of the American establishes a precedent after which it will be very difficult to prevent the penetration of the Persian administration by the citizens, and, it follows, the influence, of other Great Powers.[49]

The counsel of both Great Powers, however, was ignored, and seven Americans were invited to be financial officers of the treasury. Russia asked the American government to refuse the request, as it had convinced the Italians and French to do so before in similar situations, but Washington was not as easily swayed as Paris and Rome.[50] Five financial experts from the United States were therefore hired by the Persian government to reform the treasury.

Shuster, the leader of the American group as treasurer-general, began clashing with the established order immediately on his arrival in Persia on 12 May 1911, alienating both Persians and Europeans alike. Most conspicuously, Shuster quickly came into conflict with the Belgian head of the Persian customs bureau, Joseph Mornard, when he demanded that the latter abide by the letter of the law and deposit Persian customs receipts into the treasurer's account. Mornard refused and a crisis ensued, with Russia supporting Mornard and Britain finding in favour of Shuster.[51] Neratov insisted that Russia could not turn its back on the Belgians, who had done so much good work to restore the Persian customs administration to a semblance of order and effectiveness; the replacement of the Belgians by other individuals, which seemed the likely outcome of this stand-off, might very well undermine all the advantages that Russia currently enjoyed in its dealings with that branch of the government. Furthermore, the precedence of Russian submission to the will of citizens from 'a second-tier power' was extremely undesirable for the maintenance of Russia's leading role in Persia.[52]

The tension that the Mornard–Shuster conflict had created was nothing compared to the furore that was about to break out over Shuster's next move. The treasurer-general invited Major Claude Bayfield Stokes, the military attaché to the British legation at Teheran since 30 April 1907, to command a special treasury gendarmerie tasked with improving on the dismal estimated 16 per cent of collected inland revenue that actually made it to the central treasury.[53] The choice of Stokes was particularly unfortunate, as even the British themselves recognized that he was 'fanatically anti-Russian'.[54] Russia, as expected, was extremely opposed to the appointment of a British officer to command a security force that would operate within its sphere, and proposed either the appointment of an officer from a second-tier power or the division of the command into two positions – a Russian in the north and Stokes, if unavoidable, in the south.[55] Shuster, however, refused to split the command and insisted to Barclay that Stokes was the only man for the job, based on his 'military training, his four years' sojourn in Persia, his knowledge of the country, of the Persian language and of French, and in general of the esteem in which he is held in this community as an officer and a man.'[56]

While it was obvious that the Russian government distrusted Stokes, the British government was also not particularly enamoured of its military attaché, and vice versa. On hearing of the appointment, Charles Greenway, the managing director of the Anglo-Persian Oil Company, took aside the senior clerk in the Foreign Office, Sir Eyre Crowe, and informed him that Stokes's open identification with the extreme nationalist movements in Persia made his appointment as undesirable for Britain as it was for Russia. As Greenway cautioned, 'He was nearly as anti-British as he was anti-Russian and lost no chance of denouncing the iniquity of British policy in Persia. ... In his new position he would have every opportunity of damaging the position of Great Britain in Persia and of spreading his opinion among Persians.'[57] Barclay, corroborating Greenway's opinion, telegrammed London to inform his superiors that Stokes was not only closely identified with the extreme Nationalist party, but was often known privately to express strong condemnation of the policies of the British government.[58]

Nevertheless, the British, despite their misgivings as to the advantages of Stokes accepting the command, refused to tell Shuster that the appointment was undesirable; the American had convinced them that his decision was made without political motive, and they feared he would quit his position if his will was not satisfied. The British were, however, prepared to support a

Russian claim for a compensatory appointment of Russian officers within the Russian sphere.[59] By early August, however, it had become clear that vague British promises of compensatory support would not be sufficient. The developing plans for the treasury gendarmerie, numbering 7000 cavalry and foot soldiers, pointed towards the creation of what would be Persia's principal security force under the direction of Shuster and Stokes. Such a significant independent force, with the authority to operate throughout Persia, was considered by Russia to be unacceptable.[60] Furthermore, it was possible that Stokes, while pursuing his mandate to secure the Persian roads, might take part in military operations that would bring him into conflict with Russian officers. As Benckendorff warned Grey, 'The result would be to give the appearance of a most unfortunate breach between England and Russia in their policy with regard to Persia.'[61]

Buchanan predicted far more serious repercussions than mere appearances, telegraphing, 'I fear that unless we give some satisfaction to Russia serious breach may be made in Anglo-Russian understanding.'[62] The summer of 1911 was of course no time to risk such a breach. For while Britain and Russia had become increasingly absorbed by Shuster's Persian ventures, a crisis was once again brewing in Morocco that threatened to undermine the entente. In April 1911 the French had used unrest in the Moroccan capital of Fez to justify the dispatch of troops to the country; this move, which technically was in violation of the Algeciras settlement of the First Moroccan Crisis, had been expected for some time by the other European colonial powers, most of whom were prepared to be tolerant. But Germany felt that compensation was in order for this French colonial aggrandizement, and decided to push the French hand by sending the German gunboat *Panther* to the Moroccan Atlantic seaport of Agadir on 1 July. In exchange for the transfer of the entire French Congo to Germany, the Germans offered to withdraw the *Panther* and relinquish all claims and interests in Morocco.

For the British, the appearance of a German gunboat off the Atlantic coast of Africa was of even greater concern than for the French.[63] The very notion that a German naval base might be established so close to Gibraltar was extremely alarming, and although the Admiralty determined that a German-occupied Agadir was no strategic threat to Gibraltar, the Foreign Office overruled its own naval experts and the British navy was ordered to prepare for war. On 21 July Chancellor of the Exchequer David Lloyd George – the member of cabinet least expected to promote a Continental commitment – proclaimed in a speech at the Mansion House that Britain would not sit idly by and watch while its own vital interests were affected by others' decisions and actions. Although, in essence, Lloyd George was simply reminding both parties that Britain would not be willing to be left out of any Moroccan settlement, his speech was interpreted by both France and Germany as a British statement of support for French interests – support reinforced by the preparations of the British fleet. What had begun as a German 'table thumping' to remind the French that they were not free to act unilaterally in North Africa had quickly escalated into an Anglo-German war scare.

Germany, however, had not embarked on its Moroccan adventure with an eye towards going to war with Great Britain, France and, by extension, Russia in 1911. By November the Germans backed down from the majority of their demands and a Franco-German convention was signed, establishing a French protectorate over Morocco and giving Germany in exchange the relatively small grant of two strips of the French Congo through which it could gain access to the Congo River. War had been averted, but the result, like the last time Morocco had been the focus of Great Power attention in 1905, was a solidification of the diplomatic divisions that were becoming entrenched in Europe. Britain had visibly linked its position more firmly with France in opposition to Germany, and the move towards an alliance from an entente was accelerated.

Russia's stance during the Second Moroccan Crisis, however, was not nearly so accommodating to either of its entente partners. Rather than assuming their position as the third member of the entente troika, the Russian government decided to give France the same level of support that they had received from Paris during the Bosnian annexation crisis. The French were told in no uncertain terms that Russia was not prepared in 1911 to go to war with Germany over French colonial concerns. From Russia's point of view, Morocco was a significant distraction occupying the other Great Powers, but it was of far less national interest than the conflict growing in Persia with Shuster and Stokes. While France, Germany and Great Britain were discovering the after-effects of Lloyd George's Mansion House speech, Russia continued to insist that Britain turn its attention once again to the troubles in Teheran. In St Petersburg, a draft note to Persia was prepared, demanding compensation for Shuster's offences, and the British were informed that they were expected either to prevent Stokes from assuming his command or to support openly the Russian demands. Subsequently, in an attempt to placate Russia, Grey instructed Barclay to inform the Persians that if they persisted in Stokes's appointment, Britain would recognize Russia's right to safeguard its interests in the north.[64] The Persian government, however, adamant in its insistence that there was no difference between northern and southern Persia and determined to persist in its right to stabilize the entire country as it saw fit, refused to withdraw its offer of employment.[65]

In Grey's opinion, he had been quite accommodating towards Russian feelings concerning the Stokes affair, yet his efforts were being completely discounted by Neratov. The British had petitioned Shuster and the Persian government on behalf of the Russian position; they even refused to accept Stokes's resignation, so as to hinder him from accepting Persian employment.[66] Yet Neratov and some of the more reactionary elements of Russian public opinion seemed to be accusing Britain not only of acquiescing in the Stokes appointment, but of actual responsibility for securing the position for a British subject.[67] The British foreign secretary increasingly felt that Russia was being 'unduly sensitive,' and was particularly disappointed that Neratov had not attempted to appease Russian opinion as Grey was constantly forced to appease British concerning the continued presence of Russian troops in northern Persia. As Grey complained to Buchanan, 'I have had to defend these matters several times, and if I had been as exacting over them as Russia is now the good understanding between Great Britain and Russia would have come to an end long ago.'[68]

Shuster, however, felt that neither power had been particularly supportive of his attempts to break through the paralysis that was afflicting Persian finances. In an attempt to appease the Russians, he offered to limit Stokes's tenure in Teheran to six months, after which the British officer would be sent to the south and an officer from either a second-tier power, or even from Russia, would command in the north.[69] For Russia, however, this was insufficient. Russia demanded that the Persian government give assurances that Stokes's duties would be confined to organizational work in Teheran and that he would not be actively employed in the north. If these demands were not met, and Stokes's authority was not limited to the south, Russia would insist on the establishment of a fully equivalent position staffed by a Russian officer whose authority would also extend over the entire country – for example, a Russian chief of staff of the Persian Army, or a Russian officer charged with the reorganization of the entire Persian military.[70]

Although it appeared that Shuster was attempting to accommodate Russian concerns, his expanding vision of the security force that Stokes would command increasingly threatened the Russian position. The treasurer-general informed the British and Russian ministers in Teheran that he saw no need for two separate gendarmeries operating in Persia, and envisaged the ultimate composition of a gendarmerie that would incorporate the existing paramilitary security units into a force numbering from 12,000 to 15,000 men under his control.[71] While Barclay agreed with the inefficiency of having two separate gendarmeries, Neratov was vehemently opposed to the concentration of both Persia's finances and internal security forces in the hands of an American adviser and his British henchman; the situation would, in the acting minister of foreign affairs's opinion, realistically amount to a dictatorship. Furthermore, even if Stokes were to resign his British commission, he could be expected to behave not as a Persian official, but as a British officer; the gendarmerie would therefore be figuratively, if not literally, a tool of British policy.[72] This was entirely too much for the Russians to accept, and Poklevsky-Kozell was instructed to send Shuster a letter, the ominous tone of which would leave no question as to Russia's position on the matter: 'Make him understand that we are waiting for him ... to conscientiously conform with our interests ... and that, if he stands in open opposition to this, it will cause extreme disadvantages for this regime, the interests of which he so zealously defends.'[73]

As the Stokes affair continued to exacerbate Anglo-Russian tensions in Persia, the Persian cabinet instructed Shuster to take an action that would result in the eruption of an international crisis and, eventually, the American's own dismissal. Since his re-entrance into Persia in July, Mohammad Ali had been creating tremendous difficulties for the Persian government. His very presence in the country was a force of destabilization, and as the summer progressed and he advanced on Teheran, Persia appeared to be falling once again into a state of civil war. Shuster, as a loyal and official employee of the Persian government, was charged with the task of organizing and supplying the combat units sent to deter the counter-revolutionary forces rallying behind the ex-shah. On 4 October 1911 the Persian cabinet instructed Shuster to oversee the confiscation of the property of Malek Mansur Mirza Shoa' os-Saltaneh, younger brother of Mohammad Ali and one of the leaders of the counter-revolution. On the 9th, five treasury gendarmes and a treasury official were dispatched to make an inventory of Shoa' os-Saltaneh's property. Shoa' os-Saltaneh, however, who had recently procured for himself Turkish citizenship in an attempt to gain protection from the Persian authorities, claimed to be heavily indebted to the Russian Discount-Loan Bank.[74] Under pretence of protecting the property for the sake of the bank, Ivan Fedorovich Pokhitonov, the Russian consul-general in Teheran, independently ordered his men to prevent the confiscation of the property. The gendarmes were thwarted in their efforts by the two Russian vice-consuls, Petrov and Hildebrand, and five Cossacks, who arrested the treasury official and threatened to fire if the Persians did not withdraw. At last, the following day, the Persians sent 120 gendarmes to retake the house and drive out the Cossacks.[75]

Pokhitonov's action was clearly the rogue behaviour of a man who had refused to conform to the standards of Russian policy in the post-1907 climate. As Firuz Kazemzadeh evocatively describes in his study, *Russia and Britain in Persia*, 'Pokhitonov had had a long career in Persia and belonged to the extreme nationalist group that deplored the Anglo-Russian understanding of 1907 and yearned for a return to the glorious days of unrestrained rivalry.'[76] In Benckendorff's opinion, the consul-general's indiscriminate actions had contributed greatly towards achieving just such a regression; he openly bemoaned the fact that the excessive zeal and complete absence of tact of a consul could reverse the entire policies of the imperial government and sour the entente with Britain.[77] Poklevsky-Kozell, who had often clashed with the consul-general during Pokhitonov's tenure in Teheran and in his previous appointment at Tabriz, was livid at Pokhitonov's blatant disregard for the authority of his legation. Poklevsky-Kozell fumed in a personal and extremely secret telegram to Neratov: 'I find that the behaviour of the Consul General demonstrates not only a gross and inexplicable insult to the Persian Government, but also a serious offence in relation to the Legation, which during this was burdened with the heavy necessity of condemning and countermanding the orders of the Consul General.'[78]

The Russian minister was of course obliged publicly to defend the actions of his consul, despite his own personal outrage at the affair. When Shuster came to confront him, presenting a formal note of protest against the consul-general and requesting Pokhitonov's removal, Poklevsky-Kozell responded that the Persian government's inability to secure the Russian flag and citizens from the offensive behaviour of Persian troops rendered the country virtually lawless; therefore, he categorically refused to accept either protests or requests for the removal of Russian personnel and demanded that they be withdrawn.[79] This was not, however, simply a formulaic answer to Shuster's petition; the Russian minister's response was completely in keeping with Neratov's take on the incident. The acting minister of foreign affairs advised Poklevsky-Kozell that Pokhitonov was obliged to act in defence of the property in the interests of the bank and any connected Russian subjects. He further underscored the justice of the Russian position by pointing out to Poklevsky-Kozell that the dispatch of 120 gendarmes to drive five Cossacks out from Shoa' os-Saltaneh's house was not exactly an even match.[80] Adding fuel to Russia's fire, rumours were circulating that Stokes was secretly organizing the affairs of the gendarmerie, including the recent clash with the Cossacks, despite Russian protests and Britain's best efforts to restrain him.[81] Poklevsky-Kozell, however, refused in official correspondence to budge in his adamant denunciation of Pokhitonov's actions. He condemned once again the consul-general's personal initiative, and requested that Pokhitonov be recalled from Teheran to a posting 'closer to home', that the vice-consul, Petrov, be transferred from Persia or, even better, removed from MID's employment altogether, and that the other vice-consul, Hildebrand, be severely reprimanded for his part in the affair.[82] As Poklevsky-Kozell insisted to Neratov, 'The Consul General should always defend our interests and the interests of Russian subjects, but exclusively with words and with the pen.'[83]

At this point, the agitation unleashed by the Shoa' os-Saltaneh incident threatened to strike a mortal blow to the Anglo-Russian relationship. On 19 October Neratov informed Hugh O'Beirne, the British chargé d'affaires in St Petersburg, that the instability in Persia, stemming from the general state of unrest and Shuster's attempts to dictate in a manner completely incompatible with Russia's interests, had reached intolerable heights. Russia, he warned, could not long refrain from 'measures of extreme rigour – from an occupation, in fact, of the northern provinces of Persia.'[84] O'Beirne responded that an occupation of northern Persia would expose the entire entente to 'the gravest dangers', a sentiment echoed by Grey, who commented, 'This is very tiresome and very serious.'[85] In conversation with Benckendorff several days later, the foreign secretary warned that such a move would annul the convention and violate the independence of Persia.[86]

During Grey's talk with the Russian ambassador, however, there was evidence of a gradual shift in the British position on the treasurer-general. Since the time of Morgan Shuster's appointment, the British had maintained that the American was the right man for the job. But after O'Beirne had noted his opinion that Russian opposition to Shuster was the crux of all the current crises in Persia – most notably the Stokes affair and the Shoa' os-Saltaneh incident – Grey's enthusiasm for Shuster waned.[87] In the wake of the conflagration over Shoa' os-Saltaneh, the British foreign secretary admitted to Benckendorff that Shuster was 'not the right man for the situation'.[88] Similarly, Sir Arthur Nicolson, now permanent under-secretary at the Foreign Office, told the Russian ambassador that he thought 'Shuster had played false since he arrived.' When Benckendorff proposed that the two countries work to achieve the American's dismissal, however, Nicolson retreated, claiming that Shuster's continuing popularity within the British press and in the Houses of Parliament together with his ongoing contract made such a dismissal unattainable.[89]

Just when it seemed that Shuster could do little more to antagonize the Russians, he decided to appoint another Englishman to a position in his administration, thus demonstrating once again his blatant disregard for realpolitik.[90] When Shuster defended his decision to name the openly anti-Russian Lecoffre as director of the financial section in Azerbaijan on the grounds that there were so few suitable and qualified people in Persia to fill such a position, the Russians had had enough.[91] On 11 November they issued an ultimatum to the Persian government, threatening to dispatch troops to Qazvin if their demands were not met. These were not new demands; rather, the Russians restated their earlier calls for the replacement of Shuster's gendarmes by Persian Cossacks under Russian command and the issuing of an official apology to the officers of the Russian consulate who had been insulted and threatened during the seizure of Shoa' os-Saltaneh's house.[92] Without waiting for the Persian reply, Neratov ordered that a detachment be sent to Qazvin, where it would join the existing Russian forces there and prepare for a march on Teheran.[93] Four thousand Russian soldiers were quickly dispatched from the Caucasus to Persia.[94] Neratov was insistent in his correspondence with Benckendorff that this action did not in any way contradict Russia's agreement with Great Britain.[95]

The British, however, were less convinced that the Anglo-Russian relationship could survive a march on Teheran.[96] Richard Maxwell, senior clerk in the Eastern Department of the Foreign Office, understatedly commented on the Russian demands and preparations to dispatch troops that 'This is not moderation.'[97] Buchanan, in an attempt to make Britain's position entirely clear to the Russians, informed Neratov that an extended occupation of Qazvin or Teheran by Russian troops would be regarded as the first step towards the establishment of a Russian protectorate – an alteration of status that would constitute a direct violation of the Anglo-Russian agreement.[98] Benckendorff also predicted that a prolonged occupation of Teheran would immediately result in a rupture of the entente.[99] Although the acting foreign minister assured the British ambassador that Russia had no intention of challenging Persian integrity, he also declared that only Shuster's dismissal would induce Russia to withdraw its troops.[100]

The Persian government, recognizing the weakness of its position and urged by Sir George Barclay to comply, chose to accept the earlier Russian demands. However, despite the assurances given by Kokovtsov to Buchanan that the troops would be withdrawn from Qazvin as soon as the demands had been met, the Russians had changed their minds.[101] By 20 November the Russians decided to inform the Persians that the fulfilment of their initial demands would no longer be sufficient; the future of amicable Russo-Persian relations would need to be guaranteed.[102] Since it was obvious that the Russians considered amicable relations with Shuster impossible, it was clear that the American had to go. The Persians were soon instructed that the Russian troops would withdraw when Shuster and Lecoffre had been dismissed, when the two initial demands had been met, and when the Persian government had pledged to pay for the expedition that Russia had recently launched against them.[103] In addition, the names of all future foreign candidates for employment would have to be submitted to the Russian and British legations for approval.[104] To the British, Neratov explained that he was hesitant to recall his troops now that they had arrived in Persia; their presence was, in his opinion, too valuable a tool for the prevention of further destabilizing incidents to risk the consequences of a withdrawal.[105] The Persians were therefore given a mere 48 hours from the presentation of the new ultimatum on 29 November to respond in full.[106] The Russians were willing to extend the deadline by several days, but the Persian government did not have the means to pay the indemnity that Russia required. Therefore, the revised deadline passed and the demands were not met.

For Grey, the Russian decision to escalate their demands to Persia was extremely disturbing. As the first intimation that Russia was preparing for a march on Teheran reached London, Grey admonished Benckendorff that Russia needed to pay much greater attention to the force of British public opinion.[107] The foreign secretary's ongoing defence in the House of Commons of Russian actions in Persia had already brought upon him harsh criticism from numerous corners in Britain. Benckendorff told his government that the Shoa' os-Saltaneh incident and the resulting ultimatum were considered in Britain to be merely a pretext for a Russian occupation and partition of Persia, and that Grey was being accused of total paralysis. Between his seemingly passive stance in Persia and his strongly criticized aggressive stance during the Agadir Crisis, the foreign secretary was in danger of losing the support of several of his own cabinet colleagues.[108] The result, Benckendorff feared, would be a serious ministerial crisis that would threaten not only Grey's position, but the stability of the government itself.[109] If Grey did not openly oppose the state of affairs in Persia, he would become dangerously isolated; it was imperative, in Benckendorff's opinion, that Russia clarify its position in order to save Grey and the current relationship with Great Britain.[110]

Both Benckendorff and Buchanan continually tried to impress upon Neratov the difficult position in which Grey had been placed vis-à-vis British public opinion and Muslim sentiment in India.[111] Neratov, however, countered these protestations with a two-pronged response. First of all, he minimized what he considered to be the excessive fears that seemed to be driving British public opinion on the matter. Secondly, he fell back on the weight of Russian public opinion, which, he insisted, was equally, if not more, vociferous than opinion in Britain, and which demanded that Russia continue to pursue the course it had embarked on in Persia. As Buchanan privately admitted to Grey, Neratov's concerns could not be ignored: 'For every factor that counts as public opinion here, from the Emperor downwards, is strongly in favour of settling accounts with the Persian Government and regards the occupation of Teheran, now that the Russian demands have been rejected, as the only means of effecting such a settlement.'[112]

Grey was trying very hard to be considerate of Russian public opinion and the real challenges that Russia faced in Persia. At the same time, he was truly disappointed by the second Russian ultimatum, and informed Benckendorff quite forcefully that the demand for an indemnity, the payment of which would seriously detract from Persia's ability to establish order throughout the country, was excessive. Above all, he was extremely annoyed that Russia had responded to Persia's accession to the initial ultimatum with fresh demands; this was, in Grey's opinion, a dangerous precedent that threatened to destroy the Anglo-Russian relationship:

> If further demands were to be put forward, with regard to which we might be obliged to say that they were not justified, or inconsistent with the Anglo-Russian agreement, the Persian question would disappear, and the much more serious question of foreign policy, both for us and for Russia, would take its place. This would be most deplorable.[113]

Benckendorff, although he officially defended his government in his conversations with the British, actually agreed that the nature of his country's behaviour was deplorable, and wrote a scathing letter to Neratov: 'You give an ultimatum, Persia accepts. It would appear that it is finished. Not at all. This thing is filled with new demands which put everything into question again ... with the result that Persia, weak as she is, doesn't believe it anymore.'[114] Neratov, however, was entirely unresponsive to the condemnation of Russia's successive demands by the British foreign secretary and his own ambassador; he went on to suggest to Buchanan that Russia might even expand its demands to include the establishment of a Russian-controlled security force in Tabriz or the resolution of the outstanding railway questions in the north before he would agree to withdraw the troops.[115]

Grey decided that the illusion of tacit British approval for Russian Persian policy could continue no longer, and Buchanan was instructed to submit an aide-mémoire, formally outlining Britain's position. While the British recognized the need for the establishment of a government in Persia that would 'not disregard the special and respective interests of the two powers', and supported Russia's call for Shuster's dismissal, they felt strongly that an indemnity should be avoided. Furthermore, Britain wanted guarantees that the Russian occupation of Persian territory was provisional, and would cease immediately upon the re-establishment of order in northern Persia.[116] Buchanan further clarified this final point, explaining that Britain expected Russian troops to withdraw not only from Qazvin, where they had been sent in response to the Shoa' os-Saltaneh incident, but from Tabriz and Ardabil as well. Neratov insisted, in response, that the troops in Tabriz and Ardabil were unrelated to the current situation, so thoughts of their withdrawal could not possibly be linked to discussions of the ultimatum.[117]

Although the Persian cabinet was hesitant to accept the condition that future foreign appointments be submitted for British and Russian consideration, they at last decided to agree in full to the Russian demands.[118] Final acceptance of the ultimatum lay in the hands of the Majles, however, who promised to offer stiff resistance. The Russians, in the meantime, assured the British that the Persians would have until 21 December to meet the demands in writing before the Russian troops would advance from Qazvin to Teheran, and the commander of the detachment was ordered not to set forth from Qazvin without specific instructions from Poklevsky-Kozell.[119] Neratov also told Buchanan that Russia had no desire to send its troops to Teheran, but he warned the British ambassador that in the case of a new attack on a Russian institution or troops, it would be impossible to refrain from an occupation of the capital.[120]

At the final hour, the Majles voted to accept Russia's ultimatum on the night of 20 December. By the 24th the Majles had been disbanded by the now humbled and submissive Persian cabinet, and Shuster was dismissed.[121] Just as it appeared that the crisis that Shuster had effected would be resolved and Russia would be satisfied, exactly the kind of violent incident that Neratov had warned against erupted. Gun fighting broke out between Russian soldiers and Persian gendarmes on the evening of 20 December, and Russian troops were also attacked by Persian *fedaiyan* at Anzeli and Rasht. What began as localized quarrels escalated the following day to an armed conflict between revolutionary bands and Russian troops protecting the consulates, and the Russians bombarded the citadel in Tabriz, where approximately 200 *fedaiyan* were entrenched.[122]

The typically excitable and proactive Russian consular officials throughout the north sounded the alarm. From Tabriz, Aleksander Iakovlevich Miller, always an adamant imperialist and staunch opponent of the Persian revolution, vividly described the casualties that had resulted from what he claimed was an unprovoked assault on the consulate.[123] From Rasht, Vladimir Ivanovich Nekrasov begged for the dispatch of reinforcements 'to prevent a catastrophe'.[124] From Ardebil, Dmitrii Dmitrievich Beliaev insisted that his staff were in danger, isolated far from even the most remote possibility of assistance, and asked for his local detachment to be strengthened.[125] His fears were echoed by the numerous dispatches of his colleagues.[126] Vorontsov-Dashkov, the provincial governor of the Caucasus, recommended the transfer of troops from Qazvin to Rasht and Anzeli, if not an immediate march on Teheran, and the commander-in-chief in the Caucasus demanded an indemnity from the people of Tabriz for the families of the Russian dead and wounded.[127]

Sazonov, who had at last returned to MID on 13 December after his extended illness, had a slightly more composed reaction; he and his ministry recognized the attacks as the rogue actions of local revolutionaries, not the responsibility of the central Persian government. Therefore, Russia's responses would be local, as well.[128] Five to six hundred men would be sent to Tabriz to re-establish order.[129] When this was achieved, Miller would be instructed to arrest all Russian subjects who had participated in the attack on the Russian troops and judge them under martial law. He was also ordered to disarm the *fedaiyan* and 'the other elements of disorder in Tabriz'. Finally, he was to oversee the destruction of the arsenal and all other locations in the city from which further resistance could be mounted.[130]

Sazonov's return to his post marked the end of what had been a rather unusual time for Anglo-Russian relations. Neither government was on particularly steady ground in its conduct of international relations. Grey's ongoing support for Russian policies in Persia and commitment to the agreement had threatened his domestic position to a point of extreme weakness within cabinet, parliament and the public domain. Furthermore, Britain's Central Asian policy looked increasingly reactive rather than proactive. Even the British push for a Mohammareh–Khorramabad railway concession – the most assertive British regional policy initiative of the day – was in response to a commercial threat from Germany. Apparently, Grey's regional policy was being driven by his personal desire to maintain the relationship with Russia over all other concerns; only through the means of the 1907 agreement could Russian aspirations be contained and Persia's role as a buffer state between Russia and the Indian frontier be preserved. Towards this aim, Grey was willing to tolerate and defend Russian actions that opinion in Britain considered reprehensible.

Less obvious was the Russian commitment to the Anglo-Russian relationship as they muddled through an era of ambiguous leadership and fluctuating command at the helm of Russian foreign policy. Grey's Russian counterpart in Sazonov's absence, Neratov, so lacked authority in his position that Russia's ability to have a directed Persian policy was necessarily greatly hampered; Neratov's deficiencies were aptly demonstrated by his vacillation on questions as vital as Russian support for Mohammad Ali, his reliance on the advice of consular officials rather than his minister in Teheran, and the improper nature of Russia's increasing demands to Persia in the wake of the Shoa' os-Saltaneh incident. Furthermore, during the latter months of Neratov's watch at MID, he and the new chairman of the Council of Ministers became embroiled in a battle for control of the direction of Russian foreign policy. Kokovtsov, new in his position but determined to carry on Stolypin's established practices of united government, appealed in late October to the tsar in an attempt to force the Ministry of Foreign Affairs to present significant foreign policy issues for discussion in the Council of Ministers.[131] Nicholas concurred with Kokovtsov's argument, and MID was no longer allowed to determine unilaterally Russian foreign relations without informing and consulting the other ministry heads.

Although Kokovtsov technically appeared to be integrating the reins of Russian foreign policy with those of the united government, to the British, positive results were far from apparent. The new chairman of the Council of Ministers was, in Buchanan's opinion, entirely out of touch with the prevalent sentiments in his government and was, therefore, entirely untrustworthy. Although it was clear that Kokovtsov was favourably inclined towards Britain and was motivated by an anxious reliance on good intentions, his lack of familiarity with the views of Russian public opinion and of his colleagues rendered him a liability for good Russo-British understanding.[132] Above all, Buchanan was overwhelmingly concerned by the weakness of Kokovtsov's position:

> He is not yet firmly seated in the saddle. He is opposed by reactionaries and by the advocates of a forward policy in the Council of Ministers, as well as by the Court party, who have unfortunately in this Persian business the ear of the Emperor. He is thus unable to exercise a serious influence in foreign policy or even to induce his colleagues to confirm assurances which he gives unconditionally in the most categorical manner.[133]

The result was a situation that stretched the limits of Buchanan's patience and composure in his interaction with the Russian government and in his attempts to nurture the Anglo-Russian relationship. As he privately complained to Grey in early December, 'Kokovtsoff is utterly useless, and I have never been so disappointed with anyone as I have been with him.'[134]

Thus, throughout 1911, Anglo-Russian relations in Central Asia were encumbered by the leadership challenges that both powers faced. Russian foreign policy was suffering from the absence of a dominant authority at MID and the uncertainty surrounding the new chairman of the Council of Ministers. As a result of Kokovtsov's personal weakness, his bid for responsible control of the government he officially headed, including the traditionally independent Ministry of Foreign Affairs, exacerbated the already nebulous direction of Russian foreign policy under Neratov's leadership. British foreign policy, committed to the maintenance of a good relationship with Russia but greatly hindered by the increasing difficulties that Grey faced at home, precisely because of this commitment, was in many ways foundering on the practice of reacting to a foreign policy that was itself without true direction.

The Shuster affair is significant therefore not only because of the manner in which the American's machinations and mis-steps truly dominated the attention of both Britain and Russia's Central Asia policies for most of the year. Throughout the continuing crises that seemed to develop in conjunction with Shuster's regime, the differing methodologies and challenges of each power's foreign policy machines were underscored: the Foreign Office was lacking an independent direction, and MID was lacking any direction at all. Furthermore, the various problems that Shuster's tenure as treasurer-general created and witnessed present numerous issues vital to an understanding of the direction in which the Anglo-Russian Central Asian relationship was heading; on several occasions the 1907 agreement showed disturbing signs of breaking down under the strains of the conflicting desires of the signatory parties. And, on a regional level, the Shuster affair has meaning as a last-ditch attempt by Persia to determine its own fate; as they stood up to the demands of the Russians and the strong suggestions of Great Britain to conform to those demands, the Persian cabinet and Majles demonstrated a resolution to resist the forces of regional Great Power competition that seemed destined to swallow their country up in a steady advance towards partition. Above all, the tumultuous year in Persia had called into question not only Persia's hopes for resisting partition, but the possibility that London and St Petersburg could continue to co-operate in Central Asia at all.

CHAPTER 6

Amicable Accord or Impending Breach?: 1912

Persia's capitulation to the Russian ultimatum had narrowly averted a potential collapse of the Anglo-Russian accord in Persia. However, Shuster's dismissal from the position of treasurer-general in Persia and his subsequent departure for Baku and Batum on 11 January 1912 failed to produce the desired mitigation of Anglo-Russian tensions.[1] Public opinion in Britain was vocally opposed to the support their government had given to the Russian ultimatum. The *Daily News* reported a public meeting held at the Opera House on 15 January, condemning Britain's 'surrender to Russia' as an act 'profoundly prejudicial to [Britain's] business and Imperial interests'. The *News* continued, 'No man who believes that the honour of his country is an asset worth preserving or who is concerned for the security of our Indian Empire can be indifferent to the policy by which Russia, with our consent, is obliterating a free people whose independence we have agreed to protect, and is preparing to advance her frontiers to those of our Indian Empire.'[2] In the House of Commons, Grey came under an analogous attack, but he steadfastly maintained his support for a policy of co-operation with Russia, believing that there was no alternative than to uphold the agreement at any cost.[3]

Reaction in St Petersburg was equally sceptical about the costs or benefits achieved both for Russia's position in Persia and in its relations with Britain. At the same time, Sazonov was clearly concerned by the opposition that Grey seemed to be confronting on all sides. Labour, on whom the fragile coalition government was dependent for its parliamentary majority, was vehemently hostile to Russia. Similarly, the Conservatives, now led by Bonar Law,[4] reproached the Liberals for allowing Russia to grant Germany greater privileges in northern Persia than Britain had succeeded in securing for themselves in the 1907 agreement. All this suggested to Sazonov the possibility that the Liberal government might fall and be replaced with one much less inclined to support the rapprochement.

Having recognized Grey's precarious position, however, Sazonov did not choose to take a conciliatory stance concerning Britain's Persian policy. Instead, in late January, he wrote to Benckendorff, criticizing the British foreign secretary's hesitation at taking the appropriately severe measures for the suppression of anarchy and the establishment of order in southern Persia; Sazonov felt that Grey was being unduly swayed by fears of a sympathetic pan-Islamic uprising in India resulting from British actions in Persia. Russia, in contrast, refused to be thwarted in its attempt to re-establish and maintain order in Persia, stressing that Russian public opinion – indignant at the attacks on Russian troops executing their duty – required 'energetic measures'. The Russian foreign minister urged his ambassador to persuade Grey that Russian public opinion could be just as demanding, if not more so, than either British or Indian opinion was proving to be.[5]

That Persia remained as unstable as ever was mutually acknowledged. While the attempt of Mohammad Ali to regain his throne had foundered from a lack of clearly defined Russian support, the chaos that had been unleashed in the north by his return to Persian territory continued to run rampant. Tabriz, the most critical centre of unrest since the sacking of the citadel at the end of December, remained the focal point for Russian attempts at pacification. The Persians, in opposition to the large-scale Russian military responses to what they considered to be local and independent eruptions of violence, protested to the British that the Russians were overrunning their country. At Rasht, for example, the Russian troops 'ran amok, attacked the police force, massacred it and took possession of the telegraph office. ... The Russian consul, by authority received from St Petersburgh, has taken over the reins of government.'[6] Similarly, the Persian government reported that over 500 women and children had been massacred by the Russians in the environs of Tabriz alone.[7] Sazonov denounced the dissemination of this 'slanderous invention' by the Reuters news agency, continuing to insist that the attacks on the Russian troops at Rasht and Tabriz were entirely unprovoked and, therefore, demanded adequate response.[8] While the Russians had at first assured Britain that they remained committed to the withdrawal of their troops from Qazvin upon Shuster's dismissal,[9] public opinion in Russia became so outraged by the reported losses sustained in Tabriz that an immediate recall of the expeditionary force was clearly out of the question.[10] In Teheran, the Russian minister, Poklevsky-Kozell, not only argued against the withdrawal of the Qazvin detachment, but called for the preparation of reinforcements at Baku for possible dispatch to Qazvin.[11]

Despite the indications of growing Russian military involvement in northern Persia, Sazonov continued to disavow the idea of a permanent Russian occupation.[12] Furthermore, his professed adherence to the policy of non-intervention was not merely for the consumption of international opinion. Kokovtsov, in a letter to the provincial governor of the Caucasus, instructed the local military officials to act with moderation, working within the policy boundaries set by their ambassador in Teheran:

> Although our troops are now in Persia under conditions different than the past, when the problem was exclusively one of securing the lives and property of Russian and foreign subjects and institutions, the beliefs guiding our political principles in this country remain, in general, as before. We consider, as before, it necessary as far as possible to avoid interference in internal Persian affairs and in the struggle of the local parties ... we by no means should look on the Persian people as enemies.[13]

This did not prevent the Russian officials in the north from conducting themselves like an occupying power. Having been instructed by St Petersburg to arrest and try all Russian subjects who had participated in the attacks on their troops and to disarm the local *fedaiyan*, the Russian commanders and consuls had virtually assumed the functions of local government in an attempt to pacify the region and to promote what they perceived to be Russian imperialist interests.[14] In Rasht, Consul Nekrasov ordered the sacking of a suspected anti-Russian printing plant as a reprisal against a Persian boycott of Russian goods and trade; 30 Persians were either killed or wounded in the ensuing skirmish.[15] In a further transgression of the boundaries of his jurisdiction, Nekrasov arrested a number of Persians, intending to ship them to Baku. Although the government in St Petersburg warned him that the Caucasian authorities needed legitimate cause to detain these people, such as proof that they had participated in the attacks, and Poklevsky-Kozell had previously forbidden the arrest of religious individuals, the ranks of the arrested included members of the clergy and the *anjomans* whose connection to the violence was unclear.[16] In Tabriz, Miller proceeded to execute a number of prisoners, and courts-martial were established to try any who instigated attacks on Russian soldiers or subjects.[17] Reinforcements arrived in Tabriz, bringing the total number of Russian troops in that city to at least 4000 men. While these troops served to restore partial order, there were numerous reports of thefts and looting by Russian Cossacks throughout the city. Not all the violence and transgressions were committed by the Russians, however, and recovered bodies of Russian soldiers were reported to have been 'shockingly mutilated'.[18]

The proclivity of the Russian officials in Persia to exceed their mandate, extending Russian involvement beyond that advocated by Poklevsky-Kozell in Teheran, was one of the defining themes not only of Russo-Persian relations during this period, but Russo-British, as well. Poklevsky-Kozell's growing exasperation with his Russian colleagues in Persia was well known in St Petersburg, Teheran and London. Having seen his authority clearly undermined by Pokhitonov in October, Poklevsky-Kozell struggled to rein in the independent actions of the men-on-the-spot in Tabriz, Teheran and Rasht. He urged the Russian government to put a stop to what he called the 'orgy of indiscipline' that was running rampant among Russian consular officers in Persia. The British were conscious of the dichotomy between minister and consuls; for example, Barclay explained the strain the consular forward policy was placing on the maintenance of order: 'Russo-Persian relations are at present liable at any moment to be embittered by the provocative action of Russian consuls, who will not obey the orders of their Government. How, then, can we expect those relations to remain friendly and normal?'[19] The obvious split between the Russian legation at Teheran and the consulates, although not always mirrored by a corresponding disapproval of aggressive policy in St Petersburg, allowed Grey to perceive and defend Russia as remaining true to the principles of the 1907 agreement, while the actions of the Russian officials in Persia indicated a different reality entirely.

Further complicating the situation in Persia, Shuja ud-Dowleh, the reactionary follower of Mohammad Ali, was lurking on the outskirts of Tabriz, waiting to be recognized by the Russians as the governor-general of Azerbaijan; once there, he intended to proclaim the restoration of the ex-shah to the throne. Miller strongly urged the formal recognition of Shuja, predicting that he was the only man capable of 'achieving a peaceful change in this ungoverned city'.[20] St Petersburg soon became persuaded that Shuja's recognition as governor-general was extremely desirable, not least of all because of the excellent rapport that had developed between Shuja and their consul. The British, however, were centring their entire Persian policy on the prevention of the shah's restoration, and vociferously opposed the recognition of Shuja. In the event of the occupation of Tabriz by Shuja's tribesmen and his control of the governor-generalship, Britain asked the Russians to impel Shuja not to support Mohammad Ali's claims to the throne. Russia protested that such action would be a violation of the principle of non-interference in Persia's internal affairs, but did agree to suggest a course of moderation to its client.[21]

Although Sazonov had agreed with the British not to recognize Shuja formally and had instructed Miller in early December to avoid any action that might be construed as direct aid for the shah's cause, there was little to prevent Miller from treating Shuja as the de facto governor.[22] Miller therefore sat idly by as Shuja entered the city on 1 January and unleashed a rein of terror on his enemies that was far more brutal than anything the Russian troops had committed.[23] When the Persian cabinet protested against the Russian involvement in the Tabriz massacre and threatened to resign, the

Russian response clearly intimated that such a resignation would only bring greater troubles upon the country. While the cabinet withdrew its threat of resignation, it was not willing to concede obedient defeat and made a counter-proposal for the governorship of Azerbaijan – Mohammad Vali Khan Sepahdar. Although Sepahdar had been thrown out of the cabinet by the powerful Bakhtiari khans in July 1910, the Persian government considered him, for all his weaknesses, to be superior to the reactionary Shuja.

The Russians were unwilling to desert Shuja for Sepahdar, a man they considered far too close to Turkey, Armenia and the *fedaiyan* for the establishment of good relations between him and the Russian troops. Similarly, Sazonov feared that abandonment of Shuja might be perceived as a sign of Russia's weakness and its inability to stand up to British pressure. His anxieties were encouraged by the consuls, who actively expounded the advantages of a formal implementation of Shuja's de facto rule.[24] Poklevsky-Kozell, as expected, urged St Petersburg not to promote Shuja's appointment as governor without the official agreement of the Persian government, although he grudgingly admitted that a virtual administration with Shuja at the helm was the status quo in the province.[25]

The issue at stake, however, was more than merely which man would best restore order in the region; the governor-generalship of Azerbaijan was intricately linked with the enduring controversy over the restoration of Mohammad Ali. Although the government in St Petersburg recognized Shuja to have already 'zealously proven himself [its] ardent supporter', Neratov informed General Nikolai Pavlovich Shatilov, the assistant to the viceroy of the Caucasus, that Shuja's support of the former shah and long-term opposition to the present Persian government was an insurmountable obstacle. The Persian cabinet could not trust him without threatening their own position and prestige; the Russians were determined at this point to uphold its promise to do nothing to support the return of Mohammad Ali to the throne, provided that Shuja ud-Dowleh receive some sort of compensation. Further diminishing Shuja's case, the Russians harboured no fears that Sepahdar would side with the revolutionary elements in Tabriz.[26] Although he was not as evidently pro-Russia as Shuja, neither did he appear inclined to oppose Russian Azerbaijan policy and support the *fedaiyan*. Ultimately, the problem was resolved when Shuja agreed to serve as assistant governor – retaining the bulk of the power he had amassed during his de facto rule – under Sepahdar's nominal leadership.

Grudgingly, Russia had agreed to support the removal of Shuja in favour of Sepahdar. Sazonov had informed Buchanan that the Russians would back the Persian government's decision despite its deep-seated conviction that Shuja remained the only man capable of maintaining order. However, he warned that if disorders similar to the previous December broke out – a possibility that looked likely since Sazonov reported that over 900 *fedaiyan* had arrived in Tabriz since Sepahdar's appointment had been announced – Russia would be forced to assume the direct administration of northern Azerbaijan.[27] The British were outraged by the possibility of a permanent Russian occupation. As Sir Louis Mallet, the assistant under-secretary of state for foreign affairs in charge of the Eastern Department, noted, such an action would be a direct violation of the Anglo-Russian agreement, and would only be a prelude to the complete occupation of the whole of northern Persia; he further suggested that this would have more serious consequences for Britain than for Russia, as it would be 'out of the question that [Britain] would occupy southern Persia'.[28] The British consul at Tabriz further confirmed the deficiency of Russia's stance, reporting that the Russian government was 'grossly misinformed' by its local officials, as there had been no influx of *fedaiyan* to the city.[29] Buchanan immediately warned Sazonov of Grey's extreme displeasure at the Russian threat and his hopes that Russia would abandon the idea entirely.[30] Although Sazonov claimed that Russia had no desire to annex any part of Persia, and would only consider assumption of the Azerbaijan administration under extreme circumstances, the possibility of formal Russian absorption of northern Persia was impossible to ignore.[31]

The question of what to do with Mohammad Ali lingered on through the settlement of the Shuja–Sepahdar conflict. A plan had been formulated by which Mohammad Ali would be evacuated to the Caucasus and thence to Odessa in October 1911, but he remained at Astrabad well beyond that date, waiting for the Russian intervention he was convinced – after the deferential treatment he had received at the hands of Russia's officials – would eventually come. True to their reactionary form, the Russian consuls did their best to promote the royalist cause. At the end of January, Prince Dabizha, the Russian consul in Mashhad, informed St Petersburg that up to 90 per cent of the local population was clamouring for the return of Mohammad Ali Shah, and looked longingly to Russia for help.[32] The consulate at Astrabad went further, and devoted itself to the restoration of Mohammad Ali to the throne.[33]

Britain, in contrast, remained adamantly opposed to the shah's continuing presence in Persia. The disorder in the north of Persia had spilled over into the neutral zone and southern Persia. The British troops at Shiraz were insufficient to maintain order in the region and commerce was suffering, but Britain was reluctant to bear the increased commitment that a military occupation would entail. As Hardinge informed Grey, 'from an Indian point of view we have neither the men nor the money to do it. It would be too great a strain on our resources were occupation to become permanent.'[34] Rather than dispatching an infantry battalion to Shiraz, which was recommended by

Barclay and the consul-general in Shiraz, the Government of India proposed the landing of a battalion of infantry at Bushire, the retention of customs, and a blockade of the coast to prevent the tribesmen from obtaining ammunition.[35] In Grey's opinion, such an operation would dangerously resemble the occupation of southern Persia, and needed to be avoided at all costs.

Grey considered the chaos that racked Persia to be a direct result of Mohammad Ali's proximity and conduct in the north. Although, as the foreign secretary was quick to tell Benckendorff, there certainly existed elements within British society that were ready to place all the blame for the unrest in the neutral zone on Russia's actions in the north, Grey insisted that the fault and responsibility lay with the former shah.[36] He felt that the only way to restore order in the British zone, and thence to the whole country, was to promote a strong central government, an institution that the shah's very existence challenged. As Grey complained to Benckendorff:

> The whole resources of the Persian government had been taken up by the struggle against him, owing to the fear that his return to the throne would be followed by a series of reprisals; and one result had been the blocking of the southern roads and the stopping of British trade. We therefore had good reason to resent the action of the ex-Shah. As long as there had been in Teheran a Government not favourable to Russian interests in the north, I had felt that I could not support that Government, or expect Russia to do so. But now that this obstacle had been removed, and there was a Government who realised that they must respect Russian interests in the north and accept advice, the Government ought to be encouraged and supported. It was only by showing that such a Government could keep upon their feet, and would receive goodwill and support, that their authority could be maintained in Persia.[37]

In light of their distinct opposition to the former shah, the British were quick to protest against the support being given to him by Russian agents. The Russians, increasingly aware that any further threats to the health of Grey's Foreign Office by the ominous Persian question might lead to his departure and a possible reorientation of Anglo-Russian relations, responded with a drift towards moderation. Buchanan had complained to Sazonov that in Mashhad, for example, Russian agents and citizens were getting in the way of police efforts, and Poklevsky-Kozell was instructed to put a stop to the active pro-shah agitation by the Mashhad consulate if the English complaints proved true.[38] The policy appeared on many levels to be successful, as the Persians reported calm restored to Mashhad after Prince Dabizha had condemned such agitation by Russian subjects.[39]

In an attempt to normalize the Persian situation, Sazonov sent Buchanan a formal note on 16/29 January advocating the establishment of direct negotiations between Mohammad Ali and the Persian government. Russia felt that Mohammad Ali might be persuaded to withdraw if offered a sufficient pension, and Sazonov assured Buchanan that he was more than willing to let the former shah go. For its part, however, Russia put forward several demands, such as the preservation of the Qajar dynasty, British and Russian input on the deployment of Persian troops, additional Russian concessions in its zone, and the acceptance of land ownership by foreigners.[40] In short, Russia was asking Britain and Persia to recognize Russia's independence of action in its zone.[41] Provided that Mohammad Ali would finally be removed, Britain appeared prepared to accept Russia's conditions and at last to recognize the Russian interpretation of the Persian clauses of the 1907 agreement.

Thus, on 6 February, the Russian government intervened in mediation between the Persian cabinet and the former shah. Ivanov, the consul in Astrabad, was instructed 'to offer Mohammad Ali Shah on behalf of the Persian government a pension of 50,000 tumans a year and a full amnesty to his supporters on condition that he voluntarily and immediately leave Persia.'[42] Soon thereafter, the Russian officials were instructed to cease supporting Mohammad Ali and to notify his followers that he would be leaving Persia within days.[43] Similarly, they were encouraged to work with their British counterparts to do everything possible to discourage the shah's followers from agitating in his favour.[44] The former shah, at last coming to terms with the fact that Russian support for his restoration – without which his cause was unquestionably lost – would not be forthcoming, resigned himself to bargaining for the most lucrative pension he could obtain. Until nearly the end, he had continued to look to Russia for aid, and blamed the fall of his fortunes on Britain and the Anglo-Russian understanding. As Ivanov reported:

> To the persistent questions of the Turkmen about the reasons for his departure, Mohammad Ali Shah, also sobbing, answered one word: 'England.' A significant portion of the Persian population is also reacting in favour of Mohammad Ali Shah, employing the slogan, 'Better Mohammad Ali Shah than Russia and England.'[45]

Finally, on 29 February, Mohammad Ali left Persia for the last time.

For his part in the downfall of Mohammad Ali, Sazonov was roundly criticized in the Russian press, particularly in the reactionary *Novoe Vremia*. *Novoe Vremia* – never content with Sazonov's Persian policy – condemned the Russian foreign minister not only for not supporting the shah's restoration, which they asserted was the desire of the Persian majority, but also for actively intervening to prevent his return to power. Buchanan summarized the *Novoe Vremia* article:

> When [the Shah's] cause looked hopeless strict neutrality was preserved. When things were looking brighter for him he was strongly advised to leave Persia. Russia had thereby assumed the role of a supporter of the new regime. ... The article concludes by lamenting the fact that Russia is doing all she can to alienate the sympathies of northern Persia, which has always been friendly to Russia, and is driving the Persians into the arms of the English and the Turks, in fact of anybody except the Russians.[46]

It was clear that Sazonov was considerably irritated by *Novoe Vremia*'s campaign against him.[47] The government quickly countered the paper's allegations with an official communiqué published in the Russian press on 28 March/10 April. Stressing that the shah's position in Persia – where he was completely lacking funds – had been far from secure at the time he was advised to abandon his struggle voluntarily, the government warned against what it termed 'the mischievous enlightening of public opinion' by the newspaper. The government emphasized its commitment to restoring order in Persia as the sole motivation behind Russian actions: 'The policy of Russia in Persia follows one aim only – the speediest possible cessation in that Country of the unrest which is reflecting so ruinously on Russian economic interests and is threatening to raise fresh complications which might eventually lead to most undesirable results.'[48]

Sazonov followed this public declaration with a speech on foreign policy in the Imperial Duma on 13/26 April in which the foreign minister credited the Anglo-Russian agreement with preventing the already dangerous situation in Persia from becoming disastrous.[49] The speech, however, was harshly criticized in the Russian press: while *Rech* criticized Sazonov's 'monotonous tone' and 'colourless and dull' delivery, *Novoe Vremia* stated that the basis for Russo-Persian relations rested not on the Anglo-Russian agreement, but on geographic location and the corresponding common economic and political interests the neighbouring countries shared.[50] Sazonov's foreign policy continued to suffer under a barrage from *Novoe Vremia*, which accused both Persian and Russian policy of being dictated from London: 'We would not ask these questions if our Ministry of Foreign Affairs had a programme of its own, good or bad. But, from direct and indirect evidence, it is evident that the Ministry has hitherto had no programme whatever.'[51]

Britain's Persian policy had also come under domestic attack from the press, sections of the public and seasoned Great Gamers. The public meeting at the Opera House on 15 January had denounced the very foundations of Grey's foreign policy:

We have turned treaties into waste paper, we have deserted the little people who looked to us at least to keep our word, we have endangered the future of our most vital interests, and we have involved ourselves in an expenditure on armaments without parallel in the history of the world. And the net result is that Europe is seething with unrest and that the air is thick with rumours of impending disaster, the reason for which no man can specify. This is the situation to which Sir Edward Grey's policy has brought this country and Europe. No change for the better can come without a change of spirit in our Foreign Office – a change of spirit which will make our policy abroad a ful-filment of Liberalism and not a menace to the world.[52]

Major Stokes, whose position as military attaché had been one of the casualties of the Shuster affair but who described himself as 'strongly pro-Persian, not anti-Russian', informed Grey that the Russian influence in Persia, which had been completely destroyed by the Persian revolution, was once again threatening to pose a direct challenge to the security of India. Stokes proposed a joint Anglo-French action denying Russia access to Europe's money markets in order to prevent further Russian expansion in northern Persia. Grey responded by explaining that the aim of the agreement had never been to eradicate Russian influence from Persia, but to prevent it from being used to pose a strategic threat to the Indian frontier, a goal that he considered to have been met:

Since [the Russians] had signed the Agreement, they had not stirred up any further trouble for us in Afghanistan or anywhere else in the neighbourhood of the Indian frontier. ... To use the Anglo-Russian Agreement to destroy Russian influence in the north of Persia would be a thing that was never con-templated in the making of the Agreement, and it would put an end to the Agreement. We should then be in the position of having to prepare at once in India to resist Russian aggression. No diplomatic or local action by us could turn Russia out of northern Persia. If the Anglo-Russian Agreement failed to prevent Russia from making railways or threatening the Indian frontier, I should of course regard the Agreement as having come to an end; but other-wise its maintenance was essential.[53]

Despite the commitment of both foreign ministries to the agreement, the situation in Persia continued to provide ample fodder for criticism. The former shah's ability to promote chaos in Persia was not, unfortunately, arrested by his departure. On 19 February a group of the former shah's ardent followers had taken *bast* at the Shiite Shrine of Imam Reza in Mashhad, the holiest Shiite site in Persia. These reactionaries proceeded to demonstrate flagrantly in favour of Mohammad Ali. Although Prince Dabizha had been instructed to do nothing to aid the former shah's cause, he had continued to provide secret support to these men.[54] After Mohammad Ali departed Persia aboard a Russian ship, his dedicated followers refused to disband and remained in the sanctuary of the shrine. The situation intensified, and the shrine became a fortress from which the insurgents periodically emerged to wreak havoc on the city. According to Dabizha's report, the clergy and the *mojtaheds* – the religious scholars able to interpret Islamic law – were still supporting the former shah, trade had come to a complete standstill, and the police were overwhelmed from morning to night by a marauding and pillaging population.[55] On 24 March, the governor conceded that the Persian authorities were incapable of restoring order in the city, and by the following day Russian troops had taken over the pacification of the city. Only the shrine itself remained in reactionary hands, and their numbers had been swelled by hundreds of townspeople who had sought refuge in the shrine from the chaos raging throughout the city. By the afternoon of 30 March, the shrine had been surrounded by Russian troops and the reactionaries were ordered out. They remained convinced, however, that no one would dare violate the ancient tradition of *bast* and the sanctity of the holy place. However, now that Russia had agreed to back Mohammad Ali's departure, and his supporters were no longer publicly useful, the Russians were determined to pacify the city and dissipate the tension. In a vast miscalculation, the decision was made to bombard the fortress, and the storming troops shot and bayoneted anyone they saw. Dabizha reported 39 Persian casualties, while the Persians claimed several hundred, including women and children.

The sacking of the shrine at Mashhad served Russian purposes, as it broke the back of the Constitutionalist movement; there were no further major uprisings in northern Persia before the outbreak of the First World War. The British, who had by this time ceded much of their interest in the affairs in the north, were concerned above all by the potential spill-over effect into India and Afghanistan. The Government of India was alarmed by the serious impression the attack on a religious edifice venerated by both Sunnis and Shiites had made. Although Grey acknowledged in his conversation on the subject with Benckendorff that Mashhad was well within the Russian sphere, he took pains to point out that it was also dangerously close to Afghanistan; such actions 'taken by a Power with which England is known to have intimate relations' could only damage British prestige and stability among the Muslim populations.[56] Thus, while not going so far as to regard the loss of life in Mashhad as a purely internal Russian affair, the British chose to protest against the bombardment of the shrine insofar as it affected their own possessions and protectorates, not as an aspect of their Persian policy.

Once again, the independent action of the Russian consular officials had posed a threat to the health of the Anglo-Russian understanding in Persia. As

Buchanan confided to Grey: 'When [Sazonov] ... had told me that disorders
had broken out at Meshed or at Tabriz that had necessitated the intervention
of Russian troops, I had never felt quite sure, in my own mind, whether those
disorders had not been wilfully provoked by one or other of the consuls in
order to provide an excuse for intervention.'[57] Sazonov vehemently denied
this to be the case, and Buchanan lamented that Russo-British relations in
Persia would never be harmonious until the composition of the Russian
consular service in Persia was altered. However, Buchanan recognized that
Sazonov's position was insufficiently strong to effect such changes. As he
informed Grey, '[Sazonov] is too heavily handicapped owing to the manner in
which the consuls, as well as some of the subordinate officials in his Ministry,
disobey his instructions.'[58] For the sake of the agreement, Britain was willing
to blame Russia's men-on-the-spot for the escalating interference in northern
Persia, rather than regarding events in Persia as indicative of a general trend
in official Russian policy.

In the face of the Persian outcry against the recent events in their northern
provinces, Britain went so far as to deny any ability or interest in influencing
Russia's consular policy. When the Persian government requested that the
British intervene to rein in the '"impressions" of arbitrary action' by Russia's
subordinate agents in the north,[59] Nicolson informed the Persian minister in
London that Persia did not understand the nature of the Anglo-Russian
relationship. As Benckendorff reported the conversation back to St Petersburg: 'The British government is no more occupied with the role of the
Consuls in the north than the Russians are with the role of the British Consuls
in the middle.'[60] The Persians were roundly chastised by Nicolson, and Grey
related the rebuke to Sir Walter Townley, who was taking over from Barclay
in Teheran:

> It was not [Britain's] business to keep Russian agents 'in order'. The Persians
> should not forget that if Russia were animated with such unfriendly feelings as
> were attributed to her, the position of affairs would be far worse than it actu-
> ally was, and the difficulties of the Persian Government would have been
> increased tenfold. They ought to be grateful that the two neighbours of Persia
> were working together in the hope of finding some means of restoring order
> and security in Persia, and of strengthening the authority of the Persian Gov-
> ernment.[61]

Russia, as expected, defended its actions in Mashhad as vital to the defence
of Russian subjects, property and interests. Sazonov urged Benckendorff to
make Grey and Morley understand that, while the Russians aspired to complete co-operation with Britain concerning Persia, they considered it
necessary to assert their right to act as they saw fit in protection of their

interests within their own sphere of influence.[62] The Russians made clear their displeasure at being taken to task for affairs within their own sphere:

> Each of the two parties to the agreement of 1907 must, while adhering to its general principles, be allowed a certain latitude as to the measures which either might judge it necessary to take in its respective sphere of influence, and Russian public opinion would be estranged were it to become known that its Government was lectured whenever it took steps to safeguard its interests.[63]

Within Russia's understanding of the convention, freedom of action – even of military action – was a vital necessity. The interests of Britain and India, located at a great distance from Mashhad, were necessarily different than those of the 'bordering power' in northern Persia, and, therefore, their ability to criticize Russian policies and conduct was limited.[64] Sazonov concluded by emphasizing that while there might be unrest in Afghanistan, there was now complete peace in Mashhad. It was, in his eyes, a more than fair trade.[65]

Afghan outrage at the Russian actions at Mashhad arose within the context of ongoing unease between the two countries. Britain continued to have no success in eliciting recognition of the 1907 agreement from the emir, although, as the British readily appreciated, the Russians were willing to maintain the convention as if Habibullah Khan were more co-operative.[66] Afghanistan's attitude to Russia was not only aloof, but was inclined towards antagonism. Reports of Afghan military preparations along the Russo-Afghan border were well known in Russia and India, and the growing military relationship between Afghanistan and Turkey was looked on with much suspicion by the Russian authorities.[67]

It was clear that the Afghan government was taking the Russian actions in Persia extremely seriously. The Afghan aim was evidently to head off a Russian incursion, as demonstrated by their refusal to come to the aid of the Mashhad *anjoman*, who had requested Afghan intervention, and the decision to close the Persian–Afghan border in early February.[68] However, just because the Afghans were reluctant to provide direct assistance to the Persians in their struggle with the Russians, it did not mean that the emir was not prepared to act to secure his own position vis-à-vis the perceived Russian threat to Afghan security. The Turkestan general staff anticipated the possibility that Afghanistan, fearing a Russian defensive occupation of Khorasan, might move to take for themselves Bakherz, Pain-Khaf and parts of Qaenata along the Persian–Afghan border in an attempt to hinder the further movement of Russian troops towards Afghan territory.[69] The emir ordered the reinforcement of border posts and reoriented troop disbursement towards the frontier – first along the Persian border, and later along the Russian – in response to the rumours of Russian reinforcements in Khorasan.[70] Arms were being distributed and the export of sheep and grain was prohibited.[71] Bukharan cattle merchants were forced to sell off their livestock at the border and to return empty handed.[72] The army in Herat was promised one-sixth of the sale proceeds of any property they seized while preventing exports into Russian territory.[73] Afghanistan appeared to be gearing up for a major military struggle.

Independent of the situation in Persia, relations between Russia and Afghanistan were, as stated in a report by the governor-general of Turkestan, Aleksandr Vasilevich Samsonov, 'not only unnatural, they are *profoundly significant* for Russia.' In his extensive summary of Russo-Afghan relations, Samsonov detailed the Russian efforts being made to facilitate good relations: Afghans were allowed to cross Russian borders without formal passports; premiums were being offered and customs were being relaxed in order to encourage trade; the tax on lapis-lazuli, the Afghan royal stone, was being reduced to please the emir. Yet all these efforts were to no avail, as Samsonov complained: the Afghan officials blatantly violated the general rights of reciprocity, forbidding Russian citizens even to cross the border into Afghan territory; the export of several products vital to Russo-Afghan trade was prohibited; and Afghan border officials were forbidden to interact with their Russian counterparts for the resolution of local disputes. Even more disturbing was the potential influence of the Afghan willingness to slight and disdain Russian power on Russia's own restless Muslim populations. As Samsonov warned:

> The free appearance of Afghans in the Russian cities of Central Asia – while at the same time any Russian citizens who make the slightest attempt to penetrate Afghanistan are ruthlessly expelled in disgrace – cannot go unnoticed by the fanatical Muslim mass inhabiting Central Asia. They have begun to utter criticisms at the appearance of what strikes them as incompatible ... and is deeply offensive and harmful for our state ambitions and prestige. The reality sharply underlines in their eyes the existence of Muslim rulers who would prefer to receive everything from us, while bestowing nothing in return except humiliation.[74]

The unstable border between Afghanistan and Russia was proving to be a greater source of conflict than ever before. At the end of December, two Russian officers of the Karaul-Khanenski detachment of the 30th Transcaspian Border Brigade, Pamphil Leonenko and Ivan Kosov, had stopped an Afghan caravan loaded with contraband. The clash that ensued was brutal:

Leonenko got six gaping wounds in the head and one round in the arm, and his skull was completely crushed; Kosov got hit in the head, severing his spinal cord, his lower jaw was sliced, his right arm was cut through the elbow and hand, three fingers were cut off on his left arm and a wound was inflicted on the arm above the elbow. Kosov clearly perished after a strong resistance. Two overcoats, two rifles, 30 cartridges, two sabres, and two horses were stolen from the men. Having slain the officers, the Afghans fled.[75]

The Russian authorities in the Transcaspian province immediately demanded that their Afghan counterparts search for the murderers of the two men, threatening repressive measures against all Afghan citizens within Russian territory if the brigands were not brought to justice.[76] MID advised the Turkestan governor-general not to act against Afghans indiscriminately, and to avoid focusing reprisals on the emir's agents who were pervasive in the Russian border territories, as the Ministry feared that that would only serve to estrange the two neighbouring countries even more.[77] In accordance with Russia's commitment to the Afghan clauses of the 1907 agreement, Sazonov preferred to pursue the issue through the established British channels, and Grey promised to have the Government of India make the appropriate enquiries.[78]

The murders of Leonenko and Kosov inspired Russia to rethink its border security along the Afghan frontier in an attempt to prevent a repetition. As the arrest of all Afghans in the vicinity – by far the most prevalent suggestion among the Russian officials on the spot – was ruled out by St Petersburg, Lieutenant General Shostak of the diplomatic section of the Transcaspian District recommended the registration of all Afghans in the province. This would not be a minor undertaking, as, for example, the Merv Administration absorbed approximately 5000 migrant Afghan workers every year for the cotton harvest.[79] With the aim of developing trade relations with Afghanistan and increasing the flow of cheap manual labour, no travel visas had been necessary for Afghans; Afghans would simply arrive at the border, present their national passports, and petition for a Russian permit, which they almost always received.[80] Through this system, Afghan agents were able to slip into Russia, and it was supposed that agents from India and Turkey had also used the route.[81] Not only did such circumstances hinder the maintenance of security along the frontier, reciprocal arrangements that would actually assist in the development of trade were not in any way forthcoming from the Afghan government.

The Leonenko and Kosov incident served to underscore many of the regional obstacles that Samsonov outlined in his contemporaneous report. Because, under the terms of the 1907 agreement, Russia was required to channel all its dealings with the Afghan government through the British government in India, the Russians were unable to work directly with the local Afghan authorities to investigate the murders. Instead, all discussion of the incident was conducted via St Petersburg, through London to Simla and then, at last, on to Kabul. Samsonov was convinced that the crux of the Afghanistan issue was Russia's relations with Great Britain. He acknowledged the possibility that the emir's stubbornness concerning the 1907 agreement was a direct result of his disinclination towards facilitating a regional rapprochement of the two Great Powers; it was in Afghanistan's interest to be able to play the rivals off each other. However, Samsonov conjectured that the emir was encouraged in this position by persistent Russophobe factions within the Anglo-Indian hierarchy. Samsonov censured the folly of this policy, stressing that Russia did not, under any extreme, aspire to occupy Afghanistan. According to his view, now that Russia was no longer a threat to the buffer state and, correspondingly, to India, Britain should do everything possible to coerce the emir into working with Russia and, subsequently, to strengthen the Anglo-Russian accord.[82]

The stagnation of Russo-Afghan trade was becoming an increasingly troublesome issue for Russia. On 26 January/8 February, a special conference of the Council of Representatives of Trade and Industry met in St Petersburg to discuss the better regulation of the Afghan trade. Over the next few months, the council complained bitterly against the difficulties preventing their access to a country that they considered to be 'like a market for sale'. The most immediate obstacle, and the one that they felt was most readily correctable, was the condition of Russia's trading relationship with its own protectorate, Bukhara. Because of the prohibition on Russian admission into Afghanistan, Russo-Afghan trade depended on the commercial excursions of Afghan merchants to Bukhara. However, the Bukharan officials, in the absence of any Russian commercial agents working to regulate mercantile conditions in the khanate, did little to expedite the undertaking. The Bukharans demanded steep bribes, and the established customs schedule was prohibitive and 'irrational'. Comparing Russian trade returns with that of British India, the Council found Russia to be seriously lacking, despite the approximately 800 kilometres of frontier that Bukhara and Afghanistan shared.[83] The representatives of trade and industry concluded by calling for the normalization of both Bukharan and Afghan customs duties, demanding the establishment of Russian commercial agencies in Bukhara to promote Russo-Afghan trade, and requesting the convening of a special inter-departmental conference for the discussion of the Bukharan and Afghan trade issues.[84]

By May 1912 N. Somov, the Russian political agent in Bukhara, had embarked on a campaign to improve the climate for Russo-Afghan trade. In a series of dispatches outlining the unfavourable conditions, Somov called for the resurrection of what he considered to be 'historical, natural routes'.[85] Somov urged that the development of trade with Afghanistan demanded two fundamental courses of action: (1) Russia needed to pursue diplomatic discussions with Britain, not for the acquisition of increased rights in Afghanistan, but exclusively for the establishment in practice of the rights it had already received under the 1907 accord; and (2) Russia needed to extract from the Bukharan government cheaper and easier transit routes for Russian goods through Bukharan possessions to Afghanistan.

Like the representatives of trade and industry, Somov felt that Russia's principal concern should be the appointment of an advocate for Russian trade; however, he went one step further, and called for the establishment of a non-governmental trade agent not simply in Bukhara, but at Mazar-e Sharif, along the border within Afghan territory. This trade agent should speak the local language, in order to defend the Russian and Bukharan merchants, and must be Muslim, so as to be above any possible suspicion. Somov pointed out that Russia had long allowed the presence of an Afghan trade agent in Bukhara without accusing him of espionage,[86] and suggested that Habibullah Khan be urged by the British to reciprocate.

Whereas the normalization of trading practices with Afghanistan was dependent on British intervention, the Bukharan side of the equation lay, in principle, in Russian hands. Nevertheless, reform of the customs regime in Bukhara was as troublesome an obstruction as Afghan obstinacy. Through an excessive number of toll points and exorbitantly high duties, the Bukharan treasury and its essentially corrupt bureaucracy extracted a prohibitively high levy on Russian trade, despite an 1873 agreement that guaranteed Russian merchants the right to transport their goods through Bukhara to the neighbouring countries. Furthermore, the corruption within Bukharan bureaucracy was vastly curtailing the influx of Afghan merchants to Bukhara, as wealthy Afghans were often arrested as spies in an attempt to extort money from them. Similarly, herds were often over-appraised by customs officials, who thereby levied a greater percentage of the herd as customs duty; in response, the Afghan sheep trade in Kerch had fallen off by 75 per cent between 1911 and 1912. In the face of ongoing Bukharan governmental insolence and indolence, as marked by the Bukharan emir's unwillingness and inability to deliver the promised systemic reforms, Somov bemoaned the prospects for an immediate growth of the Russo-Afghan trade. As Somov stated, if the Afghans were afraid to come to Bukhara, the entire Russo-Afghan trading system would break down.[87]

The development of trade with Afghanistan was taken up by Governor-General Samsonov at the end of June. From the perspective of the Turkestan chancellery, Russo-Afghan trade was most significant as a means to foster a sense of comradeship between the two neighbouring countries. They opposed the introduction of extensive tariffs on Afghan goods, since the increase to the Russian treasury would be minuscule when compared to the lost opportunities for political and economic intimacy with Afghanistan. Samsonov recommended the establishment of a consulate in Afghanistan under the guise of diplomatic negotiations about the regulation of the astrakhan[*] trade. He felt that the achievement of such a concession would help Russian commerce not only in Afghanistan, but, by example, in the rest of Asia as well.[88]

While Russia concentrated on increasing its involvement with Afghanistan, Britain was striving to limit the extent to which it was being sucked into the Tibetan morass. The revolution that had broken out in China in the autumn of 1911 threatened to destabilize Britain's north-east frontier. At the end of November, the British trade agent at Yatung and the political officer in Sikkim called for an increased garrison protecting the trade agency and the lives and property of British subjects in Yatung and Gyangze and the telegraph officers at Phari.[89] The Government of India, however, in an attempt to avoid further British military commitments beyond its frontier, dismissed this proposal as unnecessary. The Dalai Lama, whose exile in Darjeeling continued, looked in turn to both Russia and Britain to protect Tibet from the Chinese onslaught. He once again wrote to the tsar, requesting his assistance in the face of Chinese persecution:

> I hope that the Government of His Majesty knows, it was conditions and events which necessitated that I set off for India, and not to the north to Russia. ... Although currently residing in holy India, I hope that according to the favour of Buddha I will be able ultimately to free my country from its difficult situation with the help of mighty Russia.[90]

The Russians, having acknowledged in May that the state of affairs in Tibet was of greater immediate interest to Britain than to themselves, fully disclosed the nature of the Dalai Lama's petition, and Benckendorff submitted their prepared response to the British for their perusal.[91] The Government of India arranged a meeting between the Russian consul-general in Calcutta, Revelioti, and the Dalai Lama and his advisers, so that the tsar's response could be presented.[92] Russia, the tsar regretfully informed the Dalai Lama, was unable to help him, especially in light of its commitments to Britain in the 1907 agreement. The Russian government was, however, convinced that he would 'triumph over his problems and predicaments'.[93] The Tibetan

---

[*] The glossy black, tightly curled skins of newborn karakul lambs.

ministers, mistakenly believing that Revelioti had come on a political mission, asked that the British and Russian governments might move quickly to negotiate a settlement of the Tibetan question; the Russian consul-general hastened to remind them that his mandate in Darjeeling was only to bear the tsar's letter, not to discuss any outstanding issues concerning Tibetan affairs.[94] But the Dalai Lama continued to push for some semblance of joint Anglo-Russian intervention up until his return to Tibet.[95]

The India Office, although unwilling to actively intervene to support Tibetan autonomy, was equally unwilling to recognize the inclusion of Tibet as an integral province of the newly formed Chinese Republic for fear that it would be a precedent to the recognition of the Republic itself. As the viceroy, Lord Hardinge, reminded the Foreign Office, 'The maintenance in Tibet of a state of political isolation is in any case absolutely necessary, owing to the geographical position of the country.'[96] While Britain was ready to accept China's continued suzerainty over Tibet, the Foreign Office, India Office, Government of India and the British ambassador in Peking unanimously agreed that they could not tolerate any interference in Tibet's internal administration, including the stationing of unlimited numbers of Chinese troops in the country.[97] British pressure forced the invading Chinese garrison to be withdrawn, and the Dalai Lama departed India for Lhasa on 24 June with best wishes from the Government of India for a safe and prosperous journey.[98]

In the meantime, Russia was taking advantage of the chaos in China to increase its influence in Kashgar and Mongolia. In light of Russia's advancing presence in Central Asia, the Foreign Office proposed that Russia be given a free hand in Kashgar in return for a compensatory arrangement in Tibet, a region that had waned in importance for Russian policy since the 1907 agreement. As a Foreign Office memorandum concerning India's northeastern frontier remarked: 'Russian interests in Thibet have never been more than hopes, and these hopes seem in the course of the last few years to have been abandoned.' Comparing Russia's extensive commercial and political interests in Kashgar with those that Britain held in Tibet, the memorandum concluded that the advantages of such a plan, which would ensure the preservation of an autonomous Tibet, would far outweigh the corresponding surrender of regional geopolitical status to Russia that might ensue:

> On the side of the Government of India the disadvantages in the proposed arrangement would lie ... in a certain loss of prestige and in the after effects of a considerable disturbance of the balance of power in Central Asia. On the other hand Russian influence and trade are already infinitely greater in this district than British. Chinese Turkestan is connected with Russian territory by good caravan routes and easy passes ... while the passes into India are difficult

and the road for most of its length is a mountain track passable only by mules.[99]

The Foreign Office, while acknowledging that the establishment of a formal British protectorate over Tibet was undesirable, pushed for the development of a relationship so near to that of a protectorate that Tibet could be readily transformed into one should any contingency ever make it expedient: 'What appears to be essential is that Thibet, while nominally retaining her position as an autonomous State under the suzerainty of China, should in reality be placed in a position of absolute dependence on the Indian Government, and that there should be set up an effective machinery for keeping out the Chinese on the one hand and the Russians on the other.' Similarly, the Foreign Office proposed that a new agreement be reached with Russia, possibly one in which they offered Russia control of Mongolia and Kashgar in exchange for Tibet. Since, as they grudgingly admitted, Britain really had nothing to offer Russia that it did not already de facto possess, they suggested that an element of bluff be employed in the negotiations; one half-baked scheme would have seen Britain sending Indian troops to Kashgar so they could later be withdrawn as a concession.[100]

In contrast, the Government of India was vehemently opposed to any quid pro quo concerning Kashgar, short of complete renunciation by Russia of all interest in Tibet, excepting the relations between Russian Buddhists and the Tibetan Lamas. They insisted that Chinese Turkestan and Kashgar were far more important to India than Tibet.[101] This stance by Britain's men-on-the-spot was interpreted by members of the Foreign Office as a reactionary response not corresponding to the contemporary regional realities. As R.T. Nugent, clerk in the Far Eastern Department, stated: 'How far this point of view is also influenced by the habit of the last 50 years during which the Russian menace from the North has been the decisive factor in Indian foreign policy, while events and interests on the eastern frontier have been relegated to an obscurity which they have not always deserved is difficult to decide.'[102] Sir Eyre Crowe, now assistant under-secretary of state for foreign affairs in the Western Department, pointed out, however, that any renegotiation of the Anglo-Russian agreement concerning Tibet would appear as though Britain was working with Russia for the dismemberment of China.[103] This more cautious stance was supported by the foreign secretary, who was as wary in this instance of antagonizing the Chinese as he was the Russians. Therefore, as Grey prepared to meet Sazonov at the end of September, the concept of trading Russian hegemony in Kashgar and Mongolia for British predominance in Tibet, while still a possibility, was not at all established British policy.

Sazonov's journey to Britain, culminating in three days spent as the guest of King George V at Balmoral, provided the two governments with an unusual opportunity to reconcile their Central Asian policies. Elements of the Russian press had been less than enthused by the prospect of Sazonov's mission. *Birzhevye Vedomosti*, for example, in an article entitled 'The Policy of Yielding', criticized Sazonov for being so quick to travel to Britain when Grey had yet to appear in St Petersburg. The French ministers, the paper admonished, would never be so rude as to leave the visits of Russian foreign ministers unreturned. Furthermore, as Russia's position was currently so favourable, there was no need for Sazonov to display such a readiness to yield.[104] The majority of the Russian press, however, was extremely enthusiastic about a meeting between the two ministers.[105] Thus, Sazonov travelled to London and then on to the king's retreat in Scotland, where he met Grey on 24 and 25 September.[106]

After spending the morning discussing the general situation in the Near East, the two foreign ministers moved on to the subject of Persia. In preparation for the meeting at Balmoral, Grey had asked his minister in Teheran to offer his opinion on a possible alteration of the Anglo-Russian agreement. Townley, reluctant to propose any alteration to the demarcated spheres of influence, conceded that if such a modification were to be achieved, it would be most advantageous if the new delineation could ensure British predominance in Fars, Bakhtiaristan and Arabistan.[107] He prefaced his remarks, however, by admitting that his perspective might be tainted by the frustrating realities of diplomatic life in Teheran:

> Perhaps the British Minister at Teheran is not the best person to express an opinion upon the Anglo-Russian understanding, as far as regards its bearing on Persian affairs. Even with a colleague like Poklewski, it is at times a bit galling to feel that the Russian has such a much more preponderating influence here than oneself from the mere fact that Teheran is in the Russian sphere, a fact that receives additional weight from the presence of Russian troops in the whole of North Persia and from the knowledge that Russian Consuls beyond the immediate reach of the Legation behave like governors, and act as if the country was under Russian jurisdiction.[108]

Sazonov's notes in preparation for the Balmoral meeting indicate that he was planning to take a page directly out of the British book by lodging a complaint with Grey about the behaviour of certain British consuls. Major Percy Sykes, the British consul-general in Mashhad, incurred the bulk of Sazonov's criticism of a group of men that he felt were incapable of relinquishing their former orientation against Russia and behaving within the context of contemporary political realities. Sykes, according to complaints from both the Russian consulate and the Russo-Persian Bank branch in Mash-had, was paramount in actively promoting and disseminating anti-Russian propaganda. Sazonov intended to suggest that Sykes, 'the old Anglo-Indian', be transferred to another position, preferably out of Persia. Sazonov had further ideas about the composition of the British consular service in Persia:

> It would, in general, be desirable that in the sphere of Russian influence in Persia the appointments of Consulate employees be made from the Foreign Office lists, and not from the ranks of the Indian Service. To date, Indian em-ployees – notwithstanding the sincere consideration towards Russia of the Viceroy, Viscount Hardinge, and his efforts to strengthen the atmosphere in India of friendship towards us – are all under the influence of the old tradition of enmity and mistrust of Russia. Analogous conditions exist in the subordi-nate employees, who should also not be of Indian origin.[109]

There is, however, no indication in either the British or the Russian records of a meeting at Balmoral at which Sazonov raised this issue with Grey.

Sazonov and Grey began their discussion by agreeing that the restoration of order in Persia was their principal concern. Mohammad Ali was mutually acknowledged as too weak to pacify the country, with Sazonov commenting, 'though there might be something to be said for a strong tyrant, there was nothing to be said for a weak one.'[110] Concurring that finances were the fundamental issue, Sazonov proposed a loan of £5–6 million sterling, pre-dicting that if the Persian government were deprived of the material means necessary to solve the country's woes, it would be able to accomplish noth-ing.[111] While Grey agreed, he was opposed to Russia and Britain taking this financial burden upon themselves, yet anticipated that Europe's financiers would not be willing to extend further loans to Persia until order had been secured. He predicted, 'We shall then be in this dilemma: that there can be no money until there is a gendarmerie, and no gendarmerie until there is money.'[112]

In order to prevent railway concessions being granted to a third power in the neutral zone, Sazonov suggested its abolition. Although Britain had been entertaining the idea of redrawing the lines in Persia, as Grey's correspon-dence with Townley demonstrates, Grey was loathe to agree at Balmoral to any further partition of the neutral zone. He advised Sazonov that the Russian sphere was already so vast that to increase it would pose tremendous difficul-ties. Furthermore, an Anglo-Russian understanding about concessions in the neutral zone would still not be binding on any non-signatory powers, and would, therefore, not serve to accomplish the stated aim.[113] It is interesting to note that while Grey felt he had been very clear in his opposition to further partition, Sazonov's interpretation of their conversation was vastly different:

he came away from their meeting convinced that Grey had in principle agreed with his speculation that the two powers would eventually have to reconsider their relations in the neutral zone if they wanted to keep any others out.[114]

Notwithstanding his opposition to further partition, Grey was committed to effecting increased stability in the neutral zone. For this purpose, Grey proposed the establishment of Persian road guards in the neutral zone under British officers. When Sazonov remarked that public opinion in Russia would interpret this as a manifestation of the cession of the entire neutral zone to Britain with Russia to receive nothing in return, Grey protested that protecting the roads on which British trade depended did not amount to absorption of the neutral zone into the British sphere. He further argued that the continuing presence of 12,000–15,000 Russian troops plus the Russian-led Persian Cossacks in the north would more than offset any influence that a few British officers might have over the trade routes in the south. Grey similarly made sure to remind Sazonov that Britain had stood by and supported Russia even in the face of Muslim opposition as he referred to the bombardment of the shrine at Mashhad, pointing out that it 'had really shocked Mussulman opinion'.[115]

In a further step designed to counter any third-party plans for acquiring railway concessions, Sazonov pressed for British commitment to the scheme for a trans-Persian railway. The foreign minister felt that it was crucial that Russia acquire a commercial outlet on the Persian Gulf in order to offset the projected construction of the German Baghdad Railway.[116] When Grey insisted that British public opinion was not yet ready to digest a connection of the Indian with the European railway systems, Sazonov maintained that Russia was prepared to let Britain set the timetable for the actual construction of the connecting lines; the northern lines could be constructed independently of the southern lines, as long as there was a commitment between the two powers for the eventual linking of the two systems. He did, however, feel it prudent at this time to secure the concession from the Persian government before someone else – namely Germany – did so.[117]

Grey agreed in principle to the idea of a trans-Persian railway, especially in light of its utility as a counterbalance to the Baghdad Railway. As Grey had conceded in his speech to Parliament on 10 July, railway construction in Persia was unavoidable, so it would be best for Britain to participate and therefore be in a position to influence its orientation.[118] Britain had earlier determined that it would only be through participation in the trans-Persian scheme from the outset that it would be able to obtain a line that would be advantageous to its strategic and commercial needs.[119] Therefore, with the caveat that Britain reserved the right to dictate the eventual orientation of such a line outside the Russian sphere, Sazonov and Grey reached an agreement to allow the Société d'Études to proceed with the trans-Persian scheme.[120]

During their meeting at Balmoral, Sazonov submitted to Grey an aide-mémoire, which presented Russia's primary complaints concerning its relations with Afghanistan. Extensive discussion of Afghanistan, however, was left for Sazonov's later meeting with the Marquess of Crewe, the secretary of state for India, as Afghanistan was considered to be principally a concern of the Government of India. The Russian memorandum outlined many of the complaints that Samsonov had documented in his February report; the stagnation of Russo-Afghan trade, the uncontrolled regulation of regional irrigation and water rights, and the locusts, which, in the words of Major Sykes, 'had no respect for frontiers' and were ravaging Russian crops, all combined in a situation that was for Russia 'gravely disadvantageous'.[121]

Above all, Sazonov bemoaned the lack of direct relations between the local officials along the Russo-Afghan frontier. He felt that the establishment of such relations was indispensable, especially in light of the damage to Russia's prestige in Central Asia that the current state of affairs was fostering.[122] In addition, Russia complained that Afghanistan was becoming a hotbed of pan-Islamic fanaticism and propaganda that, as it was penetrating into both Russian and British possessions, was equally dangerous to the interests of both powers.[123] In his conversation on Afghanistan with Lord Crewe, with which they occupied the long train journey from Balmoral to London, Sazonov urged the Government of India to press the emir into acknowledging and confronting these issues.[124] While Crewe promised to do what he could, he warned Sazonov that there was little chance of obtaining the emir's recognition of the 1907 convention, stressing, 'our own people had no general access to Afghanistan, and we could not expect more to be done for Russians at our instance than we should ask for ourselves.'[125]

Both Grey and Crewe spoke with Sazonov about the unsettled predicament of Tibet. Grey assured his Russian counterpart that Britain had no ulterior aspirations for Tibet beyond the implementation of the existing commercial treaty. However, he tried to lay the groundwork for a future relaxation of the British side of the Anglo-Russian agreement in the event that it became necessary to station some sort of agent in Lhasa 'to keep [Britain] informed'. As might have been expected, Sazonov replied that he would require a quid pro quo for Russia, but that he would be open to discussions of this nature. And in a move that simultaneously thwarted Britain's hopes for a Kashgar or Mongolian trade for British primacy in Tibet and sent tremors of alarm through the Anglo-Indian community, Sazonov flatly informed the foreign secretary that any area outside the Anglo-Russian agreement could not be regarded 'in *pari materia* with Thibet'.[126] Sazonov elaborated his position during his discussion with Crewe, remarking that if any changes were made that appeared to give Britain a solid advantage in Tibet, he would come under fierce attack at home. He felt quite strongly that it would be best to deal with events in Tibet as they arose, and not to formulate a revision at this time. At this point, Sazonov made the proposal that the British had been dreading – Afghanistan. He suggested to Crewe that he might be willing to offset British gains in Tibet with increased Russian involvement in Afghanistan, to appease Russian public opinion.[127] This proposition, indicating a distinct shift in Russia's previous Afghan policy, was not particularly welcome in London, and was even more unpopular with the Government of India.

Sazonov departed Britain for a brief stop in Paris, tired and ill but pleased overall with his visit.[128] The Russian public, however, in the heat of pan-Slavism, was outraged that so much time had been spent discussing Persia when the situation in the Balkans was so grave. Furthermore, Sazonov was criticized for not achieving a revision of the Anglo-Russian convention.[129] The British press, in contrast, was pleased with the amount of attention the critical situation in Persia had received. Similarly, Grey had found the encounter to be profitable. While he was realistic about the gravity of the outstanding issues that remained concerning Afghanistan, Tibet and, in particular, Persia, the British foreign secretary felt that much had been accomplished. Most significantly, Grey felt he had acquired ammunition should a renegotiation of the 1907 agreement become necessary.[130]

The meeting of the two statesmen at Balmoral epitomized the state of Anglo-Russian relations in Central Asia over the preceding year. Since the Shuster affair, there had been numerous minor crises that had challenged the continuing health of the accord, but no serious threat had been posed to it. Similarly, several troublesome issues inherent in the current state of Central Asian geopolitics contributed a modicum of difficulty to the proceedings at Balmoral, but, overall, the atmosphere was one of positive co-operation. Both powers continued to profess their profound commitment to the continuation of Anglo-Russian regional understanding; the maintenance of the Anglo-Russian relationship had been avowed by both foreign ministries as the foundation of their foreign policies and, while public opinion in each country often appeared less than convinced of the mutual benefits of continued concert, both governments publicly insisted that the advantages accrued through the agreement remained intact.

However, beneath the surface of the Anglo-Russian relationship, away from the public protestations of mutual admiration and accord, trouble was brewing on many levels. Continued Russian encroachments in northern Persia threatened to obliterate the pretence of non-interference upon which the Persian clauses of the agreement were based. The instability in Tibet appeared to be drawing Britain in far further than it was truly prepared to go, increasing its involvement beyond the limits dictated in the 1907 accord. Most significantly, the Tibetan crisis was providing Russia with a potential bargaining chip in its bid for increased involvement in Afghan affairs. Therefore, while the Balmoral visit had appeared to be a success, little in Central Asia had truly changed.

CHAPTER 7

'Towards a Revision of the Anglo-Russian Agreement': 1913

Soon after the meeting at Balmoral had provided the Russian and British foreign ministers with an opportunity to discuss Central Asia, the outbreak of war in the Balkans overshadowed the regional concerns. The anti-Turkish coalition that had been forged the previous spring between Bulgaria, Serbia, Greece and Montenegro refused to heed Russian and Austro-Hungarian advice to keep the peace in the Balkans, and Montenegro declared war on Turkey on 8 October 1912; the remainder of the allies followed the Montenegrin example a few days later. While the European powers watched with apprehension as the Balkan states achieved victory after victory against the crumbling Ottoman Empire, the potential repercussions in Central Asia for both Russia and Britain were alarming.

Afghanistan's proclivity towards a pan-Islamic opposition to its northern and southern neighbours was an ongoing concern for Russia. The previous summer, Afghan Islamist support of their Persian brethren had become increasingly vocal. The result, as the intelligence department of the Turkestan general staff reported, was an extremely hostile orientation towards Russia, promoted through imperial proclamations in the Afghan bazaars:

> Our principal enemy is Russia. Although the English are also our enemies, they are enemies with a distinction – their words and promises don't differ from their actions. Never completely trust the Russians.

> Unlucky Persia stands defenceless before the pretensions of Russia, who, evidently, thinks to occupy her provinces. If this happens, Muslims will not dwell in the land of Iran. In the near future, you, the people of Allah given Afghanistan, will rise to the defence of truth and the fatherland and go to Persia's aid against the nonbelievers.[1]

With the outbreak of war in the Balkans, Afghan support for Persia was quickly and easily transferred to Turkey. The Turkish sultan requested funds and troops from Afghanistan in support of the Turkish war effort and was promised in response 10,000 Afghan troops by the emir, who proclaimed that 'the interests and enemies of Turkey are Afghanistan's interests and enemies.'[2] The war in the Balkans was seen as part of a growing threat by the Christian powers – following upon the bombardment of the shrine at Mash-had – to swallow up the Muslim world.[3] Regarding the struggle in the Balkans as a conflict between Islam and all of Europe, Habibullah Khan underscored Afghanistan's readiness to stand up to Britain in defence of its religion: 'Although we officially have an agreement with the English, they are the enemies of our religion, so we at the same time and in the depth of our soul are their enemies. For the sake of Islam our life and property should be given to the struggle for the Grand Caliph, the World State of Islam.'[4]

Grey had assured Russia that the British government would remind the emir 'that it would be wise of him to act in a neighbourly spirit.'[5] It was clear to the Russians, however, that Britain's actual ability to effect such a 'neighbourly spirit' was rather dubious. In an extremely secret report of 28 November/11 December 1912, Nabokov, the Russian consul-general in India, provided an extensive critique of Anglo-Afghan relations. Although the Russian government was inclined to consider Afghanistan an 'intractable vassal' of Britain, it appeared to Nabokov that the Afghan position was more like that of a sovereign than a vassal. Even the means through which Britain ostensibly controlled Afghanistan – the yearly subsidy and the domination of the Khyber Pass – were only illusions of authority, and were actually used by the emir to exert his own independence and superior position over the British. The emir did not pay a subsidy, but received one from the government to which he was supposed to owe allegiance. Rather than using this subsidy in the pursuit of order along the Afghan–Indian border as intended, the emir spent British money to arm his troops and disseminate pan-Islamic propaganda. The Khyber Pass, which Britain officially controlled, saw numerous Afghan convoys cross the border into India, but not one English trader was allowed to pass through. As Nabokov asked, 'Is this the relationship of a vassal to a sovereign?'[6]

On several levels, the Russian consul-general had questioned Britain's ability to exert any influence on Afghanistan. As he pointed out, the British did not have an official representative in Kabul, and the Afghan 'accredited' representative in Simla – who, the Russian was well aware, was not even in India at the time – neither spoke nor understood a word of English. Furthermore, the Hardinge viceroyalty was committed to maintaining peace along the frontier. Anything that might stir up pan-Islamic sentiment in the border regions or within India itself would be extremely undesirable, especially coming so soon after the previous year's visit to India by King George and Queen Mary. Therefore, Nabokov felt that Russia could not count on active support from the Government of India for the promotion of its just interests in Kabul.[7]

In light of their inability to restrain their northern neighbour and the open opposition that Britain faced in Kabul, the surge in anti-western propaganda in Afghanistan resulting from the Balkan War was understandably trouble-some to both the Government of India and the Home Government. British worries about a pan-Islamic uprising were focused not only on Afghanistan, but on their own Muslim population within India. Lord Hardinge noted in late October the steady growth of pan-Islamic sentiment in India that was manifested in a 'very keen interest' in the war. This movement, however, vacillated in its identification of either Britain or Russia as the primary foe. In a private letter to Lord Crewe, the viceroy commented on the fickle nature of Indian public opinion, especially within the North-West Frontier Province:

> A month ago the bazaar was full of war scares, rumours of railway construc-
> tion, of an advance upon Cabul, etc. etc. These have now died down and
> their place has been taken by a widespread rumour that the Amir, in fear of
> Russia, has asked me to send troops to defend the north of Afghanistan, that
> the Amir is coming to Dakka to meet our troops, and that he has said he will
> wipe out the inhabitants of the Jellalabad valley if a shot is fired! This shows
> what extraordinary imagination these people have.[8]

In addition to the growing challenge that Russian and British regional prestige and security were facing in the wake of the Balkan crisis, the rise of pan-Islamic sentiment in Central Asia had direct implications for Anglo-Russian relations. At Balmoral, Sazonov had urged the British to convince the emir to act in accordance with Article 3 of the 1907 convention concerning direct Russo-Afghan border relations on a local level, an accomplishment that looked increasingly beyond Britain's capabilities. Afghan isolationism was a long-established reality in the region, and Afghan officials continued to be prohibited from direct intercourse with British and Russian officials alike. Therefore, as Hardinge pointed out, an attempt to compel the emir to allow free intercourse between his officials and the Russians would find Britain procuring for Russia what it was unable to achieve for itself. Furthermore, Hardinge insisted that in the current atmosphere of intense Afghan Rus-sophobia, resulting from Afghan opposition to Russian aggression in Persia and affairs in the Balkans, Britain would, in fact, only serve to imperil its own shaky relations with the Afghan government were it to press Russia's de-mands. The viceroy summarized Afghanistan's distrust of its northern neighbour and the emir's ongoing opposition to the 1907 agreement:

> The Afghan Government think they understand Russian character and Russian
> aims better than we do ourselves. They regard the Anglo-Russian Convention

merely as a subtle device on the part of Russia to hoodwink us until she is ready to move. They have refused to ratify the Afghan portion of the convention and any attempt on our part to enforce any item of it will be considered by the Afghans both as a sign of weakness on our part and a surrender, through weakness, of Afghan interests to Russia. The effect of this on our prestige and our relations with Afghanistan will be serious.[9]

The memorandum in response to Russia's aide-mémoire concerning Afghanistan, which Sazonov had presented at Balmoral, had reiterated Britain's inability and unwillingness to force the emir to recognize the terms of Article 3.[10] In spite of Britain's impotence, Russia continued to push for the formal establishment of direct relations concerning issues of plague, locusts, irrigation and border conflicts. In August the Russians had requested British intervention concerning irrigation rights on the Murghab and Tedjen rivers, whose sources lay within Afghan territory but whose waters were vital for the agriculture of Russian Central Asia.[11] The Russians felt that Afghanistan was overcultivating its provinces through which the two rivers ran, resulting in the excessive diversion of water and the diminished flow of water into Russian territory; Russia duly requested that Britain investigate the matter.[12] In early November, plague was again reported in Afghanistan, and the Russians, fearful for their lengthy frontier with Afghanistan, called for the immediate dispatch of European doctors and medicines to Herat.[13] Approximately 250 Cossacks were deployed on the Persian–Afghan frontier to enforce a quarantine, and a similar increase in the Russian guard along the Russo-Afghan frontier prompted the emir to call for Afghan military measures to counter what was perceived as a Russian threat to Afghan security.[14]

Both the plague epidemic and the irrigation questions were investigated by the Government of India, who found that Russia had 'not got a leg to stand on' in either instance.[15] The British agent at Karez, the frontier town nearest to where plague was rumoured to have erupted, related that the local Russian doctor had admitted before witnesses that he had reported an outbreak of plague without having seen a single case; he based his charge on the report of a Persian doctor, who had similarly seen no plague cases.[16] Eventually the plague rumours were traced to the death of a few of Karez's inhabitants after eating a poisoned camel.[17] The Government of India similarly questioned Russian claims concerning the Murghab and Tedjen rivers on two principal grounds: (1) protocol dictated that Russia had no overriding right to any use of the rivers' waters; and (2) there existed no indication that Afghan regional irrigation and cultivation had increased at all, especially as the authorities in the Herat province had demonstrated little, if any, initiative in the development of progressive agriculture that would have placed an increased demand on the water supply.[18]

The Government of India interpreted Russia's epidemiological claims and irrigation complaints to be indications of a more ominous trend in Russian policy. As Hardinge wrote to Crewe:

> These complaints of Russia, which appear to me to be lacking in solid foundation, indicate a frame of mind which inspires me with a certain amount of anxiety. It looks to me as though they wish us to spoil our good relations with the Amir and thus change our attitude towards him into one of hostility. They must know perfectly well that the Amir would be very indisposed to allow any interference with his water rights in North Afghanistan, and still more so the invasion of Herat and other places in the north by Russian doctors – accompanied of course by Cossack escorts.[19]

In addition to the questions of irrigation and plague, both the Government of India and the India Office were concerned by the establishment of a Russian military post at Karez and an increase in the number of arrests along the border under the suspicion of espionage. All this, coupled with the expanded diplomatic interest Russia was demonstrating in the pursuit of direct relations with the emir, seemed to point towards what the British could only interpret as an alarming development for their buffer state: 'These facts taken together appear to Lord Crewe to indicate the probability that at some time in the near future the Russian Government may directly raise the question of Afghan acceptance of the Anglo-Russian convention and may even follow up this move by action on the frontier of an even more definite nature.'[20]

While the Government of India was vociferous in its suspicions of Russian intentions concerning Afghanistan, opinion in London was less definitive. Crewe agreed in principle with the Government of India, but he did allow that the Russians might have been basing their requests for British assistance on a sincere, if ill-founded, belief that Britain was actually able to dictate policy in Kabul. As he observed in a private note to Grey: 'I am not sure that Hardinge is quite fair to the Russians in expressing this application as based on intrigue. I may be quite wrong, but I believe that they honestly cannot credit us with being such d--d fools as to be unable somehow to put the screw on the Amir as they would have retained the means of doing after a war like that of 1880.'[21] Within the Foreign Office, however, there were those who saw the stance of Crewe and Hardinge as 'an attack of Russophobia', and who stressed the extreme patience the Russian government had demonstrated concerning the deficiencies of the Afghan clauses of the Anglo-Russian agreement.[22] Nevertheless, Lord Crewe's final analysis that Britain should proceed with the utmost caution in relation to Russia's Afghan intentions was, ultimately, accepted as British policy.

After Sazonov had linked the two countries at Balmoral, Russia's apparent designs on Afghanistan continued to pose a stumbling block to any resolution of the continuing chaos in Tibet. It would clearly be futile, as Lord Hardinge admitted at the end of November 1912, for Britain to seek any alteration in Tibet's status before Russia achieved even a modicum of satisfaction for its own objectives in northern Afghanistan.[23] While both the Indian and Home Governments continued to oppose any such alteration of the status of Afghanistan, Russia's acceptance of Outer Mongolian independence from China in November 1912 further complicated the situation. The Russo-Mongol agreement of 21 October/3 November and the annexed protocol granted Russia considerable commercial and political rights in Mongolia. More significantly, the agreement subordinated Mongolian foreign relations to Russian policy. Russia thus acquired in Mongolia what Britain had failed to achieve through the Younghusband expedition in Tibet – a situation that could not fail to irritate the veteran Great Gamers in the British ranks.[24] As Major O'Connor, the recently appointed British consul in Shiraz, observed in a private letter to Lord Curzon: 'When one watches Russia's masterly tactics in Mongolia it makes one wild to see how badly we have played our cards in Tibet.'[25]

Russian provisional recognition of Mongolian independence and their assumption of control over Mongolian foreign relations did not, in itself, pose a threat to Britain's sense of stability in Central Asia; in fact, the conclusion of the Russo-Mongolian agreement appeared at first to present a golden opportunity for a revision of the Anglo-Russian Tibetan arrangement in Britain's favour, despite Sazonov's acknowledgement at Balmoral that Mongolia lay outside the Anglo-Russian convention.[26] As R.T. Nugent, third secretary in the Far Eastern Department, noted, 'Russia's hands are now fuller than they were in September and full hands might make for generosity to friends.'[27] Opinion in Russia, China and, to a degree, Britain had for some time been looking for Britain to reach an arrangement with Tibet similar to that which Russia had achieved with Mongolia.[28] Russia was actually in favour of a direct agreement between Britain and the Dalai Lama that would parallel its own, as long as it would not infringe on the Anglo-Russian convention.[29] The British were, nevertheless, wary of an anti-British backlash that would expose their vulnerable commercial interests in China to attack, and the India Office advised that every effort be taken to avoid drawing an analogy between British and Russian policy in the crumbling Chinese Empire.[30]

Britain, however, was unable to downplay the implications of Russia's new-found close connection with Mongolia. Outer Mongolia's first act as a semi-independent state in the international domain was to commence negotiations with Tibet, which was claiming a similar degree of autonomy from

China. The Tibetan–Mongol treaty that was concluded on 11 January 1913 established not only the joint recognition of the two self-proclaimed independent states, but guaranteed the mutual support 'for all time' of both signatory parties 'against dangers from without and from within'.[31] Through its relationship with Mongolia, Russia would thereby acquire direct influence in Tibetan affairs. As Nugent observed:

> [The treaty has] acquired a fresh significance in view of the large number of Russian officers who are being sent to Mongolia to organize a force on Cossack lines. This will give the Mongolians an opportunity to afford the assistance promised to the Thibetans in the event of a renewal of the Chinese attempt at reconquest, and the Russians an opportunity of introducing what will be practically a Russian force into Thibet in a manner which evades the terms of the Anglo-Russian convention.[32]

Further complicating the matter in Britain's eyes, the chief treaty negotiator on the Tibetan side was none other than the ubiquitous and troublesome Agvan Dorjiev. The Buriat had reappeared in the Dalai Lama's camp in early July, soon after the latter's return to Tibet. Dorjiev had denied having authority from the Russian government for his visit, but his arrival was still looked on with suspicion by the British, who felt strongly that Russia, in the interest of friendship, might have done more to keep him from Tibet.[33] Furthermore, while Dorjiev lacked official Russian backing, he did maintain that he was in correspondence with the Russian government and had visited the Russian capital as recently as the preceding spring.[34] Although the Dalai Lama was distinctly cold to the Buriat in their audience and instructed him to leave Tibet without delay, Dorjiev's continuing influence in Tibet seemed to be manifested by his presence on the negotiating team at Urga.[35]

There remains a great deal of question as to the validity of the Tibetan–Mongol treaty, and from the outset it came under international censure. Dorjiev, who planned to continue on to St Petersburg from Urga, was disowned by the Russian government both publicly and personally. Sazonov informed Buchanan that, as a subject of the tsar, Dorjiev could not possibly be considered a diplomatic representative of the Dalai Lama, and proceeded to speak about the Buriat in very uncomplimentary terms. Russia was committed to refraining from making a decision concerning the Tibetan–Mongol agreement without first reaching an understanding with Britain.[36] Similarly, Dorjiev was informed in no uncertain terms by the Russian representative in Urga, Ivan Iakovlevich Korostovets, that the 1907 convention precluded Russia from accepting him as the official representative of the Tibetan government.[37] Dorjiev told Korostovets that the initiative for the agreement came from the Dalai Lama himself, for the purpose of demonstrating Tibetan independence from Chinese sovereignty; the Russian official, however, assured his superiors that the agreement lacked political significance, as neither signatory possessed real legal rights.[38] Since the British were convinced that the Tibetan–Mongol treaty would not make Russia more amenable towards their Tibetan proposals, they were inclined to agree with Korostovets's analysis.[39]

Russia's initial response to the Tibetan–Mongol treaty had been completely within the confines of its obligations under the 1907 agreement. This reaction seemed to be in such stark contrast to the realities of perceived Russian interests that there were those within the Foreign Office who questioned Russia's motives, as Nugent noted: 'The Russian attitude seems to have been scrupulously correct – in fact so correct as to make one wonder whether there is not an ulterior object.'[40] Similarly, the Government of India was convinced that the inspiration for the Tibetan–Mongol agreement had Russian origins, although Nugent did acknowledge that it might have been because of the unauthorized zeal of Korostovets or some other man-on-the-spot, 'who saw in it another possible loophole for Russian or Russian inspired interference in Tibet'.[41]

Despite this distinct departure from the Tibetan status quo that the 1907 agreement was designed to maintain, the Foreign Office was extremely hesitant to request a revision of the convention in response to the altered regional geopolitical status for fear that it would unavoidably lead them to the vexatious Afghan question.[42] The India Office, however, feared that if the British did not seize the initiative and gain a foothold in Mongolia, they would miss a golden opportunity to obtain a bargaining chip that could be used in any future negotiations with Russia.[43] The Foreign Office was not convinced by the India Office's reasoning, as they felt that Mongolia was not the best sphere in which to counter the spread of Russian regional influence.[44] Both the Foreign and India Offices did agree, however, that the time had come to discuss Britain's intentions towards Tibet with the Russian government.

The precise nature of those intentions, however, remained to be determined. Britain's primary concern in formulating its Tibetan policy was to avoid any British military commitment that might lead to an occupation of the country.[45] In a memorandum on Tibet at the end of January, Sir F.A. Hirtzel, the secretary of the India Office Political Department, asked the question, '*How little need we have to do with Tibet?*' Starting from the assumption that Britain had 'no interests, commercial, political or strategical, which need compel us to have relations with Tibet for its own sake within any future that we can wisely attempt to foresee', Hirtzel considered Tibet as important only in its ability to affect the north-east frontier region of Assam, 'in which much capital, European and Indian, has been sunk.' As Hirtzel observed, were there a hostile power entrenched beyond the north-east frontier, the geostrategic landscape would come to resemble that of the far more trouble-some North-West Frontier.[46]

For India, Tibet was crucial in its relation to the buffer state of Nepal, a country over which Britain exercised no formal control save for its 'friendly arrangement with the Prime Minister'. As Hirtzel readily admitted, the continued goodwill of Nepal was vital to Britain for two principal reasons: the reliance of the Indian Army on the Nepalese Gurkha recruits, and the religious and cultural ties between the Nepalese ruling caste and the Hindus in India. In addition, Nepal was a source of concern for reasons well beyond its influence on India; were Nepal to carry out its threat to take advantage of the chaos on its borders and annex the adjoining districts of Tibet, Britain's understanding with Russia – who would never be persuaded that Nepal was acting independently of British influence and policy – might be thrown into complete disarray. Therefore, Nepal was, in Hirtzel's eyes, 'the crux of the Tibetan question'.[47]

Britain's regional standing appeared to be threatened by the actual and implied inroads that Russia was making, as the Government of India lamented in February:

> Little doubt can exist that British prestige in Thibet has been diminished, and that of Russia has been heightened by latter's forward movement in Mongo-lia, combined with British refusal to interfere in affairs of Thibet while the Dalai Lama was residing in India. Prevalent feeling is reflected by a Thibetan proverb now quoted that 'the British are the road-makers of Thibet,' to which interpretation is assigned that the British do the pioneer work in Thibet, but will not long hold the country.[48]

With this in mind, the Government of India increasingly returned to the solution they first had proposed in 1903 – the establishment of a British agent at Lhasa. As Lionel Abrahams of the India Office advised the Foreign Office at the end of March:

> The whole lesson of the last ten years, it may possibly be said, is that Thibet cannot stand alone; that it must be subject to some influence; that we cannot allow that influence to be other than British; and that British influence can only be maintained by a British agency in some form or another at the capi-tal.[49]

The Tibetan national assembly was unaware that Britain was even consid-ering the posting of a representative at Lhasa and were convinced that its reluctance to do so was grounded in the terms of the Anglo-Russian conven-tion, which the Tibetans interpreted as demanding either commensurate participation or exclusion for both Great Powers in Tibet. They therefore urged the Dalai Lama to arrange for the equal establishment of both British and Russian representatives in the capital.[50] Towards this end, the Dalai Lama entrusted Dorjiev with a letter to the tsar in which he asked for the joint protection of both Russia and England as a guarantee for Tibetan independence. He also requested arms and the dispatch of military instructors, and proposed the flotation of a loan of one million roubles to be transacted in Peking by the Russian-Asiatic Bank.[51] In contrast with Izvolskii in 1908, who had considered the Dalai Lama worthy of Russian financial support, Sazonov quickly concluded that 'this petition was without question undeserving of Russia's attention.'[52] Russia's relations with Tibet, based on the affiliation of the Kalmyks and Buriats with the Dalai Lama, were irrevocably limited by the remoteness of the country and by the difficulty of maintaining communications between the Tibetan plateau and its neighbours. Furthermore, Sazonov recognized that the promotion of Tibetan independence might encourage separatist aspirations within Russia's own Buddhist population.

The most significant stumbling block for Russian support of Tibetan independence was, in Sazonov's opinion, the certainty that any increase in Russian influence in the region – even the most limited – would result in a directly corresponding increase of British influence in Tibet. In the continued absence of any serious Russian interests in Tibet, Russia would only be surrendering Tibet for inclusion within Britain's sphere of influence, were any substantive re-evaluation of the 1907 agreement to take place. Although Sazonov recognized that Tibet could be used as a bargaining chip for compensation in another region, he felt strongly that the initiation of any discussions on this subject would have to come from the British so as to maintain Russia's strong negotiating stance according to its adherence to the 1907 agreement.[53]

As Tibet reached the conclusion that help from Russia would not be forthcoming, it turned its attention back to Britain, offering the British exclusive influence at Lhasa in exchange for support against the Chinese. The Tibetan ministers wrote to the British political officer in Sikkim at the end of June in an attempt to assuage British fears of Russian inroads:

> Please do not imagine that we are desirous of dealings with Russia. It is true that we have written to Russia proposing establishment at Lhassa of British and Russian representatives, but we did so in the belief that Great Britain was prevented by the Anglo-Russian Convention from giving us help, except with the co-operation of Russia. If, however, such co-operation is not essential to Great Britain giving us help, we have no desire for relations with Russia.[54]

Britain's immediate plans for securing stability in Tibet did incorporate an increased commitment in the affairs of that country. But the ongoing conflict between, on the one hand, the demand for Britain to control the pacification of the region through talks with the Tibetans and the Chinese and, on the

other, the need to maintain the Anglo-Russian agreement while simultaneously limiting Russia's involvement proved a major challenge to British
diplomacy. Almost from the outset of the crisis, the British had recognized
the necessity, at the very least, of keeping Russia well informed of Britain's
decided course in Tibet, although Russia's inclusion in the diplomatic process
on any level was staunchly opposed by factions within the Foreign and India
Offices. As Nugent had written in November, 'Any encouragement given to
Russian pretensions in Thibet might well lead to a situation even more incon-
venient for the Government of India than a Chinese reoccupation.'[55] The
India Office proposed that any diplomatic solution that was sought with Tibet
and China to restore the status quo be communicated to Russia as a fait
accompli, and one to which Russia, Lord Crewe was convinced, 'could not in
good faith take exception'.[56]

Sir Arthur Nicolson, however, always an advocate for Russia and for strict
adherence to the 1907 agreement that he had midwifed, vehemently questioned Britain's right to pursue a diplomatic solution to the Tibet crisis – and
what appeared to be the corresponding requirement of a British agency at
Lhasa – without Russian involvement:

> The policy ... is clearly not in harmony with our convention with Russia, and
> if we merely _inform_ Russia of what we intend to do, when we have made up
> our minds, she might point out that one party to a convention cannot go be-
> yond and behind its provisions without previous consultation with the other
> party whose concurrence should properly be solicited. Russia might also
> question the fact as stated ... that no extension of British influence will take
> place. The steps that are suggested note an undoubted extension of British
> influence.[57]

By April, the Government of India had come round to Nicolson's view, at
least insofar as they acknowledged the need for frank discussions with the
Russians as to Britain's relations towards Tibet. However, they urged that
Russia be made to understand that any increased commitment that Britain
now had in Tibet was the direct result of the alteration of the status quo
because of Russia's own actions in Mongolia and the related Tibetan–Mongol
treaty.[58] In Britain's eyes, the only solution to the unrest in Tibet that would
both limit British responsibilities and secure Tibet's northern frontiers would
be a tripartite treaty reiterating Tibetan autonomy under the strictly defined
suzerainty of China.[59]

Although the British were united in their opinion that Russia should not
be included in the tripartite talks, at the end of May 1913 Buchanan was
instructed to inform the Russian government that Britain intended to open
negotiations with China and Tibet.[60] Britain promised to keep Russia fully

informed of the course of the negotiations, in the hopes that this would appease any who might consider Britain's actions in opposition to the convention. Russia, in response, noted that it saw no objections to Britain's projected course of action in Tibet: Russian interest in the country was limited to the Anglo-Russian agreement, and went no further.[61] Sazonov did stress, however, Russia's particular satisfaction with Britain's continued recognition of the principle of international non-intervention as the policy best suited for the preservation of Tibetan stability, reminding Britain that the Imperial Government remained committed to the importance of the Anglo-Russian agreement in any consideration of Tibet's future.[62] In this way, Sazonov kept the door open for a possible pursuit of a Tibet-for-Afghanistan trade.

While Russia was insisting upon a strict interpretation of the agreement in Tibet, events in Persia continued to conspire against the well being of the Anglo-Russian relationship in that country. Although the sacking of the shrine at Mashhad had arrested the tide of armed *fedaiyan* uprisings in northern Persia, the country was far from stable. Within Persia, there was a growing fear that Russia meant to annex the north, as a virtual absorption was being gradually accomplished by the steady usurpation of local authority by the Russian consular agents. Russia was well positioned to exert an overwhelming influence over the region through its military presence and the direct interference of its consuls in local administration.[63]

Mornard, the Belgian who had been Russia's candidate to replace Shuster as treasurer-general, complained to both powers that the Russian consuls throughout the north were acting like provincial governors. In Tabriz, Preobrazhenskii controlled the administration through Shuja, and Sepahdar's authority was all but usurped. In Rasht, Nekrasov proclaimed that he, rather than the Persian treasury agent, would collect the taxes from all Russian subjects and protected persons in Gilan province. The result, as more people claimed Russian protection to avoid paying taxes, was a practical cessation of revenues from a province that had been one of the most reliable contributors to the national treasury. In Astrabad, Ivanov had also assumed gubernatorial powers, acquiring land at whim, openly supporting the return of Mohammad Ali, and hindering the collection of taxes.[64]

Although Townley acknowledged that Sazonov's protestations against plans for a Russian annexation of northern Persia were quite possibly sincere, his observations of Russian consular policy demonstrated that the local Russian officials felt otherwise. It seemed clear to the British minister that not just one, but all the Russian consuls felt strongly that the gradual absorption or 'peaceful penetration' of northern Persia, progressing rapidly southwards

to the neutral zone, fell well within the scope of their political programme.[65]
As Townley summarized the circumstances in his 1913 Annual Report for
Persia:

> The situation is perhaps understandable in so far as the provinces immediately
> bordering the Caspian Sea and Russian territory are concerned, because in
> those places the consuls are so surrounded by Russians, who do not know the
> true position of affairs at Teheran, that they are misled. In such places as As-
> trabad the consul is all supreme, sees no one but his own subordinates, or
> officers of the Russian troops across the frontier, with whom he is in constant
> contact, and only knows Teheran as a sort of mythical town that lies some-
> where behind the mountain range at his back, which he has not only never
> crossed, but never intends to cross.[66]

The independent actions of the consuls, as Townley observed, made it seem
as if north-western Persia was already a Russian possession.[67]

Poklevsky-Kozell continued to be exasperated both by his inability to
control the Russian consuls and the apparent lack of support he was receiving
from St Petersburg in his efforts to do so. In October, the Russian minister
had confided to Townley that the junior members of MID considered him a
traitor for his failure to secure the restoration of the ex-shah.[68] Furthermore,
Miller, who was now back at the Central Asia Desk at MID in St Petersburg,
was dictating consular policy directly with little concern for the position of
the Russian minister in Teheran. Even if the consuls were inclined to pursue a
policy of moderation, they were, as the acting British consul in Tabriz, N.
Patrick Cowan, noted, 'caught between two fires'.[69] As vehemently as Poklevsky-Kozell protested against the behaviour of the consuls to his superiors,
they were allowed to carry on with little more than an infrequent reprimand.
For example, Prince Dabizha, who had been directly responsible for the
sacking of the shrine in Mashhad, was returned to his post at the end of 1912
after a long leave of absence.[70] Similarly, Ivanov's blatant opposition to
Mornard's treasury regime in Astrabad was rewarded with a promise of
promotion to Tabriz.[71] All this informed the British that Sazonov was either
unwilling or unable to effect a drastic change in the composition of the Russian consular service in Persia.[72]

The interference of the consuls in the local administration of northern
Persia was coupled with a continuing Russian military presence that accomplished little, in Cowan's opinion, to pacify the country. Cowan felt that
Russian prestige was at such a high level in Azerbaijan that the show of power
stemming from an army of occupation was no longer necessary for the maintenance of order.[73] Overall, northern Persia was far more stable and
prosperous than the British and neutral zones, where, the Foreign Office

admitted, 'the feeling is that the British will do nothing to punish outrages'.[74] Hirtzel summarized the essence of the challenges facing Britain in southern Persia:

> The maintenance of order is essential to the maintenance of British trade, which is essential to the maintenance of British influence. And the maintenance of British influence inland is essential to the maintenance of the British position in the Persian Gulf, which for a century has been the keystone of our policy in the Middle East, as being essential (it has always been assumed) to the safety of India.[75]

The dangerous conditions on the roads in southern Persia and the obstacles these presented for British trade were well publicized throughout Europe, as British officers and commercial officials came under frequent attack.[76] The British consul-general in Mashhad, Percy Sykes – an ardent Russophobe and veteran Anglo-Indian whose removal Sazonov had considered requesting at Balmoral – believed these attacks to be unquestionably instigated by the Russians, and made great efforts to convince London of the validity of his convictions.[77] Townley, in contrast, did his best to counter the reports of unbridled chaos on the roads in southern Persia, claiming that there was not a marked difference between the security on the southern and northern roads; the exception, he admitted, were the two main trade routes for Russian goods (the Anzeli–Qazvin–Teheran and Jolfa–Tabriz–Qazvin–Teheran roads), which were heavily policed by Russian troops and, therefore, considerably safer.[78]

There were several theories being floated within the home and Indian governments as to what would be necessary to restore order in southern Persia and create greater parity with the north. Hirtzel, at the India Office, recognized that the question of southern Persia could not be addressed without a careful analysis of British policy in the entire region. As he saw it, there existed two primary issues for Britain: control of the Persian Gulf and the interests of the Anglo-Persian Oil Company. Primacy in the Gulf – critical for the maintenance of the Indian trade – was inextricably linked to southern Persia, which could only be controlled by subduing the entire coast. The coast, in turn, could only be managed by 'the influence that is supreme in the hinterland'.[79] Although Hirtzel was unconvinced that British influence in the Persian Gulf was not destined for extinction within the next 20 years despite Britain's best efforts to preserve it, more common opinion held that, were Britain to remain committed to the Gulf as a vital political and strategic necessity for India and the Far East, there was no escaping from a continued and possibly increased involvement in southern Persia and the neutral zone.

Therefore, an obvious solution to the unrest in the south would be an increased British military presence in the region to pacify and prevent brigandry and unrest. In the light of the successful pacification of the north that Russia was achieving through military occupation, a similar British response in the south would have appeared to have been required. But the benefits to be achieved by such a military measure were outweighed by the obvious costs even in the eyes of the most ardent advocates of a forward policy in Persia. As O'Connor privately admitted to Curzon, 'Although I, in common with every other European (and many Persians) in this part of the world, would, for personal reasons, be only too delighted to see British troops marching into the country, once in, it is impossible to say when they would be able to go out.' O'Connor's conviction that a permanent British occupation of southern Persia would be a mistake had become the dominant opinion with the Anglo-Indian community, as he explained:

> We should require a considerable force as an effective garrison, which we could ill spare from India: and whatever forces we put into the country, they could never in the last resort defend the new frontier line against Russia if it really came to a question of fighting.[80]

The British government had determined that the pacification of the trade routes in the south was far too vast a task for it to undertake at that time, but it hoped to achieve the desired end through an injection of foreign capital and officials into the south.[81] Although the further deployment of British troops in southern Persia was ruled out, the government did decide to send British officers from the Indian Army to the region to instruct and supervise the indigenous troops;[82] the first man proposed for the position at Shiraz, however, was Major Stokes, and the Russians were vocally opposed.[83]

The most immediately troubling issue that Britain and Russia needed to resolve was that of the trans-Persian railway scheme. At the beginning of 1912, a 'Committee Constituted to Represent British Interests in Relation to the Project for Linking up the Russian and Indian Railway Systems' had been assembled as a counterpart to the Russian and French Société d'Études, which had been formed to promote and study the feasibility of such a railway.[84] The committee urged the British government to recognize that unless Britain were to participate in a plan for a trans-Persian line from the outset, a line that would undoubtedly be unprofitable for Britain would be built by the Russians without them; only through an initial standing as equal partners could British commercial interests be ensured.[85]

Acknowledging the logic of this argument, by March 1912 the British government had agreed in principle with the British group, but only on the condition that the connection of the lines would not only satisfy British military and commercial interests, but would be financially practicable, as well.[86] The Treasury had strongly advised against a government guarantee for the project, especially in consideration of the fact that the Russian government appeared equally reluctant to promise direct state assistance for the undertaking.[87] The challenge, therefore, was to devise an orientation of the line that would be both strategically sound and financially viable. The Board of Trade was extremely sceptical about the profitability of any of the lines that were proposed by the Persian Railways Syndicate.[88] A line from Mohammareh (Khorramshahr) to Khorramabad appeared to be destined to fail from a lack of local traffic or export trade along that route, and a line from Mohammareh to Dezful, although more fiscally promising, remained extremely unlikely.[89] The syndicate, however, disagreed with the 'lukewarm attitude' of the Board of Trade and the Indian government towards their proposed Mohammareh–Khorramabad line, and urged the Foreign Office to reconsider its position.[90]

While the British stance on the railway's alignment was debated between the Persian Railways Syndicate and the Foreign Office, the British and Russian governments reached an agreement that the combined British, Russian and French groups of the Société d'Études should assume the Persian loan. The Russians maintained that the connection of the two issues would facilitate the attainment of concessions and prompt the Persian government to agree to immediate territorial surveys.[91] In July 1912 Russia proposed a further link between Persia's financial dependency and railway concessions, suggesting to Britain that the £25,000 advance then under discussion be linked to a concession for a Jolfa–Tabriz railway; as Acting Foreign Minister Neratov saw it, £25,000 would never be sufficient, and if they were compelled to pay more, they deserved to receive something worthwhile in return.[92] Poklevsky-Kozell felt that this was an entirely feasible proposition from the Persian side, but feared that if Russia were to withhold its support in an attempt to extract its demands, Britain might very well decide to make the advance without Russia.[93]

Such was the situation when Sazonov and Grey reached their Balmoral agreement allowing the Société to proceed with the trans-Persian scheme. The British group of the Société, however, was well on their way towards transcending the boundaries of any involvement to which the British government was prepared to commit. In a letter of 6 November 1912, Sir W. Garstin urged the dispatch of a mission to Teheran from the French, British and Russian groups for the purpose of securing concessions for the main and branch lines and for maritime facilities at the terminal points. The British government, totally unprepared to commit to any alignments or terminal points without further study of the strategic and financial concerns that dominated its policy planning, felt this went far beyond its acknowledged interests at the time and referred the matter to the Committee of Imperial Defence (CID).[94] Shortly thereafter, the Bank of England told the Foreign Office that it would be unable and unwilling to guarantee the Société d'Études's scheme. News of this decision led Russia to believe that Britain's reluctance to proceed with the construction of the railway was purely financial in origin.[95]

The British government's hesitations, however, stemmed from more than just financial concerns. It remained convinced that the scheme would sacrifice the strategic advantages of India's geographical isolation while offering the promise of profit to Britain's commercial rival alone. The Foreign Office, the India Office, and the CID each embarked upon extensive reviews and analyses of the British position on the trans-Persian railway from a strategic and commercial perspective. Drawing on the 1910 conclusions of the Board of Trade to ascertain the economic viability of the scheme, these studies called into question the commercial significance to Britain of a trans-Persian railway. The Board of Trade had anticipated that, while the construction of such a railway might benefit Indian trade to a degree, British trade would not expand, and would most likely see Russian trade in the interior of Persia gain at its expense.[96] From this critique, the India Office and the CID determined in 1913 that a favourable disposition towards the project could not be justified on commercial and economic grounds.

From a defence standpoint, the CID and the India Office remained equally uneasy about India's security after a trans-Persian railway was constructed. As the CID draft report on the question reiterated, the purpose for which the entire defensive system of buffer states had been so carefully constructed and sustained over the previous 50 years was to deny Russia the fundamental advantage of its vast population and close proximity.[97] The hindrance of transport within such a buffer system was the crux of Britain's defence of India against a numerically superior Russian advance.[98] Although it could be argued that the construction of a trans-Persian railway would promote a continued healthy Anglo-Russian relationship and thus alleviate the need to fear a Russian advance on India, no dependence could be placed on eternal friendship between these historically rival powers; the moment a through-rail connection to India was completed and India's isolation was forfeited, the security of the subcontinent would suffer an irreparable blow. As those who opposed the trans-Persian scheme on military grounds urged the government to understand, 'To abandon the great natural advantage for defence purposes which India obtains from the absence of good land communications with the rest of Asia would ... be to make too great a sacrifice in the interest of the continuance of good international relations, and would be a policy of short-sighted opportunism.'[99]

Britain was, nevertheless, committed to the project in direct conflict with its own perceived interests. Starting from the predominant – although not universal – assumption that the construction of a trans-Persian line was inevitable, British participation in the scheme was primarily a defensive measure calculated to minimize the strategic threat and the commercial challenge to Britain's position in the region. If Britain were to remain aloof, Russia would still be free to take advantage of its long-standing railway concession and construct lines through the neutral zone to within 260 miles of Seistan; Britain, in contrast, would have nothing on which to rely but its diplomatic influence in Teheran – necessarily inferior to Russia's since the Persian capital lay within the Russian sphere – to determine the orientation of any constructed lines.[100]

From a commercial standpoint, the ability to influence the alignment and administration of the through-line and its branches was considered to be requisite for the maintenance of existing British and Indian trade and for any hopes of developing British commerce in the southern and neutral spheres. Once these lines were built, as it was assumed they eventually would be, it would be impossible to prevent inequality of treatment for British trade unless Britain were represented on the board of management.[101] Therefore, unless Britain were willing to sacrifice its trade in the Russian sphere and neutral zone, it was crucial that it participate in the scheme from the out-set.[102] As Louis Mallet, assistant under-secretary of state for foreign affairs in the Eastern Department, warned in his memorandum in favour of the trans-Persian scheme: 'Abstention from construction ourselves ... would result in handing over Persia as a free gift to Russia to develop as she liked. In process of time, our trade, which principally enters Persia by the Gulf Ports, would disappear entirely and with it our influence.'[103]

In addition, not all the conclusions drawn about the commercial viability of a trans-Persian scheme had been negative. While the India Office and CID had been dwelling on the pessimistic forecasts of the Board of Trade, the Foreign Office relied upon the conclusions that the director-general of Commercial Intelligence, India, had reached in 1910: a trans-Persian railway would bring inevitable gains for British and Indian trade and a corresponding increase of British influence.[104] Furthermore, British involvement in the construction of a railway from the Gulf to the interior would appease the Manchester commercial interests who had long been lobbying against what they perceived as government indifference to the promotion of the Gulf trade.[105]

The Foreign Office's most pressing concern on the railway issue, however, proved to be neither the defence of India nor the Gulf trade. Rather, the deciding factor in Britain's decision to forge ahead with the trans-Persian railway scheme was its importance for the maintenance of the Anglo-Russian relationship. In his Balmoral memorandum on the railway project, Sazonov had warned that a decision to allow the French and Russian groups to proceed alone might have dire consequences for the health of the relationship, as it might be perceived as an indication of a '*dissentiment profond*' between the two powers.[106] The British government's biggest fear, as manifested in all the Foreign Office and CID memoranda on railway construction in Persia from the beginning of 1913, was that Russia, thwarted by Britain's refusal for railway co-operation, would turn towards Germany for assistance. What would begin as a commercial conglomeration confined to Persian railways might blossom into a political relationship in the Middle East and later even in Europe. The Potsdam Agreement of November 1910 had forced Britain to recognize that German and Russian interests in the Middle East were not irreconcilable, and Germany's steady efforts to insert itself into the Anglo-Russian exclusive Persian playing field were regarded with great apprehension by Britain.[107] At this point, in the spring of 1913, the possibility of a Russian rapprochement with Germany was sufficiently alarming that Britain was willing to sacrifice its more immediate financial and strategic concerns in an effort to offset such a realignment. As Maurice Hankey, secretary to the CID, admitted, 'The whole European situation and balance of power might be affected thereby.'[108]

Although Britain was, at last, openly committed to the construction of a trans-Persian railway by the English, Russian and French groups that comprised the Persian Railway Syndicate and the Société d'Études, the details of financing and alignment remained to be hammered out by the two regional Great Powers. The British government proposed that the English Syndicate finance their construction of the lines within the British and neutral zones by compelling the Persian government to make good its promised mineral concessions in the neutral zone.[109] This 60-year concession for mineral rights in Fars, Kannat and Kermanshah had been procured by the Syndicate in November 1912 in exchange for an offered loan of £100,000, and had been met by fierce Russian opposition.[110] The Russian branch of the Société d'Études demanded that the Russian government defend its own rights to the mineral deposits to which the English Syndicate was laying claim.[111] Furthermore, Sazonov saw the concession as a manifestation of the 'aspiration of the English to seize for themselves the exclusive use of this zone', and ordered Benckendorff to raise the matter with Grey.[112]

Grey's attention, however, was more focused on the alignment and terminus questions than on defending the Syndicate's rights to the concessions. The Russian group of the Société had proposed an alignment of Astara–Rasht–Teheran–Yezd–Kerman–Chahbar.[113] In contrast, the British Inter-Departmental Committee that had been convened to discuss the proposed trans-Persian railway was insistent that Bander-e 'Abbas was the 'least objectionable' port for the terminus, since they felt that only such a line, whose further connection with a line from Karachi would stretch across 800 miles of difficult country, would be defensible by British naval power in the Gulf. Access to the railway for a naval bombardment was considered to be a crucial security imperative, as the commander-in-chief of India predicted that the Indian Army would not be able to spare sufficient troops to participate in a defence of the line were forces required to resist a Russian advance in Afghanistan. The Committee proposed that the line follow the Astara–Rasht–Teheran–Esfahan–Shiraz–Bander-e 'Abbas route, and strongly advocated that the break of gauge be as far from India as possible or, at the very least, no nearer than the middle of the neutral zone.[114]

Sazonov adamantly objected to the majority of the recommendations of the Inter-Departmental Committee. Starting from his position that Bander-e 'Abbas was completely unacceptable as the terminus, since it could not be converted into a suitable port without enormous expense, Sazonov criticized the British proposals for an alignment from Bander-e 'Abbas through Esfahan and Shiraz. He feared that such an alignment would leave the railway open to German interference; were the Germans to construct a railway from Khanaqin to Esfahan, the trans-Persian line would be linked with the Baghdad Railway, and trade would most likely favour that route rather than the Russian. Sazonov took further exception to the circuitous nature of such a route, claiming that it would: (1) lengthen the line by approximately 350 kilometres; (2) increase the cost by approximately 50 million roubles; (3) decrease the traffic in European passengers; and (4) decrease the importance of the line for Persia. The Russian foreign minister reminded Buchanan that this would contradict the intended nature of the project as a direct transit railway through Persia to India, and concluded that the entire nature of the enterprise was in danger of falling to pieces if the British route were followed. Nevertheless the British continued to favour this route for commercial as well as strategic reasons, and Buchanan stressed that the longer length would be counterbalanced by the profitable trading centres through which it would pass.[115]

Above all, the Russians protested their utter befuddlement at Britain's strategic objections to the trans-Persian scheme. Vladimir Nikolaevich Kokovtsov, the chairman of the Council of Ministers, in a conversation with

Buchanan shortly before the British ambassador departed on a trip back to England, expressed his confusion, confessing that 'he could not imagine how anybody in their senses could attribute to Russia aggressive designs against India.' In response to Buchanan's assurances that Britain's strategic planners were simply guarding against unforeseeable circumstances that might develop 15 or 20 years hence, Kokovtsov declared that there was no possible situation in which Russia would benefit from an advance on India:

> Whatever changes might take place it would never be to Russia's interest to embark on such a very hazardous enterprise as an attack on India. She had to be on her guard on her western frontier both against Austria and Germany; she had to keep an eye on Turkey, and she had to safeguard her interests against China. Speaking entirely academically and unofficially, he thought that if Russia in twenty years' time adopted a forward policy it would not be in the direction of India but much further east.[116]

Despite Kokovtsov's assurances, the India Office and the Government of India continued to be suspicious of Russia's designs on India and were, therefore, extremely wary of the trans-Persian railway scheme. As Crewe had reminded the Foreign Office at the beginning of April, 'In existing political conditions – or, indeed, in any that he is able to forecast – the establishment of [a] through railway connection between Europe and India involves dangers to the latter, which must profoundly affect the basis upon which the military requirements of Great Britain no less than of India are at present calculated.'[117] Hirtzel was also vehement in his criticism of what he considered to be Russian bad faith and manipulation:

> I cannot help feeling that Russia is still relentlessly pursuing under cover of the convention the same ends that she was pursuing before it – i.e. the development of a fresh line of advance on the key of our position – Seistan (via Kerman) – and the acquisition of a port on the open sea. ... If we accept the Kerman alignment we admit Russia to Seistan, and it seems to me that in pressing for it Russia is trying to get back what she lost by the convention.[118]

The Inter-Departmental Committee, however, felt that Hirtzel was being alarmist and paranoid. At the end of May they recommended that Britain could concede the alignment via Yezd to Kerman without any real risks to British interests.[119]

However, Hirtzel and the Government of India refused to yield. They felt that Britain was preparing to give in to Russia's demands far too soon: 'We seem rather to be in the position of knocking down the walls of our own Jericho the very moment the Russian trumpet sounds.' Hirtzel, refusing to sign the draft report of the committee that found in favour of the Yezd–Kerman alignment, insisted that Britain was conceding far more than it could an alignment, insisted that Britain was conceding far more than it could ever hope to receive in return from Russia:

> Co-operation implies a certain community of interests, and if two parties are to co-operate in the ordinary affairs of life each must bring something to the common stock, or each must be satisfied that he will gain something by it. That, however, is very far from being the position in which we find ourselves as regards this scheme. We are simply asked to 'stand and deliver' – not our money only, but also (if the extreme military view is sound) our lives.[120]

In a similar vein, a memorandum by the chief of the Indian general staff, Lieutenant-General Percy Lake, reiterated the ongoing strategic threat of any projected Central Asian railways in the direction of Seistan. Lake argued that diplomatic understandings come and go, but 'the building of railways has an effect far beyond the present generation.' Lake warned that if the railway were constructed to Kerman, 100,000 more men would be needed to defend the line – men who would have to be drawn from Britain and the rest of the Empire, as the Indian Army would already be stretched to the limit; further-more, this number was most likely an underestimation, if the hostile attitudes of Afghanistan and the frontier tribes were taken into account. The Indian general staff, in conclusion, felt that Britain should refuse to agree to the Kerman line. Lake ventured that Russia would not be able to harm Britain without construction of railways in the British sphere – which it could not undertake without British consent – and without a direct challenge to Great Britain. In Lake's worst-case scenario, were Britain to take up such a chal-lenge, 'Russia would find herself at war with us with a railhead several hundred miles from our frontier, and possibly in difficult and barren coun-try.'[121] Therefore, in the opinion of the Indian general staff, the risks inherent in a refusal of the Kerman line were well worth taking.

Buchanan, who was then in London, and O'Beirne, the chargé d'affaires in St Petersburg, were becoming steadily exasperated by the obstinacy of the India lobby. Buchanan stressed the vital importance of the Anglo-Russian understanding and reminded the government that the supporters of the railway were among Russia's most ardent Anglophiles. As the ambassador asserted, 'It would be ridiculous to impute to them the Machiavellian design of forging a weapon for a Russian attack on India. They hope, on the con-trary, that the projected railway will serve to draw the two countries still closer together, while they believe that it will promote Russian interests by acting as a counterpoise to the Baghdad Railway.'[122] O'Beirne assured Grey that the Russian group 'were certainly more concerned with the commercial aspects of the matter than with any political considerations, and it is exceed-ingly difficult to imagine that these gentlemen ... took their instruction from the Russian General Staff.'[123]

By November 1913, the alignment question had been tabled, as Britain and Russia had agreed to a 'Russo-British technical commission' that would examine the two possible routes once the railway had reached the Russian frontier of the neutral sphere. However, as the War Office noted, this ostensible compromise was, in reality, a capitulation to Russian demands: 'It would appear self-evident that the Russians with a free hand as far as Yezd in their own sphere, will so align and construct the railway within that sphere as to leave no room for discussion as to the route to be followed southwards.'[124] Therefore, as 1914 began, the Kerman versus Shiraz debate was, essentially, moot. The terminal point, however, remained under contention, and Sazonov warned Buchanan that the trans-Persian scheme might break down were Britain to continue to refuse to consider any point further east than Bander-e 'Abbas.[125]

The question of Bander-e 'Abbas versus Chahbar was certainly not the only issue straining the Anglo-Russian relationship in Persia. At the end of September, Townley dispatched a lengthy lament to Grey in which he complained of the often diametrically opposed British and Russian interests in Persia:

> It is easy for us to be loyal to the Anglo-Russian 'entente' in Persia; it is as obviously against our interests to encroach on Persia as it is in the interests of Russia to do so. Russia may quite genuinely have no intention of infringing either the letter or the spirit of the 'entente', but her hand is inevitably forced by circumstances; she is a huge overwhelming power towering over the puny, effete nation on her border, and it is not in the nature of the Russian or probably of any other nationality to resist the temptation to make that power felt.[126]

Townley did not wish to lodge personal complaints against either Poklevsky-Kozell or the Russian chargé d'affaires, E.V. Sablin, who were, in his opinion, 'both charming men with whom it has been a pleasure to work'. However, he bitterly observed that Russian policy was systematically oriented towards preventing the stabilization of the Persian situation. Admitting that the opposition to Mornard's financial administration was far too methodical and prevalent to be the work of individual consuls as they had previously been led – and had chosen – to believe, Townley placed the responsibility for Persia's ongoing chaos firmly on the shoulders of the Russian government itself. He outlined the official obstructionist tactics that were running rampant at even the highest levels:

> Unless Mornard is a still greater liar than I believe him to be, there can be no
> doubt that Poklevsky gave him pretty clearly to understand that he would
> continue to enjoy the good-will and support of Russia so long as he did not
> try too hard to create a serious financial administration such as might really
> improve the status of Persia. Sablin has spoken in somewhat similar language
> to the Belgian Minister, and the financial agents in Azerbaidjan have been told
> plainly that they will meet with no Russian opposition so long as they only
> make a pretence of doing their duty!

In the face of Russian opposition at every turn, Townley felt there was little
he could do to help steer Persia on the road to recovery. As he resignedly
told Grey, 'I have daily found myself in double-harness with a jibber, whose
natural inclination was to run down hill, whilst I was laboriously striving to
drag him and the rickety Persian coach up hill.'[127]

The aggressive behaviour of the Russian consuls in northern Persia had
continued to chip away at the strength and stability of the Persian government. The spring of 1913 had brought three principal actions that were seen
by the Persian cabinet to be destructive to its position. In Astrabad, the
Russian consul, Ivanov, had refused to receive the new governor, even
though the latter's appointment had been approved by the Russian legation in
Teheran. The Russian government supported Ivanov, saying that Sablin
should have consulted the consul before he had agreed to the appointment. In
Tabriz, Shuja ud-Dowleh, the Russian protégé, told the Persian foreign
minister that he was no longer useful, and should step down. And in Kuchan,
the governor was deposed by Cossacks sent from Mashhad under orders from
Prince Dabizha, the Russian consul-general.[128] Although Dabizha was subsequently given 'a good head-washing' by Sazonov, the damage that these
incidents had inflicted on the Persian government's already tenuous position
appeared irreparable.[129] Buchanan therefore continued to remind Sazonov of
the great difficulties the actions of the Russian consuls were presenting to the
British government. As the British ambassador remonstrated, 'The spirit by
which [the] consuls were animated was illustrated by [a] remark made by one
of them that his last post was dull, as it was impossible to create incidents
there.'[130]

At this point, Buchanan and Townley were still accepting the Russian
government's pledges that the obstructionist policies of its consuls in the
north were the independent actions of rogue men-on-the-spot who were
unwilling to act within the confines of the policies dictated by the legation in
Teheran and the government in St Petersburg. By the end of the summer,
Britain's patience had run out. It had become impossible to ignore the unity
of action and policy that was being demonstrated in the Russian sphere. As
Smart, the acting British consul in Tabriz, explained, not one of the men who

comprised the Russian consular corps in Persia was sufficiently outstanding to be capable of directing such a systematic absorption of northern Persia in defiance of Russian governmental opposition:

> Preobrazhenskii here is amiable, weak, unintelligent. Vidensky, who runs the Consulate General, is an excellent machine, but, though unscrupulous and energetic, he is too insignificant socially and by his official rank to exercise a wide influence or to initiate comprehensive schemes. The Russian consul at Urni, who was formerly an unfailing source of amusement to Miller and myself at Tabriz is an absolute cretin. Iyas at Saoujboulak is a Finn and very anti-Russian. Tcherkof at Khoi appears to be the only personality of the lot, but he has only recently come to Persia and the sphere of his influence is very limited. The Consul at Ardebil, formerly second dragoman at Constantinople, drinks like a fish, but his only other claim to distinction is a quarrel with M. Tcharukof at Constantinople, which resulted in his temporary retirement from the consular service.[131]

Therefore, in Smart's opinion, which was later upheld by Townley, the steady Russification that was under way in northern Persia must be centrally directed.

The spectre of Russian absorption of northern Persia being spread by the Russian consular policies was bolstered by the statements of the government in St Petersburg. In mid-May, Sazonov had declared to the British ambassador that 'Russia desired more elbow-room and freedom of action in northern Persia'. As Buchanan recounted their conversation: '[Russia] had thousands of subjects or protected subjects, the trade was entirely in her hands, and by its geographical position Northern Persia naturally gravitated towards Russia.'[132] Although members of the Foreign Office took exception to Sazonov's assertion that the trade in northern Persia was 'entirely in Russian hands', Russia's virtual absorption of the five northern provinces, in particular Azerbaijan, was well documented by the British officials on the spot.[133] Smart outlined the extent of Russian influence in the region:

> We could not keep the Russians out of Azerbaidjan. They have killed or put to flight the active spirits among their Persian opponents. They have replaced the anti-Russian local authorities by Russian puppets. The Azerbaidjanis generally have lost the hope they had in England; they regard the Russian domination as accomplished, irretrievable. The result is general surrender.[134]

Although Sazonov repeatedly assured Buchanan that Russia had no intention of annexing any portion of Persia, he desired a much freer hand in the Russian zone without British interference. In exchange, he offered Britain a similar level of independent action in its own sphere.[135] In addition, Sazonov began to make noises about modifying the Anglo-Russian relationship con-

cerning the neutral zone. As he told Buchanan, the creation of such a large
neutral zone had been a mistake born out of the existing mutual suspicions at
the time the agreement was reached. In light of the current good relationship
between the two nations, he felt that the mistake should be rectified by a
redistribution of the neutral zone.[136] Although Sazonov was prepared to see
Britain considerably extend its admittedly smaller sphere of influence, his
greatest concern was to protect the neutral zone from a de facto incorpora-
tion into the British sphere through a British railway monopoly in the region
and the extension of British trading influence.[137]

British reaction to the Russian concept of 'elbow-room' was lukewarm at
best. Principally, greater Russian autonomy in the north with less inquisitorial
interference from Britain was immediately recognized as impractical: so long
as the capital by which the southern sphere was also governed remained well
within the Russian zone, it was impossible for Britain to ignore Teheran.[138]
Similarly, Townley felt that 'elbow-room' was in direct opposition to the
'letter and spirit' of the 1907 agreement, as it would violate the two-party
pledge 'to maintain the integrity and independence of Persia'.[139] Furthermore, a division of the neutral zone was opposed on several grounds.
Nicolson pointed out that the British sphere was already as large as the Government of India – who were opposed to any extension of their regional
responsibilities – had felt was necessary for the defence of British interests.[140]
Buchanan thought that Grey would be unwilling officially to divide the neutral zone, as such an action would appear to be the first step towards partition
and would undoubtedly weaken the Persian government's position.[141]

Townley felt that this latest diplomatic card that Russia was playing was
simply one more step towards the complete absorption of the north by
Russia, a process that Sablin had described as 'peaceful penetration under
arms'.[142] As Consul Smart had warned, unless Britain were to undertake
active measures to thwart Russian advances, such as the expansion of the
financial administration and steps to secure Azerbaijani representation in the
Majles, there would be nothing to prevent Russian absorption up to Kasr-i-
Shirin, the beginning of the neutral sphere: 'Even with the best will in the
world it is very difficult for a military force in a tribal country not to be
dragged into advances, extensions of occupation, etc. And when there is no
overwhelming distaste for such extensions, it requires very great optimism to
hope that they will not take place.'[143]

Furthermore, Townley was concerned that progressive Russian penetration would not terminate at the northern boundaries of the neutral zone, but
would continue on to include a gradual absorption of the neutral zone itself:

Russia's word is law in Isfahan, and ... unless we speedily do something to prove to the Bakhtiaris and the rest of Persia that we are faithful to our ancient friendship for the tribesmen, that we can furnish the backbone of a strong natural barrier between North Persia and that part of the country in which British interests are still predominant, we shall find the wedge of Russian influence driven down to the Karun by peaceful penetration under arms.[144]

In light of increasing Russian influence, a consideration of a revision of the neutral zone's status along the lines that Sazonov had proposed appeared to be worthwhile. Both Russia and Britain were looking to prevent the other from gaining influence and authority in the region while maintaining stability and order within Persia, and the status quo was mutually acknowledged as having only partially achieved these aims.[145] As Sir Eyre Crowe recognized at the end of November 1913, shortly after he added the Eastern Department to his portfolio upon the appointment of Louis Mallet to Constantinople, Britain was entirely incapable of preventing Russian encroachments in Persia without derailing British world strategy and endangering Indian security. Therefore, it was in Britain's best interests to do everything possible to control the pace and procedure of this Russian forward movement, in order to allow Britain time to consolidate domestic Persian opposition and to strengthen its own position in southern Persia. Only in this manner could Britain hope to defend against the 'inevitable day' when the British and Russian frontiers would become coterminous.[146]

Russia's desires for a re-evaluation of the 1907 agreement were not based solely on its insistence on the need to redraw the boundaries in Persia. Growing frustrations over the ineffectiveness of the agreement concerning Afghanistan continued to be a source of discord between the two Great Powers. The Russians were well aware of the difficulty Britain was facing in attempting to tame its so-called dependent, and had for some time been contemplating the establishment of direct relations with the emir in response to the practical failure of the agreement in Afghanistan.[147] Vasilii Oskarovich Klemm, the managing director of the Central Asian Section at MID, submitted a detailed analysis of the Afghan question in which he asserted that the 1907 agreement had created more problems for Britain in Afghanistan than it had solved:

Having definitely convinced the Emir of the absence of any aggressive intentions on our part against his khanate, this document has completely untied his arms in relation to the English. If before he barely submitted to the British Government, then now he has completely ceased, apparently, to consider it.

... Therefore, it would seem in the interests of the British Government to make the Emir understand, that the danger from the north could be renewed if he doesn't alter the manner of his actions.[148]

Klemm felt that the questions plaguing Russo-Afghan relations – most notably the irrigation issue – were too important to be treated with indifference. If, he asserted, the British were unable to obtain succour for Russia's complaints through their established influence on the emir, the only course left open to Russia would be to mount armed expeditions to the upper Murghab and Tedjen that would 'demolish every dam, fill up excessive irrigation canals and, at the risk of further repression, conclude with the local authorities a treaty concerning future crop development within the Afghan boundaries and the establishment of mandatory passage of standard amounts of water to the Transcaspian provinces.'[149]

Following upon this rather aggressive outline of Russian future action in defence of their perceived irrigation rights, Klemm did acknowledge that such an action would be disastrous for the agreement with England to which Russian policy was firmly committed and would, therefore, be 'pregnant with consequences'. In addition, Russia's desire to avoid a military expedition against Afghanistan was not based solely on its concerns for the Anglo-Russian relationship. Within the context of concern over the growing tide of pan-Islamism in Central Asia, a movement against a Muslim country was seen as guaranteed to inflame existing anti-Russian sentiments within the Russian provinces of Bukhara, Semirechensk and Fergana, and in northern Persia.[150] Therefore, Klemm concluded that Russia's aim in Afghanistan should be to promote British influence in the khanate as a means to achieve its goals, rather than pursuing an independent policy designed to bring the emir to submission.

Although Klemm had advised deference to Britain's established course of relations with the emir, Sazonov subsequently proposed to Buchanan that a warning from Russia to the local authorities might carry greater weight than the attempts of the distant British to accomplish their aims.[151] Grey feared, in response, that the Russian government would soon take matters into its own hands and settle the question 'in the manner which may suit them best'.[152] Therefore, Grey and Crewe agreed that Britain must not only attempt to solve the irrigation question, but must finally demand formal recognition of the agreement from the emir, without which the Afghan question could only lead to greater Anglo-Russian discord in the future.[153]

When Habibullah Khan at last responded to Britain's enquiries concerning the irrigation issue, however, his response did not allow Britain to demonstrate its value as an intermediary. The emir completely discounted Russia's claims of increased water use and restated Afghan rights to the exploitation of the rivers within their territory as they saw fit. Furthermore, he insisted that no large canals that might have depleted the water supply to Russia had been constructed.[154] He was supported in his position that Russia's claims were unfounded by the Government of India, who felt that Russia was pressing the issue merely as a means to effect a general change in Afghanistan's status:

> Russia has always resented – and not unnaturally – the isolation of Afghanistan – an isolation which it has been our declared policy to foster. Not only is this isolation irksome in a neighbouring State, but it effectually closes the door to the extension of political influence. Realising as they must how dear this isolation is to Afghanistan, the Russians cannot fail to know that by pressing us to break it down they will be straining our friendly relations with the Ameer.[155]

The Government of India therefore urged that Britain exercise the utmost caution in adopting a course of action that might not only damage Britain's relations with Afghanistan, but might alter the entire status quo in Central Asia in the process.

Although Afghanistan was intent upon preventing all intercourse between the kingdom and its neighbours, the established links between its economy and that of Russia were unavoidable. Not only were trade relations between the two countries continually developing on a regional level, economic refugees steadily poured into Transcaspia and Bukhara from the south.[156] Despite the emir's refusal to recognize the 1907 agreement with its corresponding guarantee for Russian trade on an equal footing with that of Indian and British, Russo-Afghan trade had been relatively healthy since the agreement. Russia, however, was convinced that the continued isolation of Afghanistan provided a significant hindrance to the expansion of trade and was determined to offset the deterrence through a policy designed to promote the development of reciprocal trading relations.

Towards this purpose, in January 1913 an interdepartmental commission was convened to consider the means available for the promotion of Russo-Afghan trade. Consisting of representatives from all the relevant ministries in conjunction with the principal leaders of Russia's commercial and industrial communities, the commission was firmly committed to achieving an increase in general trade returns between the two countries. Miller, who was representing the Ministry of Foreign Affairs, had pointed out that the growth of Russo-Afghan trade would inevitably lead to an increase in Russian regional influence; therefore, as the representative from the Ministry of Trade and Industry agreed, even if the emir never acknowledged the 1907 agreement, Russia would be well positioned to push at a later date for a rationalization of the currently unbalanced customs regime that affected trade with Afghanistan.[157] Despite the gross imbalance between Russian and Afghan customs receipts, the committee recommended the maintenance of minimal taxation on Afghan imports in order to encourage Russian exports until such a time when Afghan dependence on Russian goods would enable Russia to demand a more equitable balance of trade.[158]

The conference concentrated on two primary paths to improve the state of Russo-Afghan trade: (1) the normalization of relations with Afghanistan, which was an ongoing and expected theme; and (2) the improvement of the conveyance of Russian goods to Afghanistan. The traditional route for Russian goods bound for Afghanistan was by caravan through Bukhara. Not only was this means of transport slow and subject to brigands' attacks, but the Bukharan bureaucracy far from encouraged the passage of trade through its territory. The Treaty of Friendship of 1873 between Russia and Bukhara had guaranteed Russian merchants duty-free transit through Bukhara. But Russian goods remained subject to customs tax thanks to the ambiguous wording of one of the treaty's clauses, allowing Russian goods transported by either Bukharan or Afghan merchants to be taxable. Since Russian merchants were forbidden to enter Afghanistan, all Russian goods were by necessity transported by Afghan or Bukharan merchants and were, consequently, at the mercy of the Bukharan customs officials.[159] In response to the problems that Bukharan policies presented for Russian trade, the Interdepartmental Commission proposed the renegotiation of the treaty governing trade between Russia and Bukhara, the establishment of an agent of the Ministry of Trade and Industry in Bukhara to protect Russian commercial interests, and the construction of a railway in Bukhara.[160]

While Russia continued to insist that its trading conditions with Afghanistan were prohibitive and detrimental, Britain had concluded from an article in the *Turkestanskye Vedomosti* in November 1912 that Russia's trade with Afghanistan was flourishing, especially in comparison with the growth rates of Anglo-Afghan trade. Indeed, the volume of Russian imports and exports with Afghanistan were increasing considerably, apparently at British India's expense.[161] At the end of July 1913, Grey reminded Benckendorff that the emir was no more inclined to favour Anglo-Afghan trade than he was to promote Russo-Afghan commercial interaction. Although Grey acknowledged that both countries faced great challenges in their attempts to promote trade with Afghanistan, the Russian ambassador was informed that there was little that Britain could do without directly interfering in internal Afghan affairs to alter the commercial climate.[162]

Nevertheless, Habibullah Khan's continuing antipathy towards interaction with his neighbours was even more vexing to the Russians than it was to his putative British protectors. Within St Petersburg circles, there were calls for the taking of repressive measures against the stubborn and aloof country to the south. The government, however, insisted that countermeasures such as the closure of the Russo-Afghan frontier to Afghan subjects and goods would only further hinder the development of trade and would, at the same time, play into the hands of the isolationist Afghan government.[163] Therefore it remained committed to the promotion of trade, even if the realities of the situation ensured a temporary imbalance. Similarly, while Afghan isolationism continued to create considerable discomfort for Russia along their common border, the actual interaction between Afghan and Russian border officials rendered the mandated recourse to British intervention necessary only in extreme circumstances. Thus, the Russian government was willing, for the sake of its relationship with Britain and in opposition to vocal elements of Russian public opinion, to tolerate a little longer the continued official isolation of Afghanistan.[164]

Russia's willingness to endure what it considered to be the unnatural state of its relations with Afghanistan was in part fostered by a sense that Britain's growing embroilment in Tibet would soon preclude the need to resort to direct Russian action. Throughout MID, Central Asian experts were pushing Russia to exploit the situation in Tibet to achieve compensation along the Afghan border. As Consul-General Nabokov had advised from Calcutta early in 1913, 'If we do not take advantage of this opportunity to look again at Afghanistan and Tibet, we will lose Tibet and gain nothing from England in Afghanistan.'[165] In his opinion, Britain's ongoing commitment to the 1907 agreement would render them open to such an exchange.

Nabokov, however, had misread the situation; although both the home and Indian governments were, to varying degrees, committed to the Anglo-Russian relationship in Central Asia, Britain was not prepared to sacrifice its exclusive rights in Afghanistan as a quid pro quo for a freer hand in Tibet.[166] The omnipresent obligations of their commitment to Russia and the potential cost of altering the status quo led the British to limit any intentions of increased involvement in Tibet. Britain was further constrained in its ability to influence the outcome of events in Tibet by the impossibility of a dispatch of British troops to Lhasa in support of China's exclusion. Therefore, as a member of the British negotiating team at Simla informed the cabinet in October, a British forward policy in Tibet was both impracticable and inconceivable.[167] However, the Foreign Office acknowledged that the result of the tripartite discussions that were under way in Simla would, undoubtedly, be a partial improvement in Britain's position in Tibet, for which Russia would consider itself entitled to compensation.[168] That this compensation might be found in Afghanistan was entirely unacceptable to Britain.[169]

Thus, as 1913 drew to a close, the future of the Anglo-Russian agreement in Central Asia remained extremely nebulous. In Persia, division of the neutral zone and a push for a more formal absorption of the northern sphere by Russia seemed increasingly likely. In Afghanistan, the emir's unwillingness to recognize the convention, Britain's inability to influence its nominal vassal, and the growing exigencies of Russo-Afghan border relations and trading interests continued to exert pressures upon the Anglo-Russian regional relationship. In Tibet, the necessities of British involvement in the Tibetan–Chinese conflict persisted in upsetting the delicate balance of power and influence that had been established by the 1907 agreement. Therefore, in the eyes of both the Russian and British governments, the tide of Anglo-Russian relations in Central Asia was increasingly turning towards a revision of the agreement.

CHAPTER 8

The Death of the Anglo-Russian Agreement: 1914

The final months of 1913 had presented new challenges to the Anglo-Russian accord in Central Asia; the changing circumstances in Persia, Afghanistan and Tibet had all demanded the careful consideration of policy makers in London and St Petersburg as they pondered the future of their relationship in Asia. Yet the disagreements over affairs in Persia and the possibilities of a Tibet-for-Afghanistan quid pro quo were by no means the only concerns that the two powers faced. In late 1913, the Anglo-Russian-French entente had been seriously strained by the crisis that had followed the November appointment of the German General Liman von Sanders to a joint commission as commander of both the German military mission in Turkey and the First Ottoman Army Corps in Constantinople.

The Russians were outraged by what they saw as a blatant grab for power and prestige by Germany in what Russia considered to be its own backyard; were a German to command at Constantinople, control of the Straits would ostensibly pass into German hands.[1] Sazonov, therefore, quickly called upon Russia's entente partners to support it in its opposition to the appointment. Whereas the French immediately offered moral support to their Russian allies, this request put the British in a rather awkward position, as one of their own naval officers was in command of the Turkish fleet. They hesitated to back the Russian position, and the French were unwilling and unable to promise more than their word of support without British participation in a united front. Eventually, Britain was persuaded to help convince the Germans of the need for compromise. The Germans yielded at Britain's behest and, at the end of January, Liman von Sanders was promoted to the rank of field-marshal of the Turkish Army, a position that demanded a posting at Adrianople rather than Constantinople. The Russians were satisfied with this altered circumstance, and a more serious crisis was averted.

Even though Britain had ultimately come to Russia's aid, the Liman von Sanders affair had provided, in Sazonov's opinion, 'a test of the real value of the Triple Entente' – a test that the entente had barely passed.[2] The absence of immediate British support forced Russia to recognize the actual weakness of a Franco-Russian combination when it lacked the added weight of the third partner. Sazonov became committed to the strengthening of a formal relationship with Great Britain, and began to seek an Anglo-Russian naval agreement.[3]

Yet, despite the Russian foreign minister's stated desires for a closer relationship with Great Britain and the frequent intimations from Tsar Nicholas II of his hopes for a closer union between the two powers, the path to a greater Anglo-Russian understanding was far from clear.[4] Personnel changes both at the highest levels of the Russian government and within its diplomatic corps seemed to point towards a possible departure from the Russian drift towards a Franco-Russo-British alliance. Kokovtsov's replacement in late January 1914 by Petr Levovich Bark as minister of finance and by the old standby, Ivan Logginovich Goremykin, back for his second term as titular head of the Council of Ministers, was seen by the pro-German factions within Russia as the reassertion of autocratic conservatism and an opportunity to move Russia closer to Germany.[5] Public opinion expected Sazonov soon to follow Kokovtsov into early retirement, and many looked for his replacement to be far more inclined towards a rapprochement with Germany.[6]

Furthermore, in Teheran, Poklevsky-Kozell, who had long been accused of neglecting Russian interests and allowing the growth of British influence in Persia, was replaced by Ivan Iakovlevich Korostovets, fresh from his triumphant handling of the Russo-Mongol negotiations in Urga and suggesting a more concerted forward policy in Russo-Persian relations. In contrast to the good working relationship that had existed between the Russian and British legations since Hartwig's departure in 1908, Townley soon found Korostovets's manner and methods impossible; as he confidentially complained to Grey in April: 'Ways of [the] Russian Minister are so peculiar that nobody knows whether or not to place any confidence in what he says. He constantly contradicts himself, and rarely says the same thing to two different people.'[7]

However, the most immediate challenge to the formal extension of the Anglo-Russian relationship came from the existing uncertainty that had long dominated intercourse between the two Great Powers; the irreconcilable differences between Russian and British policies and aims in Central Asia that had plagued their association with increasing frequency throughout the preceding years threatened to undermine any efforts towards reaching a more binding accord. Troubles along the Russo-Afghan border were stretching the patience of the Russian government and placing increasing strain on its reliance upon British mediation. Furthermore, the wave of pan-Islamism that was spreading throughout the region was threatening the stability of all the regional borders, challenging the security of the positions of the two powers not only with their Persian and Afghan neighbours, but within their own Muslim-populated territories as well. In Tibet, British attempts to limit their involvement in the Sino-Tibetan conflict collided with their determination to safeguard their own regional interests and retain the last remnants of Britain's favoured position, which had survived from the Younghusband expedition through the 1907 declaration of disinterest. Russian recognition of the opportunity that these conflicting British interests provided pushed them to begin looking for compensation for Britain's altered status in Tibet in regions wherein lay the very foundations of the 1907 agreement.

The distant possibility of an increased Russian presence in Afghanistan resulting from an alteration of the 1907 agreement was echoed in the very real changes being manifested in Persia. More and more, members of both governments were discussing the obvious failings of the agreement in Persia and the need to reformulate its terms. During the previous year, Townley had begun to push for a partition and absorption of the neutral zone into the respective spheres of the two powers as a counterbalance to the steady southward encroachment of Russian influence and primacy in the neutral zone. Furthermore, he recommended the division of the country into two distinct administrations: Mohammad Ali under Russian supervision in the north, and an acceptable Persian prince under direct British supervision in the south. As Townley advised Grey, such a division was the only way to safeguard British interests and prevent future Anglo-Russian discord in Persia.[8]

In 1913 Townley's government was not at all disposed to agree with his radical plan for the solution of the Persian problem. Grey quickly pointed out to his minister in Teheran the numerous difficulties that a division of Persia would foster: it would look like the very partition that Britain was pledged to prevent; there would be protests from Europe; Britain's regional responsibilities would increase; and the Russian and British spheres would become coterminous, vastly expanding Britain's security concerns.[9] Townley immediately clarified that he was only proposing this change in the status quo in the case of a successful return of Mohammad Ali, but he urged his government once again to consider the advantages of stemming the tide of Russia's trade and influence in the neutral zone before Russian pretensions to a larger share of a divided zone expanded as well.[10] Sir Louis Mallet, shortly before his appointment to Constantinople, harshly condemned Townley's proposal as a demonstration of the minister's complete misunderstanding of the object of the Anglo-Russian agreement. A proposal to partition Persia was, in Mallet's opinion, 'all very impractical'.[11]

By early 1914, however, many within the British government had shifted their orientation, and a call was being made for active measures to safeguard the British position. In mid-January, Sir Eyre Crowe, from his authoritative position as head of both the Western and Eastern Departments of the Foreign Office, bemoaned the disturbing state of Britain's waning authority in Persia:

> The result of our whole policy in Persia is to give Russia power to get every-
> thing done she wants and place anyone relying on England in a state of
> helplessness if not oppression. So long as we are not prepared ever to assert
> ourselves, this will not merely continue but be accentuated. I feel confident
> that without a show of force of some sort we cannot hope to recover any po-
> sition in Persia and, as we have no force, we must put up with the gradual
> closing of the whole of Persia to us.[12]

Unsurprisingly, Grey and the Russophilic Nicolson did not at that time, as the latter noted, 'take quite as doleful a view' of the Persian situation, and were slower to come around to Townley's concerned stance.[13] Therefore, when Korostovets, newly installed in Teheran, met with Townley for the first time on 7 February 1914 and confided his belief that the neutral zone was a failure that only served as a tremendous source of potential Anglo-Russian friction, Townley – who had only a few months earlier informally sounded out Poklevsky-Kozell on the concept of a redistribution of the neutral zone – resisted the pull of his own convictions and responded with the party line: Britain had no interest in revising the agreement, not even as far as a limited redrawing of the neutral zone was concerned.[14]

By March, however, Grey and his government had altered their stance. There was one principal factor motivating Grey's admission that a re-evaluation was necessary – oil. As he grudgingly admitted to Buchanan in a private letter in March: 'The chief point on which we shall have to ask for a modification of the Anglo-Russian Agreement is in connection with the concessions.'[15] Russian advances in the neutral zone and steady absorption of northern Persia through their stated policy of 'peaceful penetration under arms' increasingly threatened what had become the most significant element that Persia had to offer Britain – oil.

British involvement in Persian oil began in 1901 with the acquisition by the English gold magnate, William Knox D'Arcy, of a 60-year concession for the exclusive oil production, export and selling rights in all but the five northern Persian provinces, which were to comprise the Russian sphere of the country after 1907. In addition to drilling rights, D'Arcy and whatever companies or syndicates he might found would control any pipelines and stations that would be developed, in exchange for a lump sum paid to the Persian government and a number of shares in the initial company formed plus 10 per cent of the annual net profits. D'Arcy soon found that the ex-penses of exploration and preliminary development of the Persian petroleum industry were quickly exhausting his available financial resources, and he threatened the British Admiralty and the Foreign Office in 1903 that, without government assistance, he might be obliged to sell shares in his concessionary company to foreigners. At the time, the most likely candidates to acquire the shares appeared to be the Russians, whose ardent interest in Persia during those dog days of the Great Game was a consuming concern for the British government. But the navy was still primarily powered by coal, and the Chancellor of the Exchequer, Austen Chamberlain, did not feel that the Commons would be willing to float a loan to D'Arcy's fledgling concern, despite the support from the Admiralty and Foreign Office. Nevertheless, the government was sufficiently concerned about the possibility of the concession falling under Russian control that it fervently urged the Burmah Oil Company to join forces with D'Arcy and form the Concession Syndicate. When an agreement between the two sides was reached on 15 June 1905, D'Arcy's interest became subsidiary to the Syndicate, although he remained a director.[16]

Shortly thereafter, the Syndicate reached a prospecting and drilling agreement with the Bakhtiari khans in whose territory the oil fields lay, and drilling soon began. The first significant load was discovered at Masjed-e Soleyman on 26 May 1906, and in May 1908 a paying load of oil was found at Maidan-e Minaftun.[17] Two subsidiary companies to work the concession were floated in London in May 1909 under the name of the Anglo-Persian Oil Company: the First Exploitation Company and the Bakhtiari Oil Company.[18] The Anglo-Persian Oil Company quickly became the most prevalent and influential manifestation of the British imperial presence in southern Persia and the neutral zone, financing and controlling their own security forces of Indian sowars, advancing loans to the Sheik of Mohammareh through the British government, and even offering to underwrite a considerable loan to the Persian government in exchange for further concessions.[19]

As evidenced by the government's support for and compliance with the efforts of those involved in the D'Arcy concession, it had quickly become established fact that the fate of the Anglo-Persian Oil Company was intricately linked to British governmental policy despite the Treasury's refusal to provide direct financial backing. The government was determined to ensure that the concession remained in British hands, both as a preventive means to limit foreign involvement in Persia and as a steady source for Britain's own still moderate petroleum needs. Thanks to the indefatigable efforts of the First Sea Lord, Admiral Sir John Arbuthnot Fisher, the demand for the latter was quickly to swell. 'Jacky' Fisher, obsessed with the modernization of the Royal Navy, had long been pushing for Britain to convert its fleet from coal propulsion to oil.[20] Oil had numerous advantages over coal as a fuel for fighting ships: oil-powered ships could travel further at higher speeds; burn-

ing oil produced steam more rapidly than coal did; refuelling required only a
few men, not the multitude of cokers that a coal-powered ship demanded;
and refuelling could be done at a ship's fighting position at sea rather than in
port at a coaling station, thereby increasing the strength of the fleet by at least
25 per cent.[21] There was, however, one principal disadvantage, on top of the
traditional opposition of the Royal Navy towards change – supply. As Grey
reminded the House of Commons in July 1912:

> The British Empire was never planned, and the importance of oil was never
> foreseen; so, even if it had been planned, I doubt whether this omission to
> secure a first-rate supply of oil in the British Empire would have been reme-
> died. The Admiralty cannot make arrangements within the British Empire.[22]

Britain had a more than adequate domestic supply of coal in the Welsh
coal mines but, as yet, no reliable and sufficient source of oil within the
Empire. Nevertheless, Fisher felt that the strategic advantages of oil fuel far
outweighed the disadvantages engendered by questions of supply. Oil was
already being used to fuel smaller ships in the navy, but Fisher was determined that the opposition to the use of oil for the nation's battleships be
overcome and that the technology for internal combustion engines to power
such ships be developed.[23] The First Sea Lord was convinced that Britain
needed to act quickly to secure the oil reserves that would allow these technological advances to be accomplished, and there was a growing lobby within
the Admiralty that agreed with him. Sir Francis Hopwood, the Additional
Civil Lord at the Admiralty, reported the conversation at a dinner with the
naval construction expert, Sir Philip Watts, in which his companion had
'mixed oil with the wine':

> He rather astonished me by saying that there was no difficulty whatever in
> designing a Dreadnought to use oil only (not of course with internal combus-
> tion engines at present), but that it had never been done because 'we had not
> got the oil'. – This gives me a clearer understanding of Fisher's attitude as to
> construction going hand in hand with oil purchase.[24]

Fisher's greatest ally in his quest to modernize the navy was none other
than the First Lord of the Admiralty from September 1911, Sir Winston
Churchill. Fisher had quickly won Churchill over to his position on Britain's
requirements for the defence of naval supremacy, and the latter became a
staunch proponent of Fisher's programme for naval development. In 1912
Churchill oversaw the establishment of the Royal Commission on Fuel and
Engines, charged with determining the advantages and methods of oil propulsion. The committee, with Fisher at its head, was staffed by a distinguished
group of Admiralty and oil experts: George Lambert, Civil Lord of the

Admiralty; Sir Thomas Boverton Redwood, government adviser on petro-leum; Sir Philip Watts, Admiralty adviser on naval construction; Vice-Admiral Sir Henry John Oram, engineer-in-chief of the Admiralty; and Vice-Admiral Sir John Rushworth Jellicoe.[25] The conclusion of these men was unquestionably that oil fuel possessed overwhelming advantages for use by the Royal Navy as its principal method of propulsion.[26]

The Commission's mandate included the exploration of not only the technological means of oil propulsion, but also the potential supply of petro-leum available to meet the Admiralty's projected needs. It was, as Lambert appended to the Commission's second report, crucial that Britain look to-wards the acquisition and warehousing of adequate petroleum stores.[27] Towards the aim of securing this supply, the Commission heard the testi-mony of Charles Greenway, the managing director of the Anglo-Persian Oil Company. Greenway stressed the danger that the company, which had now reached the production stage in Persia but continued to suffer from rather shaky financial circumstances, might fall to foreign control. As he saw it, either the Admiralty would assume control of the enterprise through a monumental contract or the company, the only considerable independent British oil interest in existence, would be forced to 'join hands' with the Royal Dutch Shell Company, a firm whose headquarters were in London but 60 per cent of whose stock lay in Holland. Both Greenway and Fisher insisted to the Commission that an Anglo-Persian alliance with the Royal Dutch Shell would be disastrous for British economic and military security.[28]

Once the Royal Navy had decided to base not only its future, but its present on oil-fired battleships, a reliable source for fuel became a paramount concern; the naval programmes of 1912, 1913 and 1914, with not one coal-burning ship on the list, demonstrated the navy's commitment to oil, and with it the commitment of the entire nation. The navy then set about trying to convince the Treasury, which had been so unhelpful several years earlier when D'Arcy had wanted to link his fate and his finances with that of the Admiralty, that the existing methods of procuring oil on an ad hoc basis were no longer satisfactory in light of the exponential increase in naval demand. It was mandatory that Britain obtain 'Forward Contracts' for fuel oils, to defend against the inflated prices that would necessarily accompany the establishment of the industrial and marine uses of the internal combustion engine, to prevent the hoarding of oil by potentially hostile powers, to meet the peacetime needs of the Royal Navy, and to provide for the procurement of increased supplies in times of war. The Admiralty, therefore, urged the Treasury to eliminate the Anglo-Persian Oil Company's need to sacrifice its independence and look to the Dutch or Germans for capital, and to meet

Britain's military and security needs by obtaining an exclusive relationship with that company.[29]

Furthering the Admiralty's plea for forward planning, Churchill took Fisher's case to the House of Commons:

> Our stake in oil-burning ships is becoming so important that we must have the certainty of being able to buy a steady supply of oil at a steady price. Not to take proper steps in time would mean we should gradually but rapidly get into the position of being forced purchasers. We should be grossly over-charged. It does not mean we should not get the oil. At a certain price it would pay nobody else but us to buy it. ... It would mean, however, that we should be made to pay an excessive price for it.[30]

The idea was soon floated that the British government could kill two birds with one stone: secure a steady supply of oil and solve the Anglo-Persian Oil Company's pecuniary woes by becoming a significant shareholder in the company. Subsequently, on 2 October 1913, the cabinet dispatched to Persia a commission under Rear-Admiral Sir Edmond J.W. Slade to investigate the Anglo-Persian's actual potential to deliver on the promises it was making.

Admiral Slade and his cohort of mining and geology experts visited the Anglo-Persian's oil fields and refining operations, finding the outlook in Arabistan to be 'highly favourable' for British exploitation – perhaps more favourable than it truly was.[31] As Slade wrote to Churchill in November, 'It seems to be a thoroughly sound concession, which may be developed to a gigantic extent with a large expenditure of capital. It would put us into a perfectly safe position as regards the supply of oil for naval purposes *if we had the control of the company* and at a very reasonable cost.'[32] The second report of his Commission was exactly what the Anglo-Persian and its sup-porters within the Admiralty had longed to hear: 'It would be a national disaster if the concession were allowed to pass into foreign hands, and that all possible steps should be taken to maintain the Company as an independent British undertaking.'[33]

All that remained was for the government and the company to hammer out an understanding. On 20 May 1914 an agreement was signed, through which the company was guaranteed independence from foreign intervention yet 'bound to the Government by financial and contractual obligations'. In exchange for its significant capital outlay, the British government secured direct control of sufficient oil to meet the Royal Navy's demands in peace and war.[34] Once Parliament approved the appropriation, both the Anglo-Persian's and the Admiralty's wishes would become reality.

Parliamentary approval, however, was not at all automatic. In addition to those members of Parliament who were opposed to preferential treatment

for the Anglo-Persian Oil Company – not least of whom was the member for
Wandsworth, Samuel Samuel, who had, with his brother Marcus Samuel,
created and built the Shell conglomerate that was the Anglo-Persian's greatest
competitor for Admiralty contracts – there were significant factions within
the government bureaucracy who were opposed to the extension of British
government involvement and responsibilities in Persia. From the India Office, Sir F.A. Hirtzel, the secretary of the Political Department, posed what
his branch considered to be the fundamental question: who would pay for the
defence of the newly acquired oil fields? The India Office was insistent that
the contract should not and could not result in increased military responsibilities for India; the Government of India felt overtaxed already and was not
prepared to provide Indian troops for the oil fields, even in the event of an
emergency. As Hirtzel elucidated:

> It may be assumed that if the relations of the British empire with Russia or
> Turkey became strained, the oil-field would be a probable objective for an
> enemy, and its security in advance would be a very pressing matter. The In-
> dian Government from its geographical position would be naturally looked to
> for troops. But it is clear from the Report of the recent Army in India Com-
> mittee that in the event of war the Indian Government will require every
> available soldier to provide for the internal defence of India and to place on
> the north-west frontier a field army of the necessary strength.[35]

With vocal opposition expected from various corners, the debate in the
House began with the introduction of the bill in question by Winston Churchill. Appealing to jingoist patriotism and trust-bashing sentiment, Churchill
promoted government investment in the British-owned Anglo-Persian Oil
Company not only as a prop for British industry but as a means for striking
back at the two great oil monopolies: the American-owned Standard Oil and
the Royal Dutch Shell. Ignoring the overtures that Shell had made to the
Admiralty in the past, and falsely implying in a speech redolent with strong
overtones of anti-Semitism that the Samuels' concern had unpatriotically
overcharged the Admiralty, Churchill urged his fellow members to support
the Anglo-Persian and save the Persian oil fields from 'being swallowed up by
the Shell or by any foreign or cosmopolitan companies.'[36] Numerous members objected. Samuel Samuel tried in vain to defend his firm's honour, and
he was joined by Watson Rutherford, member for Liverpool, who criticized
Churchill for a personal attack on Shell and the Samuels and for 'a little bit of
Jew-baiting'.[37] But the damage to Shell's position had already been done.

After Churchill had raised the spectre of monopolies and 'cosmopolitans',
Grey rose to discuss the implications of the Anglo-Persian issue for Britain's
foreign policy. Attempting to answer those who criticized the creation of a

British dependency on the success and security of an industry ensconced in the territory of a 'decadent empire',[38] the foreign secretary gave a rousing defence of Persian oil for Admiralty needs:

> Can anybody point to any other part where we might get oil concessions outside the British Empire where those risks would be less? Take the difficulty of protecting these wells, and, even at the worst, 150 miles of pipe-line from the coast of Persia. Would you rather have oil wells in Mexico? Would it be easier to send a British force there to protect them? People talk of the danger of the concession being threatened by Russia or by Turkey. Would you rather have the oil wells actually in Russia or Turkish territory?[39]

The persuasive words of Grey and Churchill carried the day, and the oil bill passed by an overwhelming vote of 254 to 18.

The House of Commons had been convinced of the advantages of the government's acquisition of a controlling interest in the Anglo-Persian Oil Company. Far less receptive was Russian official and public opinion. Shortly after the parliamentary debate, the *Novoe Vremia* published a scathing attack, condemning the appropriation as an extension of British exclusive influence beyond the limits of the southern sphere and a virtual British absorption of the neutral zone, wherein lay the greatest assets of the Anglo-Persian concession.[40] Grey quickly attempted to appease the Russians, insisting to Benckendorff that Britain had no plan to extend its influence in the north, and that the Admiralty had advised the company to exploit the promising fields in southern Persia rather than developing the existing fields in the northern neutral zone. The only alteration of existing circumstances would be the possible introduction of British officers for Persian troops in the neutral zone, to help secure the region; Grey reminded Benckendorff that this step had been under discussion between the two powers for more than two years, and he assured the ambassador that Britain would take no action without first consulting Russia.[41]

Sazonov was not opposed to the loan of British officers for the establishment of stability in the neutral zone. He was, however, concerned that the British acquisition of a controlling interest in the Anglo-Persian Oil Company had changed the whole character of the D'Arcy concession. He was aware that the concession granted the holder the exclusive right to exploit the oil in all but the five northern provinces, and he was more than happy to watch the British take as much oil as they wanted from the south. But Sazonov fervently hoped that Britain would avoid going anywhere near the Russian zone, and he urged the British government to state publicly that it would not take advantage of all of the rights inherent in the D'Arcy concession. Buchanan reported Sazonov's plea:

He did not want oil. Russia had enough and to spare, and we were at liberty to develop all the oil areas in the south marked on Blue Book map, but it was a different matter with those near Kermanshah. Russian public would never tolerate arrangement under which a company controlled by British Government could operate in Russian zone and virtually absorb whole of the neutral zone.[42]

Buchanan feared that the perception of a British forward policy in the neutral zone might prompt Russia to counter with its own southward penetration, and he urged the British government to grant the Russians some satisfaction concerning the oil fields in the north.[43] Grey and his advisers recognized the utility of conceding something to the Russians since, in Persia, as Crowe noted, 'in general, all the asking is on the British side.'[44] The foreign secretary therefore privately informed Benckendorff that Britain had no intention of developing the oil wells in the north, and hinted at the possible exploitation of these wells by a joint Anglo-Russian venture once the British were sure that their holdings in the south would meet the Admiralty's needs.[45]

Buchanan's fears that Russian power would extend into the neutral zone in response to Britain's own burgeoning presence were well founded. Sazonov's language was becoming increasingly expansionistic, and he often equated Russia's forward policy in Persia with that of Britain's in Baluchistan and the territories adjoining India, whose absorption had been accomplished in the name of strategic defence.[46] Members of the Russian Council of Empire were similarly complaining that the Anglo-Persian arrangement proved that British governmental expansion in Persia was far more aggressive than the gradual appropriation of property by individual Russian citizens could ever be.[47] Nicholas II had recently proposed to the British ambassador that the neutral zone be partitioned. Buchanan had responded to the tsar that his government did not want to extend its formal responsibilities; since Britain was a naval, not a military, power, the onus of defence for an aggrandized British sphere would fall on the Indian Army – a situation that Britain unconditionally wished to avoid.[48]

In correspondence with Grey, however, the ambassador questioned just how great the actual increase in responsibility would be if Britain were officially to incorporate what it already felt obliged to defend: 'If we have important interests to defend we shall have to defend them whether they lie within or without our sphere, and the mere fact that we shall have a more extensive sphere of influence than at present does not, to my mind, entail the obligation of defending it by force of arms.' Buchanan concluded with a dire warning for what might happen if the question of the neutral zone were not resolved: 'Nothing, I venture to think, is more calculated to create tension between the two countries than to leave the neutral zone, as it is at present, a debatable ground, about which there will be constant bickerings and mutual recriminations.'[49]

It was quite obvious that further strain on the already faltering Anglo-Russian Persian understanding was highly undesirable. As 1914 progressed, the Russian forward policy in northern Persia into the neutral zone was increasingly pushing the limits of British tolerance. Sazonov continued publicly to avow no intention of absorbing the neighbouring country; yet the realities of Russian policies and practice in Persia belied his claim. In Tabriz, Persians refusing to profess openly pronounced pro-Russian sympathies were being driven out of town, and those opposing the Russian military presence were threatened with confiscation of their property, the razing of their houses and personal punishment.[50] In Esfahan, on the border of the neutral zone, the Russian consul was bullying the local merchants into importing nothing but Russian goods in exchange for Russian protection and papers.[51] Throughout the region, the efforts of the Persian authorities and the gendarmerie to pacify the country were opposed by the Russian officials and the Persian Cossacks they controlled. There could only be one unfortunate explanation for this intransigence, as Townley commented in a secret dispatch to Grey:

> One is reluctantly forced to the conclusion that the Russian Government does not desire to see order re-established, either because it is in the interest of Russian trade that a valuable road into Persia should be blocked for British commerce, or because ... Russia has some ulterior political object in wishing to see a state of anarchy maintained in a district into which she may wish to penetrate later on.[52]

In addition to the apparently sanctioned prolongation of disorder and unrest, an organized project of Russian resettlement in northern Persia was under way, authorized by St Petersburg. Secret instructions for the Russian settlers in Persia were drafted by the government agency that oversaw farming and land organization, with directions for leasing land from the local consuls, information concerning from whom they should seek agricultural advice and support, and maps of the region.[53] As Townley described the wave of Russian migration overrunning northern Persia: 'Large tracts of country ... are being colonised by Russian immigrants who appear to come into the country by every mail steamer, one or two hundred at a time, and to settle down on lands illegally acquired through the instrumentality of Russian agents.'[54] As more and more land was occupied by Russian subjects and protected persons, less and less revenue was reaching the Persian treasury, since the taxes from both these categories of people were to be collected by the Russian consuls rather than the Persian treasury regime. In Azerbaijan alone, two-thirds of the revenue in 1914 was due from Russian subjects and protected persons, and was therefore considered by Persia to be, for all intents and purposes, lost.

The steady Russian acquisition of land and privileges under way in northern Persia revealed the truth that Britain had wanted so badly to overlook: official Russian policy was supporting a programme of formal colonization and absorption of Persian territory. No longer could Britain blame the realities of Russian expansion in Persia on the independent actions of rogue Russian men-on-the-spot; Vorontsov-Dashkov's proposed programme for the reorganization of the consular hierarchy in June 1914, combining the activities of the individual consular officials into one general programme subordinate to the consul-general in Tabriz, who would answer to the minister in Teheran, was a manifestation of the Russian recognition of centralized responsibility for consular action.[55] At the Foreign Office, Eyre Crowe openly charged his colleagues to act before the official Russian onslaught had pushed the British presence from Persia altogether:

> I think it is quite futile to pretend that there is any distinction between the Russian government and the Russian officials in Persia. ... Russia has – in my opinion deliberately – taken the 5 northern provinces; if we go on, as we have done, looking on and doing nothing for ourselves, Russia will within a twelvemonth have taken over the neutral zone.[56]

Britain, however, was not prepared to act. Grey had confidentially confessed to Buchanan in March what he considered to be the great weakness of Britain's position: 'The Russians are prepared to occupy Persia, and we are not.'[57] Crowe, in contrast, argued the vital imperial necessity of a strong stance against the Russian advance, no matter the potential sacrifice in money and possibly men:

> There is only one possible way now of keeping Russia out of southern Persia: we must establish our own exclusive authority there ourselves. If we take the line that we cannot afford to incur expenditure for such Imperial interests, it will be like a declaration of imperial bankruptcy in respect of those regions.

It was clear to Crowe that the only escape from the Persian morass was 'the complete separation of the South from the Power established at Teheran, whether that Power calls itself Shah or Czar', and he joined with Townley and Buchanan in a call for a renegotiation of the agreement and partition of the neutral zone. It was, he insisted, the only way to save the relationship with Russia:

> Under the conditions which now prevail in Persia, and which involve our sharing before the world the responsibility for Russia's unscrupulous pro-

ceedings in that country, the understanding will break down. No British officials can actively co-operate with Russian officials: the difference of methods
and of standards of conduct is practically unbridgeable. ... To this necessity
we must sacrifice the fiction of an independent and united Persia. ... It is not
perhaps an heroic course, but it is not open to blame and it is the only one
that will preserve us from grave political and national peril.[58]

The growing British lobby for a formal renegotiation of the terms of the
1907 agreement was not, of course, alone. Sazonov had for some time continued to press for official British recognition of Russia's predominant
interests in northern Persia; only British acknowledgement of Russia's need
for 'elbow-room' in the north could eliminate the far too frequent British
complaints concerning the actions of the Russian consular officials in the
region. While Grey had held on to his opposition towards any formal alteration of Russia's relationship with northern Persia, the gradual transformation
of circumstances throughout the region governed by the convention increasingly demanded a renegotiation and reconstruction of the agreement. In
Persia, Russia wanted 'elbow-room' and partition; Britain desired the maintenance of a neutral buffer state and practical control of the majority of the
neutral sphere for itself. In Afghanistan, Russia wanted formal relations,
influence and trade; Britain longed to have its semi-protectorate remain
unchallenged, unquestioned and unprovoked. Only in Tibet, where Britain
specifically sought a reworking of the terms of the agreement governing its
official relationship with the Dalai Lama's realm, did Russia have no outstanding wishes. Yet this absence of aspirations did not signify a dearth of
Russian desires; rather, Russia saw its acquiescence towards British policies in
Tibet as the perfect means to achieve its considerable aims in the region as a
whole. Sazonov did not consider 'elbow-room' in Persia alone to be adequate
compensation for a change of Britain's relationship with Tibet; rather, he
reminded Buchanan that circumstances in Persia, Tibet and, by extension,
Afghanistan were all linked by their mutual inclusion in the 1907 agreement.[59]

The British, however, were entirely unprepared to provide compensation
for Russia in any of the areas in question. As Grey disconsolately admitted to
Buchanan in a private letter in March 1914:

You will see, therefore, that, as regards Persia, we wish to have practically
the whole of the neutral sphere, and have nothing to concede there to Russia;
as regards Afghanistan, we cannot concede any thing to Russia, because we
cannot get the Ameer's consent; as regards Tibet, the change that we wish to
have, and to which Russia's consent is necessary, is very slight, but we have
nothing to give in return. So, all along the line we want something, and we

have nothing to give. It is therefore difficult to see how a good bargain is to be made.[60]

With the precariousness of the British position in mind, the opening of communications with Russia concerning Tibet and the tripartite talks under way in Simla was continually postponed. Finally, in May, the negotiations with the Chinese and the Tibetans had reached the point where it was no longer possible to avoid talking to Russia. Buchanan therefore informed Sazonov of the course the negotiations had taken, specifically communicating the two main points that directly affected the 1907 agreement. As a result of the Tibetan insistence that they not be limited to a Chinese monopoly on financial and industrial concessions, Britain proposed that Article 4 of the Anglo-Russian convention be cancelled; under the new terms governing Tibet's commercial relations, the continuation of the article's prohibition against Russian or British concessions in Tibet would leave them at a distinct disadvantage in an environment where all other powers were free to seek concessions. Secondly, the proposed tripartite agreement called for the occasional visit of a British agent to Lhasa to facilitate communication concerning trade issues.[61]

Sazonov decided that this was the time to play his hand. He immediately responded to Buchanan that the British proposal 'constituted the abrogation of the Thibetan Agreement and established a British protectorate'.[62] While admitting that he personally did not care what Britain did with Tibet, he maintained that public opinion would denounce him were he not to obtain a quid pro quo. He claimed that Russia was equally entitled to send a commercial agent to Lhasa, although he assured the British ambassador that he had no intention of exercising that right. Instead, Sazonov insisted that, in exchange for Russian acquiescence to British agents in Tibet, Britain must allow Russia to send agents into Afghanistan – a region where Russia had far greater economic interests than Britain had in Tibet. If Britain were to demand an alteration of the status quo in Tibet, Russia must insist on a corresponding modification in Afghanistan.

Buchanan told Sazonov that he was 'greatly disappointed by his unconciliatory attitude'. The British ambassador pointed out that Russia seemed to be concerned with observing the letter of the agreement only when convenient; clearly the military occupation of northern Persia by some 12,000 Russian troops and the steady encroachment upon Azerbaijan through a process of land-purchase was in violation of the letter of the agreement, yet Britain had been willing to overlook such infractions for the sake of the spirit of the rapprochement.[63] At this, Sazonov softened considerably. Claiming again the difficulty of his position vis-à-vis Russian public opinion, he offered not to oppose the Tripartite Agreement provided the convention was kept secret.[64] However, he continued to push for corresponding rights in Afghanistan, threatening to extract a monumental quid pro quo were Britain's involvement in Tibet to be extended to include a permanent presence in Lhasa. Buchanan feared that the foreign minister was preparing to request more than Britain would be able to concede, and that the Anglo-Russian understanding would break down for the sake of Sazonov's 'pound of flesh'.[65]

Finally, on 19 May, Sazonov made what he claimed was his final offer concerning Russian recognition of the initialled but unsigned tripartite convention. He insisted that he could only accede to the provision allowing for a British trade agent in Lhasa if the two powers signed notes guaranteeing that such an agent would not be sent without Russia's prior consent.[66] Furthermore, he demanded at the very least the appearance of a counter-concession in Afghanistan, calling for a note addressed to the Russian government promising British governmental support for the exclusion of British irrigation works, railways or preferential commercial or industrial rights in northern Afghanistan.[67] Britain agreed in principle to Sazonov's requirements, proposing that the two governments make a joint declaration concerning Afghanistan that would state the aforementioned qualification of concessions in northern Afghanistan and would restate that Afghanistan was not in Russia's sphere of political influence.[68] In addition, Britain attempted to define informally the boundaries of northern Afghanistan, being careful to ensure that Russia could not 'have even a shadowy claim' to the area surrounding Herat and the crest of the Hindu Kush westward from Nawak.[69]

Sazonov, however, refused to accept the British definition of the region, and returned to his conviction that, since he had allowed Britain virtually to tear up their Tibetan convention, Britain needed to be more accommodating. He insisted that the boundaries of northern Afghanistan be extended beyond those proposed by Great Britain to include the Hari Rud River. Furthermore, he proposed that Britain and Russia reach a public agreement concerning the construction of railways and irrigation works in the region. Finally, Sazonov requested the inclusion of a clause granting the right of Russian Buddhist pilgrims to travel to Lhasa via India, rather than the more difficult routes through Chinese Turkestan and Mongolia.[70]

These new conditions were extremely unpalatable to the British; the first and second might alarm the emir as indicative of a division of Afghanistan into spheres of influence along the Persian model, while the last would make it even easier for Russian citizens of possibly dubious intentions to enter India and Tibet. The Marquess of Crewe, secretary of state for India, insisted that Sazonov's professed fears of appearing to have ceded Russian interests whilst receiving nothing in return were entirely unfounded; in fact, these fears were far more appropriate for the British government than for the Russian.[71] In all, the British were becoming extremely put off by Russia's insatiable appetite. R.T. Nugent of the Foreign Office Far Eastern Department complained, 'M. Sazonoff is behaving very badly. He makes proposals and, as soon as they are agreed to, raises fresh demands.'[72]

Sazonov, in contrast, did not feel his approach to the Tibetan question was at all underhand. Rather, he was convinced that he was proceeding with considerable deference to Britain's needs. As he wrote to Benckendorff at the end of June:

> I hope that the British Government recognizes the good will which I bring to a revision or rather – because the word must be said, the <u>annulment</u> of our arrangement concerning Tibet. I am guided in this question by the considerations springing from Britain's special circumstances in her role as the neighbouring Power of Tibet. You well understand that I would employ the same title when they talk of our rights in Persia.[73]

Sazonov reiterated his determination to cultivate and reassert the ties of friendship with Great Britain, the maintenance of which, he claimed, 'at all times dominates my political preoccupations'. At the same time, he at last began to align his Central Asian policies with his European goals, laying the foundations of a further extension of the Tibetan bargain beyond even the confines of Central Asia. As he told his ambassador, it would be impossible to demand the tsar's consent for Russian compliance in Tibet while Britain continued to defer signing the entente naval convention that France had initiated – an arrangement to which Grey's government seemed in no great hurry to agree.[74]

In addition to defending his stance concerning the Tibet-for-Afghanistan trade, Sazonov virulently denounced what he considered to be British obstructionism in Persia. Greeting Buchanan with what the latter called 'a violent attack' on the constant complaints against the Russian consuls in Persia that filled the British press, Sazonov warned that he could not go on indefinitely making 'great sacrifices' for the sake of friendship with Britain.[75] The British responded with a formal memorandum, underscoring the de facto acquisition by Russia of supreme political power and influence in northern Persia in strict violation of the Persian independence and integrity guaranteed in the 1907 agreement; Britain had been willing to overlook the gradual Russification of northern Persia, but the extension of Russian predominance into the neutral zone was entirely unacceptable. Therefore, the British government proposed that both governments consider the revision of the agreement that had been so battered over the preceding seven years.[76]

The Russian Ministry of Foreign Affairs was irritated by many of the suggestions contained in this memorandum, taking considerable offence at the implication that Russia had supported rebellious and dishonest people and had crippled the Persian financial administration by diverting tax revenues from the Persian treasury. Unsigned marginalia to this memorandum, which most likely were penned by the foreign minister, point out what the Russians considered to be the hypocrisy of the British position. The British were accused of the same appropriation of influence in portions of the neutral zone – an area that the notes emphasize 'is open to everybody' – that Buchanan claimed the Russians were inappropriately acquiring for themselves. The control of local officials by Russian consuls was vehemently defended: 'It has always been so and can't be otherwise. And don't the British Consuls do the same in their region f.i [sic] in Seistan?' And the suggestion that the Russian activity in the north combined with the chaos that reigned in the south had created a veritable monopoly for Russian trade was met with a fierce 'Nonsense!'[77]

The official Russian response to the British memorandum was prompt. In a point-by-point rebuttal, Russia explained the geographical necessities that demanded its interference in northern and north-western Persia, especially in Azerbaijan. Defending the Russian activities as necessary protection for Russian and other foreign interests in Persia, the Russian government insisted that its involvement in the neighbouring country had actually entailed considerable Russian sacrifices all for the sake of the preservation of order. Only the Russian presence was saving the country from complete economic and political chaos. The government regretted that Russian actions in Persia had been met with such extreme opposition from Great Britain, but insisted that the maintenance of order was in the interests of both powers. And, as in his correspondence concerning the reworking of the Tibetan agreement, Sazonov suggested that any revision of the arrangement in Persia be linked to a widening of the Anglo-Russian relationship in Europe and the movement of the entente towards an alliance relationship as well.[78]

These, therefore, were the considerations that the two powers would bring to any discussions of a renegotiated agreement. While Russia was looking to expand the very nature of the Anglo-Russian relationship, in Britain, concern for the state of affairs in Central Asia was so concentrated that Benckendorff feared that only the amicable resolution of the conflicts in Persia could preserve the entente at all.[79] Difficulties and disagreements in Persia were serving to distract the two powers from the important questions of naval co-operation.[80] In two lengthy and personal appeals to Sazonov, Benckendorff urged his government to look beyond the limited confines of Central Asia and recognize the risks it was running by not being more flexible. If Russia did not temper its progression in northern Persia, Britain would be forced to undertake a similar absorption in the middle of Persia, and the convention would be a failure and its political foundation lost.

Furthermore, Benckendorff attempted to smooth over the personal relations between the British foreign secretary and Sazonov, which were becoming increasingly strained by what Sazonov considered to be excessive British interference in what were, in principle, solely Russian concerns:

> When he [Grey] orders Buchanan to speak with you, it is because he is persuaded that in principle you share his opinion and his point of view. He sees this choice as a call and a cry of alarm, and not as meddling. Be absolutely persuaded that I am not deluding myself on this point. There is nothing, absolutely nothing else hidden beneath this.[81]

Sazonov responded confidentially that the sacrifices the British demanded in Persia and Tibet were too great. He complained to his ambassador that the British were asking of Russia limitations that they had not imposed on themselves: 'The English should not forget Kuwait, all of the Persian Gulf, Afghanistan and Baluchistan. Remind them from time to time the role to which these countries have been enslaved. It is far from London to Teheran, but from Moscow to Tabriz the distance is not so great.'[82]

But the realities of British desires contrasted sharply with Sazonov's apprehension of an ever-increasing extension of British power outwards from its Indian nucleus. Only grudgingly, the home and Indian governments were coming to terms with a growing awareness of the need to surpass the limitations that had been placed upon their Central Asian expansion by security requirements and budgetary constraints. The Anglo-Persian Oil Agreement had completely altered the demands placed on the British presence in Persia, the Russian advance in Persia seemed irreversible, and the inevitability of partition became more and more apparent.[83] At the end of July, a Foreign Office memorandum prepared by G.R. Clerk of the Eastern Department outlined the realities of the Persian situation and the necessities for British policy if both a British presence and any semblance of an understanding with Russia were to be maintained: Persia must be partitioned if the Russian advance were to be checked. An outline for discussions with Russia on this subject was drawn up, and Crowe offered his vociferous approval and agreement. Even Sir Arthur Nicolson, the principal architect of the 1907 agreement and long the most vocal advocate for its preservation, urged immediate action in accordance with Clerk's and Crowe's suggestions for partition.[84]

Thus, the 1907 Anglo-Russian agreement, guaranteeing the status quo in Persia, Afghanistan and Tibet, was dead. In Persia, both parties, each for their own reasons, longed for the alteration of the terms of the agreement: the Russians to solidify their presence and to legitimize their exclusive right to conduct their operations in their sphere as they saw fit; the British to stave off the Russian advance and to protect their trade, their increasingly vital concessionary interests in the Persian oil fields, and their strategic concerns tied to the demands of the defence of India. In Afghanistan, Russia clamoured for direct intercourse and the acknowledged right to pursue and protect its own interests in the emirate whose territories it bordered; the emir's continuing refusal to recognize the agreement only served to underscore the absence of applicability for the agreement in Afghanistan. And in Tibet, Britain's need to appease its own north-east frontier protectorates by pacifying the Tibetan plateau and bolstering its official presence in the Dalai Lama's realm offered the opportunity and the cause to redress the balance in the Anglo-Russian Central Asian situation.

European matters intervened before Britain and Russia could hammer out their differences in Central Asia and strengthen the relationship in Europe with the conclusion of a naval agreement. Shortly after the two powers had each recognized the need to rework the agreement, tensions in Europe intensified, forcing Central Asian issues into the background for what was expected to be only a temporary pause. At first, the assassination on 28 June of the Austrian Archduke Franz Ferdinand in Sarajevo did not directly impact upon Anglo-Russian relations. Zara Steiner states in her *Britain and the Origins of the First World War* that Grey immediately recognized the magnitude of the crisis.[85] While that may have been true, the senior officials by whom Grey was surrounded at the Foreign Office were inclined to believe that this was a crisis no more urgent than those that Europe had already weathered during the preceding years, from Fashoda to Morocco to Bosnia-Herzegovina.[86] The makers of British official policy towards Russia during the period immediately following the assassination were far more wrapped up in their concerns over Persia than with any sense that the situation developing in the Balkans would grow into a crisis that would envelop all of Europe and transform the entente into an alliance.[87]

The immediate Russian reaction to the assassination of the Hapsburg archduke was equally composed. For the first three weeks of July, the Russian government was lulled into a sense of complacency by Austro-Hungarian reassurances that the Dual Monarchy would not harshly discipline Serbia.[88] As Austria-Hungary prepared its response, Anglo-Russian discussions were focused first and foremost on the outstanding issues in the Persian question, and only secondarily on Austro-Serbian relations.[89] The Turkestan general staff even commissioned a study of the Afghan theatre in preparation for an increasingly possible struggle against an Afghan-Anglo-Indian combination, fully anticipating the event when the Anglo-Russian '"friendship" could suddenly and quickly transform into a quarrel'. Rather than envisaging an imminent transition to a wartime alliance, important and influential factions within the Russian military were focused on predictions of future conflicts between Russia and Britain in Central Asia, motivated by the same issues that had aggravated Anglo-Russian regional relations for decades.[90]

The Austro-Hungarian ultimatum to Serbia on 23 July, therefore, took Russia and Britain very much by surprise.[91] It is at this point that the affairs in the Balkans came to dominate Anglo-Russian relations. The Russians quickly moved to secure the support of their entente partners in their expression of 'strong reprobation' against the Austro-Hungarian demands, expressing 'the hope that His Majesty's Government would proclaim their solidarity with France and Russia.'[92] Yet, even at this late hour, as Britain contemplated the possibility of joining its Franco-Russian partners in a European war against the Central Powers, Central Asian concerns were not left behind. Buchanan, in an effort to persuade Grey of the importance of maintaining a united front with Russia on the Serbian issue, relied on the requirements of their Asian relationship to underscore the crucial nature of continued friendship: 'If we fail her now we cannot hope to maintain that friendly co-operation with her in Asia that is of such vital importance to us.'[93]

The proclamations of general mobilization on 30 July and the European war that followed distracted Russian and British attention from Central Asia for obvious reasons. Discussions of a revised Anglo-Russian convention were placed on the back burner while the members of the Triple Entente at last banded together to fight the Central Powers; war had produced what peace could not – a common interest in Europe that outweighed the seemingly irreconcilable differences faced by Russia and Britain in Asia. The outbreak of war in 1914 saved Britain and Russia from the necessity of once again working through their many disagreements in Central Asia, disagreements that the 1907 convention had temporarily suppressed, but which were now bubbling to the surface with a vengeance. Nowhere did the agreement that had been forged in 1907 remain intact. In Persia, Afghanistan and Tibet, circumstances and priorities had so altered as to demand either the revision of the convention or the acknowledgement that British and Russian goals could not be made to correspond.

The plans to renegotiate the Anglo-Russian convention of 31 August 1907 were not in any way the first step towards a global Anglo-Russian alliance. For Grey, the move resulted from the recognition that the agreement, as it stood, was no longer serving its purpose. Central Asian stability, however, remained a crucial concern for the British government, one that could even prompt British support for Russia on the Continent, if necessary, for the maintenance of amicable relations. For Sazonov, Central Asian policies were clearly distinct from European concerns. While he sought more formal and binding Anglo-Russian ties in Europe, he remained willing to antagonize Great Britain in Afghanistan and Persia in pursuit of an advancing Russian presence in Central Asia. By the summer of 1914, both men had admitted – each for their own reasons – the need to rework the agreement. But the outbreak of the First World War and the Russian Revolution that toppled the Romanov regime irrevocably interfered. Whether or not a new agreement could ever have been moulded from the conflicting aims and desires of the two powers will forever remain a cause for speculation.

Conclusion

The Great Power war that broke out in 1914 was not a Central Asian war. It was not a war between Russia and Great Britain on the steppes, plains and mountains of Central Asia. It was not the war for regional hegemony and imperial supremacy that so many had anticipated in the late nineteenth century. And because this war in 1914 was not fought between the Russian bear and the British lion, the 1907 Anglo-Russian agreement can be considered to have been a success.

But such a limited appraisal of the 1907 agreement would be flawed for several reasons. Firstly, although predicated on the accurate premise that the 1907 Treaty of Rapprochement was designed to relieve the regional tension between Britain and Russia in Central Asia that had been building throughout the latter half of the nineteenth century, this assessment presumes that the absence of armed conflict alone indicates a solution to the Anglo-Russian Central Asian contest. Yet, for both Britain and Russia, the 1907 agreement proved to be not a solution, but a temporary bridge over the gaping divide that separated British and Russian aims and desires in Central Asia.

The British had sought a rapprochement with Russia in an attempt to alleviate the pressure on India's defence capabilities and to buttress their overstretched imperial resources through a diplomatic agreement preserving the Central Asian status quo. Regional circumstances and Russia's objective in first achieving this convention, however, made just such a preservation of the status quo impossible. Russia's principal aim in reaching a Central Asian rapprochement with Great Britain in 1907 was to buy time for the battered Romanov Empire to recover from the trauma of Tsushima and the lingering wounds from Bloody Sunday and the Revolution of 1905. Once Russia had regrouped, its government was prepared to resume the forward policy in Central Asia that had so characterized its late nineteenth-century imperial policy, in an attempt to re-establish and solidify its place at the Great Power table.

Almost from the agreement's inception, the Russian government was prepared to take advantage of the various opportunities that Central Asian circumstances offered them. In Persia, where revolution and unrest created a power vacuum and demanded the securing of established Russian interests, the Russian diplomatic and military men-on-the-spot, supported ultimately by their government in St Petersburg, were quick to promote Russian interests and work towards the gradual absorption of the northern provinces into the Russian Empire. In Afghanistan and Tibet, where the Russian government had acknowledged the absence of any outstanding interests, Russia was content at first to work within the confines of the agreement. But as the Russian occupation of northern Persia became a de facto if not yet de jure reality, the next obvious outlet for Russian influence in Central Asia was northern Afghanistan. The twofold expansion of the Russian presence and influence into Persia and Afghanistan was guaranteed to bring Britain and Russia into conflict. Therefore, it is clear that the 1907 Anglo-Russian agreement neither provided the solution to regional security concerns for which Britain longed, nor the possibility for an unencumbered continued advance in Central Asia that Russia desired.

If the Treaty of Rapprochement did not answer British and Russian requirements in Central Asia, then perhaps it should be examined as part and parcel of the European foreign policy agendas of the two Great Powers. The 1907 agreement has been traditionally considered one of the principal diplomatic foundations of the European alliance structure that so vividly contributed to the outbreak of the Great War. In this picture, the rapprochement early in the twentieth century between Russia and Britain was important because it allowed Britain, Russia and their entente partner, France, to align themselves against the Central Powers of Germany and Austria-Hungary. The maintenance of the relationship in Asia was, therefore, essential precisely because it allowed the members of the entente to face the growing German threat.

This analysis of the success and significance of the 1907 Anglo-Russian Treaty of Rapprochement is equally flawed. While the agreement allowed for the creation of the Triple Entente and offered the opportunity for an ever closer relationship between the entente's partners, the difficulties and challenges faced by Britain and Russia in Persia, Afghanistan and Tibet did little to foster a greater understanding between the two regional Great Powers beyond Central Asia. By the outbreak of the European war in 1914, on numerous fronts the Anglo-Russian Central Asian accord was on the verge of collapsing, threatening any further affinity in Europe. The British government's overriding concerns for the defence of India and the determination to maintain Britain's imperial power had brought it to the point where it was no longer willing or able to tolerate further 'peaceful penetration' by the Russian regional presence; Britain would need to take a strong stance in defence of its

interests and either hammer out a new agreement with Russia or acknowledge the end of their co-operation in Central Asia. On the Russian side,
Sazonov's willingness to antagonize Great Britain by pushing the unmistaka-
bly vexatious Afghan question distinctly indicates that the idea of a Russian
forward policy in Central Asia not only survived the 1907 agreement, but
was in many ways a more vital policy concern for Russia than the buttressing
of entente relations. Furthermore, such a Eurocentric analysis as one focused
around the origins of the First World War overlooks the reality that for the
makers of Russian and British policy, the relationship in Central Asia was,
first and foremost, directed towards addressing regional, not European,
concerns.

To look for the agreement's significance in its direct contribution to the
origins and outbreak of the First World War, therefore, would be to evaluate
the treaty's success far in excess of its realistic value and to place the focus of
the agreement in a region and conflict that was distinctly separate in the
foreign policies of the day. Yet, as Keith Neilson has underscored, the history
that has been written of the period before the onset of war in 1914 has so
often been skewed by the knowledge that war broke out when it did, between whom it did.[1] The vital need to understand why and how war came has
led historians to place excessive emphasis on the relationships of the various
European powers with Germany and to see the relations of the entente
members as leading directly towards the alliance that evolved with the onset
of war.

This is not to say that Germany was not the crucial factor in the outbreak
of the First World War, nor that the origins of the war that began in the
summer of 1914 do not lie in the Anglo-German naval arms race, in Russian
aspirations in the Straits and the exigencies of the crumbling Hapsburg Empire, in a general European commitment to military timetables, or in German
Weltpolitik or social imperialism, to offer just a few of the explanations that
contribute to an understanding of the origins of the First World War. Keith
Wilson's thesis that Asia was the determining factor in Britain's decision to
enter the war is an overstatement; it is a considerable stretch to posit, as he
does, that Grey and his advisers were only incidentally thinking of Europe in
the years leading up to 1914.[2] But one must remember as one looks at the
pre-war years, that the makers of policy throughout Europe did not know if
or when war would come. It is true that they had their theories and suspicions, but there had also been theories and suspicions throughout much of the
late nineteenth century that the next European war would be an armed
settlement of the Great Game, fought between Britain and Russia over the
buffer zones of Persia, Afghanistan and Tibet, with the ultimate prize being
India and imperial hegemony. Diplomacy and circumstances had averted that

conflict, and there was no reason to expect that diplomacy and circumstances would not avert other growing European conflicts in the new century.

On the domestic front, Russia and Britain each faced numerous challenges in 1914 which distracted their attention from the world stage. Russia, battered by revolutionary unrest and the steady deterioration of the Romanov autocracy and internal stability, found the pursuit of Great Power foreign policy to be increasingly difficult as it was embroiled in troubles at home. The British government was similarly distracted by domestic issues, facing unrest in Ulster over Home Rule, violent suffragette protests, and a looming budgetary crisis that threatened to limit British naval defence spending. Clearly, foreign affairs were not the only tests that Britain and Russia faced in the years before the outbreak of the First World War, and neither power had the luxury to concentrate exclusively on the growing tensions on either the European or Asian continents.

But even within the sections of government that were directly focused upon the international stage, the possibility of imminent war with Germany was not the solitary hazard with which the makers of foreign policy were confronted. The potential breakdown of the Anglo-Russian mutual accord in Central Asia was as vital a concern in the years from the agreement to the Great War as the threat in Central Europe. The conflicting regional interests of both powers did not disappear with the advent of the rapprochement. British requirements for the defence of India, augmented by the critical need for oil resources to support the Royal Navy's commitment to oil propulsion, demanded that Britain do all that could be done to secure its imperial position in the region. Russian interests in defending and expanding the presence of its trade and influence in Persia and Afghanistan, with an eye towards the possible absorption of further Central Asian territory, inclined the Russian government towards a policy destined to threaten the status quo that Britain was so desperate to preserve. In addition, the growth of pan-Islamism throughout Asia – especially within the three semi-independent countries in question and in the bordering territories of the Russian and British Empires – severely endangered regional stability. Therefore, the relations between Britain and Russia before 1914 were not all about the coming war. For Grey, Izvolskii, Sazonov, Buchanan, Benckendorff and all the other men involved with steering British and Russian foreign policy, the ongoing relationship in Central Asia was crucial in its own right for all of the reasons of imperial defence, prestige and economic security that had first required the conclusion of the agreement in 1907.

Thus the Anglo-Russian convention of 1907 should be considered neither as the end of the Great Game nor as the beginning of the Triple Entente. The period from the conclusion of the agreement to the outbreak of the First

World War was marked by continued Anglo-Russian tensions and regional manoeuvring, in the same vein as that which had characterized the era before the rapprochement. In Persia, Afghanistan and Tibet, the competition between the two Great Powers for hegemonic influence and strategic position remained heated, albeit relatively obscured by the veil of the existing mutual accord. Both Britain and Russia had hoped that the 1907 agreement would satisfy their objectives and secure their imperial position, and, throughout the years before the War, both governments professed their commitment to the maintenance of their amicable relationship. By the summer of 1914, however, the realities of their conflicting goals and the changing strategic landscape in Central Asia had brought the makers of British and Russian policy to the conclusion that the 1907 agreement's applicability and utility had long since passed. But with the outbreak of hostilities in Europe, British and Russian difficulties in Central Asia were set aside while the Great Powers addressed the far more urgent crises of world war. Once again, a conflagration of Anglo-Russian regional animosity had been averted, this time by the advent of a war in which their individual interests demanded that they band together against a common enemy. Had war not intervened, the Anglo-Russian accord, which had persisted in the face of adversity through seven years of Persian revolutionary unrest, Afghan obstructionism and the Tibetan geostrategic void, would have faced the challenge of re-evaluation and revision – a challenge it might not have survived.

Notes

Scholars who are interested in more detailed notes and bibliographic references are referred to my dissertation, '"Peaceful Penetration under Arms": Anglo-Russian Relations in Central Asia, 1907–1914' (Yale University, 1998).

Abbreviations and Terms

Archival citations

f.	*fond* – collection
op.	*opis* – subgroup within the collection
d.	*delo* – file
l.	*list* – page
ob.	*obratnaia* – reverse side of the page

Archives

AVPRI	*Arkhiv Vneshnei Politiki Rossisskoi Imperii* – Archive of the Russian Imperial Foreign Ministry, Moscow
GARF	*Gosudarstvennyi Arkhiv Rossiiskoi Federatsii* – State Archive of the Russian Federation, Moscow
IO	India Office, London
PRO	Public Record Office, Kew
RGIA	*Rossisskii Gosudarstvennyi Istoricheskii Arhkiv* – Russian State Historical Archive, St Petersburg
RGVIA	*Rossisskii Gosudarstvennyi Voenno Istoricheskii Arhkiv* – Russian State Military Historical Archive, Moscow

Published Document Collections

BD	*British Documents on the Origins of the War, 1898–1914*
BDFA	*British Documents on Foreign Affairs: Reports and Papers from the Foreign Office Confidential Print*
KA	*Krasnyi Arkhiv*
PD	*Hansard Parliamentary Debates*

General Abbreviations

MID   *Ministerstvo Inostrannykh Del* – Russian Ministry of Foreign Affairs

CID   British Cabinet – Committee of Imperial Defence

Introduction

[1] George N. Curzon, *Persia and the Persian Question* (London, 1892), vol i, p 4.

[2] A.E. Snesarev, *Indiia kak glavnii faktor v sredne-aziatskom voprose* (St Petersburg, 1906), p 173.

[3] The two most notable advocates of the equivalence, if not the primacy, of the Anglo-Russian relationship are Keith Wilson and Keith Neilson, both of whom urge the reader to remember that the makers of Great Power policy before 1914 did not know that a war with Germany would break out in the summer of 1914. See Keith M. Wilson, *Empire and Continent* (London, 1987); *The Policy of the Entente* (Cambridge, 1985); 'Imperial Interests in the British Decision for War, 1914: The Defence of India in Central Asia', *Review of International Studies*, 10 (1984), pp 189–203; Keith Neilson, *Britain and the Last Tsar* (Oxford, 1995).

Chapter 1: The Great Game and the 1907 Agreement

[1] Aaron L. Friedberg, *The Weary Titan* (Princeton, 1988), p 219; P.J. Cain and A.G. Hopkins, *British Imperialism: Innovation and Expansion, 1688–1914* (London, 1993), p 333; Ronald Robinson and John Gallagher with Alice Denny, *Africa and the Victorians*, 2nd ed. (London, 1981), p 11.

[2] D.R. Gillard, 'Salisbury and the Indian Defence Problem, 1885–1902', in K. Bourne and D.C. Watt (eds) *Studies in International History* (London, 1967), p 238.

[3] Firuz Kazemzadeh, *Russia and Britain in Persia, 1864–1914* (New Haven, 1968), pp 4–5.

[4] The genesis of the expedition is often considered to lie in Paul's planned co-operation with Napoleon. But Roderick E. McGrew, in his *Paul I of Russia, 1754–1801* (Oxford, 1992), p 316, insists that this was not the case. Rather, McGrew, with Muriel Atkin, 'The Pragmatic Diplomacy of Paul I: Russia's Relations with Asia, 1796–1801', *Slavic Review*, 38 (March 1979), pp 60–74, sees Paul's Indian policies as exemplifying his prescient, if ill-timed, awareness of British vulnerabilities and Russian possibilities in Central Asia.

[5] PRO/FO65/1640/56: 'Anglo-Japanese Agreements'. Sir Charles Scott to the Marquess of Lansdowne, St Petersburg, 17 February 1902.

[6] General Skobelev, quoted in George N. Curzon, *Russia in Central Asia* (London, 1967), pp 323–4.

[7] Prince Esper Ukhtomsky, quoted in Andrew Malozemoff, *Russian Far Eastern Policy, 1881–1904* (Berkeley, 1958), p 44.

[8] Constantine Leontiev, quoted in Robert Wesson, *The Russian Dilemma* (New Brunswick, NJ, 1974), p 9. Leontiev, although ostracized by the Ministry of Foreign

Affairs after his open support for the Ottoman Empire, was relatively influential in Russian literary circles. Therefore, while his writings had virtually no impact on foreign policy, his calls for the spread of Russian Orthodoxy to the East did contribute to the Asianist ideology that promoted Russian eastward expansion.

[9] Prince Gorchakov, 21 November 1864, in Dominic Lieven (ed), *BDFA*, Part I, Series A, vol 1 (University Publications of America, 1983), p 287.

[10] PRO/FO65/1419/17 March 1892: A.B. on the subject of the influence of India on the Eastern Question in *Novoe Vremia* of 4/16 March 1892.

[11] David N. Druhe, *Russo-Indian Relations, 1466–1917* (New York, 1970), pp 215–16.

[12] PRO/FO65/1599/116: Summary of Rittich's pamphlet on 'Railways in Persia', Part I. Enclosure in Scott to the Marquess of Salisbury, St Petersburg, 2 May 1900.

[13] Captain E. Peach, Sir William Nicholson, and Earl Roberts, 'Russia's Offensive Strength', 29 April, 17 May and 10 June 1901, Document 120, in David Gillard (ed), *BDFA,* Part I, Series B, vol 12 (University Publications of America, 1985), p 352.

[14] Beryl J. Williams, 'The Strategic Background to the Anglo-Russian Entente of August 1907', *The Historical Journal,* ix, 3 (1966), pp 363–4.

[15] Peach et al, 'Russia's Offensive Strength', p 352.

[16] Friedberg, *The Weary Titan,* p 220 and note p 220.

[17] PRO/CAB38/4/39: 'Defence of India: Comments by his Excellency the Commander-in-Chief on the War Office Memoranda on the Defence of India, 15 February 1904', p 4.

[18] For discussions within the Russian government and press on the need to take advantage of Britain's preoccupation in South Africa, see Kazemzadeh, *Russia and Britain in Persia, 1864–1914,* pp 332–40. See also 'Tsarskaia diplomatiia o zadachakh Rossii na Vostoke v 1900 g.', *KA*, 5 (18) (Moscow, 1926), pp 3–29.

[19] IO/L/P&S/18/A141: Abstract and Extracts of Translation by Robert Michell of 'To India, A military statistical and strategical sketch. A project of a future campaign', by Captain W. Lebedeff, Grenadier Guards, St Petersburg, 1898.

[20] PRO/FO65/1599/178: Scott to Salisbury, 'Russia and Afghanistan': copy of instructions to the Governor of Turkestan in case of war with England, St Petersburg, 27 June 1900.

[21] General L.N. Sobolev, *Is an Advance by the Russians to India Possible* (1901), quoted in Druhe, *Russo-Indian Relations, 1466–1917,* p 250.

[22] For the Russian and British views of Britain's position in India, see PRO/CAB38/1/2: 'General Kouropatkine's Scheme for a Russian Advance upon India, with notes thereon by Lord Roberts, the Commander-in-chief in India, and the other members of the Governor-General's Council', August 1891.

[23] PRO/FO65/1593/2 September 1899: 'To India', p 26.

[24] Dufferin to Kimberley, 3 February 1885, Dufferin Papers, quoted in Ira Klein, 'The Anglo-Russian Convention and the Problem of Central Asia, 1907–1914', *The Journal of British Studies,* xi, 1 (November 1971), p 127.

[25] IO/L/P&S/18/A110: Note by W. Lee-Warner, on the Afghan succession and Russia's advance, 26 August 1896, p 2.

[26] See Druhe, *Russo-Indian Relations, 1466–1917*, pp 210–12.

[27] PRO/FO65/1598/103: Precis from the *St Petersburger Zeitung*, 26 March/8 April 1900, Enclosure in Scott to Salisbury.

[28] PRO/FO65/1577/1: 'The Anglo-Russian Problem in Afghanistan and Persia', *Novoe Vremia*, 18/30 December 1898.

[29] PRO/FO371/324/19553: 'Question of Direct Relations between Russia and Afghanistan', Political Department, India Office, 10 June 1907.

[30] PRO/FO539/85/6: Lansdowne to Scott, 29 January 1902.

[31] IO/L/P&S/18/A110: Note by Lee-Warner, 26 August 1896, p 12.

[32] IO/L/P&S/18/C106: Lee-Warner, 'Russia and the Indian Empire', 6 November 1902.

[33] Kimberley to Lansdowne, 3 February 1893, quoted in Rose Louise Greaves, 'British Policy in Persia, 1892–1903', I and II, in *Bulletin of the School of Oriental and African Studies*, 28 (1965), p 41.

[34] Lamsdorff, Proceedings of Special Council, 7 June 1904, on the question of Russia's financial and economic policy in Persia, *KA*, 56, p 50.

[35] Salisbury, quoted in Gillard, *Struggle*, p 165.

[36] Gillard, *Struggle*, p 165.

[37] PRO/FO65/1599/116, Enclosure 1: Summary of Rittich's Pamphlet on 'Railways in Persia', Part II.

[38] Greaves, 'British Policy in Persia, 1892–1903', p 304.

[39] Salisbury, quoted in David McLean, *Britain and Her Buffer State: The Collapse of the Persian Empire, 1890–1914* (London, 1979), p 25.

[40] Alastair Lamb, *The McMahon Line* (London, 1966), vol i, p 5.

[41] See Great Britain Foreign Office Historical Section, *Tibet* (London, 1920), p 37, and Lamb, *The McMahon Line*, pp 6–7. See also AVPRI, f. 144, op. 488, d. 4143, ll. 36–9 ob. and AVPRI f. 144, op. 488, d. 4147 II, ll. 312–26: Draft circular letter to Russian representatives abroad.

[42] See Evgenii Aleksandrovich Belov, *Russko-Kitayskie Otnosheniia v 1911–1915 gg* (Moskva, 1993), p 31.

[43] See John Snelling, 'Agvan Dorjiev: Eminence Grise of Central Asian Politics', *Asian Affairs*, 21, 1 (1990), pp 37–8. For Ukhtomsky's 'Asianist Vision', see David Schimmelpenninck van der Oye, *Oriental Dreams: Ideologies of Empire and Russia's Far East* (DeKalb, IL, 2001), chapter 3.

[44] Sir Francis Younghusband, *India and Tibet* (London, 1910), pp 68–9.

[45] See Younghusband, *India and Tibet*, p 73 and Lamb, *The McMahon Line*, p 9.

[46] Parshotam Mehra, *The McMahon Line and After* (Madras, 1974), p 19.

[47] Younghusband, *India and Tibet*, pp 74–5.

[48] Convention between Great Britain and Thibet. Signed at Lhasa on September 7, 1904. Document 298, in G.P. Gooch and Harold Temperley (eds), *BD* (London, 1929), iv, pp 314–16.

[49] Lansdowne to Sir Cecil Spring-Rice, 17 November 1903, Document 289, in *BD*, iv, p 306.

[50] Lansdowne to Hardinge, 2 June 1904, Document 293, in *BD*, iv, p 310.

[51] Lansdowne to Hardinge, 27 September 1904, Document 301, in *BD*, iv, pp 319–20.

[52] Lord George Hamilton, November 1899, quoted in Bernard Porter, *The Lion's Share* (London, 1975), p 123.

[53] Hugh Arnold-Forster, Diary entry, 28 April 1904, quoted in Keith Neilson, '"Greatly Exaggerated": The Myth of the Decline of Great Britain before 1914', *International History Review*, XIII (4 November 1991), p 716.

[54] I. Reisner, 'Anglo-Russkaia Konventsiia 1907 g. i Razdel Afganistana', *KA*, 10 (1925), p 54.

[55] MacDonald to Lansdowne, 25 May 1905, quoted in Williams, 'The Strategic Background to the Anglo-Russian Entente of August 1907', p 362.

[56] MacDonald to Lansdowne, 15 July 1905, quoted in Williams, 'The Strategic Background to the Anglo-Russian Entente of August 1907', p 362.

[57] William C. Fuller, Jr., *Strategy and Power in Russia, 1600–1914* (New York, 1992), p 395. See also RGVIA, f. 2000, op. 1, d. 3737, ll. 10–41: Extract from a summary of the staff of the Turkestani Military District on the internal politics and economic situation of Afghanistan; description of plans for the Afghan theatre of military action, 1912.

[58] S. Iu. Witte, *Vospominaniia* (Moscow, 1994), vol iii, pp 438–9.

[59] Campbell-Bannerman, quoted in Bernard Mallet, *British Budgets, 1887–88 to 1912–13* (London, 1913), pp 233–4.

[60] PRO/FO371/124/9907: Sir Edward Grey to Spring-Rice, 19 March 1906.

[61] See V.P. Potemkin, *Istoriia Diplomatii* (Moskva, 1945), p 178.

[62] See Keith Neilson, *Britain and the Last Tsar* (Oxford, 1995), pp 277–9.

[63] AVPRI f. 144, op. 488, d. 4147 II, ll. 312–26: Draft circular letter to the Russian representatives abroad; Lettre du Comte Benckendorff, en date de Londres, le 7–20 Juin 1906, in Alexandre Iswolsky, *Au Service de la Russie. Correspondance Diplomatique, 1906–1911* (Paris, 1939), vol i, p 309.

[64] PRO/FO371/322/10140: A. Godley, India Office to Foreign Office, 27 March 1907; PRO/FO371/322/12116: Godley to Foreign Office, 13 April 1907.

[65] Izvolskii, in the protocol of 'The Journal of the Special Committee on the Conclusion of an Agreement with England on the Question of Afghanistan', 11/24 August 1907, *KA*, 69–70 (1935), pp 32–9; see also Neilson, *Britain*, pp 286–7.

[66] Kokovtsov, in the protocol of 'The Journal of the Special Committee on the Afghan Question', 14 April 1907, quoted in Reisner, *KA*, 10 (1925), p 55.

[67] PRO/CAB37/89/80: 'Anglo-Russian Convention of 31 August 1907: Persia, Afghanistan & Tibet', 3 September 1907.

[68] AVPRI f. 133, op. 470, d. 72: Note remise par Nicolson à Izvolskii en date de St Pétersbourg le 18/31 août 1907.

Chapter 2: Triumph or Tribulation?

[1] AVPRI f. 144, op. 488, d. 4147, ll. 312–26: Draft Circular Letter to the Russian Representatives abroad.

[2] I.A. Zinoviev, *Rossiia, Angliia i Persiia* (St Petersburg, 1912).

[3] S. Iu. Witte, *Vospominaniia* (Tallinn and Moscow, 1994), vol iii, p 437.

[4] *Moskovskie Vedomosti*, 22–23 September/5–6 October 1907, quoted in Igor Vasilevich Bestuzhev, *Borba v Rossii po Voprosam Vneshnei Politiki* (Moscow, 1961), p 147.

[5] See P.N. Efremov, *Vneshniaia politika Rossii (1907–1914 gg.)* (Moscow, 1961), pp 65–6.

[6] 'The Anglo-Russian Agreement and Public Opinion', *The Times*, 6 September 1907, p 7; 'The Anglo-Russian Convention', Leader, *The Times*, 25 September 1907, p 7.

[7] 'The Anglo-Russian Agreement', *The Economist*, 28 September 1907, pp 1618–19.

[8] Leader, *The Guardian*, 26 September 1907, p 6.

[9] National Administrative Council of the Independent Labour Party, *The Times*, 8 July 1907, p 7.

[10] AVPRI f. 144, op. 488, d. 4143, ll. 273–4 ob.: Secret dispatch from Benckendorff, London, 31 October/12 November 1907, No. 56.

[11] Curzon, 'The Anglo-Russian Convention', maiden speech in the House of Lords, 6 February 1908, in *The Times*, 7 February 1908, pp 8–9.

[12] PRO/FO371/514/5877: Extract from *The Times* re debate in House of Commons of 17 February 1908, 18 February 1908.

[13] Spring-Rice to Grey, 13 September 1907, in Stephen Gwynn (ed), *The Letters and Friendships of Sir Cecil Spring-Rice* (London, 1929), vol 2, pp 103–5.

[14] Grey, 'Foreign Relations', Corn Exchange, Berwick-on-Tweed, 19 December 1907, in P. Knaplund (ed), *Speeches on Foreign Affairs, 1900–14 by Sir Edward Grey* (London, 1931), pp 40–1; see also AVPRI f. 144, op. 488, d. 4143, l. 312: Télégramme secret de Benckendorff, Londres, le 7/20 Déc 1907.

[15] IO/L/P&S/18/C/140: Memorandum respecting the Anglo-Russian Convention, Foreign Office, 29 January 1908 (confidential).

[16] AVPRI f. 147, op. 486, d. 2326, l. 346: Promemoria, 16/29 August 1907; AVPRI f. 144, op. 488, d. 4143, l. 103: Izvolskii, Carlsbad, 2 September 1907, No. 327.

[17] AVPRI f. 147, op. 485, d. 748, ll. 92–3: Report of agent A.M.Kh. from 10/23 September 1907.

[18] PRO/FO371/514/10133: Fakir Syed Iftikhar-ud-Din, British Agent at Kabul, to Government of India, 25 January 1908.

[19] IO/L/P&S/18/C/140: Memorandum respecting the Anglo-Russian Convention, Foreign Office, 29 January 1908 (confidential).

[20] AVPRI f. 147, op. 486, d. 232b, ll. 372–3 ob.: Benckendorff to Izvolskii, 23 March/5 April 1908.

[21] PRO/FO371/516/17778: O'Beirne to Grey, St Petersburg, 21 May 1908.

[22] PRO/FO800/73: Nicolson to Grey, 19 July 1908. See also PRO/FO371/514/26711: Morley to Government of India, 30 July 1908.

[23] PRO/FO371/514/32895: Government of India to Morley, 21 September 1908.

[24] PRO/FO371/514/33705: Government of India to Morley, 28 September 1908.

[25] PRO/FO371/514/35858: Morley to Government of India, 14 October 1908.

[26] PRO/FO371/514/26711: Morley to Government of India, 30 July 1908.

[27] PRO/FO371/311/38680: No. 40: Diary of Captain Smyth (military attaché at Mashhad) for week ending 5 October 1907.

[28] AVPRI f. 147, op. 486, d. 232b, ll. 355–6: Copy of Memorandum by the Official for Border Relations under the Chief of the Transcaspian District (A. Baranovskii) to the Diplomatic Section of the Turkestan Governor-Generalship from 30 September/13 October 1907, No. 435.

[29] AVPRI f. 147, op. 486, d. 232b, l. 368: Izvolskii to N.I. Grodekov, 6/19 March 1908, No. 290.

[30] RGVIA f. 400, op. 1, d. 3692, ll. 5–5 ob.: Izvolskii to A.A. Polivanov, 5/18 July 1908, No. 660.

[31] PRO/FO371/518/25278: O'Beirne to Grey, St Petersburg, 20 July 1908; PRO/FO371/518/26282: Government of India to Morley, 23 July 1908.

[32] PRO/FO371/518/27161: Government of India to Morley, 3 August 1908 (telegraphic). For confirmation of local involvement of Russian frontier authorities in Jamshedi raids, see PRO/FO371/518/28790: Grey to Nicolson (telegraphic), 19 August 1908.

[33] PRO/FO371/518/28723: Nicolson (telegram), 17 August 1908.

[34] PRO/FO371/518/29128: Government of India to Morley (telegraphic), 20 August 1908; AVPRI f. 147, op. 486, d. 232b, l. 382: Secret telegram to General-Adjutant Mishenko in Tashkent, St Petersburg, 11/24 August 1908.

[35] PRO/FO371/518/29128: Minute by H.C. Norman on Government of India to Morley, 20 August 1908.

[36] AVPRI f. 147, op. 486, d. 232b, l. 382: Secret telegram to Mishenko, St Petersburg, 11/24 August 1908.

[37] PRO/FO371/518/32377: Government of India to Morley (telegraphic), 17 September 1908.

[38] PRO/FO371/727/6057: Russia. Annual Report (1908), 8 February 1909.

[39] PRO/FO371/518/33404: Nicolson to Grey, St Petersburg, 22 September 1908; PRO/FO371/724/658: Nicolson to Grey, No. 445, St Petersburg, 7 October 1908.

[40] PRO/FO371/724/658: Nicolson to Grey, No. 445, St Petersburg, 7 October 1908; PRO/FO371/518/44390: Nicolson to Grey, St Petersburg, 16 December 1908.

[41] PRO/FO371/311/38680: No. 40: Diary of Captain Smyth for week ending 5 October 1907.

[42] RGVIA f. 400, op. 1, d. 3733, ll. 1–4 ob.: F.F. Palitsyn to A.F. Roediger, 31 October/13 November 1908, No. 2354 (secret).

[43] See RGVIA f. 400, op. 1, d. 3757: Collected information about neighbouring countries, prepared by the intelligence agents of the staff of the Turkestan Military District. These digests cover Afghanistan, India, China and Persia.

[44] RGVIA f. 400, op. 1, d. 3733, ll. 1–4 ob.: Palitsyn to Roediger, 31 October/13 November 1908, No. 2354 (secret).

[45] IO/L/MIL/7/7811: Major-General A.A. Pearson, C.B., Officiating Adjutant General in India, to the Secretary of the Government of India, Military Department, Simla, 26 September 1904.

[46] PRO/WO106/6148: 'Secret Service'. Lecture delivered by Captain C.H.G. Black, 34th Horse, Staff College, Quetta, p 13.

[47] For an example of the type and scope of intelligence gathered by the British in Afghanistan, see IO/L/MIL/17/14/2: Gazetteer of Afghanistan (4th edition), compiled in the Division of the Chief of the Staff, Calcutta, 1907. This is a four-volume account of Afghanistan, detailed province by province. However, it was only updated approximately once every ten years.

[48] PRO/FO371/502/9460: 'Appointment of a Permanent Military Attaché at Meshed', Army Department, Dispatch No. 115, Simla, 7 November 1907.

[49] PRO/FO371/502/9460: Minute by Hardinge.

[50] PRO/FO371/502/23647: India Office to Foreign Office, 8 July 1908.

[51] PRO/FO371/502/32315: War Office to Foreign Office, 16 September 1908.

[52] PRO/FO371/502/39418: Treasury to Foreign Office, Treasury Chambers, 11 November 1908.

[53] AVPRI f. 144, op. 488, d. 4146, ll. 197–8: Sir C. Spring-Rice to the Persian Minister of Foreign Affairs, 4 September 1907. Enclosure in Secret report of Poklev-sky-Kozell, Teheran, 24 March/5 April 1912; AVPRI f. 144, op. 488, d. 4143, l. 51: No. 1853, 21 August/3 September 1907.

[54] PRO/FO371/312/32434: Nicolson to Grey, re conversation with the Mushir-ul-Mulk, Persian Minister in St Petersburg, St Petersburg, 24 September 1907.

[55] PRO/FO371/312/32478: Spring-Rice to Grey, No. 203, Gulahek, 13 September 1907.

[56] See E.G. Browne, *The Persian Revolution of 1905–09* (Cambridge, 1910), pp 112–19. Although the author is at times rather impassioned in his liberal defence of Persian constitutionalism and the revolution, his chronicle of the course of the revolution remains one of the best major works on the subject.

[57] See Kazemzadeh, *Russia and Britain in Persia, 1864–1914*, pp 495–7.

[58] See Bestuzhev, *Borba v Rossii po Voprosam Vneshnei Politiki*, pp 148–50.

[59] PRO/FO371/313/38674: Marling to Grey, No. 243, Teheran, 7 November 1907.

[60] RGIA f. 560, op. 28, d. 375, l. 53: Journal of a Special Conference on the question of measures called for by the situation in Persia, 30 November/13 December 1907.

[61] See Kazemzadeh, *Russia and Britain in Persia, 1864–1914*, pp 512–14.

[62] AVPRI f. 144, op. 488, d. 4143, ll. 299–301: Lettre privée de Benckendorff, Londres, 30 November/13 December 1907.

[63] AVPRI f. 144, op. 488, d. 4143, l. 324: Izvolskii to Hartwig, St Petersburg, 14/27 December 1907 (telegram); AVPRI f. 144, op. 488, d. 4143, ll. 310–11: Lettre de Benckendorff, Londres, 7/20 December 1907.

[64] AVPRI f. 144, op. 488, d. 4143, l. 305: Télégramme secret de Benckendorff, Londres, 4/17 December 1907.

[65] AVPRI f. 144, op. 488, d. 4147, ll. 264–9: Russian policies in Persia and the mutual relations of Russia and England in Persian Affairs.

[66] AVPRI f. 144, op. 488, d. 4147, l. 237: Copy of a circular letter from Izvolskii to the Russian Ambassadors in Berlin, Paris, London and Constantinople, 20 December 1907/3 January 1908.

[67] RGIA f. 560, op. 28, d. 401, l. 44: Izvolskii to Vorontsov-Dashkov, St Petersburg, 31 March/13 April 1908.

[68] PRO/FO371/516/15992: Marling to Grey, Teheran, 23 April 1908; Hartwig was supported by the Russian consuls in northern Persia in his call for direct military intervention in Azerbaijan. See RGIA f. 560, op. 28, d. 401, l. 52: Secret telegram from Pokhitonov, Tabriz, 4/17 April 1908.

[69] RGIA f. 560, op. 28, d. 375, ll. 191–3 ob.: Excerpts from the Approved Commander in Chief of the Troops of the Caucasian Military District of the Considerations Concerning Military Influence on Persia, 20 March/2 April 1908.

[70] PRO/FO371/516/15261: O'Beirne to Grey, St Petersburg, 30 April 1908; For Vorontsov-Dashkov's instructions to the detachment, see RGIA f. 560, op. 28, d. 401: Instructions to the Commander of the Diman Detachment.

[71] PRO/FO371/516/17677: Consul Stevens to Grey, Batum, 13 May 1908.

[72] RGIA f. 560, op. 28, d. 401, l. 64: Izvolskii to Vorontsov-Dashkov, St Petersburg, 7/20 April 1908.

[73] RGIA f. 560, op. 28, d. 401, ll. 82–3: Secret dispatch from Hartwig, No. 64, Teheran, 24 April/7 May 1908.

[74] PRO/FO371/516/17624: O'Beirne to Grey, St Petersburg, 22 May 1908.

[75] RGIA f. 560, op. 28, d. 401, ll. 140–1: Secret telegram from Kokhanovskii, Tiflis, 25 May/7 June 1908, No. 291.

[76] RGIA f. 560, op. 28, d. 401, ll. 105–105 ob.: Secret dispatch from Hartwig, Teheran, 10/23 May 1908, No. 227.

[77] PRO/FO371/516/19681: Marling to Grey, Gulahek, 20 May 1908.

[78] RGIA f. 560, op. 28, d. 401, ll. 128–9: Secret telegram from Vorontsov-Dashkov, Tiflis, 21 May/3 June 1908, No. 290.

[79] PRO/FO371/516/18730: Marling to Grey, Teheran, 30 May 1908.

[80] PRO/FO371/516/20077: Marling to Grey, Gulahek, 29 May 1908.

[81] RGIA f. 560, op. 28, d. 401, l. 142: Secret telegram from Hartwig, Teheran, 29 May/11 June 1908.

[82] RGIA f. 560, op. 28, d. 401, ll. 157–157 ob.: Secret telegram from Vorontsov-Dashkov, Tiflis, 2/15 June 1908, No. 312.

[83] AVPRI f. 144, op. 488, d. 4143, l. 430: 'Foreign News. Foreign Survey. In Persia and Afghanistan', *Slova*, 438 (23 April/6 May 1908).

[84] 'Russia and Persia', *The Times*, 38, 655 (25 May 1908), p 9.

[85] AVPRI f. 144, op. 488, d. 4143, l. 430: 'Foreign News. Foreign Survey. In Persia and Afghanistan', *Slova*, 438 (23 April/6 May 1908).

[86] PRO/FO371/517/19621: O'Beirne to Grey, St Petersburg, 2 June 1908.

[87] Kazemzadeh, *Russia and Britain in Persia, 1864–1914*, p 520.

[88] PRO/FO371/517/20885: Memorandum by Hardinge, HM yacht *Victoria & Albert*, 12 June 1908, p 8.

[89] PRO/FO371/516/15846: Government of India to Morley, 24 April 1908.

[90] PRO/FO371/516/15846: Government of India to Morley (telegraphic), 28 April 1908.

[91] PRO/FO371/516/15846: Morley to Government of India, 29 April 1908; AVPRI f. 147, op. 485, d. 749, ll. 39–39 ob.: Dispatch from Benckendorff, London, 16/29 April 1908, No. 24.

[92] PRO/FO371/516/15846: Government of India to Morley, 2 May 1908.

[93] PRO/FO371/516/17207: Government of India to Morley, 10 May 1908.

[94] PRO/FO371/516/17207: Government of India to Morley, 18 May 1908.

[95] AVPRI f. 147, op. 485, d. 749, ll. 46–7: Diplomatic Official in the Turkestan Governor-Generalship to the First Department of MID, Tashkent, 20 June/3 July 1908, No. 243.

[96] PRO/FO371/517/20885: Memorandum by Hardinge, HM yacht *Victoria & Albert*, 12 June 1908, pp 11–12.

[97] AVPRI f. 147, op. 485, d. 749, ll. 74–5 ob.: Excerpts from the report of the staff of the Turkestan Military District to Palitsyn, 17/30 July 1908, No. 1502.

[98] PRO/FO371/516/29443: Government of India to Morley, 23 August 1908.

[99] AVPRI f. 144, op. 488, d. 4143, l. 472: Izvolskii to Hartwig, St Petersburg, 13/26 June 1908. Communicated to Benckendorff; AVPRI f. 144, op. 488, d. 4143, l. 483: Télégramme secret de Benckendorff, Londres, 17/30 June 1908 (Personnel), No. 2.

[100] AVPRI f. 144, op. 488, d. 4143, l. 492: Izvolskii to Hartwig, St Petersburg, 19 June/2 July 1908 (telegram).

[101] AVPRI f. 144, op. 488, d. 4143, l. 473: Télégramme secret à Benckendorff et à Hartwig en date de St Pétersbourg, 12/23 June 1908.

[102] PRO/CAB37/94/95: Grey to O'Beirne (private) (telegraphic), 1 July 1908.

[103] AVPRI f. 144, op. 488, d. 4143, l. 484: Télégramme secret de Benckendorff, Londres, 17/30 June 1908, No. 3 (Très confidentiel et personnel).

[104] AVPRI f. 144, op. 488, d. 4143, l. 479: Télégramme secret à Benckendorff, Londres, 16/29 June 1908.

[105] AVPRI f. 144, op. 488, d. 4143, l. 482: Télégramme secret de Benckendorff, Londres, 17/30 June 1908 (Personnel).

[106] AVPRI f. 144, op. 488, d. 4143, l. 479: Télégramme secret à Benckendorff, Londres, 16/29 June 1908.

[107] AVPRI f. 144, op. 488, d. 4143, l. 482: Télégramme secret de Benckendorff, Londres, 17/30 June 1908 (Personnel).

[108] AVPRI f. 144, op. 488, d. 4143, l. 484: Télégramme secret de Benckendorff, Londres, 17/30 June 1908, No. 3 (Très confidentiel et personnel).

[109] AVPRI f. 144, op. 488, d. 4143, l. 490: Secret telegram from Hartwig, Teheran, 18 June/1 July 1908, No. 349.

[110] AVPRI f. 144, op. 488, d. 4143, l. 495: Secret telegram from Hartwig, Teheran, 19 June/2 July 1908; AVPRI f. 144, op. 488, d. 4143, l. 496: Télégramme secret de Benckendorff, Londres, 19 June/2 July 1908.

[111] AVPRI f. 144, op. 488, d. 4143, l. 495: Secret telegram from Hartwig, Teheran, 19 June/2 July 1908.

[112] PRO/FO371/956/8668: Persia. Annual Report (1908), 10 February 1909, p 9.

[113] AVPRI f. 144, op. 488, d. 4143, l. 497: Izvolskii to Hartwig, St Petersburg, 20 June/3 July 1908 (telegram).

[114] PRO/FO371/727/6057: Russia. Annual Report (1908), 8 February 1909, p 19.

[115] PRO/FO371/507/37030: Marling to Grey, No. 265, 30 September 1908 (very confidential); Hartwig thought much more highly of his English colleague than Marling did of him, describing Marling as 'an honest and conscientious man', AVPRI f. 144, op. 488, d. 4144, l. 49: Secret report from Hartwig, Zergendeh, 25 September/8 October 1908, No. 136.

[116] Lettre de Benckendorff, en date de Londres, le 23 juin/6 juillet 1908, in Alexandre Iswolsky, *Au Service de la Russie* (Paris, 1939), vol 2, pp 177–82.

[117] PRO/FO371/506/31808: Nicolson to Grey, No. 400, St Petersburg, 7 September 1908.

[118] RGIA f. 560, op. 28, d. 398, ll. 202–3: Copy from a secret letter from Izvolskii to Roediger, 26 January/8 February 1908, No. 157.

[119] PRO/FO371/727/6057: Russia. Annual Report (1908), 8 February 1909, p 20; Soviet historians have extensively explored the relationship between Russian and Caucasian revolutionaries and the Persian revolution of 1905–11. See, for example, Mikhail Sergeevich Ivanov, *Iranskaia Revoliutsiia 1905–1911 godov* (Moscow, 1957), or E. Bor-Ramenskii, 'K voprosu o roli bolshevikov zakavkazia v iranskoi revoliutsii 1905–1911 godov', *Istorik marksist*, 11 (1940). Although it is unquestionable that the Caucasian revolutionary movement was extremely influential in the course of the Persian revolution, Kazemzadeh stresses that this movement was not a Bolshevik one. See Kazemzadeh, *Russia and Britain in Persia, 1864–1914*, pp 527–8, n. 56.

[120] RGIA f. 560, op. 28, d. 376, l. 8: Copy of a telegram from Hartwig, Teheran, 1/14 October 1908, No. 578.

[121] AVPRI f. 144, op. 488, d. 4144, ll. 57–8: Secret telegram from Hartwig, Tehe-ran, 8/25 October 1908, No. 596; PRO/FO371/727/6057: Russia. Annual Report (1908), 8 February 1909, p 20.

[122] RGIA f. 560, op. 28, d. 401, ll. 190–5 ob.: Journal of the Special Confidential Session of the Council of Ministers on the question of stabilizing the situation on the Caucasian–Persian border, 27 August/9 September 1908.

[123] RGIA f. 560, op. 28, d. 398, l. 213: Kokovtsov to Izvolskii, 7/20 February 1908, No. 97; RGIA f. 560, op. 28, d. 398, ll. 210–12: Izvolskii to Kokovtsov, 5/18 February 1908, No. 206.

[124] RGIA f. 560, op. 28, d. 398, ll. 230–230 ob.: Chairman of the Board of Direc-tors of the Tabriz and Anzeli-Teheran Road Company, Podgurskii, to the Director of the Chancellery of the Ministry of Finance, E.D. Lvov, St Petersburg, 1/14 July 1908, No. 187.

[125] RGIA f. 560, op. 28, d. 376, ll. 10–10 ob.: Acting Minister of Foreign Affairs (Charikov) to Hartwig, St Petersburg, 2/15 October 1908 (telegram).

[126] RGIA f. 560, op. 28, d. 376, ll. 24–31: Special Session of the Council of Minis-ters, 3/16 October 1908. On measures to secure in the Persian Province of Azerbaijan, Russian subjects and their property, and also the property of Russian institutions and industries.

[127] AVPRI f. 144, op. 488, d. 4144, ll. 57–8: Secret telegram from Hartwig, Tehe-ran, 8/25 October 1908, No. 596.

[128] AVPRI f. 144, op. 4144, l. 80: Télégramme secret de Benckendorff, Londres, 23 October/5 November 1908.

[129] AVPRI f. 144, op. 488, d. 4144, l. 65: Charikov to Hartwig, St Petersburg, 11/24 October 1908, No. 1475; AVPRI f. 144, op. 488, d. 4144, l. 87: Izvolskii to Hartwig, St Petersburg, 28 October/10 November 1908, No. 1580 (telegram).

[130] It is interesting to note that after Hartwig left Teheran, he was appointed to the post of Russian minister in Serbia. Once in Belgrade, he proceeded to behave much as he had in Persia, working steadily and often independently to attach Serbia to Russia. For a more extensive discussion of Hartwig's activity in Belgrade and his blatant disregard for overall Russian foreign policy after his tenure in Persia, see D.C.B. Lieven, *Russia and the Origins of the First World War* (London, 1983), pp 41–2.

[131] PRO/FO371/727/6057: Russia. Annual Report (1908), pp 22–3.

[132] PRO/FO371/514/3643: Russia. Annual Report (1907), pp 29–30.

[133] PRO/FO371/727/6057: Russia. Annual Report (1908), p 26.

[134] RGVIA f. 400, op. 1, d. 3547, ll. 42–6: Izvolskii to the Council of Ministers, 26 July/8 August 1908, No. 1114.

[135] See 'Last Year's Trade. Official Report', *The Indian Trade Journal*, Rangoon, 20 July 1908.

[136] See Alastair Lamb, *The McMahon Line* (London, 1966), chapter x, for a full discussion of the Tibet Trade Regulations negotiations of 1908.

[137] PRO/FO371/412/17309: E.C. Wilton, British Commissioner, China Consular Service, to Government of India, Calcutta, 23 April 1908.

[138] PRO/FO371/412/1520: Government of India to Morley, 11 January 1908.

[139] PRO/FO371/412/704: Government of India to Morley, 4 January 1908. Enclosure in India Office to Foreign Office, 7 January 1908.

[140] Morley Papers (D.573/3), Morley to Minto, 3 January 1908, quoted in Lamb, *The McMahon Line*, p 149.

[141] PRO/FO371/727/6057: Russia. Annual Report (1908), p 26; see also Mehra, *The McMahon Line and After*, p 44.

[142] PRO/FO371/412/17309: Thibet Trade Regulations, Calcutta, 20 April 1908.

[143] AVPRI f. 144, op. 488, d. 4143, l. 364: Draft Note from HMG to the Imperial Russian Government, no date.

[144] RGIA f. 560, op. 28, d. 1123, ll. 26–26 ob.: Secret report of Baron Heyking, 22 August/4 September 1908, No. 382.

[145] PRO/FO371/513/40797: Summary of Events in Russia during the fortnight ending 19 November 1908.

[146] For the implications of the Bosnian crisis for Anglo-Russian relations, see Keith Neilson, *Britain and the Last Tsar* (Oxford, 1995), pp 298–305. For the state of Russian military preparedness and inability to go to war, see William C. Fuller, Jr., *Strategy and Power in Russia, 1600–1914* (New York, 1992), pp 420–2.

[147] PRO/FO371/513/40797: Summary of Events in Russia during the fortnight ending 19 November 1908.

[148] IO/L/MIL/17/5/1745: Kitchener, 'Consideration of the Effect of the Anglo-Russian Convention on the Strength of the Army in India', 21 October 1907, p 1.

[149] IO/L/MIL/17/5/1745: Kitchener, pp 3–5.

[150] AVPRI f. 144, op. 488, d. 4147, l. 66: Morning Bulletin (telegram and overland), London, 18 February/2 March, House of Commons, 19 February/3 March 1908.

[151] IO/MSS Eur/D573/37/104: Military (Secret) No. 50. Letter from the Secretary of State, John Morley, to the Governor-General of India in Council, 20 March 1908.

[152] IO/MSS Eur/D 573/37/62: Minute. Note on reduction of British Army, L. Abrahams, 2 June 1908 (confidential).

[153] PRO/CAB37/94/89: 'A Note upon British Military Needs', W.S.C, 27 June 1908.

Chapter 3: Old Designs under a New Cover?

[1] Bülow to Pourtalès (St Petersburg) (drafted by Kiderlen), 21 March 1909, quoted in A.J.P. Taylor, *The Struggle for Mastery in Europe 1848–1918* (Oxford, 1954), p 455.

[2] PRO/FO371/507/44366: Official Communiqué which appeared in the Russian press, 23 November 1908. Enclosure in Nicolson to Grey, St Petersburg, 28 November 1908; see also PRO/FO371/513/42578: Summary of Events in Russia during the fortnight ending 3 December 1908.

[3] PRO/FO371/507/44366: Official Communiqué which appeared in the Russian Press, 23 November 1908. Enclosure in Nicolson to Grey, St Petersburg, 28 November 1908.

[4] See RGIA f. 560, op. 28, d. 376 for various discussions outlining the unrest, such as reports of revolutionaries seizing guns and threats to the property of Russian subjects, in northern Persia.

[5] RGIA f. 560, op. 28, d. 376, ll. 95–103 ob.: Journal of a Meeting of the Special Conference on the question of the direction of Russian politics in relation to Persia, 17/30 December and 19 December 1908/2 January 1909.

[6] M. Grulev, *Sopernichestvo Rossii i Anglii v Srednei Azii* (St Petersburg, 1909), p 230.

[7] N.N. Shavrov, *Vneshniaia Torgovlia Persii i uchastie v ney Rossii. Izdania zhurnala 'Russkyi Eksport'* (St Petersburg, 1913), p 65.

[8] See Kh. Ataev, *Politicheskie i Torgovlo-Ekonomicheskie Otnosheniia Severo-Vostochnogo Irana i Rossii v Nachale XX Veka (1900–1917 gg.)* (Ashkhabad, 1989), pp 29–36; on the development of the Russo-Persian trade, see also B. Mannanov, *Iz Istorii Russko-Iranskikh Otnoshenii v Kontse XIX-Nachale XX Veka* (Tashkent, 1964), pp 86–130.

[9] Ataev, *Politicheskie*, pp 46–55.

[10] See Zh. Ia. Kassis, *Ekonomicheskoe polozhenie sovremennoy Persii* (Kiev, 1915), p 78.

[11] RGIA f. 560, op. 28, d. 398, l. 279–80 ob.: Memorandum on the organization of security of the Tabriz road in Persia, by Kokovtsov at Tsarskoe Selo, 24 December 1908/6 January 1909.

[12] RGIA f. 560, op. 28, d. 376, ll. 191–191 ob.: Copy of a letter from the Commander-in-Chief of the troops of the Caucasian Military District to Izvolskii, 14/27 February 1909, No. 652.

[13] RGIA f. 560, op. 28, d. 376, ll. 140–140 ob.: Secret telegram from Sablin, Teheran, 13/26 February 1909, No. 62.

[14] RGIA f. 560, op. 28, d. 377, l. 17: Izvolskii to Sablin, St Petersburg, 7/20 April 1909, No. 633 (telegram).

[15] RGIA f. 560, op. 28, d. 377, l. 55: Secret telegram to Vorontsov-Dashkov, St Petersburg, 9/22 April 1909, No. 658.

[16] RGIA f. 560, op. 28, d. 377, l. 64: Secret telegram from Vorontsov-Dashkov, Tbilisi, 10/23 April 1909, No. 303.

[17] AVPRI f. 144, op. 489, d. 594b, l. 202: Instructions to the Tabriz Detachment, 12/25 April 1909.

[18] RGIA f. 560, op. 28, d. 377, l. 136: Secret telegram from Miller, Tabriz, 16/29 April 1909, No. 74.

[19] Grey, 'Russia, Persia, and the King's Visits Abroad', The House of Commons, 24 March 1909, in P. Knaplund (ed) *Speeches on Foreign Affairs, 1900–14 by Sir Edward Grey*, pp 115–16.

[20] PRO/FO371/717/21106: Barclay to Grey, Teheran, 30 April 1909; see also PRO/FO371/717/39626: Barclay to Grey, Teheran, 9 October 1909.

[21] RGIA f. 560, op. 28, d. 377, l. 222: Secret telegram from Vorontsov-Dashkov, Tbilisi, 25 April/8 May 1909, No. 11699.

[22] PRO/FO371/717/17243: Barclay to Grey (telegraphic), Teheran, 7 May 1909.

[23] RGIA f. 560, op. 28, d. 378, ll. 6–8 ob.: Journal of a Session of the Special Committee on Persian Affairs, 25 April/8 May 1909.

[24] PRO/FO371/717/17243: Grey to Nicolson (telegraphic), 7 May 1909.

[25] AVPRI f. 144, op. 488, d. 4144, l. 133: Stolypin to Vorontsov-Dashkov, St Petersburg, 25 May/7 June 1909, No. 984 (telegram).

[26] AVPRI f. 144, op. 488, d. 4144, l. 163: Aide-Mémoire, St Petersburg, 22 May/4 June 1909.

[27] AVPRI f. 144, op. 488, d. 4144, ll. 131–131 ob.: Izvolskii to Benckendorff, St Petersburg, 23 May/5 June 1909, No. 969 (telegram No. 1).

[28] PRO/FO371/504/8975: Consul Haworth to Major Cox, Kermanshah, 22 October 1907. Enclosure 1 in Marling to Grey, Teheran, 28 February 1908.

[29] PRO/FO371/504/30126: Marling to Grey, Gulahek, 13 August 1908.

[30] PRO/FO378/210/16003: 'Mr. Marling reports on openings for British trade in Persia', 20 April 1908.

[31] PRO/FO371/504/30126: Haworth to Cox, Kermanshah, 6 August 1908. Enclosure 7 in Marling to Grey, Gulahek, 13 August 1908.

[32] RGIA f. 560, op. 28, d. 528, ll. 217–18 ob.: Secret report from Reshetov, Ardebil, 18 February/3 March 1909, No. 54.

[33] IO/L/P&S/18/C/140: Memorandum respecting the Anglo-Russian Convention, Foreign Office, 29 January 1908 (confidential).

[34] PRO/FO371/1427/49756: Trade in ports in Southern Persia. Extracted from Consular Reports.

[35] PRO/FO371/718/29933: Memorandum respecting the Disorders on the Trade Routes of Southern Persia. H.G. Chick, Vice-Consul at Bushire, 18 July 1909.

[36] PRO/FO371/718/25139: Barclay to Grey, No. 122, Gulahek, 15 June 1909.

[37] PRO/CAB37/97/23: Memorandum to be communicated by Nicolson to Izvolskii, 3 February 1909.

[38] AVPRI f. 144, op. 488, d. 4144, ll. 189–189 ob.: Acting Minister of Foreign Affairs to Benckendorff, St Petersburg, 13/26 June 1909, No. 1092 (telegram); RGIA f. 560, op. 28, d. 379, l. 92: Acting Minister of Foreign Affairs to Sablin, St Petersburg 13/26 June 1909, No. 1093.

[39] RGIA f. 560, op. 28, d. 376, ll. 113–113 ob.: Secret telegram from Sablin, Teheran, 3/16 February 1909, No. 38.

[40] RGIA f. 560, op. 28, d. 376, ll. 123–123 ob.: Izvolskii to Sablin, St Petersburg, 10/23 February 1909, No. 230 (telegram).

[41] PRO/FO371/717/18282: Nicolson to Grey, No. 298, St Petersburg, 10 May 1909.

[42] AVPRI f. 144, op. 488, d. 4144, ll. 189–189 ob.: Acting Minister of Foreign Affairs to Benckendorff, St Petersburg, 13/26 June 1909, No. 1092 (telegram).

[43] RGIA f. 560, op. 28, d. 379, l. 129: Secret telegram from Sablin, Teheran, 18 June/1 July 1909, No. 314.

[44] AVPRI f. 144, op. 488, d. 4144, l. 202: Télégramme secret de Benckendorff, Londres, 17/30 June 1909, No. 114.

[45] AVPRI f. 144, op. 488, d. 4147, l. 225: Télégramme secret de Benckendorff, Londres, 20 June/3 July, No. 125.

[46] PRO/FO800/73: O'Beirne to Grey (telegraphic), St Petersburg, 2 July 1909.

[47] AVPRI f. 144, op. 488, d. 4144, l. 223: Izvolskii aux Représentants de Russie à l'étranger, St Pétersbourg, 20 June 1909 (télégramme).

[48] AVPRI f. 144, op. 488, d. 4144, l. 265: Telegram from Sablin, Teheran, 30 June/13 July 1909, No. 885.

[49] AVPRI f. 144, op. 488, d. 4144, l. 276: Secret telegram from Sablin, Teheran, 2/15 July 1909, No. 350.

[50] AVPRI f. 144, op. 488, d. 4144, l. 277: Secret telegram from Sablin, Teheran, 2/15 July 1909, No. 349.

[51] AVPRI f. 144, op. 488, d. 4144, l. 276: Secret telegram from Sablin, Teheran, 2/15 July 1909, No. 350.

[52] RGIA f. 560, op. 28, d. 380, l. 51: Telegram from the Director of the Discount-Loan Bank of Persia to the Director of the General Chancellery of the Ministry of Finance, Teheran, 3/16 July 1909.

[53] AVPRI f. 144, op. 488, d. 4144, l. 289: Secret telegram from Sablin, Teheran, 4/17 July 1909, No. 356.

[54] AVPRI f. 144, op. 488, d. 4144, l. 282: Télégramme de Sablin, Téhéran, 3/16 July 1909.

[55] AVPRI f. 144, op. 488, d. 4144, l. 279: Secret telegram from Sablin, Teheran, 3/16 July 1909, No. 353; AVPRI f. 144, op. 488, d. 4144, l. 302: Secret telegram from Sablin, Teheran, 6/19 July 1909, No. 363.

[56] RGIA f. 560, op. 28, d. 380, ll. 111–111 ob.: Secret telegram from Sablin, Teheran, 7/20 July 1909, No. 366.

[57] Kazemzadeh sees Sablin in this period as insufficiently strong to pursue a policy independent from that of Izvolskii (see Kazemzadeh, *Russia and Britain in Persia, 1864–1914*, p 532). The correspondence in the Russian archives, however, appears to point towards Sablin's actual commitment to non-intervention and the ideas of Russian restraint and Anglo-Russian co-operation.

[58] AVPRI f. 144, op. 488, d. 4144, l. 338: Secret telegram from Sablin, Teheran, 17/30 July 1909, No. 381.

[59] AVPRI f. 144, op. 488, d. 4144, ll. 366–7: Secret telegram from Sablin, Teheran, 24 July/6 August 1909, No. 401.

[60] PRO/FO800/73: Grey to O'Beirne (private), 9 July 1909.

[61] AVPRI f. 147, op. 485, d. 750, ll. 36–43: Copy of a secret report from Captain Gias to the District Staff Quartermaster-General of the Turkestan Military District,

5/18 March 1909, No. 23. See also RGVIA f. 400, op. 1, d. 3757, ll. 35–50: Collected information on neighbouring countries, prepared by the intelligence agents of the staff of the Turkestan Military District, 1909, No. 3. 1/14 March–1/14 April 1909.

[62] PRO/FO371/516/22955: Government of India to Morley, 20 June 1908.

[63] PRO/FO371/516/36869: Government of India to Morley, 22 October 1908; Soviet historians have made much of Sardar Nasrollah Khan's opposition to Habibullah's rule, calling him the centre of a national-patriotic 'Young Afghan' movement, along the lines of the Young Turks and the other nascent nationalist movements in the region. (See, for example, D. Ia. Ochildiev and M.A. Babakhodzhaev, 'Politika Anglii v Afganistane i Borba Afganskogo Naroda za Nezavisimost v Nachale XX Veka', in *Strani Blizhnego Vostoka v Mezhdunarodnikh Otnosheniiakh (XIX–XX vv.)* (Tashkent, 1984), pp 36–40.) Nasrollah's opposition, however, appears to be more along the lines of the kind of dynastic rivalry from which Afghanistan had long suffered than any nationalist or patriotic uprising.

[64] PRO/FO371/728/9654: Government of India to Morley (telegraphic), 12 March 1909.

[65] AVPRI f. 147, op. 485, d. 750, ll. 36–43: Report from Agent M.S., in Copy of a secret report from the Commander of the Pamir Detachment (Lithuanian Life-Guards Captain Gias) to the District Staff Quartermaster-General of the Turkestan Military District, 5/18 March 1909, No. 23.

[66] PRO/FO800/98: Memorandum on the Present Situation in Afghanistan (secret), A.H. McMahon, Quetta, 31 May 1909.

[67] PRO/FO371/727/15712: Ritchie to Mallet, India Office, 24 April 1909.

[68] PRO/FO371/514/34509: Government of India to Morley, 3 October 1908.

[69] PRO/FO371/724/4749: Government of India to Morley (telegraphic), 3 February 1909.

[70] AVPRI f. 147, op. 485, d. 750, ll. 36–43: Copy of a secret report from Captain Gias to the District Staff Quartermaster-General of the Turkestan Military District, 5/18 March 1909, No. 23.

[71] PRO/FO371/724/6056: Nicolson to Grey, No. 91, St Petersburg, 7 February 1909.

[72] PRO/FO371/730/17375: Nicolson to Grey, No. 241 (telegraphic), St Petersburg, 7 May 1909.

[73] AVPRI f. 144, op. 488, d. 4144, l. 181: Secret telegram from Sablin, Teheran, 11/24 June 1909, No. 279. In addition to their periodic public meetings, the Persia Society published numerous pamphlets promoting their cause. See, for example, H.F.B. Lynch, 'The Importance of Persia', or Lord Curzon, 'Persian Autonomy', both published in 1912. The visibility of this group was so great that by 1914, the Russian government expressed concern that British policy in Persia was being driven by the Society, rather than the government. See, for example, AVPRI f. 133, op. 470, d. 192, ll. 1–15: Benckendorff to Sazonov, London, 29 May/11 June 1914.

[74] 'The Position in Persia', Letter to the editor by Lamington, E.G. Browne, H.F.B. Lynch, and James O'Grady, *The Times*, 14 July 1909.

[75] IO/L/MIL/17/15/26: Russian military designs in Persia: a strategical fragment, Simla, Intelligence Branch Division of the Chief of the Staff, 1909.

[76] RGIA f. 560, op. 28, d. 379, ll. 11–11 ob.: Secret telegram from Miller, Tabriz, 29 May/11 June 1909, No. 203.

[77] AVPRI f. 144, op. 488, d. 4144, l. 146: Secret telegram from Sablin, Teheran, 28 May/10 June 1909, No. 252.

[78] RGIA f. 560, op. 28, d. 380, ll. 34–5: Informational memorandum, St Petersburg, 30 June/13 July 1909.

[79] PRO/FO371/718/29177: Barclay (private and confidential), Teheran, 1 August 1909.

[80] PRO/FO371/718/29178: Barclay (private), Teheran, 1 August 1909.

[81] PRO/FO371/718/32744: Barclay to Grey, No. 704 (telegraphic), Gulahek, 30 August 1909.

[82] AVPRI f. 144, op. 488, d. 4144, ll. 388–388 ob.: Secret telegram from Sablin, Teheran, 18/31 August 1909, No. 438.

[83] PRO/FO371/718/35185: Barclay to Grey, No. 733 (telegraphic), Gulahek, 20 September 1909. Sadovskii, however, was dead within nine months, and the Russians were once again pressing that he be replaced only by a Russian (AVPRI f. 144, op. 488, d. 4145, ll. 337–8: Confidential report from Poklevsky-Kozell, Zergendeh, 18 June/1 July 1910).

[84] RGIA f. 560, op. 28, d. 381, l. 101: Copy of a letter from Acting Minister of Foreign Affairs (S.D. Sazonov) to P.A. Stolypin, 1/14 September 1909, No. 922.

[85] RGIA f. 560, op. 28, d. 381, ll. 106–106 ob.: Review of a ciphered telegram from Tbilisi from Infantry General Shatilov to Stolypin, No. 2618, 4/17 September 1909.

[86] RGIA f. 560, op. 28, d. 381, l. 127: Izvolskii to Poklevsky-Kozell, St Petersburg, 12/25 September 1909, No. 1741.

[87] RGIA f. 560, op. 28, d. 381, l. 132: Secret telegram from Poklevsky-Kozell, Teheran, 16/29 September 1909, No. 479.

[88] *Novoe Vremia*, 16/29 October 1907, quoted in PRO/FO371/327/36063: Russian and Indian Railway systems.

[89] *Daily Telegraph*, 11 January 1908, quoted in AVPRI f. 214, op. 779, d. 154, ll. 56–7: 'Russo-Indian Railroad', January 1908.

[90] See PRO/FO371/503/13229: Memorandum communicated by J.D. Rees, MP, 16 April 1908; AVPRI f. 144, op. 488, d. 3015, ll. 55–113: A. Samov, The Railroad Question in Persia, 18 April/1 May 1908; PRO/FO371/538/17606: 'The Baghdad Railway', translated from the *Novoe Vremia* of 16 May 1908. A.L. Popov sees the desire to counter the Baghdad Railway with Persian railway construction as the principal motivating factor behind Russia's entire Persian policy, including the 1907 agreement itself. See A.L. Popov, 'Stranitsa iz Istorii Russkoy Politicheski v Persii', *Mezhdunarodnaia Zhizn*, 4–5 (1924), pp 133–64.

[91] PRO/FO371/538/6101: Hardinge to Grey, 18 February 1908.

[92] RGIA f. 23, op. 8, d. 24, ll. 4–7: Secret report from Hartwig, Zargandeh, 28 May/10 June 1908, No. 75.

[93] AVPRI f. 144, op. 488, d. 3015, ll. 205–6 ob.: Izvolskii to D.A. Filosofov, N.K. Shaufus, A. F. Redichev, etc, 8/21 July 1908 (secret).

[94] AVPRI f. 144, op. 488, d. 3015, ll. 224–32 ob.: Draft Journal of the Special Committee, established on 11/24 July 1908, on the question of Persian railroads.

[95] PRO/FO800/98: Morley to Grey (private), 9 October 1907.

[96] PRO/FO371/503/33769: India Office to Foreign Office, 28 September 1908.

[97] PRO/FO371/503/23132: Memorandum by Percy L. Loraine, Gulahek, 16 June 1908.

[98] PRO/FO371/503/23132: Marling to Grey, No. 157, Teheran, 17 June 1908.

[99] AVPRI f. 144, op. 488, d. 3015, ll. 259–60: Copie d'un aide-mémoire confidentiel adressé à l'Ambassade de la Grande Bretagne, 2/15 August 1908.

[100] PRO/FO371/503/33780: Memorandum respecting Railway Construction in Persia, Foreign Office, 29 September 1908.

[101] AVPRI f. 144, op. 488, d. 4144, ll. 60–2: Memorandum, Foreign Office, 9 October 1908.

[102] PRO/FO371/717/43527: Barclay to Grey, No. 206, Teheran, 8 November 1909.

[103] PRO/FO371/503/40837: Barclay to Grey, No. 288 (secret), Teheran, 4 November 1908.

[104] AVPRI f. 147, op. 485, d. 750, ll. 109–109 ob.: Extraction from a note for 1908 about the state of the Transcaspian province. Enclosure in Pleve to Sazonov, Council of Ministers, 27 October 1909, No. 4441.

[105] AVPRI f. 147, op. 485, d. 750, ll. 106–7 ob.: Informational memorandum, St Petersburg, 17/30 September 1909.

[106] AVPRI f. 147, op. 485, d. 750, ll. 109–109 ob.: Extraction from a note for 1908 about the state of the Transcaspian province.

[107] RGVIA f. 2000, op. 1, d. 961, ll. 57–8 ob.: Samsonov on the question of the possibility of independent action against us by Afghanistan. Letter to the Chief of the General Staff, 4/17 October 1909, No. 2596.

[108] RGVIA f. 2000, op. 1, d. 961, ll. 1–13 ob.: General Considerations on the Turkestan Operational Front, Colonel Novitsyi, St Petersburg, 3/16 March 1908.

[109] RGVIA f. 2000, op. 1, d. 961, ll. 57–8 ob.: Samsonov to the Chief of the General Staff, 4/17 October 1909, No. 2596.

[110] RGVIA f. 2000, op. 1, d. 961, ll. 35–9: Status of Operational Works on the Turkestani Front. M.V. Report for the Commander in Chief of the General Staff, 11/14 February 1909.

[111] RGVIA f. 2000, op. 1, d. 961, ll. 44–9: On the Development of an Operational Plan on the Turkestani Front. M.V. Report for the Commander in Chief of the General Staff, 23 September/6 October 1909, No. 17; and RGVIA f. 2000, op. 1, d. 3737, ll. 10–41: Extract from a summary of the Staff of the Turkestani Military District on the internal politics and economic situation of Afghanistan; description of plans for the Afghan theatre of military action, 1912.

[112] RGVIA f. 2000, op. 1, d. 961, ll. 44–9: On the Development of an Operational Plan on the Turkestani Front, 23 September/6 October 1909, No. 17.

[113] RGVIA f. 2000, op. 1, d. 3737, ll. 10–41: Extract from summary on the internal politics of Afghanistan.

[114] RGVIA f. 2000, op. 1, d. 961, ll. 57–8 ob.: Communication from Samsonov on the question of the possibility of independent action against us by Afghanistan. Letter to the Chief of the General Staff, 4/17 October 1909, No. 2596.

[115] AVPRI f. 147, op. 485, d. 750, ll. 83–5 ob.: Political agent in Bukhara to Sazonov, 14/27 August 1909, No. 169.

[116] AVPRI f. 147, op. 485, d. 750, ll. 26–7: Political agent in Bukhara to Charikov, 21 March/3 April 1909, No. 63.

[117] RGVIA f. 400, op. 1, d. 3757, ll. 171–83: Collected information about the neighbouring countries, compiled by the intelligence agents of the Staff of the Turkestan Military District, 1909, No. 11. 1/14 November to 1/14 December 1909.

[118] AVPRI f. 147, op. 485, d. 750, ll. 26–7: Political agent in Bukhara to N.V. Charkov, 21 March/3 April 1909, No. 63.

[119] Fedorov (Podporuchik), *Otchet o poezdke v Vostochnuiu Persiiu 2-go Zakaspyiskago strelkovago bataliona Podporuchika* (Tashkent, 1910), p 2.

[120] Fedorov, p 75.

[121] PRO/FO371/718/34173: Barclay to Grey, No. 162, Gulahek, 24 August 1909; AVPRI f. 144, op. 488, d. 4141, l. 294: Izvolskii to Poklevsky-Kozell, St Petersburg, 3/16 November 1909, No. 1964 (telegram).

[122] PRO/FO371/718/42639: Aide mémoire communicated to Izvolskii by Nicolson, St Petersburg, 2/15 November 1909; AVPRI f. 144, op. 488, d. 4141, l. 294: Izvolskii to Poklevsky-Kozell, St Petersburg, 3/16 November 1909, No. 1963 (telegram).

[123] RGIA f. 560, op. 28, d. 382, l. 115: Urgent telegram from Poklevsky-Kozell, Teheran, 12/25 November 1909; PRO/FO371/719/43169: Barclay to Grey, No. 790 (telegraphic), Teheran, 25 November 1909.

[124] *Novoe Vremia*, quoted in PRO/FO371/719/43584: Nicolson to Grey, No. 625, St Petersburg, 26 November 1909.

[125] *Birzhevye Vedomosti*, quoted in PRO/FO371/719/44009: Nicolson to Grey, No. 625, St Petersburg, 27 November 1909.

[126] PRO/FO371/719/43446: Nicolson to Grey, No. 498 (telegraphic), St Petersburg, 28 November 1909.

[127] AVPRI f. 144, op. 488, d. 4145, ll. 2–2 ob.: Aide Mémoire, St Petersburg, 23 December 1909/5 January 1910; AVPRI f. 144, op. 489, d. 2976, l. 1: Secret telegram from Poklevsky-Kozell, Teheran, 5/18 January 1910, No. 3.

[128] AVPRI f. 144, op. 489, d. 2956, ll. 20–20 ob.: Kokovtsov to Izvolskii, 27–28 November/10–11 December 1909, No. 752.

[129] AVPRI f. 144, op. 489, d. 2956, ll. 26–26 ob.: Izvolskii to Poklevsky-Kozell, St Petersburg, 31 December 1909/13 January 1910, No. 2287 (telegram).

[130] AVPRI f. 144, op. 488, d. 4141, l. 331: Secret telegram from Poklevsky-Kozell, Teheran, 30 November/13 December 1909, No. 621.

[131] RGIA f. 560, op. 28, d. 1123, ll. 51–51 ob.: Secret report from Chirkin, Bombay, 14/27 October 1909, No. 728.

[132] Grulev, *Sopernichestvo Rossii i Anglii v Srednei Azii*, pp 360–1.

[133] AVPRI f. 144, op. 488, d. 4144, ll. 376–8: Lettre de Benckendorff, Londres, 3/16 August 1909.

[134] PRO/FO371/732/30519: Memorandum (Grey), 6 August 1909.

Chapter 4: Conflicting Motivations

[1] PRO/FO371/732/29593: Press extracts respecting the visit of the Tsar to Cowes. Enclosure in O'Beirne's dispatch No. 452 of 3 August 1909.

[2] See PRO/FO371/634 for correspondence concerning Colonel Kozlov's unauthorized mission to Tibet.

[3] See Alastair Lamb, *The McMahon Line* (London, 1966), vol i, chapter viii; N.S. Kuleshov, *Rossia i Tibet v nachale XX veka* (Moscow, 1992), pp 141–5.

[4] Lamb, *The McMahon Line*, p 193.

[5] PRO/FO371/853/4577: Diary of Captain R.S. Kennedy, officiating British trade agent, and Lieutenant J.L.R. Weir, British trade agent at Gyangze for the month of December 1909, 3 January 1910.

[6] Lamb, *The McMahon Line*, p 194.

[7] PRO/FO371/853/3543: Telegram from the Viceroy, 30 January 1910.

[8] PRO/FO371/853/4722: India Office to Foreign Office, 9 February 1910.

[9] PRO/FO371/853/11015: India Office to Foreign Office, 31 March 1910.

[10] PRO/FO371/853/11535: Memorandum for the perusal of Lieutenant-Colonel J. Manners-Smith, by Chandra Shum Shere, Prime Minister of Nepal, 11 March 1910.

[11] PRO/FO371/853/7546: Max Müller to Grey, No. 41 (telegraphic), Peking, 4 March 1910.

[12] PRO/FO371/853/9582: Nicolson to Grey, No. 103 (telegraphic), St Petersburg, 20 March 1910.

[13] PRO/FO371/854/16787: Minute by Hardinge on India Office to Foreign Office, 11 May 1910.

[14] 'Great Britain and Tibet', *The Times*, 15 July 1910, p 5.

[15] See PRO/FO371/854/15282: 'Notes on Tibetan Affairs'. Major W.F. O'Connor, Consul for Seistan and Qaen, Seistan, 20 March 1910; PRO/FO371/854/19526: C.A. Bell, Political Officer in Sikkim, to the Secretary to the Government of India in the Foreign Department, No. 507, Camp Darjeeling, 30 April 1910. For the exploits of Bell and O'Connor in Tibet, see the entertaining accounts in Peter Hopkirk, *Trespassers on the Roof of the World* (Oxford, 1982).

[16] PRO/FO371/854/20646: Government of India to Morley (telegraphic), 9 June 1910.

[17] PRO/FO371/854/21086: Morley to Government of India (telegraphic), 10 June 1910.

[18] PRO/FO371/854/23729: Morley to Government of India (telegraphic), 29 June 1910.

[19] See PRO/FO371/854/24446: Government of India to Morley (telegraphic), 5 July 1910.

[20] PRO/FO371/854/26989: Minute by Grey on Government of India to Morley (telegraphic), 23 July 1910.

[21] 'India and Tibet. Orders to British Troops', Simla, 29 July 1910, *The Times*, 30 July 1910, p 5.

[22] PRO/FO371/854/27682: Nicolson to Grey, No. 215 (telegraphic), St Petersburg, 1 August 1910.

[23] AVPRI f. 147, op. 486, d. 235b, l. 5: 'Reexamination of the Anglo-Russian Agreement', *Russkoe Slovo*, 21 July/3 August 1910.

[24] PRO/FO371/854/27682: Grey to Nicolson, No. 411 (telegraphic), 2 August 1910.

[25] PRO/FO371/855/30123: Müller to Grey, No. 146 (telegraphic), Peking, 18 August 1910.

[26] PRO/FO371/855/31256: India Office to Foreign Office, 27 August 1910.

[27] AVPRI f. 147, op. 485, d. 60 (3), l. 221: Memorandum. Foreign Office to Russian Embassy, London, 8/21 September 1910.

[28] RGVIA f. 400, op. 1, d. 3757, l. 129: Secret letter from the Turkestan Governor-General to Sukhomlinov, 5/18 November 1909, No. 559.

[29] AVPRI f. 147, op. 485, d. 751, ll. 68–70 ob.: Political agent in Bukhara to Sazonov, 16/29 June 1910.

[30] PRO/FO539/95/20: Izvolskii to O'Beirne, St Petersburg, 13/26 May 1910; see also PRO/FO371/725/44747: Nicolson to Grey, No. 502 (telegraphic), St Petersburg, 8 December 1909.

[31] PRO/FO539/95/8: Ameer of Afghanistan to Government of India, 25th Muharram, 1327 Hijra (6 February 1910).

[32] AVPRI f. 147, op. 485, d. 750, l. 123: Samsonov to Izvolskii (telegraphic), Tashkent, 1/14 December 1909; PRO/FO371/725/45950: Nicolson to Grey, No. 510 (telegraphic), St Petersburg, 18 December 1909.

[33] AVPRI f. 147, op. 485, d. 60 (1), l. 139: Concerning rumours in India about Russia's preparations to construct a bridge at the Kelif crossing. Secret report from Chirkin, Bombay, 9/24 December 1909, No. 855.

[34] AVPRI f. 147, op. 485, d. 749, l. 94: 'Russia in Central Asia', Newspaper article (no date).

[35] RGVIA f. 2000, op. 1, d. 7646, ll. 99–101 ob.: Report. Chief of Staff of the Turkestan Military District. Reconnaissance, to the Commander in Chief of the General Staff, 5/18 March 1910, No. 864.

[36] See, for example, RGVIA f. 2000, op. 1, d. 3721, ll. 1–63: Notes on a trip to Turkey and Afghanistan by Lieutenant Chanishev of the First Turkestani Cavalry Battalion, 1910.

[37] PRO/FO371/981/47037: Note re: conversation with Miller. J.L. Maffey, political agent, Khyber, 26 November 1910.

[38] AVPRI f. 147, op. 485, d. 60 (2), ll. 86–7 ob.: Secret report from Arseniev to Izvolskii, Calcutta, 18/31 March 1910, No. 1.

[39] AVPRI f. 147, op. 485, d. 60 (3), ll. 196–203 ob.: Secret report from Arseniev, Simla, 1/14 August 1910, No. 16.

[40] Arkadyi Petrov, *Kak Zashchishchaiut svoi interesi v Azii Angliia i Rossiia* (St Petersburg, 1910).

[41] RGVIA f. 2000, op. 1, d. 3681, ll. 122–35 ob.: Collected periodical press on relations with neighbouring countries, No. 1, from 1/14 to 15/28 December 1910. Published by the Staff of the Turkestan Military District, 4th Department, Tashkent, 1910.

[42] PRO/FO371/978/4746: 'An Old but not Harmless Delusion'. Extract from *Golos Pravdy* of 25 January/7 February 1910.

[43] G.I. Ter-Gukasov, *Ekonomicheskie interesi Rossii v Persii. Redaktsia periodicheskikh izdanyi Ministerstva Finansov: 'Vestnik Finansov' i 'Torgovaia Promishelanaia Gazeta'* (St Petersburg, 1915), p 39.

[44] PRO/FO371/717/39626: Barclay to Grey, Teheran, 9 October 1909.

[45] 'The Situation in Southern Persia. Effect on British Trade, Bushire, 2 February 1910', *The Times*, 17 May 1910, p 5.

[46] AVPRI f. 291, op. 614, d. 1050, ll. 27–8 ob.: To the Supreme Committee of the Official Society for the Promotion of Russian Trade and Industry, Tbilisi Stock Exchange Committee (no date).

[47] PRO/FO371/717/47161: 'Russian Influence in Persia', in *The Caucasian Press*, translated by P. Stevens. British Consulate, Batum, 21 December 1909.

[48] RGIA f. 22, op. 3, d. 96, ll. 63–63 ob.: Bureau of the Persian Transport Society of the Caucasus and Mercury, Eastern, Russian to the Department of Customs Collection, 20 December 1909/2 January 1910, No. 42193.

[49] PRO/FO371/818/44307: Nicolson to Grey, No. 632, St Petersburg, 1 December 1909. For Russian concerns over growing German involvement in Persia see AVPRI f. 144, op. 488, d. 4145.

[50] AVPRI f. 144, op. 488, d. 4145, ll. 168–9: Secret letter from Sazonov, 6/19 April 1910, No. 304; AVPRI f. 147, op. 485, d. 60(2) l. 24: Télégramme secret de Benckendorff, Londres, 21 April/4 May 1910, No. 35.

[51] Perceval Landon, 'New Persian Question. German Activity. Threatened Russian Interests', *The Daily Telegraph*, 22 April 1910.

[52] AVPRI f. 144, op. 488, d. 4145, ll. 186–90 ob.: Extremely secret letter from Kokovtsov to Sazonov, 11–12/24–25 April 1910, No. 291. For German offers of financial assistance to the Persian government, see AVPRI f. 144, op. 488, d. 4145, l. 86: Aide mémoire, Remis par l'Ambassade d'Angleterre, 5/18 March 1910.

[53] PRO/WO106/52: Strategic Railways in Persia. General Staff Note dated 16 June 1910. Precis of railway projects in Persia, 1870–1910. Colonel G. Richardson, Major, General Staff.

[54] PRO/FO371/1178/2803: Lieutenant-Colonel Sir H. McMahon to Government of India, Calcutta, 20 December 1910.

[55] IO/L/MIL/5/730: Lieutenant-Colonel Cox to Government of India, Bushire, 20 December 1910; PRO/PRO/FO371/1178/2803: McMahon to Government of India, Calcutta, 20 December 1910.

[56] IO/L/MIL/5/730: Memorandum by the General Staff on the Proposed Trans-Persian Railway, D. Haig, 3 January 1911.

[57] PRO/FO371/717/46604: India Office to Foreign Office, 23 December 1909.

[58] PRO/FO371/717/46604: Foreign Office to India Office, 19 January 1910.

[59] PRO/CAB16/26: Memorandum by the Director-General of Commercial Intelligence, F. Noël Paton, 31 December 1910.

[60] For a contemporary analysis of Russia's position on the Trans-Persian Railway project, see P.A.T., 'Zheleznodorozhnyi Vopros v Persii i Velikyi Indyiskii Put', *Velikaia Rossiia*, II (Moscow, n.d.), pp 243–82.

[61] Sazonov was a protégé of both Izvolskii and Stolypin, who was Sazonov's brother-in-law. For the close and admiring relationship between Sazonov and Izvolskii, see S.D. Sazonov, *Vospominaniia* (Paris, 1927), pp 7–28. However, the replacement of Izvolskii – with his acknowledged Francophile and Anglophile tendencies – by Sazonov marked a clear shift in Russian policy towards a better understanding with Germany.

[62] AVPRI f. 144, op. 488, d. 4145, ll. 549–50 ob.: Secret letter from Sazonov to Kokovtsov, 1/14 December 1910, No. 1109.

[63] RGIA f. 560, op. 28, d. 382, l. 23: Secret telegram from Poklevsky-Kozell, Teheran, 23 October/5 November 1909, No. 539.

[64] AVPRI f. 147, op. 485, d. 60 (1), l. 248: Stolypin to Vorontsov-Dashkov, St Petersburg, 25 February/10 March 1910, No. 316; AVPRI f. 147, op. 485, d. 60 (1), l. 252: Izvolskii to Benckendorff, St Petersburg, 26 February/11 March 1910, No. 315.

[65] See, for example, AVPRI f. 147, op. 485, d. 60 (1), l. 266: Izvolskii to the Ambassador in Paris, St Petersburg, 2/15 March 1910, No. 332.

[66] AVPRI f. 144, op. 488, d. 4145, l. 196: Lettre de Benckendorff, Londres, 13/26 April 1910.

[67] AVPRI f. 147, op. 485, d. 60 (1), l. 420: Secret telegram from Poklevsky-Kozell, Teheran, 12/25 May 1910, No. 274.

[68] AVPRI f. 144, op. 488, d. 4145, ll. 326–7: Secret letter from Poklevsky-Kozell to Izvolskii, 12/25 June 1910.

[69] AVPRI f. 147, op. 485, d. 60 (2), l. 244: Télégramme secret de Benckendorff, Londres, 22 June/5 July 1910, No. 171.

[70] PRO/FO371/962/27728: Marling to Grey, No. 117, Gulahek, 4 July 1910.

[71] AVPRI f. 144, op. 489, d. 2966, ll. 12–13: Aide Mémoire, St Petersburg, 30 July/12 August 1910; AVPRI f. 144, op. 488, d. 4145, l. 383: Sazonov to Poklevsky-Kozell, St Petersburg, 31 July/13 August 1910, No. 1218.

[72] AVPRI f. 144, op. 488, d. 4145, l. 471: Barclay to the Persian government, Teheran, 15 October 1910.

[73] AVPRI f. 144, op. 489, d. 2966, ll. 12–13: Aide Mémoire, St Petersburg, 30 July/12 August 1910.

[74] AVPRI f. 144, op. 489, d. 2966, l. 8: Secret telegram from Poklevsky-Kozell, Teheran, 9/22 August 1910, No. 530.

[75] AVPRI f. 144, op. 488, d. 4145, ll. 493–4: Secret telegram from Poklevsky-Kozell, Teheran, 16/29 October 1910, No. 58.

[76] Edward G. Browne, 'The Problem of Persia', *The Daily Chronicle*, 31 October 1910.

[77] AVPRI f. 144, op. 488, d. 4145, l. 482: Secret telegram from Poklevsky-Kozell, Teheran, 12/25 October 1910, No. 657.

[78] AVPRI f. 144, op. 488, d. 4145, l. 478: Secret telegram from Poklevsky-Kozell, Teheran, 12/25 October 1910, No. 2.

[79] AVPRI f. 144, op. 488, d. 4145, l. 515: Memorandum remis par le Foreign Office à Etter en date de Londres, le 5 November 1910.

[80] AVPRI f. 144, op. 489, d. 296b, ll. 48–50 ob.: Response from Sazonov, St Petersburg, December 1910.

[81] AVPRI f. 144, op. 489, d. 2976, ll. 2–2 ob.: Aide Mémoire, Remis par l'Ambassade Britannique, St Petersburg, 16/29 July 1910.

[82] AVPRI f. 144, op. 489, d. 2976, l. 5: Izvolskii to Poklevsky-Kozell, St Petersburg, 17/30 July 1910, No. 1114.

[83] See, for example, RGIA f. 560, op. 28, d. 383, ll. 196–8: Memorandum from the Staff of the Caucasian Military District to the Commander of the 16th General Mingrelski Regiment, Colonel Averianov, 19 January/1 February 1910, No. 12.

[84] AVPRI f. 144 op. 488, d. 4145, l. 375: Aide-Mémoire, Remis à l'Ambassade Britannique, St Petersburg, 24 July/6 August 1910.

[85] PRO/FO371/1214/11045: Annual Report for Russia (1910), 22 March 1911. See also Maybelle Kennedy Chapman, *Great Britain and the Baghdad Railway, 1888– 1914* (Northampton, MA, 1948), chapter 7.

[86] PRO/FO371/981/40354: O'Beirne to Grey, No. 430, St Petersburg, 28 October 1910.

[87] For Stolypin's influence over Sazonov, see David MacLaren McDonald, *United Government and Foreign Policy in Russia, 1900–1914* (Cambridge, MA, 1992), pp 157–61. Sazonov, in his memoirs, insisted that his appointment was not dependent on Stolypin's patronage. See Sazonov, *Vospominaniia*, pp 22–3.

[88] See Judith A. Head, 'Public Opinions and Middle Eastern Railways: The Russo-German Negotiations of 1910–11', *The International History Review*, vi, i (February 1984), p 31.

[89] Although the tsar had appointed Sazonov as minister of foreign affairs in October, he did not officially assume the position until after the trip to Potsdam. Sazonov had asked Nicholas to defer the appointment so as to avoid having his first official visit as foreign minister being to Germany, instead of to one of the entente partners (Sazo-

nov, *Vospominaniia*, p 41). Despite this precaution, Pichon, the French minister for foreign affairs, openly expressed his displeasure that Sazonov's debut as foreign minister was in Berlin rather than Paris or London, and Sazonov was branded for some time as a Germanophile (see Bertie to Grey, Paris, 16 November 1910, No. 611 in *BD*, x, 1, p 563). For a discussion and documentation of the shift in Russian policy and Sazonov's preparation for Potsdam, see 'K istorii Potsdamskogo soglasheniia 1911 g.', *KA*, 3 (58) (1933), pp 46–57.

[90] AVPRI f. 144, op. 488, d. 4148, ll. 28–36: Journal of the meeting of the Special Committee on Persian Affairs, 15/28 October 1910.

[91] O'Beirne to Grey, St Petersburg, 17 October 1910, No. 599, in *BD*, x, 1, pp 550–1.

[92] O'Beirne to Grey, St Petersburg, 19 October 1910, No. 600, in *BD*, x, 1, pp 552–3.

[93] Sir George Buchanan, *My Mission to Russia* (London, 1923), vol i, p 95.

[94] See Keith Neilson, *Britain and the Last Tsar* (Oxford, 1995), pp 310–12.

[95] Goschen to Grey, Berlin, 9 November 1910, No. 607, in *BD*, x, 1, pp 557–8.

[96] Buchanan to Nicolson (private), St Petersburg, 10 December 1910, No. 619, in *BD*, x, 1, pp 576–7; Buchanan to Grey, St Petersburg, 10 December 1910, No. 618, in *BD*, x, 1, p 574.

[97] Buchanan to Grey, St Petersburg, 18 December 1910, No. 620, in *BD*, x, 1, pp 577–9. For further examples of Sazonov's 'rather careless habit of doing business', see Buchanan to Grey, St Petersburg, 26 December 1910, No. 630, in *BD*, x, 1, pp 589–91.

[98] See Buchanan to Nicolson (private), St Petersburg, 16 December 1910, No. 624, in *BD*, x, 1, pp 585–6.

[99] Buchanan to Nicolson (private), St Petersburg, 29 December 1910, No. 635, in *BD*, x, 1, pp 597–8.

[100] Grey to Buchanan, 15 December 1910, No. 621, in *BD*, x, 1, pp 581–2.

[101] Nicolson to Buchanan (private), 3 January 1911, No. 637, in *BD*, x, 1, pp 599–601. In addition, Kaiser Wilhelm's open support for the Islamic movement in Persia was one of the main bones of contention between him and the Russians and British. See *Novoe Vremia*, 19 October 1910.

[102] Edward G. Browne, 'The Problem of Persia', *The Daily Chronicle*, 31 October 1910.

[103] RGVIA f. 2000, op. 1, d. 3681, ll. 122–35 ob.: Collected periodical press on relations with neighbouring countries, No. 1. From 1/14 to 15/28 December 1910. Published by the Staff of the Turkestan Military District, 4th Department, Tashkent, 1910.

[104] AVPRI f. 147, op. 485, d. 751, ll. 79–88: Information on Afghanistan, collected and developed at the Russian-Imperial Consulate General in Khorasan by Captain Skurat, May 1910, No. 8.

[105] RGVIA f. 2000, op. 1, d. 3721, ll. 1–63: Notes on a journey to Turkey and Afghanistan by Lieutenant Chanishev of the 1st Turkestan Cavalry Regiment, 1910.

[106] IO/L/MIL/17/14/15/1: Final report on Afghanistan, 1907–1910 by Fakir Saiyid Iftikhar-ud-Din, British Agent at Kabul, 19 September 1910.

[107] AVPRI f. 147, op. 485, d. 751, l. 98: Report by the Official for border relations under the Chief of the Transcaspian Region to the Chief of the Merv District, 8/21 June 1910, No. 460.

[108] AVPRI f. 147, op. 485, d. 752, ll. 3–27: Information on Afghanistan, collected and developed by Captain Skurat, No. 9, December 1910.

[109] RGVIA, f. 2000, op. 1, d. 3681, ll. 67–104: Information about neighbouring countries, collected by intelligence agents, January 1911, No. 1.

[110] AVPRI f. 147, op. 486, d. 16, l. 58 ob.: Telegram from Samsonov, Tashkent, 10/23 November 1910, No. 776. The Hazarahs, who live in the Hazarajat, are customarily said to be descended from garrison troops left by Genghis Khan in the thirteenth century; modern scholars, however, have rejected this theory as oversimplification, seeing no present link between Mongols and Hazarahs. See Mary Louise Clifford, *The Land and People of Afghanistan* (New York, 1989), pp 20–1; Vartan Gregorian, *The Emergence of Modern Afghanistan* (Stanford, 1969), pp 33–4.

[111] PRO/FO371/1213/271: Viceroy of India to Habibullah Khan, Fort William, 9 December 1910; AVPRI f. 147, op. 485, d. 684, ll. 6–6 ob.: Samsonov to Sazonov, Tashkent, 8/21 December 1910, No. 839.

[112] RGVIA f. 4000, op. 1, d. 3991, ll. 2–3: Samsonov to Sazonov, Tashkent, 7/20 January 1911, No. 225.

[113] AVPRI f. 147, op. 485, d. 684, ll. 22–22 ob.: Report of the Pendinskiy Police Officer (Captain Moskalenko) to the Official for Border Relations under the Chief of the Transcaspian District, 14/27 January 1911, No. 5.

Chapter 5: The Strangling of Anglo-Russian Foreign Policy

[1] PRO/FO371/1213/8933: India Office to Foreign Office, 10 March 1911; PRO/FO371/1213/10516: Extract from News-letter from the British News-writer at Herat (translation), 5 January 1911.

[2] For many months the British had no idea who the 'Mishmez' or 'Michmez' were, having never heard of any Afghan tribe with a name in any way resembling that which the Russians were reporting (PRO/FO371/1213/8933: India Office to Foreign Office, 19 March 1911). Finally in April, Benckendorff explained to the British government that the Michmez were a semi-nomadic, Persian-speaking tribe related to the Jamshedi (PRO/FO371/1213/14689: Note communicated by Benckendorff, 19 April 1911). The Government of India subsequently determined that the Russians were referring to the Meshmasts, a tribe who complained that they were being oppressed by the governor of Herat and had fled to Qaen (PRO/FO371/1213/15406: India Office to Foreign Office, 24 April 1911).

[3] AVPRI f. 147, op. 486, d. 26, l. 7 ob.: Telegram from Samsonov, Tashkent, 19 February/4 March 1911, No. 79; AVPRI f. 147, op. 485, d. 684, l. 16: Samsonov to Sazonov, Tashkent, 19 February/4 March 1911.

[4] AVPRI f. 147, op. 485, d. 684, l. 33: Telegram from Samsonov to Neratov, 23 March/5 April 1911.

[5] PRO/FO371/1213/14689: Note communicated by Benckendorff, 19 April 1911.

[6] IO/L/MIL/17/14/15/1: Final report on Afghanistan (1907–1910) by Fakir Saiyid Iftikhar-ud-Din, British Agent at Kabul, 19 September 1910.

[7] AVPRI f. 147, op. 485, d. 73 (2), l. 127: Secret report from Arseniev, Simla, 12/25 April 1911, No. 16. For a discussion of the import of arms to Afghanistan through Persia, see also AVPRI f. 147, op. 485, d. 749, ll. 79–88 ob.: Some information about the condition of affairs in Herat and Qandahar, according to the reports of agents and the information of border chiefs, Captain Iasa, Russian Consulate in Turbat-i-Haidari, Persia, 26 August/8 September 1908.

[8] AVPRI f. 147, op. 485, d. 684, ll. 35–6 ob.: Neratov to Benckendorff (secret draft), 24 March/7 April 1911, No. 256; PRO/FO371/1216/14690: Note communicated by Benckendorff, 19 April 1911; PRO/FO371/1217/17088: India Office to Foreign Office, 5 May 1911.

[9] AVPRI f. 147, op. 485, d. 684, ll. 44–5: Copie d'un Memorandum de Grey à Benckendorff, 2/15 May 1911.

[10] PRO/FO371/1237/1435: Buchanan to Grey, No. 13 (telegraphic), St Petersburg, 12 January 1911.

[11] PRO/FO371/1237/1983: Secretary of State for India to Viceroy (telegraphic), 14 January 1911; PRO/FO371/1237/5122: Buchanan to Grey, No. 33 (secret) (telegraphic), St Petersburg, 11 February 1911; AVPRI f. 144, op. 489, d. 280b, l. 26: Télégramme secret de Benckendorff, Londres, 4/17 February 1911, No. 38.

[12] PRO/FO371/1237/5122: Buchanan to Grey, No. 33 (secret) (telegraphic), St Petersburg, 11 February 1911; PRO/FO371/1237/5394: Buchanan to Grey, No. 36 (telegraphic), St Petersburg, 13 February 1911.

[13] PRO/FO371/1185/8929: Buchanan to Grey, No. 54 (telegraphic), St Petersburg, 10 March 1911.

[14] AVPRI f. 144, op. 489, d. 280b, ll. 31–3 ob.: Lettre de Benckendorff, Londres, 13/26 February 1911; PRO/FO371/1185/8929: Buchanan to Grey, No. 54 (telegraphic), St Petersburg, 10 March 1911.

[15] PRO/FO371/1185/7212: Barclay to Grey, No. 68 (telegraphic), Teheran, 27 February 1911.

[16] PRO/FO371/1185/8929: Minute by R.P. Maxwell on Buchanan to Grey, No. 54 (telegraphic), St Petersburg, 10 March 1911. For a discussion of the commercial advantages of the proposed Mohammareh to Khorramabad rail line, see PRO/FO371/1185/3606: Mr. C. Greenway, Managing Director Anglo-Persian Oil Company, to Foreign Office, Steam-ship 'Dwaika' (off Karachi), 7 January 1911.

[17] AVPRI f. 144, op. 489, d. 280b, l. 29: Sazonov to Benckendorff, St Petersburg, 10/23 February 1911, No. 182 (Telegram).

[18] PRO/FO371/1185/9984: Buchanan to Grey, No. 58 (telegraphic), St Petersburg, 19 March 1911.

[19] PRO/FO371/1185/10827: Grey to Buchanan, No. 87, 22 March 1911; PRO/FO371/1185/9984: Buchanan to Grey, No. 58 (telegraphic), St Petersburg, 19 March 1911.

[20] AVPRI f. 144, op. 489, d. 280b, l. 60: Télégramme secret à Benckendorff, St Pétersbourg, 14/27 March 1911, No. 330.

[21] PRO/FO371/1185/10573: Buchanan to Grey, No. 65 (telegraphic), St Petersburg, 22 March 1911.

[22] PRO/FO371/1185/11413: Buchanan to Grey, No. 74 (telegraphic), St Petersburg, 28 March 1911.

[23] AVPRI f. 147, op. 485, d. 73 (1), l. 178: Secret telegram from Poklevsky-Kozell (completely confidential), Teheran, 21 March/3 April 1911, No. 224; PRO/FO371/1186/39496: Barclay to Grey, No. 173, Gulahek, 11 September 1911.

[24] PRO/FO371/1185/8929: Buchanan to Grey, No. 54 (telegraphic), St Petersburg, 10 March 1911.

[25] Buchanan to Grey, St Petersburg, 31 January 1911, No. 667, in *BD*, x, 1, pp 640–1.

[26] Derek Spring considers the Société d'Études to be an excellent example of the driving force of Russian private finance and industry behind significant Russian foreign policy initiatives. See D.W. Spring, 'The Trans-Persian Railway Project and Anglo-Russian Relations, 1909–14', *Slavonic and East European Review*, LIV, 1 (January 1976), pp 60–82. For the composition of the Russian committee, see PRO/FO371/1433/3668: 'Brief Notes on the Preliminary Expenses for the Construction of a Transcontinental Railway through Persia (prepared by the Russian Committee)', translated from the Russian, May 1911.

[27] PRO/FO371/1178/19356: Buchanan to Grey, No. 134 (secret), St Petersburg, 16 May 1911.

[28] PRO/FO371/1178/16485: War Office to Foreign Office, 26 April 1911.

[29] Foreign Office to War Office. Memorandum for the Chief of the Imperial General Staff, 15 May 1911, No. 722, in *BD*, x, 1, p 700.

[30] PRO/FO371/11788/15143: Grey to Buchanan, No. 129 (secret), 10 May 1911.

[31] PRO/FO371/1178/25701: O'Beirne to Grey, No. 181 (secret), St Petersburg, 28 June 1911.

[32] AVPRI f. 147, op. 485, d. 73 (1), l. 205: Neratov to Benckendorff, St Petersburg, 5/18 July 1911, No. 907.

[33] For a discussion of the difficulties and necessities for Russian trade with Persia in 1911, see RGIA f. 23, op. 11, d. 109, ll. 11–14 ob.: T-vo Prokhorovskoi Trekhgornoi Manufaktury in Teheran to Pokhitonov, Teheran, 20 October/2 November 1911.

[34] PRO/FO371/1187/6833: Barclay to Grey, No. 61 (telegraphic), Teheran, 23 February 1911.

[35] PRO/FO371/1179/9546: Barclay to Grey, No. 84 (telegraphic), Teheran, 15 March 1911; AVPRI f. 147, op. 485, d. 73 (1), l. 188: Secret telegram from Poklevsky-Kozell, Teheran, 29 March/11 April 1911, No. 251.

[36] AVPRI f. 147, op. 485, d. 73 (1), l. 263: Secret telegram Poklevsky-Kozell, Teheran, 19 July/1 August 1911, No. 499.

[37] AVPRI f. 147, op. 485, d. 73 (1), l. 229: Secret telegram from Poklevsky-Kozell, Teheran, 7/20 July 1911, No. 568.

[38] AVPRI f. 147, op. 485, d. 73 (1), l. 292: Secret telegram from Poklevsky-Kozell, Teheran, 12/25 July 1911, No. 601; PRO/FO371/1187/6833: Barclay to Grey, No. 61 (telegraphic), Teheran, 23 February 1911.

[39] AVPRI f. 147, op. 485, d. 73 (1), l. 292: Secret telegram from Poklevsky-Kozell, Teheran, 12/25 July 1911, No. 601.

[40] AVPRI f. 138, op. 467, d. 300/3, ll. 2–9 ob.: Extremely secret letter from Neratov to Poklevsky-Kozell, St Petersburg, 14/27 June 1911, No. 449.

[41] AVPRI f. 147, op. 485, d. 73 (1), l. 209: Télégramme secret de Benckendorff, Londres, 5/18 July 1911, No. 152.

[42] AVPRI f. 147, op. 485, d. 73 (1), l. 216: Neratov to Benckendorff, St Petersburg, 6/19 July 1911.

[43] For Mohammad Ali's return to Persia, see Firuz Kazemzadeh, *Russia and Britain in Persia* (New Haven, CT, 1968), pp 597–612.

[44] AVPRI f. 147, op. 485, d. 73 (1), l. 321: Télégramme secret de Benckendorff, Londres, 15/28 July 1911, No. 167.

[45] AVPRI f. 147, op. 485, d. 73 (1), l. 403: Secret telegram from Poklevsky-Kozell, Teheran, 4/17 August 1911, No. 683.

[46] AVPRI f. 147, op. 485, d. 73 (1), l. 369: Secret telegram from Poklevsky-Kozell, Teheran, 27 July/9 August 1911, No. 664.

[47] For a straightforward narrative of Shuster's financial regime, see B.M. Dantsig, 'Finansi Persii', *Novyi Vostok*, 18 (1927), pp 120–43; Shuster's own account of his tenure in Persia, vividly subtitled 'Story of the European diplomacy and Oriental intrigue that resulted in the denationalization of twelve million Mohammedans', was published soon after his return to America in 1912. See W. Morgan Shuster, *The Strangling of Persia* (New York, 1912).

[48] AVPRI f. 147, op. 485, d. 60 (3), l. 15: Sazonov to the Ambassador in Paris, St Petersburg, 6/19 August 1910, No. 1261.

[49] AVPRI f. 147, op. 485, d. 60 (3), l. 97: Sazonov to Poklevsky-Kozell, St Petersburg, 26 August/8 September 1910, No. 1358.

[50] AVPRI f. 147, op. 485, d. 60 (3), l. 123: Sazonov to the Ambassador in Washington, St Petersburg, 28 August/10 September 1910, No. 1365; AVPRI f. 147, op. 485, d. 60 (3), l. 214: Report of Baron Rosen, Manchester, 1/14 September 1910, No. 52.

[51] AVPRI f. 147, op. 485, d. 73 (1), l. 273: Secret telegram from Poklevsky-Kozell, Teheran, 25 June/8 July 1911, No. 523; AVPRI f. 147, op. 485, d. 73 (1), l. 274:

Neratov to Benckendorff, St Petersburg, 26 June/9 August 1911, No. 855; Grey to Buchanan, 10 July 1911, No. 779, in *BD*, x, 1, p 767.

[52] AVPRI f. 147, op. 485, d. 73 (1), l. 274: Neratov to Benckendorff, St Petersburg, 26 June/9 August 1911, No. 855.

[53] PRO/FO371/1192/28641: Telegram from Mr. Brown (Teheran) to Mr. Greenway (London), 20 July 1911. Enclosure in Anglo-Persian Oil Company to Foreign Office, London, 20 July 1911.

[54] PRO/FO371/1192/26457: Minute on Barclay to Grey (telegraphic), Teheran, 7 July 1911, No. 234. It is unclear who authored this minute.

[55] AVPRI f. 144, op. 489, d. 296b, l. 67: Secret telegram from Poklevsky-Kozell, Teheran, 25 June/8 July 1911, No. 525; AVPRI f. 144, op. 489, d. 298b, l. 11: Neratov to Poklevsky-Kozell, St Petersburg, 28 June/11 July 1911, No. 872.

[56] PRO/FO371/1192/27787: Extract from Shuster to Barclay, in Barclay to Grey, Teheran, 14 July 1911, No. 252.

[57] PRO/FO371/1192/27787: Minute by Crowe on Barclay to Grey, Teheran, 14 June 1911, No. 252.

[58] PRO/FO371/1192/28250: Decipher of telegram from Barclay, Teheran, 18 July 1911.

[59] PRO/FO371/1192/30212: Grey to Buchanan, Foreign Office, 26 July 1911, No. 210.

[60] AVPRI f. 144, op. 489, d. 298b, l. 35: Secret telegram Poklevsky-Kozell, Teheran, 21 July/3 August 1911, No. 645.

[61] PRO/FO371/1192/30228: Grey to Buchanan, Foreign Office, 28 July 1911, No. 216.

[62] PRO/FO800/74: Buchanan to Grey (telegraphic), 6 August 1911.

[63] A.J.P. Taylor writes that the appearance of the *Panther* did not cause much stir in France. See A.J.P. Taylor, *The Struggle for Mastery in Europe 1848–1918* (Oxford, 1954), pp 467–8.

[64] AVPRI f. 144, op. 489, d. 298b, l. 47: Télégramme secret de Benckendorff, Londres, 25 July/7 August 1911, No. 176, No. 2.

[65] PRO/FO371/1192/31422: Barclay to Grey, No. 318 (telegraphic), Teheran, 9 August 1911.

[66] PRO/FO371/1192/32475: Grey to Barclay, No. 242 (telegraphic), 18 August 1911.

[67] PRO/FO371/1192/30826: Buchanan to Grey, No. 175 (telegraphic), St Petersburg, 4 August 1911; PRO/FO371/1192/30667: Buchanan to Grey, No. 174 (telegraphic), St Petersburg, 3 August 1911.

[68] PRO/FO371/1182/32367: Grey to Buchanan, Foreign Office, No. 441 (telegraphic), 16 August 1911; see also AVPRI f. 144, op. 489, d. 298b, ll. 107–107 ob.: Buchanan to Neratov (personal), St Petersburg, 4/17 August 1911.

[69] AVPRI f. 144, op. 489, d. 298b, ll. 114–15: Secret telegram from Poklevsky-Kozell, Teheran, 8/21 August 1911, No. 702.

[70] AVPRI f. 144, op. 489, d. 298b, ll. 79–81 ob.: Information on the affair of the invitation for Persian service of the English military attaché in Teheran, Major Stokes, with his appointment as commander of the financial gendarmerie (secret), St Petersburg, August 1911.

[71] AVPRI f. 144, op. 489, d. 296b, l. 89: Secret telegram from Poklevsky-Kozell, Teheran, 27 August/9 September 1911, No. 746; PRO/FO371/1192/33674: Barclay to Grey, No. 359 (telegraphic), Teheran, 26 August 1911.

[72] AVPRI f. 144, op. 489, d. 298b, ll. 125–125 ob.: Neratov to Poklevsky-Kozell, St Petersburg, 31 August/13 September 1911, No. 1229.

[73] AVPRI f. 144, op. 489, d. 593b, l. 110: Neratov to Poklevsky-Kozell, St Petersburg, 29 September/12 October 1911, No. 1466.

[74] AVPRI f. 144, op. 489, d. 594b, ll. 26–26 ob.: Secret telegram from Poklevsky-Kozell, Teheran, 29 September/12 October 1911, No. 924, No. 1.

[75] PRO/FO371/1196/43360: Barclay to Grey, No. 533 (telegraphic), Teheran, 2 November 1911; AVPRI f. 144, op. 489, d. 594b, ll. 27–9: Secret telegram from Poklevsky-Kozell, Teheran, 30 September/13 October 1911, No. 924, No. 2.

[76] Kazemzadeh, *Russia and Britain in Persia, 1864–1914*, p 614.

[77] AVPRI f. 138, op. 467, d. 706/7, ll. 97–101 ob.: Benckendorff to Neratov (personal), London, 26 October/8 November 1911.

[78] AVPRI f. 144, op. 489, d. 594b, ll. 27–9: Secret telegram from Poklevsky-Kozell, Teheran, 30 September/13 October 1911, No. 924, No. 2.

[79] AVPRI f. 144, op. 489, d. 594b, ll. 30–1: Secret telegram from Poklevsky-Kozell, Teheran, 30 September/13 October 1911, No. 924, No. 3.

[80] AVPRI f. 144, op. 489, d. 594b, ll. 35–35 ob.: Neratov to Poklevsky-Kozell, St Petersburg, 2/15 October 1911, No. 1498.

[81] AVPRI f. 144, op. 489, d. 298b, l. 138: Neratov to Poklevsky-Kozell, St Petersburg, 11/24 October 1911, No. 1578; AVPRI f. 144, op. 489, d. 279b, l. 17: Secret telegram from Poklevsky-Kozell, Teheran, 22 October/4 November 1911, No. 1040.

[82] AVPRI f. 144, op. 489, d. 594b, ll. 40–5: Secret telegram from Poklevsky-Kozell, Teheran, 4/17 October 1911, No. 957a.

[83] AVPRI f. 144, op. 489, d. 594b, ll. 47–9 ob.: Secret telegram from Poklevsky-Kozell, Teheran, 5/18 October 1911, No. 957b.

[84] PRO/FO371/1199/41203: O'Beirne to Grey, No. 252 (telegraphic), St Petersburg, 19 October 1911.

[85] PRO/FO371/1199/41203: Minute by Grey on O'Beirne to Grey, No. 252 (telegraphic), St Petersburg, 19 October 1911.

[86] AVPRI f. 144, op. 489, d. 298b, ll. 136–136 ob.: Télégramme secret de Benckendorff, Londres, le 11/24 October 1911, No. 246.

[87] PRO/FO371/1199/41203: O'Beirne to Grey, No. 252 (telegraphic), St Petersburg, 19 October 1911.

[88] AVPRI f. 144, op. 489, d. 298b, ll. 136–136 ob.: Télégramme secret de Benckendorff, Londres, le 11/24 October 1911, No. 246.

[89] AVPRI f. 138, op. 467, d. 706/7, ll. 95–6: Lettre de Benckendorff, Londres, le 12/25 October 1911 (très confidentiel).

[90] AVPRI f. 144, op. 489, d. 279b, l. 16: Secret telegram from Poklevsky-Kozell, Teheran, 21 October/3 November 1911, No. 1023.

[91] AVPRI f. 144, op. 489, d. 279b, l. 31: Secret telegram from Poklevsky-Kozell, Teheran, 27 October/9 November 1911, No. 1071.

[92] PRO/FO371/1196/44586: O'Beirne to Grey, No. 271 (telegraphic), St Petersburg, 10 November 1911.

[93] AVPRI f. 144, op. 489, d. 594b, l. 96: Neratov to Poklevsky-Kozell, St Petersburg, 3/16 November 1911, No. 1796 (telegram).

[94] AVPRI f. 144, op. 489, d. 594b, ll. 182–182 ob.: Ciphered telegram from the Commander-in-Chief of the Troops of the Caucasian Military District to Sukhomlinov, 5/18 November 1911, No. 31564.

[95] AVPRI f. 144, op. 489, d. 594b, ll. 98–9: Neratov to Benckendorff, St Petersburg, 3/16 November 1911, No. 1798.

[96] RGIA f. 560, op. 28, d. 387, ll. 118–21: Secret telegram from Neratov to Benckendorff, 5/18 November 1911, No. 1810.

[97] PRO/FO371/1196/44586: Minute by Richard Ponsonby Maxwell on O'Beirne to Grey, No. 271 (telegraphic), St Petersburg, 10 November 1911.

[98] PRO/FO371/1196/46034: Buchanan to Grey, No. 286 (telegraphic), St Petersburg, 15 November 1911.

[99] AVPRI f. 144, op. 489, d. 279b, l. 81: Télégramme secret de Benckendorff, Londres, 12/25 November 1911, No. 289, No. 3.

[100] PRO/FO371/1196/46034: Buchanan to Grey, No. 286 (telegraphic), St Petersburg, 15 November 1911.

[101] PRO/FO371/1196/46682: Buchanan to Grey, No. 294 (telegraphic), St Petersburg, 22 November 1911. After Stolypin had been assassinated on 14 September 1911, Count Vladimir Nikolaevich Kokovtsov had assumed the position of chairman of the Council of Ministers, while maintaining the portfolio of the Ministry of Finance.

[102] AVPRI f. 147, op. 485, d. 73 (2), l. 102: Neratov to Poklevsky-Kozell, St Petersburg, 7/20 November 1911, No. 1833.

[103] AVPRI f. 144, op. 489, d. 594b, l. 281: Neratov to Poklevsky-Kozell, St Petersburg, 15/28 November 1911, No. 1898 (telegram).

[104] PRO/FO371/1196/47134: Buchanan to Grey, No. 303 (telegraphic), St Petersburg, 26 November 1911.

[105] PRO/FO371/1196/46539: Buchanan to Grey, No. 291 (telegraphic), St Petersburg, 21 November 1911.

[106] PRO/FO371/1196/47134: Buchanan to Grey, No. 303 (telegraphic), St Petersburg, 26 November 1911.

[107] AVPRI f. 144, op. 489, d. 279b, l. 48: Télégramme secret de Benckendorff, Londres, le 4/17 November 1911, No. 279.

[108] AVPRI f. 144, op. 489, d. 594b, l. 189: Télégramme secret de Benckendorff, Londres, le 10/23 November 1911, No. 286.

[109] AVPRI f. 147, op. 485, d. 73 (2), l. 155: Télégramme secret de Benckendorff, Londres, le 12/25 November 1911, No. 288, No. 2.

[110] AVPRI f. 144, op. 488, d. 4146, ll. 6–12 ob.: Benckendorff to Neratov, 21 November/4 December 1911.

[111] See, for example, PRO/FO371/1197/48347: Buchanan to Grey, No. 349, St Petersburg, 29 November 1911; and AVPRI f. 144, op. 488, d. 4146, ll. 2–5: Benckendorff to Neratov, London, 16/29 November 1911.

[112] PRO/FO800/74: Buchanan to Grey (private), St Petersburg, 4 December 1911.

[113] PRO/FO371/1197/48522: Grey to Buchanan, No. 315, 2 December 1911.

[114] AVPRI f. 340, op. 812, d. 10, ll. 126–9: Benckendorff à Neratov, Londres, 22 November/5 December 1911.

[115] AVPRI f. 144, op. 489, d. 279b, l. 109: Neratov to Benckendorff, St Petersburg, 21 November/4 December 1911, No. 1951 (telegram).

[116] PRO/FO371/1197/49055: Grey to Buchanan, No. 779 (telegraphic), 7 December 1911; for the text of the aide-mémoire, which was delivered on 8 December 1911, see AVPRI f. 144, op. 489, d. 594b, ll. 480–1 ob.

[117] AVPRI f. 144, op. 489, d. 594b, l. 537: Neratov to Benckendorff, St Petersburg, 30 November/13 December 1911, No. 2028.

[118] AVPRI f. 144, op. 489, d. 577b, l. 34–34 ob.: Secret telegram from Poklevsky-Kozell, Teheran, 25 November/8 December 1911, No. 1216; AVPRI f. 144, op. 489, d. 279b, l. 132: Secret telegram from Etter, London, 25 November/8 December 1911, No. 315.

[119] AVPRI f. 144, op. 489, d. 279b, l. 154: Neratov to Poklevsky-Kozell, St Petersburg, 27 November/10 December 1911, No. 2010 (telegram); AVPRI f. 144, op. 489, d. 594b, l. 15 (part 2): Sazonov to Vorontsov-Dashkov, St Petersburg, 1/14 December 1911, No. 2046.

[120] AVPRI f. 144, op. 489, d. 279b, l. 154: Neratov to Poklevsky-Kozell, St Petersburg, 27 November/10 December 1911, No. 2010 (telegram).

[121] See Kazemzadeh, *Russia and Britain in Persia, 1864–1914*, pp 644–5; for Shuster's impassioned retelling of the circumstances of his dismissal, see Shuster, chapters 7 and 8.

[122] PRO/FO371/1198/51329: Barclay to Grey, No. 728 (telegraphic), Teheran, 22 December 1911.

[123] AVPRI f. 144, op. 489, d. 594b, l. 636: Secret telegram from Miller, Tabriz, 10/23 December 1911, No. 734; AVPRI f. 144, op. 489, d. 279b, l. 193: Secret telegram from Miller, Tabriz, 10/23 December 1911, No. 740.

[124] AVPRI f. 144, op. 489, d. 279b, l. 206: Secret telegram from Nekrasov, Rasht, 14/27 December 1911, No. 343.

[125] AVPRI f. 144, op. 489, d. 594b, l. 635: Telegram from Beliaev, Ardebil, 10/23 December 1911, No. 1093.

[126] See for example AVPRI f. 144, op. 489, d. 594b, l. 671: Secret telegram from Preobrazhenskyi, Khoy, 13/26 December 1911, No. 69; AVPRI f. 144, op. 489, d. 279b, l. 211: Secret telegram from Dolgopolov, Esfahan, 15/28 December 1911, No. 655.

[127] AVPRI f. 147, op. 485, d. 73 (2), l. 361: Secret telegram from Vorontsov-Dashkov, Tbilisi, 15/28 December 1911, No. 7892; RGIA f. 560, op. 28, d. 388, l. 65: Ciphered telegram from the Commander-in-Chief of the Troops of the Caucasian Military District to Sukhomlinov, 11/24 December 1911, No. 7785.

[128] AVPRI f. 144, op. 489, d. 594b, l. 645: Sazonov to the Consul in Tabriz, St Petersburg, 10/23 December 1911, No. 2116.

[129] PRO/FO371/1198/51477: Buchanan to Grey, No. 347 (telegraphic), St Petersburg, 23 December 1911.

[130] AVPRI f. 144, op. 489, d. 594b, l. 645: Sazonov to Miller, St Petersburg, 10/23 December 1911, No. 2116.

[131] See David MacLaren McDonald, *United Government and Foreign Policy in Russia, 1900–1914* (Cambridge, MA, 1992), pp 172–6.

[132] PRO/FO371/1196/46682: Buchanan to Grey, No. 294 (telegraphic), St Petersburg, 22 November 1911.

[133] PRO/FO800/74: Buchanan to Grey (private), St Petersburg, 4 December 1911.

[134] PRO/FO800/74: Buchanan to Grey (private), St Petersburg, 4 December 1911. Buchanan was later taken to task by Sazonov for having discussed matters of foreign affairs with the chairman of the Council of Ministers at all. Sazonov categorically informed Buchanan that only the minister of foreign affairs was responsible to the tsar for the direction of foreign policy, and the chairman of the council had no authority over Russia's foreign policy. See Sir George Buchanan, *My Mission to Russia* (London, 1923), vol i, pp 102–3.

Chapter 6: Amicable Discord or Impending Breach?

[1] AVPRI f. 144, op. 489, d. 594b, l. 704: Secret telegram, Poklevsky-Kozell, Teheran, 29 December–11 January 1912, No. 1362.

[2] 'Persia and Sir E. Grey', *Daily News*, 16 January 1912, in AVPRI f. 144, op. 488, d. 414b, l. 38.

[3] PRO/FO800/93 (Grey MSS): Grey to Hardinge, 28 January 1912, in D.W. Sweet and R.T.B. Langhorne, 'Great Britain and Russia, 1907–1914', in F.H. Hinsley (ed), *British Foreign Policy under Sir Edward Grey* (Cambridge, 1977), p 251.

[4] It seems that Sazonov did not believe that to be his actual name, as 'Bonar Law' appears in quotation marks in a draft letter to Benckendorff. See RGIA f. 560, op. 28, d. 388, ll. 26–9: Draft Letter, Sazonov to Benckendorff (secret), n.d.

[5] RGIA f. 560, op. 28, d. 388, ll. 26–9: Draft Letter, Sazonov to Benckendorff (secret), n.d.

[6] PRO/FO371/1198/51329: Barclay to Grey, No. 728 (telegraphic), Teheran, 22 December 1911.

[7] AVPRI f.144, op. 489, d. 279b, l. 197: Télégramme secret de Benckendorff, Londres, 12/25 December 1911, No. 327.

[8] PRO/FO371/1198/51477: Buchanan to Grey, No. 347 (telegraphic), St Petersburg, 23 December 1911; AVPRI f. 144, op. 489, d. 279b, l. 200: Télégramme à Benckendorff, St Petersburg, 13 December 1911.

[9] PRO/FO371/1198/51477: Buchanan to Grey, No. 347 (telegraphic), St Petersburg, 23 December 1911.

[10] PRO/FO371/1422/96: Buchanan to Grey, No. 392, St Petersburg, 27 December 1911; PRO/FO371/1422/3: Buchanan to Grey, No. 356 (telegraphic), St Petersburg, 30 December 1911.

[11] RGIA f. 560, op. 28, d. 388, ll. 156–8. Sazonov to Kokovtsov, 17/30 December 1912, No. 1310.

[12] PRO/FO371/1422/3: Buchanan to Grey, No. 356 (telegraphic), St Petersburg, 30 December 1911.

[13] RGIA f. 560, op. 28, d. 387, ll. 136–136 ob.: Kokovtsov to Vorontsov-Dashkov, Tiflis (no date – some time after 11/24 November 1911).

[14] AVPRI f. 144, op. 489, d. 594b, l. 645: Sazonov to Miller, St Petersburg, 10/23 December 1911, No. 2116.

[15] Kazemzadeh, *Russia and Britain in Persia, 1864–1914*, p 645. See also AVPRI f. 144, op. 489, d. 594b, l. 568: Telegram from the Moscow Manufacturers, Moscow, 2/15 December 1911. For complaints of Russian merchants about the boycott of Russian goods in the north of Persia and the effect it had on Russian trade, see RGIA f. 23, op. 11, d. 8.

[16] AVPRI f. 147, op. 485, d. 73 (2), l. 217: Secret telegram from Poklevsky-Kozell, Teheran, 21 November/4 December 1911, No. 1196; AVPRI f. 144, op. 489, d. 594b, l. 612: Secret telegram to Nekrasov, communicated to Poklevsky-Kozell, St Petersburg, 8/21 December 1911, No. 2096.

[17] See Kazemzadeh, *Russia and Britain in Persia, 1864–1914*, pp 650–1.

[18] PRO/FO371/1422/281: Barclay to Grey, No. 3 (telegraphic), Teheran, 1 January 1912.

[19] PRO/FO371/1422/1870: Barclay to Grey, No. 41 (telegraphic), Teheran, 14 January 1912.

[20] AVPRI f. 144, op. 489, d. 279b, l. 245: Secret telegram from Miller, Tabriz, 22 December 1911/4 January 1912, No. 796.

[21] AVPRI f. 144, op. 489, d. 279b, l. 237: Sazonov to Poklevsky-Kozell, St Petersburg, 20 December 1911/2 January 1912, No. 2194 (telegram).

[22] AVPRI f. 144, op. 489, d. 279b, l. 169: Secret telegram to Miller, St Petersburg, 2/15 December 1911, No. 2053 (personal).

[23] See Kazemzadeh, *Russia and Britain in Persia, 1864–1914*, p 652.

[24] AVPRI f. 144, op. 488, d. 4146, l. 118: Secret telegram from Miller, Tabriz, 31 January/12 February 1912, No. 87.

[25] AVPRI f. 144, op. 488, d. 4146, l. 94: Secret telegram from Poklevsky-Kozell, Teheran, 22 January/4 February 1912, No. 70.

[26] RGIA f. 560, op. 28, d. 388, ll. 134–5: Copy of a secret letter from Neratov to the Infantry General Shatilov, 7/20 August 1912, No. 926.

[27] PRO/FO371/1440/15842: Buchanan to Grey, No. 149 (telegraphic), St Petersburg, 15 April 1912.

[28] PRO/FO371/1440/15842: Minute by Mallet on Buchanan to Grey, No. 149 (telegraphic), St Petersburg, 15 April 1912.

[29] PRO/FO371/1440/16224: A. Young to Grey, No. 266 (telegraphic), Teheran, 18 April 1912.

[30] AVPRI f. 144, op. 488, d. 4146, ll. 231–2 ob.: Buchanan to Sazonov, St Petersburg, 4/17 April 1912.

[31] Buchanan to Grey, in Sir George Buchanan, *My Mission to Russia* (London, 1923), p 110.

[32] AVPRI f. 144, op. 488, d. 4146, l. 108: Secret telegram from Prince Dabizha, Mashhad, 25 January/7 February 1912, No. 5.

[33] Kazemzadeh, *Russia and Britain in Persia, 1864–1914*, p 656.

[34] PRO/FO800/98: Hardinge to Grey (private), Viceroy's Camp, India, 12 February 1912.

[35] IO/L/P&S/18C/125: Memorandum on the situation in Southern Persia, J.E. Ferard, 16 February 1912 (secret).

[36] AVPRI f. 144, op. 488, d. 4146, ll. 58–58 ob.: Télégramme secret de Benckendorff, Londres, le 10/23 Janvier 1912, No. 10.

[37] PRO/FO371/1423/6205: Grey to Buchanan, No. 41, 8 February 1912.

[38] AVPRI f. 144, op. 488, d. 4146, l. 101: Sazonov to Poklevsky-Kozell, St Petersburg, 24 January/6 February 1912, No. 148 (telegram).

[39] AVPRI f. 144, op. 488, d. 4146, l. 119: Secret telegram from Poklevsky-Kozell, Teheran, 1/14 February 1912.

[40] AVPRI f. 138, op. 467, d. 300/303, ll. 50–4 ob.: Note of Sazonov to Buchanan, St Petersburg, 16/29 January 1912.

[41] Kazemzadeh, *Russia and Britain in Persia, 1864–1914*, p 659.

[42] Poklevsky-Kozell to Sazonov, Telegram No. 75, 25 January/7 February 1912, quoted in Kazemzadeh, *Russia and Britain in Persia, 1864–1914*, p 660.

[43] AVPRI f. 144, op. 488, d. 4146, l. 134: Manager of the Central Asian Department of MID to Prince Dabizha, St Petersburg, 11/24 February 1912, No. 279 (telegram).

[44] AVPRI f. 144, op. 488, d. 4146, l. 146: Sazonov to Poklevsky-Kozell, St Petersburg, 16/29 February 1912, No. 310.

[45] AVPRI f. 144, op. 488, d. 4146, l. 152: Secret telegram from Ivanov, Astrabad, 24 February/8 March 1912, No. 35.

[46] PRO/FO371/1424/14642: Buchanan to Grey, summarizing *Novoe Vremia* article of 3 April 1912, No. 104, St Petersburg, 3 April 1912.

[47] PRO/FO371/1424/15859: Buchanan to Grey, No. 117, St Petersburg, 10 April 1912.

[48] PRO/FO371/1424/15859: Translation of an official communiqué published in the Russian press on 28 March/10 April 1912. Enclosure in Buchanan to Grey, No. 117, St Petersburg, 10 April 1912.

[49] PRO/FO371/1469/18331: Translation of the speech delivered by Sazonov in the Imperial Duma on the 13/26 April 1912. Enclosure in Buchanan's dispatch No. 137 of 27 April 1912.

[50] PRO/FO371/1469/19025: Buchanan to Grey, No. 140, St Petersburg, 29 April 1912.

[51] PRO/FO371/1444/21342: O'Beirne to Grey, summarizing *Novoe Vremia* article of 12 May 1912, No. 156, St Petersburg, 16 May 1912.

[52] 'Persia and Sir E. Grey', *Daily News*, 16 January 1912.

[53] PRO/FO800/70: Grey to Barclay (private), 10 January 1912.

[54] AVPRI f. 144, op. 488, d. 4146, l. 134: Manager of the Central Asian Department of MID to Prince Dabizha, St Petersburg, 11/24 February 1912, No. 279 (telegram).

[55] AVPRI f. 144, op. 488, d. 4146, l. 164: Secret telegram from Prince Dabizha, Mashhad, 10/23 March 1912.

[56] AVPRI f. 144, op. 488, d. 4146, ll. 209–209 ob.: Télégramme secret de Benckendorff, Londres, le 30 mars/12 avril 1912, No. 95; AVPRI f. 144, op. 488, d. 4146, l. 180: Télégramme secret de Benckendorff, Londres, le 21 mars/3 avril 1912, No. 94.

[57] Buchanan to Grey, in Buchanan, *My Mission to Russia*, p 112.

[58] Buchanan to Grey, *ibid.*, p 113.

[59] PRO/FO371/1424/19922: Grey to Townley, No. 91. 14 May 1912.

[60] AVPRI f. 144, op. 488, d. 4146, l. 287–9 ob.: Une Lettre secrète de Benckendorff adressée à Sazonov, Londres, le 28 avril/11 mai 1912.

[61] PRO/FO371/1424/19922: Grey to Townley, No. 91, 14 May 1912.

[62] AVPRI f. 144, op. 488, d. 4146, l. 224: Sazonov to Benckendorff, St Petersburg, 2/15 April 1912, No. 680.

[63] PRO/FO371/1743/6216: Annual Report on Russia for the year 1912, 17 January 1913.

[64] AVPRI 144, op. 488, d. 4146, ll. 241–241 ob.: Télégramme secret de Benckendorff, Londres, le 6/19 Avril 1912, No. 103.

[65] AVPRI f. 144, op. 488, d. 4146, l. 224: Sazonov to Benckendorff, St Petersburg, 2/15 April 1912, No. 680.

[66] AVPRI 144, op. 488, d. 4146, ll. 241–241 ob.: Télégramme secret de Benckendorff, Londres, le 6/19 avril 1912, No. 103.

[67] RGIA f. 560, op. 28, d. 467, ll. 2–2 ob.: Secret report of Revelioti, Calcutta, 14/27 February 1912.

[68] The Mashhad *anjoman* stated that the Persians would rather be citizens of the Afghan emir than of Russia. AVPRI f. 147, op. 485, d. 753, ll. 46–7: Copy of secret information from the Commander of the troops of the Turkestan Military District, to the Director of the General Staff, 30 January/12 February 1912, No. 585.

[69] AVPRI f. 147, op. 485, d. 753, ll. 55–55 ob.: Headquarters of the Turkestan Military District Intelligence Department to the Director in Chief of the General Staff, Department of the General-Quartermaster, Tashkent, 27 February/11 March 1912, No. 919.

[70] AVPRI f. 147, op. 485, d. 753, ll. 74–92: Information about Afghanistan. Collected by the first officer of the military attaché in Khorasan, Lieutenant Colonel Skurat, No. 16, February 1912; AVPRI f. 147, op. 486, d. 36, l. 13: Secret telegram from Revelioti, Simla, 15/28 April 1912, No. 20.

[71] PRO/FO418/51/31: Grey to Buchanan, Foreign Office, 1 May 1912, No. 142.

[72] RGVIA f. 2000, op. 1, d. 3724, l. 41: Copy of a secret dispatch from the Acting Chubai customs post to the Director of the Turkestan Customs District, 2/15 May 1912, No. 6.

[73] PRO/FO371/1470/39700: Extract from Diary of the British Agent at Kabul, No. 85 for the period ending 11 August 1912.

[74] AVPRI f. 147, op. 486, d. 239b, ll. 49–54 ob.: A. Samsonov, Turkestan Governor-General, to Sazonov, Tashkent, 29 January/12 February 1912, No. 92.

[75] AVPRI f. 147, op. 485, d. 753, ll. 104–104 ob.: Copy of a report of the Pendinskii police officer, Captain Moskalenk, to the Chief of the Merv District, 30 December 1911/12 January 1912, No. 6766.

[76] AVPRI f. 147, op. 485, d. 762, l. 7: Urgent secret telegram from Samsonov, Tashkent, 26 January/9 February 1912, No. 68.

[77] AVPRI f. 147, op. 485, d. 762, l. 9: Sazonov to Samsonov, St Petersburg, 28 January/11 February 1912, No. 166 (telegram); for information about Afghan agents, see AVPRI f. 147, op. 485, d. 753, ll. 74–92: Information about Afghanistan, Collected by Skurat, No. 16, February 1912.

[78] PRO/FO371/1468/9639: Benckendorff to Grey, London, 2 March 1912.

[79] AVPRI f. 147, op. 485, d. 753, ll. 102–3 ob.: Lieutenant General Shostak, Director, Diplomatic Section of the Transcaspian District, to Samsonov, Ashkhabad, 17/30 January 1912, No. 62.

[80] AVPRI f. 147, op. 485, d. 753, ll. 107–8: Copy of letter from Shostak, to the Manager of the Chancellery of the Turkestan Governor Generalship, 6/19 June 1912, No. 512.

[81] AVPRI f. 147, op. 485, d. 753, ll. 109–109 ob.: Official for border relations under the Director of the Transcaspian District, Colonel Palchevskyi, Merv, 17/30 May 1912, No. 8582.

[82] AVPRI f. 147, op. 486, d. 239b, ll. 49–54 ob.: Samsonov to Sazonov, Tashkent, 29 January/12 February 1912, No. 92.

[83] AVPRI f. 147, op. 486, d. 239b, ll. 55–8 ob.: N. Iasa. Memorandum. Council of Representatives of Trade and Industry, 1/14 March 1912, No. 25199; RGIA f. 560, op. 28, d. 455, ll. 13–13 ob.: Political agent in Bukhara to the Director of the Transcaspian District, 6/19 May 1912, No. 153. Enclosure in Secret report of Somov, Novaia Bukhara, 10/23 May 1912, No. 9.

[84] PRO/FO368/718/6111: 'Russo-Afghan Trade, application for an inter-Departmental Conference at St Petersburg to regulate various impediments to.' Memorandum by Henry Cooke, commercial attaché, St Petersburg, 8 February 1912. Enclosure in Buchanan's Dispatch No. 42, 9 February 1912; AVPRI f. 147, op. 486, d. 239b, ll. 55–8 ob.: Iasa. Memorandum.

[85] AVPRI f. 147, op. 486, d. 239b, ll. 36–44 ob.: Secret report of Somov, Novaia Bukhara, 10/23 May 1912, No. 9.

[86] When the gendarme in Old Bukhara requested permission from Somov to arrest the departing Afghan commercial agent on suspicion of being a spy, Somov refused the petition for fear of possible repercussions against Russian and Bukharan traders. The gendarme, however, circumvented the refusal by detaining the agent on the railway zone over which Somov had no authority (AVPRI f. 147, op. 486, d. 36, l. 15 ob.: Secret telegram from Somov, Bukhara, 14/27 May 1912).

[87] AVPRI f. 147, op. 486, d. 239b, ll. 36–44 ob.: Secret report of Somov, Novaia Bukhara, 10/23 May 1912, No. 9; AVPRI f. 147, op. 486, d. 239b, ll. 41–41 ob.: Political agent in Bukhara to Samsonov, 5/18 May 1912, No. 146.

[88] RGVIA f. 400, op. 1, d. 4140, ll. 2–4: Confirmation by Samsonov, 31 July/12 August 1912. Excerpts from the Journal of the Chancellery of the Turkestan Governor-Generalship, 14/27 June 1912, No. 17.

[89] PRO/FO371/1326/347: British Trade Agent to Government of India (telegraphic), Yatung, 30 November 1911.

[90] Dalai Lama, quoted in N.S. Kuleshov, *Rossia i Tibet v nachale XX veka* (Moscow, 1992), p 160.

[91] PRO/FO371/1078/19979: Buchanan to Grey, No. 116 (telegraphic), St Petersburg, 24 May 1911; PRO/FO371/1078/50894: Aide-mémoire communicated by Benckendorff, 18 December 1911; see also Kuleshov, pp 193–4.

[92] RGVIA f. 2000, op. 1, d. 4198: Secret telegram from MID to Benckendorff, St Petersburg, 24 January/6 February 1912, No. 143; PRO/FO371/1326/9614: C.A. Bell, Political Officer in Sikkim, to the Secretary to the Government of India in the Foreign Department, Darjeeling, 10 February 1912.

[93] PRO/FO371/1078/50894: Aide-mémoire communicated by Benckendorff, 18 December 1911.

[94] PRO/FO371/1326/9614: C.A. Bell to the Secretary to the Government of India in the Foreign Department, Darjeeling, 10 February 1912.

[95] PRO/FO535/15/67: Jordan to Grey, 22 February 1912, quoted in Amar Kaur Jasbir Singh, *Himalayan Triangle. A Historical Survey of British India's Relations with Tibet, Sikkim and Bhutan, 1765–1950* (London, 1988), pp 63–4.

[96] PRO/FO371/1326/12818: Telegram from Viceroy, 23 March 1912.

[97] PRO/FO371/1348/34756: Memorandum respecting the Situation in the Countries bordering on the North-Eastern Frontier of India, R.T. Nugent, Foreign Office, 26 August 1912.

[98] PRO/FO371/1327/25530: Memorandum communicated to Benckendorff, 25 June 1912.

[99] PRO/FO371/1348/34756: Memorandum respecting the Situation in the Countries bordering on the North-Eastern Frontier of India, R.T. Nugent, Foreign Office, 26 August 1912.

[100] PRO/FO371/1348/34756: Memorandum respecting the Status of Thibet, J.D. Gregory, Foreign Office, 1 September 1912.

[101] PRO/FO371/1348/38535: Government of India to the Marquess of Crewe (telegraphic), 12 September 1912.

[102] PRO/FO371/1348/38535: Nugent. Minute on Government of India to Crewe (telegraphic), 12 September 1912.

[103] PRO/FO371/1328/38627: Crowe. Minute on Buchanan to Grey, No. 279, St Petersburg, 11 September 1912.

[104] PRO/FO371/1470/33896: Buchanan to Grey, No. 245, St Petersburg, 8 August 1912.

[105] Buchanan to Grey, St Petersburg, 9 October 1912, No. 811, in *BD*, ix, i, pp 769–70.

[106] For Sazonov's reminiscences of his trip to Britain, see S.D. Sazonov, *Vospominania* (Moscow, 1991), pp 66–72.

[107] PRO/FO371/1447/37616: Telegram from Townley (private and confidential), Teheran, 5 September 1912.

[108] PRO/FO800/70: Townley to Grey (private and confidential), Gulahek, 5 September 1912.

[109] AVPRI f. 144, op. 488, d. 4146, ll. 511–12: Sazonov's notes for his conversations with Grey at Balmoral, St Petersburg, 3/16 September 1912.

[110] PRO/FO371/1447/40566: Memorandum respecting Conversations between Sazonov and Grey at Balmoral, 24 September 1912.

[111] AVPRI f. 144, op. 488, d. 4146, ll. 499–500: Persian Affairs. Sazonov's notes from his conversations with Grey at Balmoral, September 1912.

[112] PRO/FO371/1448/41470: Memorandum respecting Conversations at Balmoral between Sazonov and Grey, 25 September 1912.

[113] PRO/FO371/1435/41468: Note on Conversations at Balmoral between Sazonov and Grey, 25 September 1912.

[114] AVPRI f. 144, op. 488, d. 4146, ll. 489–92 ob.: Persian Affairs. Sazonov's notes from his conversations with Grey at Balmoral, September 1912.

[115] PRO/FO371/1447/40566: Memorandum respecting Conversations between Sazonov and Grey at Balmoral, 24 September 1912.

[116] AVPRI f. 144, op. 488, d. 4146, ll. 528–528 ob.: Chemin de fer Transpersique. In Sazonov's notes for his conversations with Grey at Balmoral, St Petersburg, 5/18 September 1912.

[117] AVPRI f. 144, op. 488, d. 4146, ll. 489–92 ob.: Persian Affairs. Sazonov's notes from his conversations with Grey at Balmoral, September 1912.

[118] Grey, 'Persia, the Anglo-Russian Convention, Egypt, Naval Strength', The House of Commons, 10 July 1912, in P. Knaplund (ed), *Speeches on Foreign Affairs, 1900–14 by Sir Edward Grey* (London, 1931), p 196.

[119] PRO/FO371/1433/3668: 'The Trans-Persian Railway Scheme: Draft Memorandum for the consideration of the Committee constituted to represent British Interests in relation to the Project for linking up the Russian and Indian Railway systems', Sir Walter Hughes, 15 January 1912.

[120] Grey, Minute on 'Chemin de Fer Transiraneien'. Memorandum communicated by Sazonov, 24 September 1912, No. 803 (5), in *BD*, ix, i, p 754.

[121] AVPRI f. 147, op. 486, d. 235b, ll. 8–9: Aide-mémoire transmis par Sazonov à Grey à Balmoral, août 1912; Brigadier-General Sir Percy Sykes, *A History of Afghanistan* (London, 1940), vol ii, p 242.

[122] AVPRI f. 147, op. 486, d. 235b, ll. 8–9: Aide-mémoire transmis par Sazonov à Grey à Balmoral, août 1912.

[123] PRO/FO371/1468/40428: Memorandum respecting the Question of Afghanistan, Communicated by Sazonov, 24 September 1912.

[124] AVPRI f. 147, op. 486, d. 235b, l. 57 and AVPRI f. 144, op. 488, d. 4146, ll. 492 ob. and 493 ob.: Sazonov's notes on Afghanistan, September 1912.

[125] PRO/FO371/1448/41472: Extract of Note of Conversation between Crewe and Sazonov at Crewe Hall, 29 September 1912.

[126] PRO/FO371/1328/40435: Note on the Question of Thibet (Grey), 24 September 1912.

[127] PRO/FO371/1328/41188: Extract from Note of Conversation between Crewe and Sazonov, 29 September 1912.

[128] Buchanan to Grey (private), St Petersburg, 17 October 1912, No. 812, in *BD*, ix, i, p 771.

[129] No. 811, in *BD*, ix, i, pp 769–70.

[130] Keith Neilson, *Britain and the Last Tsar* (Oxford, 1995), p 327.

Chapter 7: Towards a Revision

[1] RGVIA f. 2000, op. 1, d. 3724, ll. 47–9 ob.: Report. Chief of Staff of the Turkestan Military District. Intelligence Department. To the Director in Chief of the General Staff, Department of the General-Quartermaster, 9/22 August 1912, No. 3770.

[2] AVPRI f. 147, op. 485, d. 753, ll. 212–13: Intelligence about Afghanistan, 7/20 October 1912.

[3] AVPRI f. 147, op. 485, d. 753, ll. 222–41: Information about Afghanistan, collected and developed by Skurat, No. 20, October 1912.

[4] AVPRI f. 147, op. 485, d. 753, ll. 212–13: Intelligence about Afghanistan, 7/20 October 1912.

[5] PRO/FO371/1468/40428: Memorandum communicated to Sazonov respecting Afghanistan, 4 October 1912.

[6] AVPRI f. 147, op. 486, d. 235b, ll. 18–23: Consul General in India Nabokov to V.O. von Klemm (extremely secret), Simla, 28 November/11 December 1912, No. 37.

[7] AVPRI f. 147, op. 486, d. 235b, ll. 18–23: Nabokov to von Klemm (extremely secret), Simla, 28 November/11 December 1912, No. 37.

[8] PRO/FO800/98: Extract from a letter from Hardinge to Crewe (private), Viceroy's Camp, India, 30 October 1912.

[9] PRO/FO800/98: Extract from a letter from Hardinge to Crewe (private), Viceroy's Camp, India, 30 October 1912.

[10] PRO/FO371/1468/40428: Memorandum communicated to Sazonov respecting Afghanistan, 4 October 1912.

[11] For the Russian position on Afghan misuse of regional water rights, see RGVIA 400, op. 1, d. 4137, ll. 1–2: Turkestan Governor General, Diplomatic Section to the Minister of War, 4/17 July 1912, No. 511.

[12] PRO/FO371/1470/35494: Note communicated by the Russian Chargé d'Affaires, 20 August 1912.

[13] PRO/FO371/1472/47200: Russian Government to Benckendorff. Communicated by the Councillor of the Russian Embassy, 6 November 1912. For discussions of the Russian measures taken against the outbreak of plague epidemics in Central Asia in 1912, see AVPRI f. 147, op. 486, d. 36.

[14] PRO/FO368/707/53090: Telegram from Townley, No. 631, Teheran, 12 December 1912.

[15] PRO/FO800/98: Letter from Hardinge to Crewe (private), 27 November 1912. Enclosure in Crewe to Grey (private), 16 December 1912.

[16] PRO/FO368/707/53090: Telegram from Townley, No. 631, Teheran, 12 December 1912.

[17] PRO/FO371/1472/54206: India Office to Foreign Office, 18 December 1912.

[18] PRO/FO371/1470/51195: Government of India to Crewe (telegraphic), 29 November 1912.

[19] PRO/FO800/98: Letter from Hardinge to Crewe, 27 November 1912.

[20] PRO/FO371/1472/54206: India Office to Foreign Office, 18 December 1912.

[21] PRO/FO800/98: Crewe to Grey (private), 16 December 1912.

[22] PRO/FO371/1470/52924: Minute by H. Norman on India Office to Foreign Office, 10 December 1912.

[23] PRO/FO800/98: Letter from Hardinge to Crewe, 27 November 1912.

[24] See Alastair Lamb, *The McMahon Line* (London, 1966), vol ii, pp 438–41 and Appendices XIII and XV.

[25] IO/MSS Eur/F 112/251: Major O'Connor to Curzon (private letter), Shiraz, 21 March 1913.

[26] PRO/FO371/1329/48911: Sir J. Jordan to Grey, No. 237 (telegraphic), Peking, 16 November 1912.

[27] PRO/FO371/1329/51749: Minute by R.T. Nugent on India Office to Foreign Office, 3 December 1912.

[28] RGVIA f. 2000, op. 1, d. 4198: Unsigned letter to Oskar Karlovich (last name unknown), 10/23 April 1912; PRO/FO371/1329/55070: Jordan to Grey, No. 271 (confidential) (telegraphic), Peking, 26 December 1912; RGVIA f. 2000, op. 1, d.

7915, l. 1: Secret telegram from the Envoy in Peking (Krutsenskii), 13/26 December 1912, No. 1017.

[29] RGIA f. 560, op. 28, d. 64, l. 104: Secret telegram from Sazonov to Benckendorff, 11/24 December 1912, No. 3012.

[30] PRO/FO371/1329/53945: Jordan to Grey, No. 262 (telegraphic), Peking, 17 December 1912; PRO/FO371/1326/12818: Telegram from Viceroy, 23 March 1912; PRO/FO371/1329/55420: India Office to Foreign Office, 27 December 1912.

[31] 'Treaty between Tibet and Mongolia, said to have been signed at Urga on 11 January 1913', in Lamb, *The McMahon Line*, Appendix XIV, pp 612–14.

[32] PRO/FO371/1609/9276: Minute by Nugent on the Transmitted text of Tibetan-Mongolian Treaty. Enclosure in Jordan to Grey, No. 72, Peking, 10 February 1913.

[33] PRO/FO371/1327/29267: Government of India to Crewe (telegraphic), 9 July 1912.

[34] PRO/FO371/1327/31836: India Office to Foreign Office, 26 July 1912.

[35] PRO/FO371/1327/32864: Government of India to Crewe (telegraphic), 2 August 1912; PRO/FO371/1328/36999: Government of India to Crewe (telegraphic), 31 August 1912.

[36] PRO/FO371/1609/2600: Buchanan to Grey, No. 19 (telegraphic), St Petersburg, 17 January 1913.

[37] RGIA f. 560, op. 28, d. 64, l. 106: Secret telegram from Sazonov to Korostovets in Urga, 22 December 1912/4 January 1913, No. 3082.

[38] PRO/FO371/1609/7144: Dispatch from Korostovets, Urga, 6/19 January 1913. Enclosure in Buchanan to Grey, No. 52, St Petersburg, 11 February 1913.

[39] PRO/FO371/1609/7144: Minute on Buchanan to Grey, No. 52, St Petersburg, 11 February 1913.

[40] PRO/FO371/1609/7222: Minute by Nugent on Buchanan to Grey, No. 55 (telegraphic), St Petersburg, 14 February 1913.

[41] PRO/FO371/1613/55748: Government of India to Crewe (telegraphic), 9 December 1913.

[42] PRO/FO371/1610/12462: Foreign Office to India Office (confidential), 17 March 1913.

[43] PRO/FO371/1608/13846: India Office to Foreign Office, 25 March 1913.

[44] PRO/FO371/1608/13846: Foreign Office to India Office, 29 March 1913.

[45] PRO/FO371/1609/2534: Government of India to Crewe (telegraphic), 16 January 1913.

[46] IO/L/P&S/18/B/191: Tibet (Hirtzel), 27 January 1913.

[47] IO/L/P&S/18/B/191: Tibet (Hirtzel), 27 January 1913.

[48] PRO/FO371/1609/8917: Government of India to Crewe (telegraphic), 23 February 1913.

[49] PRO/FO371/1610/13816: India Office to Foreign Office, 25 March 1913.

[50] PRO/FO371/1609/8917: Government of India to Crewe (telegraphic), 23 February 1913.

[51] RGIA f. 560, op. 28, d. 64, ll. 116–17: Dalai Lama to the Imperial Government (n. d.).

[52] RGIA f. 560, op. 28, d. 64, ll. 118–20: Sazonov to Kokovtsov, 25 April/8 May 1913, No. 366.

[53] RGIA f. 560, op. 28, d. 64, ll. 118–20: Sazonov to Kokovtsov, 25 April/8 May 1913, No. 366.

[54] PRO/FO371/1611/29020: Government of India to Crewe (telegraphic), 24 June 1913.

[55] PRO/FO371/1329/48911: Minute by Nugent on Jordan to Grey, No. 237 (telegraphic), Peking, 16 November 1912.

[56] PRO/FO371/1329/51749: India Office to Foreign Office, 3 December 1912.

[57] PRO/FO371/1329/51749: Minute by Nicolson on India Office to Foreign Office, 3 December 1912.

[58] PRO/FO371/1610/17717: Government of India to Crewe (telegraphic), 15 April 1913.

[59] PRO/FO371/1610/17717: Government of India to Crewe (telegraphic), 15 April 1913; PRO/FO371/1610/16537: Foreign Office to India Office, 30 April 1913.

[60] PRO/FO371/1610/20005: Foreign Office to India Office, 15 May 1913.

[61] PRO/FO371/1611/25215: O'Beirne to Grey, No. 175, St Petersburg, 29 May 1913.

[62] RGIA f. 560, op. 28, d. 64, ll. 122–122 ob.: Memorandum, presented to the British Government, 14/27 June 1913.

[63] PRO/FO371/1706/1653: Acting Consul N. Patrick Cowan to Townley, No. 9 (confidential), Tabriz, 25 November 1912.

[64] AVPRI f. 144, op. 488, d. 4146, l. 582: Sazonov to Poklevsky-Kozell, St Petersburg, 24 December/5 January 1912, No. 3103 (telegram); PRO/FO371/1449/49699: Townley to Grey, No. 232 (very confidential), Teheran, 7 November 1912.

[65] PRO/FO371/1721/39074: Townley to Grey, No. 166 (very confidential), Teheran, 1 August 1913.

[66] PRO/FO371/2073/10393: Annual Report for Persia (1913), 18 February 1914.

[67] PRO/FO371/1449/49699: Townley to Grey, No. 232 (very confidential), Teheran, 7 November 1912.

[68] PRO/FO800/70: Townley to Grey (private and confidential), Gulahek, 8 October 1912.

[69] PRO/FO371/1721/11022: Cowan to Townley, No. 1, Tabriz, 20 January 1913.

[70] PRO/FO371/1743/6216: Annual Report on Russia for the year 1912, 17 January 1913.

[71] PRO/FO371/1449/52795: Townley to Grey, No. 626 (telegraphic), Teheran, 10 December 1912.

[72] PRO/FO371/1743/6216: Annual Report on Russia for the year 1912, 17 January 1913.

[73] PRO/FO371/1706/1653: Cowan to Townley, No. 9 (confidential), Tabriz, 25 November 1912.

[74] PRO/FO371/1449/49699: Minute by Parkes on Townley to Grey, No. 232 (very confidential), Teheran, 7 November 1912.

[75] IO/L/P&S/18/C/127: The Attack on the 39th Central India Horse, Hirtzel, 6 January 1913.

[76] See IO/L/P&S/18/C/125: Memorandum on the situation in Southern Persia, J.E. Ferard, 16 February 1912 (secret).

[77] PRO/FO371/1720/15861: Consul-General Sykes to Townley, No. 5 (confidential), Mashhad, 22 January 1913.

[78] PRO/FO371/1725/11024: Townley to Grey, No. 34, Teheran, 16 February 1913.

[79] IO/L/P&S/18/C/127: 'The Attack on the 39th Central India Horse', Hirtzel, 6 January 1913.

[80] IO/MSS Eur/F 112/251: O'Connor to Curzon (private letter), Shiraz, 21 March 1913.

[81] IO/MSS Eur/F 112/251: Cox to Curzon (private letter), Bushire, 10 April 1912.

[82] AVPRI f. 144, op. 489, d. 296b, ll. 102–102 ob.: Aide-Mémoire, British Embassy, St Petersburg, 20 April/3 May 1913.

[83] AVPRI f. 144, op. 489, d. 298b, l. 153: Secret telegram from Sablin, 8/21 May 1913, No. 210.

[84] PRO/FO371/1433/3668: A.J. Barry to Foreign Office (confidential), 25 January 1912.

[85] PRO/FO371/1433/3668: 'The Trans-Persian Railway Scheme: Draft Memorandum for the consideration of the Committee constituted to represent British Interests in relation to the Project for linking up the Russian and Indian Railway systems.' Sir Walter Hughes, 15 January 1912.

[86] IO/L/P&S/18/C/131: Memorandum by Mr. Parker respecting Railway Construction in Persia, Foreign Office, 13 January 1913.

[87] PRO/FO371/1178/45231: Treasury to Foreign Office, Treasury Chambers, 13 November 1911.

[88] PRO/FO371/1433/12866: Board of Trade to Foreign Office (confidential), 25 March 1912.

[89] PRO/FO371/1433/15203: Foreign Office to Mr. Greenway, Persian Railways Syndicate (confidential), 19 April 1912.

[90] PRO/FO371/1434/23863: Persian Railways Syndicate to Foreign Office, London, 3 June 1912.

[91] PRO/CAB16/26: Aide-mémoire, St Petersburg, 4/17 April 1912.

[92] AVPRI f. 144, op. 488, d. 4146, l. 341: Neratov to Poklevsky-Kozell, St Petersburg, 14/27 July 1912, No. 1413.

[93] AVPRI f. 144, op. 488, d. 4146, l. 347: Secret telegram from Poklevsky-Kozell, Teheran, 16/29 July 1912, No. 594.

[94] IO/L/MIL/5/730: Standing Sub-Committee of the CID. The Trans-Persian Railway. Note by the Secretary (MPA Hankey), 7 January 1913; PRO/CAB16/26: Draft Report (Hankey) Standing Sub-Committee of the CID. The Trans-Persian Railway, 12 April 1913.

[95] AVPRI f. 144, op. 488, d. 4146, l. 465: Télégramme secret de Benckendorff, 21 November/4 December 1912.

[96] Board of Trade, 13 September 1910, quoted in PRO/FO371/1709/902: Memorandum respecting the Trans-Persian Railway (Hirtzel), India Office, 3 January 1913.

[97] PRO/CAB16/26: Draft Report, 12 April 1913.

[98] PRO/FO371/1712/33730: Memorandum by the Indian General Staff on the Trans-Persian Railway. Percy Lake, Lieutenant-General, Chief of the General Staff, 6 June 1913.

[99] PRO/CAB16/26: Draft Report, 12 April 1913.

[100] PRO/CAB16/26: Draft Report, 12 April 1913.

[101] PRO/CAB16/26: Draft Report, 12 April 1913.

[102] IO/L/P&S/18/C/131: Memorandum by Parker, 13 January 1913.

[103] PRO/FO371/1709/3227: 'Trans Persian Railway'. Memorandum by Louis Mallet, 20 January 1913.

[104] F. Noel Paton, Director-General of Commercial Intelligence, India, 31 December 1910, quoted in PRO/FO371/1709/902: Memorandum, 3 January 1913.

[105] PRO/FO371/1709/3227: 'Trans Persian Railway', 20 January 1913.

[106] Sazonov, 27 September 1912 quoted in IO/L/P&S/18/C/131: Memorandum by Parker, Foreign Office, 13 January 1913.

[107] IO/L/P&S/18/C/131: Memorandum by Parker, 13 January 1913; PRO/FO371/1709/3227: 'Trans Persian Railway', 20 January 1913.

[108] PRO/CAB16/26: Draft Report, 12 April 1913.

[109] AVPRI f. 133, op. 470, d. 96, l. 8: Secret telegram from Poklevsky-Kozell, 16/29 January 1913, No. 17.

[110] AVPRI f. 144, op. 488, d. 4146, l. 469: Secret telegram from Poklevsky-Kozell, 28 November/11 December 1912, No. 919.

[111] AVPRI f. 144, op. 488, d. 4438, l. 20: Sazonov to Sablin, St Petersburg, 6 May 1913, No. 1297 (telegram).

[112] AVPRI f. 144, op. 488, d. 4146, l. 476: Sazonov to Benckendorff, St Petersburg, 30 November/13 December 1912, No. 2879 (telegram).

[113] PRO/FO371/1712/22761: Aide-Mémoire communicated to Buchanan by Sazonov, St Petersburg, 1/14 May 1913.

[114] PRO/FO371/1711/15016: Government of India to Crewe, Simla, 13 February 1913.

[115] PRO/FO371/1710/8687: Buchanan to Grey, No. 63, St Petersburg, 20 February 1913; PRO/FO371/1712/22761: Aide-Mémoire communicated to Buchanan by Sazonov, St Petersburg, 1/14 May 1913.

[116] PRO/FO371/1745/22759: Buchanan to Grey, No. 158, St Petersburg, 15 May 1913.

[117] PRO/FO371/1711/15016: India Office to Foreign Office (secret), 1 April 1913.

[118] IO/L/P&S/10/122/2276: Note by Hirtzel on PRO/FO371/1729/23129, 27 May 1913.

[119] PRO/FO371/1712/27788: Memorandum concerning the Inter-Departmental Committee on the Trans-Persian Railway's consideration of the Russian aide-mémoire of 14 May 1913, 29 May 1913.

[120] PRO/FO371/1712/27788: Hirtzel to Nicolson, 3 June 1913.

[121] PRO/FO371/1712/33730: Memorandum by the Indian General Staff on the Trans-Persian Railway. Percy Lake, Lieutenant-General, Chief of the General Staff, 6 June 1913.

[122] PRO/FO371/1712/27788: Memorandum by Buchanan on Hirtzel's Letter, London, 7 June 1913.

[123] PRO/FO371/1712/43384: O'Beirne to Grey, No. 277 (secret), St Petersburg, 17 September 1913.

[124] PRO/FO371/1712/56211: Memorandum respecting Effect on the Defence of India of an Alignment, viâ Kerman, of the Trans-Persian Railway, War Office, November 1913.

[125] PRO/FO371/2059/3508: Buchanan to Grey, No. 21 (telegraphic), St Petersburg, 25 January 1914.

[126] PRO/FO371/1731/50317: Townley to Grey (private letter), Teheran, 30 September 1913.

[127] PRO/FO371/1731/50317: Townley to Grey (private letter), Teheran, 30 September 1913.

[128] PRO/FO371/1720/20780: Townley to Grey, No. 188 (telegraphic), Teheran, 5 May 1913.

[129] PRO/FO371/1720/21118: Buchanan to Grey, No. 182 (telegraphic), St Petersburg, 7 May 1913.

[130] PRO/FO371/1730/27406: Buchanan to Grey, No. 216 (very confidential) (telegraphic), St Petersburg, 15 June 1913.

[131] PRO/FO371/1731/50317: Extracts from Acting Consul Smart to Townley, Tabriz, 6 September 1913. Enclosure in Townley to Grey (private letter), Teheran, 30 September 1913.

[132] PRO/FO371/1729/23129: Minute of Buchanan's conversation with Sazonov on 14 May 1913.

[133] PRO/FO371/1729/23129: Minute by Lancelot Oliphant on Minute of Buchanan's conversation with Sazonov on 14 May 1913.

[134] PRO/FO371/1721/39074: Smart to Townley (private letter), Tabriz, 20 July 1913.

[135] PRO/FO371/1729/23129: Minute of Buchanan's conversation with Sazonov on 14 May 1913; PRO/FO371/1730/27406: Buchanan to Grey, No. 216 (very confidential) (telegraphic), St Petersburg, 15 June 1913.

[136] PRO/FO371/1729/23129: Minute of Buchanan's conversation with Sazonov on 14 May 1913.

[137] AVPRI f. 144, op. 489, d. 286b, ll. 1–32: Towards a revision of the Anglo-Russian Agreement of 1907; PRO/FO371/1729/23129: Minute of Buchanan's conversation with Sazonov on 14 May 1913.

[138] PRO/FO371/1729/23129: Minute by Oliphant on Minute of Buchanan's conversation with Sazonov on 14 May 1913.

[139] PRO/FO371/1721/43225: Townley to Grey, No. 181 (very confidential), Teheran, 15 August 1913.

[140] PRO/FO371/1729/23129: Minute by Nicolson on Minute of Buchanan's conversation with Sazonov on 14 May 1913.

[141] PRO/FO371/1729/27406: Buchanan to Grey, No. 216 (very confidential) (telegraphic), St Petersburg, 15 June 1913.

[142] PRO/FO371/1721/42706: Townley to Grey, No. 325 (telegraphic), Teheran, 17 September 1913.

[143] PRO/FO371/1731/50317: Townley to Grey (private letter), Teheran, 30 September 1913.

[144] PRO/FO371/1731/43231: Townley to Grey, No. 188 (secret), Teheran, 30 August 1913.

[145] AVPRI f. 144, op. 489, d. 286b, ll. 1–32: Towards a revision of the Anglo-Russian Agreement of 1907.

[146] PRO/FO371/2069/1481: Minute by Sir Eyre Crowe on Smart to Townley, No. 14 (confidential), Tabriz, 18 November 1913.

[147] AVPRI f. 147, op. 486, d. 239b, ll. 49–54 ob.: Samsonov, Turkestan Governor-General, to Sazonov, Tashkent, 29 January/12 February 1912, No. 92.

[148] AVPRI f. 147, op. 486, d. 235b, ll. 32–3 ob.: From the notes of von Klemm on the Afghan question, St Petersburg, 1/14 February 1913.

[149] AVPRI f. 147, op. 486, d. 235b, ll. 32–3 ob.: From the notes of von Klemm on the Afghan question, St Petersburg, 1/14 February 1913.

[150] RGVIA f. 2000, op. 1, d. 7664, ll. 7–8 ob.: Neratov to V.A. Sukhomlinov, 20 February/5 March 1913, No. 95341.

[151] PRO/FO371/1743/7221: Buchanan to Grey, No. 54 (telegraphic), St Petersburg, 14 February 1913.

[152] PRO/FO371/1743/5856: Foreign Office to India Office, 24 February 1913.

[153] PRO/FO371/1743/5856: Foreign Office to India Office, 24 February 1913; PRO/FO371/1744/11173: Crewe to the Government of India (telegraphic), 4 March 1913.

[154] PRO/FO418/52/29: Emir Afghanistan to the Viceroy of India, 5 March 1913.

[155] PRO/FO371/1744/24295: Government of India to Crewe, Simla, 10 April 1913.

[156] AVPRI f. 133, op. 470, d. 191, ll. 15–18: Memorandum. 1913; AVPRI f. 147, op. 486, d. 235b, ll. 53–6: Notes concerning Afghanistan, 18 January 1913.

[157] Goods entering Afghanistan along the Russian border were taxed anywhere from 20 per cent to 60 per cent the cost, depending upon the point of entry. Along the Persian border, the rate was lower than 10 per cent, and along the Indian border, the tax was only 5 per cent (AVPRI f. 147, op. 486, d. 239b, ll. 159–90: Memorandum on the question of the development of Russia's trading relations with Afghanistan).

[158] AVPRI f. 147, op. 486, d. 239b, ll. 78–124: Journal of the conference on the question of the possible measures towards the development of our trading relations with Afghanistan and Bukhara, 17/30 January and 25 January/7 February 1913.

[159] AVPRI f. 147, op. 486, d. 239b, ll. 63–8: A. Baranevskii, MID, Diplomatic Official in the Turkestan Governor-Generalship. To the Chancellery of the Turkestan Governor-General. Enclosure in Baranevskii to the First Department of MID, 11/14 October 1912, No. 717.

[160] AVPRI f. 147, op. 486, d. 239b, ll. 78–124: Journal of the conference on the question of the possible measures towards the development of our trading relations with Afghanistan and Bukhara, 17/30 January and 25 January/7 February 1913.

[161] N.M. Gurevich, *Vneshniaia Torgovlia Afghanistana* (Moscow, 1959), p 21.

[162] PRO/FO418/52/51: Grey to Benckendorff, 25 July 1913.

[163] AVPRI f. 133, op. 470, d. 191, ll. 15–18: Memorandum, 1913.

[164] AVPRI f. 147, op. 486, d. 239b, ll. 78–124: Journal of the conference on the question of the possible measures towards the development of our trading relations with Afghanistan and Bukhara, 17/30 January and 25 January/7 February 1913.

[165] RGIA f. 560, op. 28, d. 64, ll. 109–11: Secret telegram from Nabokov, Calcutta, 27 December 1912/9 January 1913.

[166] PRO/FO371/1610/20005: India Office to Foreign Office, 38 April 1913.

[167] L/P&S/18/B/201: Tibet: The Simla Conference. J.E. Shuckburgh, 17 October 1913, Prepared for the Cabinet (secret).

[168] PRO/FO371/1613/53755: Minute by Nugent on Jordan to Grey, No. 254 (telegraphic), Peking, 27 November 1913.

[169] PRO/FO371/1613/58687: Government of India to Crewe (telegraphic), 11 December 1913.

Chapter 8: The Death of the Anglo-Russian Agreement

[1] For Sazonov's personal reaction and reminiscences of the Liman von Sanders affair, see S.D. Sazonov, *Vospominaniia* (Paris, 1927), pp 139–54.

[2] O'Beirne to Grey, St Petersburg, 9 December 1913, No. 412, in *BD*, x, pp 365–6.

[3] Sazonov, *Vospominaniia*, pp 153–4.

[4] For Nicholas's suggestions to Buchanan for an Anglo-Russian defensive alliance, see, for example, PRO/FO371/2092/15312: Buchanan to Grey, No. 100 (secret), St Petersburg, 3 April 1914.

[5] For an example of this trend, see the conversations with Witte published in *Novoe Vremia* in March, as discussed in PRO/FO371/2092/15087: Buchanan to Grey, No. 93, St Petersburg, 31 March 1914.

[6] David MacLaren McDonald, *United Government and Foreign Policy in Russia, 1900–1914* (Cambridge, MA, 1992), pp 199–202.

[7] PRO/FO371/2066/16099: Townley to Grey, No. 103 (telegraphic), Teheran, 12 April 1914.

[8] PRO/FO371/1706/15874: Townley to Grey, No. 64 (confidential), Teheran, 17 March 1913.

[9] PRO/FO371/1706/15874: Grey to Townley, No. 66, 7 May 1913.

[10] PRO/FO371/1729/24053: Townley to Grey, No. 215 (telegraphic), Teheran, 26 May 1913.

[11] PRO/FO371/1729/24053: Minute by Mallet on Townley to Grey, No. 215 (telegraphic), Teheran, 26 May 1913.

[12] PRO/FO371/2071/1492: Minute by Crowe, 16 January 1914.

[13] PRO/FO371/2071/1492: Minute by Nicolson on Minute by Crowe, 16 January 1914.

[14] PRO/FO371/2072/6122: Townley to Grey, No. 40 (telegraphic), Teheran, 9 February 1914.

[15] PRO/FO800/74: Grey to Buchanan (private), 18 March 1914.

[16] PRO/FO371/1720/2770: 'Mr. W. K. D'Arcy's Oil Concession in Persia', Gaston de Bernhardt, Foreign Office, 3 January 1913.

[17] PRO/FO371/956/8669: Persia. Annual Report (1909).

[18] PRO/FO371/1720/2770: 'Mr. W. K. D'Arcy's Oil Concession in Persia', Gaston de Bernhardt, Foreign Office, 3 January 1913.

[19] PRO/FO371/713/16185: Grey to Barclay (telegraphic), 28 April 1909; AVPRI f. 144, op. 488, d. 4145, ll. 87–8: Poklevsky-Kozell to Sazonov, Teheran, 5/18 May 1910; AVPRI f. 144, op. 488, d. 4145, l. 450: Secret telegram from Poklevsky-Kozell, Teheran, 13/26 September 1910, No. 591.

[20] See his self-proclaimed 'exuberant outburst' of 1912, 'Oil and the Oil Engine', reprinted in Admiral Lord Fisher, *Memories and Records* (New York, 1920), vol 2, pp 188–93.

[21] Admiralty Library: Second Report of the Royal Commission on Fuel and Engines. Appointed to Inquire into and Report on the Means of Supply and Storage of Liquid Fuel in Peace and War and Its Application to Warship Engines, Whether Indirectly or By Internal Combustion, 27 November 1912.

[22] Grey, 'Persia, the Anglo-Russian Convention, Egypt, Naval Strength', The House of Commons, 10 July 1912, in Paul Knaplund (ed), *Speeches on Foreign Affairs, 1900–14 by Sir Edward Grey* (London, 1931), pp 190–207.

[23] See Daniel Yergin, *The Prize* (New York, 1991), p 155.

[24] PRO/CAB1/33/2: Sir Francis Hopwood to Winston Churchill, Admiralty (no date – sometime before 29 May 1912).

[25] Admiralty Library: First Report of the Royal Commission on Fuel and Engines.

[26] Admiralty Library: Final Report of the Royal Commission on Fuel and Engines, 10 February 1914, p 4.

[27] Admiralty Library: Appendix by George Lambert, Civil Lord of the Admiralty, to Second Report of the Royal Commission on Fuel and Engines, 27 February 1913.

[28] Admiralty Library: Greenway's Testimony to the Royal Commission, 19 November 1912. First Report of the Royal Commission on Fuel and Engines, pp 334–7.

[29] ADM116/3806: Case 11508: Draft Letter from Director of Navy Contracts (F.W. Black) to the Secretary of the Treasury, 19 June 1913; ADM116: Proposed Arrangement with the Anglo-Persian Oil Company for the Supply of Fuel Oil. Supplementary Note, Admiralty, 4 July 1913.

[30] Admiralty Library: Extracts from Speeches of Churchill in Regard to Oil Fuel, 17 July 1913, in debate in Committee of the House of Commons, on the Navy Estimates for 1913–14.

[31] PRO/FO371/2076/29456: Lieutenant-Colonel Sir P. Cox to Government of India, Bushire, 7 December 1913.

[32] ADM116/3486: Slade to Churchill, Mohammareh, 8 November 1913. In Anglo-Persian Oil Company. Proposed Agreement, Admiralty, S.W., December 1913.

[33] ADM116/3806: Case 11508: Second Interim Report of the Admiralty Commission on the Petroleum Resources of the Countries Adjoining the Persian Gulf, 26 January 1914; for the final report of the Slade Commission, see IO/L/P&S/10/410 pt. 1/1831: Final Report of the Admiralty Commission on the Persian Oil fields, 6 April 1914.

[34] ADM116: Agreement with the Anglo-Persian Oil Company (Limited). Explanatory Memorandum, Admiralty, S.W., 5 May 1914, pp 5–7.

[35] IO/L/P&S/10/410 pt. 2/2248: Persian Oil fields: Admiralty Contract with Anglo-Persian Oil Co. Draft. Hirtzel. [16] June 1914; Final copy in PRO/FO800/98: pp 340–5.

[36] *Parliamentary Debates*, 5, 1914, LXIII, pp 1131–53.

[37] *Parliamentary Debates*, 5, 1914, LXIII, pp 1219–22 and 1228–35.

[38] PRO/FO371/2076/29456: Cox to Government of India, Bushire, 7 December 1913.

[39] *Parliamentary Debates*, 5, 1914, LXIII, pp 1178–87.

[40] PRO/FO371/2077/28134: Buchanan to Grey, No. 190, St Petersburg, 20 June 1914.

[41] AVPRI f. 133, op. 470, d. 192, l. 27: Télégramme secret de Benckendorff, 11/24 June 1914, No. 164; PRO/FO371/2077/28760: Grey to Buchanan, No. 283 (telegraphic), 25 June 1914; AVPRI f. 144, op. 489, d. 287b, ll. 34–5 ob.: Lettre de Benckendorff, 14/27 June 1914; This plan for the exploitation of Persian oil had been the conclusion of the Oil Conference which had been held at Delhi in early January 1914. See IO/L/P&S/10/410 pt. 1/771: Proceedings of the Oil Conference which was held at Delhi, 5 & 7 January 1914.

[42] PRO/FO371/2077/30746: Buchanan to Grey, No. 151 (telegraphic), St Petersburg, 7 July 1914.

[43] PRO/FO371/2077/30747: Buchanan to Grey, No. 152 (telegraphic), St Petersburg, 7 July 1914.

[44] PRO/FO371/2077/30747: Minute by Crowe on Buchanan to Grey, No. 152 (telegraphic), St Petersburg, 7 July 1914.

[45] PRO/FO371/2077/33658: Grey to Buchanan, No. 290, 22 July 1914.

[46] PRO/FO371/2076/29082: Buchanan to Grey, No. 192, St Petersburg, 25 June 1914.

[47] IO/L/P&S/10/410 pt. 3/2580: Buchanan to Grey, No. 145 (telegraphic), St Petersburg, 30 June 1914.

[48] PRO/FO371/2076/29082: Buchanan to Grey, No. 192, St Petersburg, 25 June 1914.

[49] PRO/FO371/2076/29082: Buchanan to Grey, No. 192, St Petersburg, 25 June 1914; see also PRO/FO371/2076/27927: Buchanan to Grey, No. 138 (telegraphic), St Petersburg, 21 June 1914.

[50] PRO/FO371/2069/8849: Townley to Grey, No. 64 (telegraphic), Teheran, 27 February 1914; PRO/FO371/2076/24869: Townley to Grey, No. 161 (telegraphic), Teheran, 3 June 1914.

[51] PRO/FO371/20731/10391: Acting Consul-General Bristow to Townley, No. 2 (confidential), Esfahan, 27 January 1914.

[52] PRO/FO371/2066/6895: Townley to Grey, No. 29 (secret), Teheran, 4 February 1914.

[53] RGVIA f. 400, op. 1, d. 4341, ll. 1–5: Draft of short secret instructions to the ranks of the resettlement administration, dispatched to northern Persia. Chief of the Agency for Land Organization and Farming, 31 March/13 April 1914, No. 444.

[54] PRO/FO371/2059/24443: Townley to Grey, No. 143 (confidential), Teheran, 13 May 1914.

[55] AVPRI f. 144, op. 489, d. 592b, ll. 40–1: Vorontsov-Dashkov, Report, 25 May/7 June 1914.

[56] PRO/FO371/2059/24443: Minute by Crowe, 2 June 1914.

[57] PRO/FO800/74: Grey to Buchanan (private), 18 March 1914.

[58] PRO/FO371/2059/24443: Minute by Crowe, 2 June 1914.

[59] PRO/FO371/1930/22567: Buchanan to Grey, No. 117 (telegraphic), St Petersburg, 19 May 1914.

[60] PRO/FO800/74: Grey to Buchanan (private), 18 March 1914.

[61] PRO/FO371/1929/18917: Grey to Buchanan, No. 162, 4 May 1914.

[62] PRO/FO371/1930/21986: Buchanan to Grey, No. 113 (telegraphic), St Petersburg, 17 May 1914.

[63] PRO/FO371/1930/21986: Buchanan to Grey, No. 113 (telegraphic), St Petersburg, 17 May 1914.

[64] PRO/FO371/1930/22413: Buchanan to Grey, No. 115 (telegraphic), St Petersburg, 18 May 1914.

[65] IO/L/P&S/10/455/2223: Buchanan to Grey, No. 148, St Petersburg, 19 May 1914.

[66] PRO/FO371/1930/22413: Buchanan to Grey, No. 115 (telegraphic), St Petersburg, 18 May 1914.

[67] PRO/FO371/1930/22567: Buchanan to Grey, No. 117 (telegraphic), St Petersburg, 19 May 1914.

[68] AVPRI f. 147, op. 486, d. 235b, l. 38: Buchanan to Neratov, St Petersburg, 26 May/8 June 1914. From Klemm's notes on the Afghan question.

[69] IO/L/P&S/10/455/2160: Viceroy to Secretary of State for India (telegraphic), 4 June 1914.

[70] AVPRI f. 147, op. 486, d. 235b, l. 41: Sazonov to Buchanan, St Petersburg, 28–29 May/10–11 June 1914, re: Buchanan to Neratov, 26 May/8 June; PRO/FO371/930/26093: Buchanan to Grey, No. 131 (telegraphic), St Petersburg, 10 June 1914.

[71] PRO/FO371/1930/27131: India Office to Foreign Office, 16 June 1914.

[72] PRO/FO371/930/26093: Minute by R.T. Nugent on Buchanan to Grey, No. 131 (telegraphic), St Petersburg, 10 June 1914.

[73] AVPRI f. 133, op. 470, d. 192, ll. 25–6 ob.: Lettre confidentielle de Sazonov à Benckendorff, le 11/24 juin, 1914.

[74] AVPRI f. 133, op. 470, d. 192, ll. 25–6 ob.: Lettre confidentielle de Sazonov à Benckendorff, le 11/24 juin, 1914. In late April, while Grey had been visiting Paris, (his first ever trip outside the Empire) he had agreed to the opening of Anglo-Russian naval talks in an attempt to appease the French. By the end of June, talks had still not begun, although the British cabinet had agreed to the principle of non-binding naval discussions. Nicholas II was anxious that they should begin immediately, but Grey seemed in no great hurry to commit. See A.J.P. Taylor, *The Struggle for Mastery in Europe, 1848–1918*, pp 512–13; Keith Neilson, *Britain and the Last Tsar*, pp 336–8.

[75] PRO/FO371/2076/25927: Buchanan to Grey, No. 130 (telegraphic), St Petersburg, 9 June 1914.

[76] AVPRI f. 144, op. 489, d. 287b, ll. 31–31 ob. and PRO/FO371/2076/26283: Memorandum communicated to Sazonov, 10 June 1914.

[77] AVPRI f. 144, op. 489, d. 287b, ll. 42–3: Memorandum communicated to Sazonov, 10 June 1914, with margin notes, possibly by Sazonov.

[78] AVPRI f. 144, op. 488, d. 4147, ll. 313–19: Copy of a Memorandum of the IMPERIAL Government to the British Ambassador in St Petersburg, 1/14 June 1914.

[79] AVPRI f. 133, op. 470, d. 192, ll. 1–15: Benckendorff to Sazonov, London, 29 May/11 June 1914.

[80] AVPRI f. 138, op. 467, d. 706/7, ll. 280–5: Lettre de Benckendorff, Londres, le 16/29 juin 1914.

[81] AVPRI f. 133, op. 470, d. 192, ll. 16–20: Benckendorff to Sazonov, Windsor, 4/17 June 1914.

[82] AVPRI f. 133, op. 470, d. 192, ll. 25–6 ob.: Lettre confidentielle de Sazonov à Benckendorff, le 11/24 juin 1914.

[83] PRO/FO371/2076/29456: India Office to Foreign Office. 29 June 1914; PRO/FO371/2059/32826: Townley to Grey, No. 196, Teheran, 6 July 1914; PRO/FO371/2076/33486: Townley to Grey, No. 203 (telegraphic), 23 July 1914.

[84] PRO/FO371/2076/33484: 'Anglo-Russian Relations in Persia'. Confidential Memorandum by G.R. Clerk, Foreign Office, 21 July 1914. Minutes by Crowe and Nicolson, 23 July 1914.

[85] Zara Steiner, *Britain and the Origins of the First World War* (London, 1977), p 220.

[86] Steiner's study of the Foreign Office, *The Foreign Office and Foreign Policy, 1898–1914* (Cambridge, 1969), pp 155–6, presents a British Foreign Office and press calmly reacting to the news of the assassination in the early days of July. Neilson, pp 338–9, also supports this view, suggesting that the July crisis only slowly intruded on Britain's relations with Russia.

[87] J.W. Headlam-Morley, in his introduction to volume XI of *British Documents on the Origins of the War*, points out that the grave difficulties which were arising in the Anglo-Russian relationship in Asia were, 'the subject of constant telegrams, dispatches and private letters, which continued as late as the 22nd July'. Although, as Headlam-Morley writes, these challenges in the Anglo-Russian relationship 'had no immediate connection with the outbreak of the war', this ongoing flurry of diplomatic traffic and interdepartmental correspondence provides an important example of the reality that, even as Europe moved towards war, the possible collapse of the Anglo-Russian Central Asian agreement remained a vital concern (*BD*, xi, pp x–xi).

[88] D.C.B. Lieven, *Russia and the Origins of the First World War* (London, 1983), p 140.

[89] See, for example, Buchanan to Nicolson (private), St Petersburg, 23 July 1914, No. 164, in *BD*, xi, pp 117–18.

[90] RGVIA f. 2000, op. 1, d. 3722, l. 64–64 ob.: Chief of Staff of the Turkestan Military District to the Acting Chief of the General Staff. Department of the Quartermaster-General, 26 June/9 July 1914, No. 3257.

[91] Lieven, *Russia and the Origins of the First World War*, p 140.

[92] Buchanan to Grey, St Petersburg, 24 July 1914, No. 101, in *BD*, xi, pp 80–1; see also telegram from Sazonov to London, 12/25 July 1914, No. 1489, in *KA*, 4 (1923), p 11.

[93] Buchanan to Grey (very confidential), St Petersburg, 25 July 1914. Document No. 125, in *BD*, xi, pp 93–4.

Conclusion

[1] Keith Neilson, *Britain and the Last Tsar*, pp 339–40.

[2] Keith M. Wilson, *The Policy of the Entente* (Cambridge, 1985), p 77.

Bibliography

I. Official Sources: Unpublished

Public Record Office (PRO), Kew

Admiralty

ADM 116 – Admiralty and Secretariat Papers
ADM 127 – Naval Stations – Persian Gulf

Cabinet Papers

CAB 1 – Miscellaneous Records
CAB 6 – Committee of Imperial Defence – Defence of India Memorandum
CAB 16 – Committee of Imperial Defence – Ad Hoc Sub-Committee Records
CAB 37 – Cabinet Minutes
CAB 38 – Committee of Imperial Defence to 1914

Foreign Office

FO 65 – Consular and Diplomatic Correspondence of the Russia Office, pre-1906
FO 368 – Commercial Department: General Correspondence
FO 369 – Consular Department: General Correspondence
FO 371 – Consular and Diplomatic Correspondence, post-1906
FO 372 – Treaty Department: General Correspondence
FO 418 – Confidential Print – Russia
FO 535 – Confidential Print – Tibet
FO 539 – Confidential Print – Central Asia
FO 800 – 35–113, Grey MSS
         336–381, Nicolson MSS

War Office

WO 106 – Directorate of Military Operations and Intelligence
WO 287 – B Papers (Military or Intelligence Reports on Foreign Countries)

India Office (IO), London

Military Department Records

L/MIL/1 – Committee Records, 1809–1937
L/MIL/5 – Compilations and Miscellaneous
L/MIL/7 – Military Collections
L/MIL/17/5 – Indian Army
L/MIL/17/14 – Afghanistan, Central Asia, Tibet
L/MIL/17/15 – Iran, Iraq, Persian Gulf

Parliamentary Branch Records 1772–1952

L/PARL/2/438 – Parliamentary Papers Relating to Persia, etc., 1904–1912

Political and Secret Department Records, 1756–1950

L/P&S/10 – Departmental Papers: Political and Secret Separate (or Subject) Files,
    1902–1931
L/P&S/11 – Political and Secret Subject Files, 1912–1930
L/P&S/18 – Political and Secret Memoranda, c.1840–1947

Private Papers Collections

MSS Eur/F 112 – Curzon MSS
MSS Eur/D 573 – Morley MSS

Admiralty Library, London

Royal Commission on Fuel and Engines

Arkhiv Vneshnei Politikii Rossisskoi Imperii (AVPRI), Moscow

Fond	Opis	Title
133	470	Kantseliariia ministra inostranikh del
138	467	Sekretnyi arkhiv ministra
144	1/488	Persidskii stol
	2/489	
147	485	Sredne-Aziatskii stol
	486	
214	779	Rossiskoe generalnoe konsulstvo v Bombe
291	614	Rossiskoe genkonsulstvo v Tegerane
340	812	Sergei Dimitrievich Sazonov
	584	N.G. Hartwig
	835	Aleksei Petrovich Izvolskii
	797	B.V. Miller

Rossiskii Gosudarstvenyi Istoricheskii Arhkiv (RGIA), St Petersburg

Fond	Opis	Title
22	3	Tsentralnie uchrezhdeniia M.F. Torgovli i promyshlennosti
23	8	Ministerstvo torgovli i promyshlennosti

	11	
95	18	Otdeli Torgovogo Moreplavaniia Torgovikh Portov Ministerstva Torgovli i Promyshlennosti
350	64	Plani chertezhi po stroitelstvu zheleznikh dorog i iskusstvennikh sooruzheni. Sredne-Aziatskaia Zheleznaia Doroga.
560	22	Obshaia kantseliariia ministra finansov
	26	
	28	

Rossiskii Gosudarstvenii Voenii Istoricheskii Arhkiv (RGVIA), Moscow

Fond	Opis	Title
280	1	A. F. Roediger
400	1	Glavnyi shtab. Aziatskaiia chast
1396	2	Shtab Turkestanskogo Voennogo Okruga-Upravlenie oruzhnogo general-kvartirmeistera
1396	2, dop.	Shtab Turkestanskogo Voennogo Okruga-Upravlenie oruzhnogo general-kvartirmeistera
2000	1	Glavnoe upravlenie Generalnogo shtaba

II. Official Sources: Printed

Great Britain

Gillard, David (ed), *British Documents on Foreign Affairs*. Part I, Series B, 'The Near and Middle East, 1856–1914' (University Publications of America, 1985)

Gooch, G.P. and Temperley, H. (eds), *British Documents on the Origins of the War, 1898–1914*, 11 vols (London, 1926–38)

Great Britain, Foreign Office, Historical Section, *Tibet* (London, 1920)

Grey, Sir Edward, *Speeches on Foreign Affairs, 1904–1914*, edited by Paul Knaplund (London, 1937)

Hansard. Parliamentary Debates, 4th and 5th series.

Lieven, Dominic (ed), *British Documents on Foreign Affairs*. Part I, Series A, 'Russia, 1859–1914' (University Publications of America, 1983)

Public Record Office Handbooks, *Records of the Foreign Office, 1782–1939* (London, 1969)

Russia

Adamov, E.A (ed), and I.V. Kozmenko (comp), *Sbornik dogovorov Rossii s drugimi gosudarstvami. 1856–1917* (Moscow, 1952)

'Doklady v ministra inostrannykh del S.D. Sazonova Nikolaiu Romanovu, 1910–1912 gg.' *Krasnyi Arkhiv*, 3 (1923)

'Doklady V.N. Kokovtsova Nikolaiu II.' *Krasnyi Arkhiv*, 11–12 (1925), pp 1–25

Fedorov (Second Lieutenant), *Otchet o poezdke v Vostochnuiu Persiiu 2-go Zakaspyisk-ago strelkovago bataliona Podporuchika*, Shtaba Turkestanskogo Voennogo Okruga 4-e Otdelenie (Tashkent, 1910)

Grimm, E.D., *Sbornik Dogovorov i Drugikh Dokumentov po Istorii Mezhdunarodnikh Otnoshenii na Dalnem Vostoke (1842–1925)* (Moscow, 1927)

Iswolsky, Alexandre, *Au Service de la Russie: Correspondance Diplomatique*, 2 vols (Paris, 1939)

'K istorii Potsdamskogo soglasheniia 1911 g.', *Krasnyi Arkhiv*, 3 (58) (1933), pp 46–57

Kliuchnikov, I.V., and A. Sabanin, *Mezhdunarodnaia politika noveishego vremeni v dogovorakh, notakh i delkaratsiiakh*, 3 parts in 4 vols (Moscow, 1925–29)

Materialy po izucheniiu Vostoka, First Issue, Confidential, 1909; Second issue, Secret, 1915 (St Petersburg, Ministry of Foreign Affairs)

Mezhdunarodnye otnosheniia v epokhu imperializma, 2nd series (Leningrad, 1939)

Ministry of Foreign Affairs, *Sbornik diplomaticheskikh dokumentov kasaiushchikhsia sobytii v Persii s kontsa 1906 g. po iiul 1909 g*, 7 vols (St Petersburg, 1911–13)

'Pis'ma I.I. Vorontsova-Dashkova Nikolaiu Romanovu', *Krasnyi Arkhiv*, 1 (26) (Moscow, 1928), pp 97–124.

Razvedka Shtaba Turkestanskago Voennago Okruga (Afganistan), Svodka svedenii, dobitikh k 1-mu dekabria 1913 goda (Tashkent, 1913)

Razvedka Shtaba Turkestanskago Voennago Okruga (Zapadnii Kitai i Anglo-India), No. 3, Ne podlezhit oglasheniiu (Tashkent, 1914)

Rossiia Soviet Ministrov, *Osovie Zhurnali Sovieta Ministrov Tsarskoi Rossii 1906–1917 gg.* (Redkol: Bovykin Sotv. red.) i dr (Moscow, 1982–88)

Rossiiskie Puteshestvenniki v Indii XIX-nachalo XXv. Dokumenti i Materiali, edited by N.A. Khalfin (Moskva, 1990)

III. Autobiographies, Memoirs, Contemporary Monographs and Articles

Asquith, H.H., *Memories and Reflections, 1852–1927*, 2 vols (London, 1928)

Bailey, F.M., *Mission to Tashkent* (Oxford, 1992)

Brailsford, H.N., *The Fruits of Our Russian Alliance* (London, 1912)

Browne, E.G., *The Persian Revolution of 1905–1909* (Cambridge, 1910; new edition edited by Abbas Amanat, Washington DC, 1995)

Buchanan, Sir G., *My Mission to Russia and Other Diplomatic Memories* (London, 1923)

Chirol, Sir Valentine, *Fifty Years in a Changing World* (London, 1927)

Churchill, Winston S., *The World Crisis, 1911–1918*, vol i (London, 1938)

Curzon, George N., *Persia and the Persian Question* (London, 1892)

——, *Russia in Central Asia* (London, 1967)

Fisher, John Arbuthnot, *Memories and Records*, 2 vols (New York, 1920)

Glinka, G.V. (ed), *Aziatskaia Rossiia* (St Petersburg, 1914; reprint, Cambridge, 1974)

Graham, Stephen, *Through Russian Central Asia* (New York, 1916)

Grey, Sir Edward, *Twenty-Five Years: 1892–1916*, 2 vols (London, 1925)

Grey, Viscount, *Fallodon Papers* (London, 1926)

Grulev, M. (Agent of the Military-Studies Institute), *Sopernichestvo Rossii i Anglii v Srednei Azii* (St Petersburg, 1909)

Gwynn, S. (ed), *The Letters and Friendships of Sir Cecil Spring-Rice*, 2 vols (London, 1929)

Haldane, R.B., *Before the War* (London, 1920)

——, *An Autobiography* (New York, 1929)

Hardinge, Sir Arthur H., *A Diplomatist in the East* (London, 1928)

Izvolskii, Aleksandr Petrovich, *The Memoirs of Alexander Iswolsky*, translated and edited by Charles Louis Seeger (London, 1920)

Kassis, Zh. Ia, *Ekonomicheskoe polozhenie sovremennoi Persii. Torgovie i finansovie interesi Rossii na persidskom rinke* (Kiev, 1915)

Kokovtsov, V.N., *Iz moevo proshlovo. Vospominaniia 1903–1919 gg*, 2 vols (Moscow, 1992)

Lynch, H.F.B., *Sir Edward Grey in Persia* (London, 1912)

Lyons, Captain Gervais, *Afghanistan: The Buffer State* (Madras, 1910)

P.A.T., 'Zhelezno-dorozhnyi vopros v Persii i Velikii Indiskii put' *Velikiaia Rossiia*, II (Moscow, n.d.)

Petrov, A.N., *Kak Zashchishchaiut svoi interesi v Azii Angliia i Rossiia* (St Petersburg, 1910)

Rittikh, Petr Aleksandrovich, *Zheleznodorozhnyi put cherez Persiiu* (St Petersburg, 1900)

Sazonov, S.D., *Vospominaniia* (Moscow, 1991)

Sazonov, Serge, *Fateful Years, 1909–1916* (London, 1928)

Shavrov, N.N., *Vneshniaia torgovlia Persii i uchastie v ne Rossii v Persii* (St Petersburg, 1913)

Shipov, N.N., *Rossiia i Angliia* (St Petersburg, 1908)

Skiff, *Persidskii Vopros* (St Petersburg, 1912)

Snesarev, A.E. (Lieutenant Colonel, Russian General Staff), *Indiia kak glavnii faktor v sredne-aziatskom voprose* (St Petersburg, 1906)

——, *Anglo-Russkoe soglashenie 1907 goda* (St Petersburg, 1908)

Taube, Baron M. de, *La politique russe d'avantguerre et la fin de l'Empire des tsars* (Paris, 1928)

Ter-Gukasov, G.I., *Ekonomicheskie interesy Rossii v Persii. Redaktsia periodicheskikh izdanyi Ministerstva Finansov: 'Vestnik Finansov' i 'Torgovaia Promyshelanaia Gazeta'* (St Petersburg, 1915)

Witte, Count Sergei Iulievich, *Vospominaniia*, 3 vols (Moscow, 1994)

Younghusband, Sir Francis, *India and Tibet* (London, 1910)

Zinovev, I.A., *Rossiia, Angliia i Persiia* (St Petersburg, 1912)

IV. Monographs

Adamec, Ludwig W., *Afghanistan, 1900–1923* (Berkeley, 1967)

——, *Afghanistan's Foreign Affairs to the Mid-Twentieth Century* (Tucson, AZ, 1974)

——, *Dictionary of Afghan Wars, Revolutions, and Insurgencies* (Lanham, MD, 1996)

Akhmedzhanova, Z.K., *K Istorii Stroitelstva Zheleznikh Dorog v Srednei Azii (1880–1917 gg.)* (Tashkent, 1965)

Allworth, Edward (ed), *Central Asia: 120 Years of Russian Rule* (Durham, 1989)

Ataev, Khommat, *Politicheskie i torgovo-ekonomicheskie otnosheniia severo-vostochnogo Irana i Rossii v Nachale XX veka (1900–1917 gg.)* (Ashkhabad, 1989)

Avetian, A.S., *Russko-germanskie diplomaticheskie otnosheniia nakanune pervoi mirovoi voiny, 1910–1914* (Moscow, 1985)

Banusevich, Anthony Michael, 'Anglo-Russian Relations Concerning the Origin and Effects of the Persian Question, 1906–1911', unpublished M.A. thesis (Georgetown University, April 1950)

Beloff, Max, *Britain's Liberal Empire, 1897–1921* (London, 1987)

Belov, Evgenii Aleksandrovich, *Russko-Kitaiskie Otnosheniia v 1911–1915 gg* (Moskva, 1993)

——, *Rossiia i Kitai v Nachale XX Veka* (Moskva, 1997)

Bestuzhev, Igor Vasilevich, *Borba v Rossii po voprosam vneshnei politiki, 1906–1910* (Moscow, 1961)

Bogdanovskii, S., *Neftianoi Imperializm* (Moskva–Leningrad, 1926)

Bovykin, V.I., *Ocherki istorii vneshnei politiki Rossii* (Moscow, 1960)

——, *Iz istorii vozniknoveniia pervoi mirovoi voiny: otnosheniia Rossii i Frantsii v 1912–1914 gg* (Moscow, 1961)

Buchanan, Meriel, *Diplomacy and Foreign Courts* (London, 1928)

Busch, Briton Cooper, *Britain and the Persian Gulf, 1894–1914* (Berkeley, 1967)

Butler, Sir J. and C.E. Carrington (eds), *Cambridge History of the British Empire*. vol. iii, 'The Empire-Commonwealth, 1870–1919' (Cambridge, 1959)

Cecil, Algernon, *British Foreign Secretaries, 1807–1916: Studies in Personality and Policy* (London, 1927)

Chapman, M.K., *Great Britain and the Baghdad Railway, 1888–1914* (Northampton, MA, 1948)

Churchill, Rogers Platt, *The Anglo-Russian Convention of 1907* (Cedar Rapids, Iowa, 1939)

Das, M.N., *India under Morley and Minto* (London, 1964)

Davenport-Hines, R.P.T. and Geoffrey Jones (eds), *British Business in Asia since 1860* (Cambridge, 1989)

Dilks, David, *Curzon in India*, 2 vols (London, 1970)

Dockrill, Michael Lawrence, *The Formulation of a Continental Foreign Policy by Great Britain, 1908–1912* (New York, 1986)

Druhe, David N., *Russo-Indian Relations, 1466–1917* (New York, 1970)

Efremov, P.N., *Vneshniaia politika Rossii (1907–1914 gg.)* (Moscow, 1961)

Emchenko, Rima Moiseevna, *Anglo-Russkie Otnosheniia v Irane v 1907–1914 godakh* (Tashkent, 1979)

Entner, M.L., *Russo-Persian Commercial Relations, 1828–1944* (Gainesville, 1965)

Fatemi, Nasrollah Saifpour, *Oil Diplomacy* (New York, 1954)

Ferrier, R.W., *The History of the British Petroleum Company* (Cambridge, 1982)

Fox, Martyna Agata, *The Eastern Question in Russian Politics: Interplay of Diplomacy, Opinion and Interest, 1905–1917*, unpublished Ph.D. thesis (Yale University, 1993)

Friedberg, Aaron L., *The Weary Titan* (Princeton, 1988)

Fuller, William C. Jr., *Strategy and Power in Russia 1600–1914* (New York, 1992)

Galperin, A., *Anglo-iaponskii soiuz. 1902–1921 gody* (Moscow, 1947)

Gankovsky, Iu. V. et al, *A History of Afghanistan*, translated by Vitaly Baskakov (Moscow, 1985)

Gatrell, Peter, *The Tsarist Economy, 1850–1917* (London, 1986)

Geyer, Dietrich, *Russian Imperialism*, translated by Bruce Little (New Haven, 1987)

Gillard, David, *The Struggle for Asia* (London, 1977)

Gilmour, David, *Curzon* (London, 1994)

Gleason, John Howes, *The Genesis of Russophobia in Great Britain* (Cambridge, 1950)

Graves, Philip, *The Life of Sir Percy Cox* (London, 1941)

Gregorian, Vartan, *The Emergence of Modern Afghanistan* (Stanford, CA, 1969)

Gurevich, N.M., *Vneshniaia Torgovlia Afghanistana* (Moscow, 1959)

Habberton, W., *Anglo-Russian Relations Concerning Afghanistan 1837–1907* (Urbana, IL, 1937)

Hamer, D.A., *John Morley: Liberal Intellectual in Politics* (Oxford, 1968)

Hauner, Milan, *What is Asia to Us?* (Boston, 1990)

Hopkirk, Peter, *Trespassers on the Roof of the World* (Oxford, 1982)

Howard, Michael, *The Continental Commitment* (London, 1972)

Ibragimov, M. Zh, *Neftianaia promyshlennost' Azerbaidzhana v period imperializma* (Baku, 1984)

Ignatev, Anatolii Venediktovich, *Russko-angliiskie otnosheniia nakanune pervoi mirovoi voiny. (1908–1914 gg.)* (Moscow, 1962)

Ismatov, Irkin, *Rol Nizhegorodskoi Iarmarki v Torgovikh Sviaziakh Rossii so Srednei Azie i Iranom (XIX-nachalo XX vv.)* (Tashkent, 1973)

Ispahani, Mahnaz Z., *Roads and Rivals* (Ithaca, 1989)

Ivanov, Mikhail Sergeevich, *Iranskaia Revoliutsiia 1905–1911 godov* (Moscow, 1957)

Jelavich, Barbara, *A Century of Russian Foreign Policy, 1814–1914* (Philadelphia, 1964)

——, *Russia's Balkan Entanglements, 1806–1914* (Cambridge, 1991)

Jones, Geoffrey, *The State and the Emergence of the British Oil Industry* (London, 1981)

——, *Banking and Empire in Iran (The History of the British Bank of the Middle East)*, vol i (Cambridge, 1986)

Kashani-Sabet, Firoozeh, *Frontier Fictions: Shaping the Iranian Nation, 1804–1946* (Princeton, 1999)

Kazemzadeh, Firuz, *Russia and Britain in Persia, 1864–1914* (New Haven, 1968)

Kennedy, Paul, *The Realities Behind Diplomacy* (London, 1981)

——, *Strategy and Diplomacy* (London, 1983)

Khalfin, N.A., *Proval Britanskoi Agressii v Afganistane XIX v.-nachalo XX v.* (Moskva, 1959)

——, *Prisoedinenie srednei azii k Rossii* (Moscow, 1965)

Khan, Chandra Kanta, *Trans-Himalayan Politics: China, Britain and Tibet, 1842–1914*, unpublished Ph.D. thesis (Pennsylvania State University, 1984)

King, Peter (ed) *Curzon's Persia* (London, 1986)

Koss, Stephen E., *John Morley at the India Office 1905–1910* (New Haven, 1969)

Kuleshov, N.S., *Tibetskii Vopros i Pozitsiia Rossii v Nachale XX v.* (Moskva, 1987)

——, *Rossiia i Tibet* (Moscow, 1992)

Lamb, Alastair, *The McMahon Line: A Study in the Relations between India, China and Tibet 1904–1914* (London, 1966)

——, *British India and Tibet, 1766–1910* (London, 1986)

Lederer, I.J. (ed), *Russian Foreign Policy* (New Haven, 1962)

Leontiev, V.P., *Angliiskaia agressiia protiv Kitai v Tibete v period 1888–1917 godov*, dissertation (Moscow, 1954)

——, *Inostrannaia Ekspansiia v Tibete v 1888–1919 gg.* (Moskva, 1956)

Lieven, D.C.B., *Russia and the Origins of the First World War* (London, 1983)

——, *Nicholas II* (New York, 1993)

Longrigg, Stephen Hemsley, *Oil in the Middle East*, 2nd edition (London, 1961)

MacCarthy, M., *Anglo-Russian Rivalry in Persia*, The University of Buffalo Studies, vol 4, no. 2, 1925

Mallet, Bernard, *British Budgets, 1887–88 to 1912–13* (London, 1913)

Malozemoff, Andrew, *Russian Far Eastern Policy, 1881–1904* (Berkeley, 1958)

Mannanov, B., *Iz Istorii Russko-Iranskikh Otnosheni v Kontse XIX-Nachale XX Veka* (Tashkent, 1964)

Marshall, Julie G., *Britain and Tibet 1765–1947* (Bundoora, 1977)

Martirosov, S.Z., *Anglo-russkie protivorechiia v Srednei Azii v dorevoliutsionnoi i sovietskoi istoricheskoi literature* (Chardzhou, 1962)

McDonald, David MacLaren, *United Government and Foreign Policy in Russia, 1900–1914* (Cambridge, MA, 1992)

McLean, David, *Britain and Her Buffer State: The Collapse of the Persian Empire, 1890–1914* (London, 1979)

Mehra, Parshotam, *The McMahon Line and After* (Delhi, 1974)

Metzer, Jacob, *Railroad Development and Market Integration: The Case of Tsarist Russia* (Jerusalem, 1973)

——, *Some Economic Aspects of Railroad Development in Tsarist Russia* (New York, 1977)

Neilson, Keith, *Britain and the Last Tsar* (Oxford, 1995)

Nicolson, Harold, *Portrait of a Diplomatist. Sir Arthur Nicolson, Bart., First Lord Carnock: A Study in the Old Diplomacy* (New York, 1930)

Nizamutdinov, Ilias, *'Seistanski vopros.' Iz Istorii vmeshatelstva Anglii v Irano-Afganskie dela* (Tashkent, 1958)

Ostaltseva, A.F., *Anglo-Russkoe Soglashenie 1907 goda*, dissertation (Moscow, 1962)

Panin, S.B., *Rossiia i Afganistan 1905–1918* (Irkutsk, 1995)

Pierce, Richard A., *Russian Central Asia, 1867–1917* (Berkeley, CA, 1960)

Pokrovskii, S.A., *Vneshniaia torgovlia i vneshniaia torgovaia politika Rossii* (Moscow, 1947)

Popplewell, Richard J., *Intelligence and Imperial Defence* (London, 1995)

Potemkin, V.P., *Istoriia Diplomatii* (Moscow, 1945)

Pubaev, R.E., *Ekspansiia Anglii v Tibete i Borba Tibetskovo Naroda Protiv Angliskikh Zakhbatchikov (konets XVIII v.-nachalo XXV.)*, Avtoreferat diss. (Leningrad, 1955)

Robbins, Keith, *Sir Edward Grey: A Biography of Lord Grey of Fallodon* (London, 1971)

Ronaldshay, Earl of, *The Life of Lord Curzon*, 3 vols (London, 1928)

Rose, Kenneth, *Superior Person: A Portrait of Curzon and His Circle in Late Victorian England* (London, 1969)

Rossiia i Afganistan (Moscow, 1989)

Rossiia i Indiia (Moscow, 1986)

Schimmelpenninck van der Oye, David, *Oriental Dreams: Ideologies of Empire and Russia's Far East* (DeKalb, IL, 2001)

Schmitt, Bernadotte, *The Annexation of Bosnia, 1908–1909* (New York, 1970)

Schultze, Ernest, *Borba za persidsko-mesopotamskuiu nefti*, Russian translation from the German by N.M. Kachkacheva (Moskva, 1924)

Shteinberg, E. L., *Istoriia britanskoi aggressii na Srednem Vostoke* (Moscow, 1951)

Sineokow, Vladimir, *La Colonisation Russe en Asie* (Paris, 1929)

Singh, Amar Kaur Jasbir, *Himalayan Triangle: A Historical Survey of British India's Relations with Tibet, Sikkim and Bhutan 1765–1950* (London, 1988)

Stanwood, Frederick, *War, Revolution & British Imperialism in Central Asia* (London, 1983)

Steiner, Zara S., *The Foreign Office and Foreign Policy, 1898–1914* (Cambridge, 1969)

——, *Britain and the Origins of the First World War* (London, 1977)

Sumner, B.H., *Tsardom and Imperialism in the Far East and Middle East 1880–1914* (Oxford, 1968)

Sykes, Brig-Gen Sir Percy, *A History of Afghanistan*, vol ii (London, 1940)

Tompkins, R.O., *Anglo-Russian Diplomatic Relations*, unpublished Ph.D. thesis (North Texas State University, 1975)

Trevelyan, George Macaulay, *Grey of Fallodon* (Boston, 1937)

Venn, Fiona, *Oil Diplomacy in the Twentieth Century* (Basingstoke, 1986)

Wesson, Robert, *The Russian Dilemma* (New Brunswick, NJ, 1974)

Westwood, J.N., *A History of Russian Railways* (London, 1964)

Wilson, Keith M., *The Policy of the Entente* (Cambridge, 1985)

——, *Empire and Continent* (London, 1987)

Wolpert, Stanley A., *Morley and India 1906–1910* (Berkeley, 1967)

Woodman, Dorothy, *Himalayan Frontiers* (New York, 1969)

Wright, Denis, *The English Amongst the Persians During the Qajar Period, 1787–1921* (London, 1977)

Yergin, Daniel, *The Prize: The Epic Quest for Oil, Money, and Power* (New York, 1991)

Zhigalina, O. I., *Velikobritaniia na Srednem Vostoke* (Moskva, 1990)

Zvonarev, K.K., *Agenturnaia Razvedka* (Moskva, 1929)

V. Articles

Bhutani, V.G., 'Source of Frontier Studies: The North-East Frontier of India', *China Report*, 24, 3 (1988), pp 299–375

Bor-Ramenskii, E., 'K voprosu o roli bolshevikov zakavkazia v iranskoi revoliutsii 1905–1911 godov', *Istorik marksist*, 11 (1940)

Chapman, S.D., 'British-Based Investment Groups before 1914', *Economic History Review*, 38, 2 (1985), pp 230–51

Dantsig, B.M., 'Finansi Persii', *Novyi Vostok*, 18 (1927), pp 120–43

Dillon, E., 'Russia, Germany and Persia', *Contemporary Review*, 54 (1911)

Georgiev, A.V., 'Dokumenty Posolstv i Missii Rossii Kak Istochnik Dlia Izucheniia Roli Zagranichnoi Sluzhby MID vo Vneshnepoliticheskom Apparate Samoderzhaviia', *Istoriia SSSR*, 4 (1988), pp 135–49

——, 'Tsarizm i Rossiiskaia Dilomatiia Nakanune Pervoi Mirovoi Voiny', *Voprosy Istorii*, 1988, pp 58–73

Gooch, G.P., 'Continental Agreements, 1902–1907', in Sir A.W. Ward and G.P. Gooch (eds), *The Cambridge History of British Foreign Policy, 1783–1919*, vol iii (Cambridge, 1923)

Greaves, Rose L., 'Seistan in British Indian Frontier Policy', *Bulletin of the School of Oriental and African Studies*, 49, 1 (1986), pp 90–102

——, 'Themes in British Policy Towards Persia in Relation to Indian Frontier Defence 1798–1914', *Asian Affairs*, 22, 1 (1991), pp 35–45

Hamilton, A., 'The Anglo-Russian Agreement: The Question of Persia', *Fortnightly Review*, 28 (1967)

Hauner, Milan, 'Central Asian Geopolitics in the Last Hundred Years: A Critical Survey from Gorchakov to Gorbachev', *Central Asian Survey*, 8, 1 (1989), pp 1–19

Head, Judith A., 'Public Opinion and Middle Eastern Railways: The Russo-German Negotiations of 1910–1911', *International History Review*, 6, 1 (1984), pp 28–47

Ingram, Edward, 'Approaches to the Great Game in Asia', *Middle Eastern Studies*, 18, 4 (1982), pp 449–457

Jack, Marian, 'The Purchase of the British Government's Shares in the British Petroleum Company 1912–1914', *Past and Present*, 39 (1968), pp 139–68

Jones, Geoffrey and Clive Trebilcock, 'Russian Industry and British Business 1910–1930: Oil and Armaments', *Journal of European Economic History*, 11, 1 (1982), pp 61–103

Kazemzadeh, Firuz, 'Russian Imperialism and Persian Railways', in *Russian Thought and Politics*, Harvard Slavic Studies, 4 (Cambridge, MA, 1957), pp 355–73

——, 'Russia and the Middle East', in Ido J. Lederer (ed), *Russian Foreign Policy: Essays in Historical Perspective* (New Haven, CT, 1962), pp 489–530

Klein, Ira, 'The Anglo-Russian Convention and the Problem of Central Asia, 1907–1914', *Journal of British Studies*, XI, 1 (November 1971), pp 126–47

——, 'British Intervention in the Persian Revolution 1905–1909', *Historical Journal*, XV (1972)

Koroleva, I.G., 'Soviet Ministrov Rossii v 1907–1914 gg.' *Istoricheskie zapiski*, 110 (1984), pp 114–53

Kuleshov, Nikolai Stepanovich, 'Rossiia i Tibetskii Krizis Nachala XX Veka', *Voprosy Istorii*, 11 (November 1990), pp 152–60

——, 'Agvan Dorjiev, the Dalai Lama's Ambassador', *Asian Affairs*, 23, 1 (1992), pp 20–33

Leshchilovskaia, I.I., 'Vneshniaia Politika Rossii XIX i Nachala XX veka. Dokumenty Rossiiskogo Ministerstva Inostrannykh Del', *Sovetskoe Slavianovedenia*, 5 (1984), pp 113–15

Mahajan, Sneh, 'The Defence of India and the End of Isolation. A Study in the Foreign Policy of the Conservative Government, 1900–1905', *Journal of Imperial and Commonwealth History*, X (January 1982) pp 168–93

McDonald, David M., 'A Lever without a Fulcrum: Domestic Factors and Russian Foreign Policy, 1905–1914', in Hugh Ragsdale (ed), *Imperial Russian foreign policy* (Washington DC, 1993), pp 268–311

Mendelson, V.I., 'Anglo-russkoe soglashenie 1907 g. v osveschenii sovetskikh istorikov', *Istoricheskii zapiski*, 104 (1979), str. 268–81

Morris, L.P., 'British Secret Service Activity in Khorassan, 1887–1908', *Historical Journal*, 27, 3 (1984), pp 657–75

Mosely, Philip E., 'Russian Policy in 1911–1912', *Journal of Modern History*, 12 (1940), pp 69–86

Neilson, Keith, '"My Beloved Russians": Sir Arthur Nicolson and Russia, 1906–1916', *International History Review*, 9, 4 (1987), pp 521–54

——, '"Greatly Exaggerated": The Myth of the Decline of Great Britain before 1914', *The International History Review*, XIII, 4 (November 1991), pp 695–725

Ochildiev, D.Ia and M.A. Babakhodzhaev, 'Politika Anglii v Afganistane i borba afganskogo naroda za nezavisimost v nachale XX veka', *Strani Blizhnego i Srednego Vostoka v Mezhdunarodnikh Otnosheniiakh* (Tashkent, 1984), pp 36–46

Popov, A.L., 'Stranitsa iz istorii russkogo imperializma v Persii', *Mezhdunarodnaia Zhizn*, 4–5 (1924), pp 133–64

——, 'Anglo-russkoe sopernichestvo na putiakh Irana', *Novyi Vostok*, 12 (1926), pp 127–53.

——, 'Rossiia i Tibet', *Novyi Vostok*, (Part I) 18 (1927); (Part II) 20–21 (1928)

——, 'Iz istorii zavoevaniia Srednei Azii', *Istoricheskie zapiski*, 9 (1940), pp 198–242

Reisner, I., 'Anglo-Russkaia Konventsiia 1907 g. i Razdel Afganistana', *Krasnyi Arkhiv*, 10 (1925), pp 54–66

Rieber, Alfred J., 'The Historiography of Imperial Russian Foreign Policy: a Critical Survey', in Hugh Ragsdale (ed), *Imperial Russian Foreign Policy* (Washington DC, 1993), pp 360–443

Robbins, Keith, 'Sir Edward Grey and the British Empire', *Journal of Imperial and Commonwealth History*, 2 (1973), pp 213–21

Shteinberg, E.L., 'Angliiskaia versiia o "russkoi ugroze" Indii v. XIX–XX v.v.' *Istoricheskie zapiski*, 33 (1950), pp 47–66

Snelling, John, 'Agvan Dorjiev: Eminence Grise of Central Asian Politics', *Asian Affairs*, 21, 1 (1990), pp 38–43

Sontag, John P. with commentary by Paul R. Gregory, 'Foreign Trade and Tsarist Policy Before World War I: An Exchange', *Slavic Review*, 40, 2 (1981), pp 264–8

Spring, D.W., 'The Trans-Persian Railway Project and Anglo-Russian Relations, 1909–14', *Slavonic and East European Review*, 54 (1976), pp 60–82

——, 'Russian Imperialism in Asia in 1914', *Cahiers du Monde Russe et Sovietique*, XX (1979)

Sweet, D.W. and R.T.B. Langhorne, 'Great Britain and Russia, 1907–1914', in F.H. Hinsley (ed), *British Foreign Policy Under Sir Edward Grey* (Cambridge, 1977), pp 236–55

Vekselman, M.I., 'Rossiskii Monopolisticheskii i Inostrannyi Kapital v Toplivnoi Promyshlennosti Srednei Azii v Kontse XIX-Nachale XX v.', *Istoricheskie Zapiski*, 1986, pp 283–304

Verrier, Anthony, 'Francis Younghusband and the Great Game', *Asian Affairs*, 23, 1 (1992), pp 34–43

Warikoo, K., 'Central Asia and Kashmir: A Study in Political, Commercial and Cultural Contacts During the 19th and Early 20th Centuries', *Central Asian Survey*, 7, 1 (1988), pp 63–83

Wheeler, W.E., 'The Control of Land Routes: Russian Railways in Central Asia', *Journal of the Royal Central Asian Society*, XXI (October 1934)

Williams, Beryl J., 'The Strategic Background to the Anglo-Russian Entente of August 1907', *Historical Journal*, ix, 3 (1966), pp 360–73

——, 'The Revolution of 1905 and Russian Foreign Policy', in C. Abramsky and B. Williams (eds) *Essays in Honour of E.H. Carr* (London, 1974), pp 101–25

Wilson, Keith M., 'Imperial Interests in the British Decision for War, 1914: the Defence of India in Central Asia', *Review of International Studies*, 10 (1984), pp 189–203

Yapp, M.A., 'British Perceptions of the Russian Threat to India', *Modern Asian Studies*, 21, 4 (1987), pp 647–65

VI. Newspapers and Contemporary Serial Publications

The Anglo-Russian Gazette (Anglo-Russkaia Gazeta)
Birzhevye Vedomosti
The Contemporary Review
The Indian Trade Journal (Rangoon)
Manchester Guardian
Novoe Vremia
Russkoe Slovo
The Times (London)
Torgovlia i promyshlennost
Torgovo-promyshlennaia Gazeta

Index

Emerson 1/08